ANIMALS AND

THE ANIMAL TURN

SERIES EDITOR
Linda Kalof

SERIES ADVISORY BOARD
Marc Bekoff and Nigel Rothfels

Making Animal Meaning
    Edited by Linda Kalof and Georgina M. Montgomery

Animals as Domesticates: A World View through History
    Juliet Clutton-Brock

Animals as Neighbors: The Past and Present of Commensal Species
    Terry O'Connor

French Thinking about Animals
    Edited by Louisa Mackenzie and Stephanie Posthumus

Animals as Food: (Re)connecting Production, Processing, Consumption, and Impacts
    Amy J. Fitzgerald

Mourning Animals: Rituals and Practices Surrounding Animal Death
    Edited by Margo DeMello

Whose Dog Are You? The Technology of Dog Breeds and the Aesthetics of Modern Human–Canine Relations
    Martin Wallen

Hats: A Very Unnatural History
    Malcolm Smith

Spanish Thinking about Animals
    Edited by Margarita Carretero-González

Animal Resistance in the Global Capitalist Era
    Sarat Colling

Animals, Mind, and Matter: The Inside Story
    Josephine Donovan

Animals and Race
    Edited by Jonathan W. Thurston-Torres

ANIMALS AND RACE

EDITED BY Jonathan W. Thurston-Torres

Michigan State University Press
East Lansing

Copyright © 2023 by Michigan State University

♾ The paper used in this publication meets the minimum requirements of ANSI/NISO Z39.48-1992 (R 1997) (Permanence of Paper).

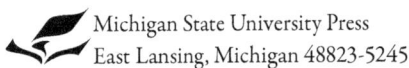
Michigan State University Press
East Lansing, Michigan 48823-5245

Library of Congress Cataloging-in-Publication Data
Names: Thurston-Torres, Jonathan W., editor.
Title: Animals and race / edited by Jonathan W. Thurston-Torres.
Description: East Lansing : Michigan State University Press, [2023] |
Series: The animal turn | Includes bibliographical references.
Identifiers: LCCN 2022017884 | ISBN 978-1-61186-445-8 (paperback) |
ISBN 978-1-60917-715-7 (PDF) | ISBN 978-1-62895-483-8 (epub) |
ISBN 978-1-62896-477-6 (Kindle)
Subjects: LCSH: Race. | Racism. | Animals—Symbolic aspects. | Speciesism.
Classification: LCC HT1523 .A75 2023 | DDC 305.8—dc23/eng/20220611
LC record available at https://lccn.loc.gov/2022017884

Cover design by Erin Kirk
Cover art is The Flemish farrier © The Trustees of the British Museum, released as CC BY-NC-SA 4.0.

Visit Michigan State University Press at www.msupress.org

Contents

vii   Introduction: A Racial History of Animals

Of Domestication and Violence

3   This Is a Thoroughbred Boy: Exploring the Lives of Slave Children and Animals, *Rachael L. Pasierowska*

15   The Double Standard: German Shepherds, Race, and Violence, *Silke Hackenesch and Mieke Roscher*

33   Sheep Trouble on Clifton Beach: Sacrificial Sheep Exorcising the Demon of Racism? *Benita de Robillard*

Of Menageries and Empires

53   Llamas, Snakes, and Indigenous Colonial Equivalency in the Andes, *Rachel Sarah O'Toole*

73   Disguise Hunting and Indian Otherness in Theodor de Bry's *Brief Narration of What Befell the French in Florida* (1591), *Thomas Balfe*

97   Reframing Whiteness in the Zoo: Snowflake the Gorilla in Modern Media, *Elizabeth Tavella*

Of Prey, Sex, and Gender

117   The Miseducation of Henrietta Forge: Whiteness and the Equestrian Imagination in C. E. Morgan's *The Sport of Kings*, *Angela Hofstetter*

133   From Apes to Stags: Black Men, White Women, and the Animals That Code Them in Horror Cinema, *Jonathan W. Thurston-Torres*

147 Queer Trouble at the Origin: Steven Cohen's *Cradle of Humankind* (2012), *Ruth Lipschitz*

159 #RateASpecies: Reviewing Animal Commodities on the Internet, *Soledad Altrudi*

Of Food and Kin

175 Civil Rats and the Human Exceptional: A Vegan-Historical Account of the Rat Extermination Act of 1967, *Thomas Aiello*

191 The Cry of the Wolf: Exposing the Peril of Racism Lurking in the White Sheep Complex, *Rajesh K. Reddy*

205 Contributors

209 Index

Introduction

A Racial History of Animals

When I visited the 2019 Cleveland Museum of Art's exhibit "Medieval Monsters," I saw countless depictions of the *cynocephali*, a "monstrous race" of dog-headed people mentioned in several Middle Ages texts, and they were often depicted alongside Black, Jewish, and Muslim people. Even the travel narratives of John Mandeville and Marco Polo spoke at least briefly about the cynocephali. It was clear: cynocephali were a race of man that had monstrous attributes. What that meant for the Black, Jewish, and Muslim people portrayed with them, however, was less clear, and the cynocephali were but one of many monstrous races that became exoticized to Europe throughout the Middle Ages.[1]

When I moved into the Renaissance texts, the cynocephali started to die out. Then I found them again in Edward Topsell's *History of Four-Footed Beasts*, where there was a section on the cynocephali: "Cynocephales, are a kind of Apes, whose heads are like Dogs, and their other parts like a mans; wherefore Gaza translateth them Canicipites, (to wit) dog-heads. In the French, German, and Illyrian tongues, they are called of some Babion, and Babuino in Italian, is a small kind of Ape; but Aristotle saith, that a Cynocephale is bigger then [sic] an Ape. In English they are called Babouns."[2] Somehow, rather than being a race of humans, this centuries-long racialized other turned out to be a literal baboon.

Animality and race are entangled in interesting ways in premodern history. For example, in the Renaissance, English writers believed Ezekiel 23:20, a metaphorical verse about a woman who sought Egyptian men with penises like that of stallions and seed like that of donkeys, "proved" the fact that Black men *literally* had horse penises, as is seen in many period racial texts, such as those by Richard Jobson in 1620 and John Bulwer in 1650.[3] These entanglements have changed, but they still exist today in the stereotypical claim that Black men are "hung like horses." Likewise, just as early modern authors compared Black voices to those of "apes," in the twentieth and twenty-first centuries we have films such as *Tarzan* and *The Jungle Book* positioning racialized others alongside primates, as if they are one and the same.

The intersection of animality and race has a long and problematic history, and that intersection is the focus of this book. At the crux of these chapters, two questions emerge: why does this intersection exist, and how can we challenge it moving forward?

Working through animal meanings in culture and literature, I often find myself addressing the term "representation." What does it mean to represent something? What does it mean to be represented? When race is represented through animals, this is inherently problematic, a sleight of hand: when you take a social construct—race—and give it a strictly biological analogy, one that can be defined taxonomically by species or other categories—you dismantle the idea that race is a constructed phenomenon. You are rooting perceived social difference in genetics, committing a form of rhetorical eugenics. When I presented at the Medieval and Renaissance Graduate Students Association conference in 2019, I talked about representations of black animals in the early modern period. One scholar asked me afterward if the very intersection of race and species wasn't problematic. I responded that it absolutely was. Defining race through species and removing it from culturally defined stereotypes is inherently problematic and not a useful biological category, either. And yet, it has been an ongoing Western practice for centuries. The intersection's existence implies a societal need to try to conceive of race as a purely biological fact rather than a social construct. However, even in premodern times, the animal-based stereotyping is linked to cultural understandings of and representations of animals, not actual scientific knowledge. Even the "scientific" works of early modern zoology writers like Leonard Mascall rely more on hearsay and folklore than they do empirical observation and rigorous study. And if we refuse to attend to the animal layers of premodern racial thinking, we will struggle with understanding how humans defined themselves in the period, how race transformed from a *strictly* animal term to a term that encompassed both animals and humans, and how our relationships with animals became codified in such a way that would leave lasting impressions on even our current understandings of race.

Studying animality and race together not only promotes critical thinking about this discourse; it also establishes a framework for thinking through premodern race. This book, then, strives to unpack the animal-race intersection, acknowledge its problematization, and critique its use in constructing a hierarchy of race that encourages discrimination. For the scholars in this book, anti-racist activism is important, and addressing this core element of historical and current race discourse allows us to tackle race from a significant but rarely discussed angle.

THE RACIAL HISTORY

Playing off Linda Kalof's *Cultural History of Animals*, I examine history over six different periods to show how Westerners connected race and animals early on in formations of race and how they still play out today. Each of these periods reveals something new to us: a culture, rhetoric, and philosophy that entangle animals and race in wholly unexpected ways.[4] By way of introduction to the topic and to set the stage for the chapters that follow, I will give only the briefest of surveys of ways that race and animals have been entangled over the past several centuries.

The first period is Antiquity, focusing on the Mediterranean and the Greek and Roman Empires. The next era is the Middle Ages, going up to roughly the War of the Roses. The Renaissance or early modern period follows that. Here is where I diverge from Kalof's work, thinking through agriculture and technology instead of political or artistic markers for period demarcation. Rather than calling what follows the Age of Enlightenment, Age of Empire, and Modern Age, I look at what are called the Industrial Revolution, the Machine Age, and the Information Age. This diversion from Kalof's frame is useful for a racial lens of animals: rather than looking at dominant white cultural markers like the Enlightenment (whose voices appear here?) or empires (who is colonizing whom?), my selection of periods assumes trends in both slavery and animal welfare.

For example, when thinking about the treatment of cattle alongside treatment of slaves, I find it more productive to track such treatments in research on the Industrial Revolution as opposed to the Enlightenment. That said, Kalof's work provides models for ways to survey a period at a glance for its animals, showing a portrait that does not try to be either complete or definitive but is still an important and productive survey of human-animal interactions.

In general, race as a premodern term has been contested. As Geraldine Heng notes in *The Invention of Race in the European Middle Ages* (2018), "Medievalists in general were not convinced the concept of race had any purchase for the medieval period. Race theorists also deemed the project presentist, convinced that race was a modern phenomenon and that they could safely ignore the Middle Ages."[5] Despite the criticisms that "race" as a term is anachronistic for the far-off past, I hold with scholars like Heng, who believe in what Kim Hall has called "strategically anachronistic" reading: "demonstrat[ing] the historical construction of a category while providing an oppositional viewpoint rooted in the present."[6] Using race as a term for the past allows for making productive connections to the present and having productive conversations about race-making. And, as Heng has said, "The refusal of race destigmatizes the impacts and consequences of certain laws, acts, practices, and institutions" of the past, disallowing us from naming them what they are and making it "impossible to bear adequate witness to the full meaning of the manifestations and phenomena they installed."[7] In these historical periods, animals and race did connect, and ignoring those connections would mean omitting the historical foundations for today's animal-race intersections.

In the period of Antiquity (800 BCE–600 CE), race was early in its discursive tradition, but we can examine three major cases where animal-race intersections appear. First, in the slave trade, even Aristotle claimed that many people born outside of Greece—racialized Others of the period, albeit before modern formulations of whiteness—were literally born for slavery, that it was part of their natural essence.[8] Thus, in these places of Antiquity, slavery was seen as a normalized element of agriculture and economy, with slaves sold alongside cows at the market.[9] In this way, race could determine one's status: free human or captive animal. Similarly, in the Roman Colosseum, there were contests held between wild animals and *bestiarii*, people who went against the animals. But there were two kinds of contestants: *venatio*, people who would be armed and would fight for money or fame, and *damnatio ad bestias*, where the *bestiarii* were slaves or enemies of the state, and would be stripped and tied to a pole while wild animals were let loose on them—their position in the "natural order" being food and entertainment.[10] And finally, Pliny wrote in *Naturalis Historia* of monstrous races. Some of these featured people whose faces were on their chests, people with one leg, and the cynocephali, all of which originated on Pliny's authority from foreign places.[11]

The Middle Ages (600–1487) is where race formation started evolving. The monstrous races appeared increasingly throughout Medieval art and literature, and they made white English writers wonder if nonwhites were sons of Adam (real humans) or sons of Cain/Ham (some kind of hybrid between animals and humans).[12] The poem *The King of Tars* had a Black Muslim sultan called a hound, from the old word for Muhammed, Mahounda, until the moment he converts to Christianity, when he magically turns white. And the word "race" appeared during this time. It originally referred to enclosures used to separate animals, especially horses, for selective breeding, later including "breeds" of people, indicating that even the discourse of race-making originated with animality and domestication.[13] We also had an emergent Spanish word *moro*, in English "the moor," used to describe Black people (such as the titular Moor in Shakespeare's later play *Othello*, *the Moor of Venice*), black dogs, and black horses. Slavery, too, was becoming an increasingly racialized practice in this period.

In the Renaissance (1487–1760), drama frequently connected Black Africans to the monstrous races or primates. For example, a cast of children performed in blackface, occasionally donning ape costumes, in the play *Mr. Moore's Revels* to illustrate an early modern view that Black men and apes were one and the same.[14] Other plays throughout the period work to create an allegorical discourse for talking about race through animals: Marlowe's *Tamburlaine the Great*, Shakespeare's *Othello*, and Webster's *The White Devil* are just examples. Edward Topsell shows how the cynocephali were literally baboons.[15] The church weaponized Ezekiel 23:20 to show how Black men not only were "hung like horses" but that they were hung because they were part horse, isolating whiteness as being more "human" and therefore closer to God.[16]

During the Industrial Revolution (1760–1880), race and racism became more of what we know today, with standard slurs and specific stereotypes based on location or skin color. In chattel slavery, racialized others were forced to work alongside animals to help build an industrial age in the West. So, enslaved Black people had this complex paradigm: even as frequent caretakers of animals, they were granted near-animal (if not total animal) status themselves. In many plantations, for example, slaves were expected to maintain large numbers of hogs or horses, perhaps separating the labor of being close to animals from whiteness. As Matthew Quallen notes in *Making Animals, Making Slaves*, "Some masters forced their slaves to feed alongside the animals and to eat what the animals ate. . . . Many sold their slaves alongside animals. . . . And many slavers housed their slaves adjacent to their animals. . . . Many slaves found themselves forced to rely on animals to survive."[17] Despite dogs being trained to catch runaway slaves, for example, horses were often used to escape, as we can see in the 1862 painting by Eastman Johnson, *The Fugitive Slaves*. Horses were animals of freedom for many Black slaves. William Billy Lee, a slave to George Washington, was a renowned horseman, for instance. Henry Bib too escaped his enslaver on horseback. And horsemanship in general seemed to have racialized codings. In the first Kentucky Derby in 1875, thirteen of the fifteen jockeys were Black.[18] In this period, animals increasingly became associated with labor, and so too was the racial Other relegated to a status of working animal.

During the Machine Age (1880–1945), race was very much theorized to be biologically and anatomically defined through eugenics work. Other races were seen as taxonomically closer to nonhuman primates, while whites were theorized by white scholars to be the most evolved form. Literature loved to place racialized others against animals as a means of pointing out differences—and similarities. *The Jungle Books*, *The Last of the Mohicans*, the *Tarzan* books, and Jack London's *Call of the Wild* and *White Fang* all worked to elide animals and racialized others. And as whites came to portray Blackness comedically, we see depictions like Disney's *Dumbo*, where Black characters are depicted as literal Jim Crows. And even during the later Civil Rights Movement, dogs were still trained to attack Black civilians specifically, commonly called "white dogs."[19] In some ways, one could argue that Black people were taught they were comparable to animals, and animals were taught they were above Black people. The animal-race entanglements here are messy, and we can start to see the intersections that last today, especially when we get to Michael Vick's legal case, where the media frequently pitted animality against race.

In the Information Age, Michael Vick's cruelty was frequently attributed to his race, and media debated over whether animal lives or Black lives mattered more through their frequent attribution of animal cruelty to a perceived intrinsic Blackness.[20] Previously, in the '90s, Hillary

Clinton called Black children "super predators," operating on the same racist, essentialist logic that marks POC boys as violent and dangerous at a young age while white adult men in their twenties are called "young boys" by the same forces. This term took on a whole new meaning when we reached the recent animated film *Zootopia*. In this film, an anthropomorphic rabbit police officer works with a lower-class, racialized fox to solve a mystery, in which it is later revealed that a city administrator has been drugging predator species to ostensibly "devolve" into their older biology by exhibiting violent, feral behaviors. Race here is again connected to species, specifically predators.[21] While the film shows that predators have evolved to be civilized, the film grounds race (and arguably defends certain microaggressions) on a historical, evolutionary precedent, and goes against the work of bell hooks in *Killing Anger*.[22]

GOOD FOR THINKING

While focus on the animal-race intersection remains uncommon, some scholars, such as Bénédicte Boisseron, Luis Cordeiro-Rodrigues, Les Mitchell, Glen Elder, Jennifer Wolch, and Jody Emel, have broached the subject before, and sometimes this discourse around the relation of animalization and racialization becomes itself unsettling due to the ways in which race is often deployed as a prop for animal suffering. But it is productive to examine that work and see what needs the most clarification.

I find it fruitful to couch my discussion of animals and race in a framework of theory from Bénédicte Boisseron against Cordeiro-Rodrigues, Mitchell, and Probyn-Rapsey to address the dominant questions and concerns as well as show the importance of such work. Then, reading these scholars with Elder, Wolch, and Emel's concept of *le pratique sauvage* [sic], I will show how that modern framework, productive for the twenty-first century, also applies easily to the Renaissance. Beginning the book with these frameworks sets up the chapters that follow in multiple ways: It introduces Boisseron, a fundamental scholar for many of the authors in this book. It sets up a mode of reading that many of the authors take on. And it sets the discursive scene for the conversations contained within this book.

In *Afro-Dog: Blackness and the Animal Question*, Boisseron addresses the intersection of animal studies and race studies as a pervasive aspect of Western culture. In her work, she analyzes the claims by media during the infamous Michael Vick dog abuse case that Vick's cruelty was derivative of his race. She also follows the legal debates around Marjorie Spiegel's 1988 *The Dreaded Comparison: Human and Animal Slavery* and PETA's campaign "Are Animals the New Slaves?" and she critiques the practice of having police dogs in courts, where racial memory associates them with the violence from police dogs during the Civil Rights Movement. How Boisseron's theorizing most informs my work, however, and allows it to be something not only defensible and justifiable but also significant and productive in understanding and challenging Western racial formation and its lasting effects in today's society, is in how she addresses a common problem of academic animal-race intersections: "The risk in the race-animal combination," Boisseron says, "is to see race only as a platform to set the scene of animal studies rather than viewing it as a permanent presence inextricably part of the animal question. The race-animal question begs to be addressed as a true combination rather than as a succession of thoughts that, as in academia, look at race first and then move on to the animal question." A word she uses a few times to address current scholarship is "instrumentalization," that is, animal studies scholars frequently instrumentalize race as a means of forwarding animal causes.[23] Boisseron's sentiments are echoed, too, in Alexander G. Weheliye's *Habeas Viscus*: "It is remarkable . . . how the (not so) dreaded comparison between human and animal slavery is brandished about in the field of animal studies and how black liberation struggles serve as both the positive and negative foil for making a case for the sentience and therefore emancipation of nonhuman beings."[24]

This "foiling" or instrumentalizing appears in several scholarly works. In the edited volume *Animals, Race, and Multiculturalism*, one can see the slant it has just by looking at the titles in the book: "Is Multiculturalism *Good* for Animals? [original emphasis]"; "Animals and the Challenges of Ethnocentrism"; "Animals Off the Menu: A Racist Proposal?"; and "Duties Toward Animals versus Rights to Culture."[25] Not only do these titles reveal an instrumentalizing of race—considering race only as a side aspect, or worse a problem, to thinking about veganism and animal ethics—but they also show a prioritizing of animals with the consequence of trivializing racial experience and oppression. Comparing speciesism to racism as one of the above authors does mirrors a move by Fiona Probyn-Rapsey in *Critical Terms for Animal Studies*, eliding anthropocentrism, a focus on humans being inherently above nonhuman animals, with both racism and sexism.[26] These scholars, however well-meaning, minimize race as a legitimate concern and try to prioritize the animal in such a way that overrides any room for intersectional discussion. Their methodological approaches *instrumentalize* race as a means of getting to animal activism, operating from an almost post-race framework. It is with this instrumentalizing in mind that Boisseron attempts to tip the scales: the trick is to "engage in a corrective tactic as it seeks to counterbalance a recent discourse that has served the animal cause by utilizing race as a leverage point. The challenge, however, is to be mindful of not overcorrecting this imbalance by emphasizing Black suffering to the detriment of animal suffering, and thus re-inscribing the contention."[27] Thus, in many ways, addressing this discourse is not just about contributing to discussions about the intersection between animals and race, but also about shifting the balance to advocate for a racially aware literacy.

Representations of animals hence connote certain racial struggles, and the resultant codification becomes tough to manage. Glen Elder, Jennifer Wolch, and Jody Emel address these concerns in "*Le Pratique sauvage*: Race, Place, and the Human-Animal Divide." They break this representation down into three major segments:

> First, animals serve as absent referents or models for human behavior. Being treated "like an animal" is typically interpreted as a degrading and dehumanizing experience, and such treatment is therefore a powerful tool for subjugation of others. . . . Second, people are dehumanized by virtue of imputed similarities in behavior or bodily features and/or associations with the animal world in general or certain animals in particular. . . . The third and least explored manner in which animals play a role in the social construction of racial difference, and the one which we argue characterizes the postcolonial, postmodern moment, involves specific human practices on animal bodies.[28]

Elder et al. show the numerous representational layers in play when it comes to addressing animals as racial codes, which I connect with a lot of Boisseron's arguments, demonstrating the multiple rhetorics for animalizing race, in some ways dehumanizing, in other ways subjugating, and yet in other ways doing both. Tackling the race-animal question in the twenty-first century relies on being aware of these multiple layers and attending to them with care, concern, and efficiency.

While Elder, Wolch, and Emel treat these representational concerns as fundamental to the race-animal question in the "postcolonial, postmodern" world, I aim to apply their theorizing to the Renaissance. While the general category of "animal" was less frequently invoked in the premodern period, individual species nevertheless became denigrating monikers for racialized others. These early discursive codes for race through animal analogy or animal co-hierarchization built the foundations for a naturally—as in, through the natural world—defined hierarchy that crystallized over time into the racist structures of the Industrial, Machine, and Information Ages.

THE CHAPTERS

And so, this brings me to the chapters of this book and the work that these authors are contributing to this emergent discourse.

The first section is called "Of Domestication and Violence" and looks at violence, familiar animals, and slavery. Rachael L. Pasierowska focuses in on the bullwhip and how enslaved Black children in the nineteenth century saw it used against both themselves and animals, and read that alongside stories of Brer Rabbit to learn about their social status. Silke Hackenesch and Mieke Roscher address police brutality toward African Americans in the 1960s, focusing on the use of German shepherds by the police. Finally, Benita de Robillard analyzes the intersectionality of race, animal slaughter, and space in post-apartheid South Africa to argue for anti-racist animal studies on the government front.

The next section, "Of Menageries and Empires," focuses on postcolonial theory regarding race-animal studies. Rachel Sarah O'Toole starts by holding a magnifying glass to colonial Peru and the ways that Afro-Andeans used their natural knowledge against European colonizers, especially when European animal language sought to demonize them. Thomas Balfe close-reads the art of Theodor de Bry in terms of hunting customs and Amerindian otherness. Last, Elizabeth Tavella reads Italo Calvino's *Mr. Palomar* against albinism, colonialism, and disability studies, and connects that case study to the multimodal corpus of work surrounding Snowflake the Gorilla.

The third section, entitled "Of Prey, Sex, and Gender," looks at race-animal studies against gender, sex, and sexuality studies. It starts with Angela Hofstetter's work in *The Sport of Kings*, examining the intersection of rape, race, and animality. Next, I argue in "From Apes to Stags" that animals have factored into horror cinema's constructions of racialized others through conflation of racial discourses and discourses of what is "natural." Ruth Lipschitz reads queerness in natural origins in Steven Cohen's *Cradle of Mankind*, and Soledad Altrudi discusses communication trends around cuteness of specific species on the Internet.

The final section is "Of Food and Kin," looking most closely at consumerism and animal ethics. Thomas Aiello conducts what he calls a vegan-historical account of the Rat Extermination Act of 1967, and Rajesh Reddy closes the book with what he calls a "critique of the animal rights movement as the ultimate opt-out" of anti-racism.

CONCLUSION

When talking with the authors of this book, many commonalities arose. Many of the authors view this collection as bridging the gap between academics and activism. Whether racial minorities are excluded from discussions of animal rights and ethics or animal rhetoric is weaponized against people of color as a form of oppression, these authors see their work as contesting many of these public and academic norms. Other authors saw many of the chapters as actively combating and dismantling systems of whiteness, white supremacy, and institutionalized racism. All the authors, though, follow in the tradition of Boisseron's *Afro-Dog* and Elder et al.'s "*Le Pratique sauvage*" in the hopes of further challenging the elision of animals and race.

As we delve deeper into the twenty-first century, hopefully we will challenge the elision of animals and race. The authors here do not advocate for a perpetuation of reading race through an animal lens. However, as it is a dominant cultural phenomenon when it comes to creating racial categories, it is necessary to identify the intersection, understand it, analyze it, and then critique it. The chapters that follow engage in anti-racist activism through these kinds of critiques, and they bring these discussions forward to critique the dominant white rhetorics of animalizing race. With lots of hope and energy, the Information Age could be the last age of a racial history of animals.

NOTES

1. Friedman, *The Monstrous Races*, 19–21.
2. Topsell, *A History of Four-Footed Beasts*, 10.
3. Loomba and Burton, *Race in Early Modern England*, 206.
4. Note that animals are living beings, while race is a concept. While many of the authors, including myself, use the eponymous "animals and race" as a typical shorthand, we do not use it to imply a categorical equivalency between the two.
5. Heng, *Invention of Race*, 3.
6. Hall, *Things of Darkness*, 261.
7. Heng, *Invention of Race*, 4.
8. Aristotle, *Politics*, 1.1254b16–21.
9. De Ste. Croix, *The Class Struggle in the Ancient Greek World*, chap. 4.
10. Futrell, *Blood in the Arena*, 28–29.
11. Friedman, *The Monstrous Races*, 19–21.
12. Ramey, *Black Legacies*, chap. 5; Friedman, *The Monstrous Races*, 101–3.
13. Eliav-Feldon, Isaac, and Ziegler, *The Origins of Racism in the West*, 202.
14. Elliott, *Mr. Moore's Revels*.
15. Topsell, *History*, 10.
16. Some examples of this include Richard Jobson's *The Golden Trade* (1623), Samuel Purchas's reprint of Jobson in 1625 where he identifies Black gentiles with "Priapian Stallions," and John Bulwer's *Anthropometamorphosis* (1650).
17. Quallen, *Making Animals, Making Slaves*, 83.
18. Gates Jr., *100 Amazing Facts about the Negro*, 41–42.
19. Romain, *White Dog*.
20. Boisseron, *Afro-Dog*, chap. 1.
21. For the exact quote from Clinton, see Hillary Clinton, "1996: Hillary Clinton on 'Superpredators.'" Bryan Howard, director, *Zootopia*.
22. Sandlin and Snaza, "'It's Called a Hustle, Sweetheart.'"
23. Boisseron, *Afro-Dog*, x, xiii, 2, 46–47, 77–79.

24. Weheliye, *Habeas Viscus*, 10.
25. Cordeiro-Rodrigues and Mitchell, *Animals, Race, and Multiculturalism*, xii–xiv.
26. Probyn-Rapsey, "Anthropocentrism," 48, 53.
27. Boisseron, *Afro-Dog*, xiv.
28. Elder, Wolch, and Emel, "*Le Pratique sauvage*," 82–83.

WORKS CITED

Aristotle. *The Politics*. Translated by H. Rackham. Vol. 21 of *Aristotle in 23 Volumes*. Cambridge, MA: Harvard University Press, 1944.

Boisseron, Bénédicte. *Afro-Dog: Blackness and the Animal Question*. New York: Columbia University Press, 2018.

Bulwer, John. *Anthropometamorphosis*. London, 1650.

Clinton, Hillary. "1996: Hillary Clinton on 'Superpredators.'" *C-Span*, 1996. Available at https://www.YouTube.com.

Cordeiro-Rodrigues, Luis, and Les Mitchell, eds. *Animals, Race, and Multiculturalism*. New York: Palgrave, 2017.

De Ste. Croix, G. E. M. *The Class Struggle in the Ancient Greek World from the Archaic Age to the Arab Conquests*. Ithaca, NY: Cornell University Press, 1989.

Elder, Glen, Jennifer Wolch, and Jody Emel. "*Le Pratique sauvage*: Race, Place, and the Human-Animal Divide." In *Animal Geographies: Place, Politics, and Identity in the Nature-Culture Borderlands*. London: Verso, 1998.

Eliav-Feldon, Miriam, Benjamin Isaac, and Joseph Ziegler. *The Origins of Racism in the West*. Cambridge: Cambridge University Press, 2013.

Elliott, John. *Mr. Moore's Revels*. London, 1636.

Friedman, John. *The Monstrous Races in Medieval Art and Thought*. Cambridge, MA: Harvard University Press, 1981.

Futrell, Alison. *Blood in the Arena: The Spectacle of Roman Power*. Austin: University of Texas Press, 2010.

Gates, Henry Louis, Jr. *100 Amazing Facts about the Negro*. New York: Knopf, 2017.

Hall, Kim. *Things of Darkness: Economies of Race and Gender in Early Modern England*. Ithaca, NY: Cornell University Press, 1995.

Heng, Geraldine. *The Invention of Race in the Middle Ages*. Cambridge: Cambridge University Press, 2018.

Howard, Bryan, director. *Zootopia*. Disney, 2016.

Jobson, Richard. *The Golden Trade*. London, 1623, 1625.

Kalof, Linda. *A Cultural History of Animals*. Vols. 1–6. Oxford: Berg, 2007.

Loomba, Ania, and Jonathan Burton. *Race in Early Modern England: A Documentary Companion*. New York: Palgrave, 2007.

Probyn-Rapsey, Fiona. "Anthropocentrism." In *Critical Terms for Animal Studies*, edited by Lori Gruen. Chicago: University of Chicago Press, 2018.

Quallen, Matthew. "Making Animals, Making Slaves: Animalization and Slavery in the Antebellum United States." Honors thesis, Georgetown University, 2016.

Ramey, Lynn. *Black Legacies: Race and the European Middle Ages*. Gainesville: University Press of

Florida, 2016.

Romain, Gary. *White Dog*. Chicago: University of Chicago Press, 2004.

Sandlin, Jennifer, and Nathan Snaza. "'It's Called a Hustle, Sweetheart': Black Lives Matter, the Police State, and the Politics of Colonizing Anger in *Zootopia*." *Journal of Popular Culture* (2018).

Topsell, Edward. *A History of Four-Footed Beasts*. London: William Jaggard, 1607.

Weheliye, Alexander G. *Habeas Viscus: Racializing Assemblages, Biopolitics, and Black Feminist Theories of the Human*. Durham, NC: Duke University Press, 2014.

Of Domestication and Violence

This Is a Thoroughbred Boy
Exploring the Lives of Slave Children and Animals

Rachael L. Pasierowska

IN THE LATE 1930S, GEORGE WOMBLE, FORMERLY ENSLAVED IN THE STATE OF GEORGIA, was still but a "small boy." Keen to ensure that his purchase was not defective in any way, Mr. Womble closely inspected young George, in the company of three doctors, beginning with his physiology: teeth, muscles, and eyes. George Womble's description of the occasion underlines the parallels between his future master's inspection of the child slave and the way in which one would examine an animal: looking at the physiological characteristics of the animal prior to finalizing his purchase. Moreover, Womble recalled the words of one of the local doctors: "This is a thoroughbred boy." The doctor's language denoted an equine beast, not a young, enslaved child. How the boy received this glowing assessment of his physical appearance and health, and later his presumed intelligence, is unknown. But being both sold and separated from the life that he had previously known would have undoubtedly been unsettling for a young child who now found himself alone in the world.

In this chapter I look at the experiences of enslaved children such as Womble, and explore the extent to which young African Americans from the U.S. South constructed a knowledge or an understanding of their social standing through the lens of the animal world. The chapter builds on research for an earlier article in which I argued that North American slave children became aware of their slave status in what was in effect a three-part process—of blissful unawareness, to then a realization of their enslavement, and finally a coming to terms with said revelation. I posit that the animal world offered enslaved children a means of exploring their social standing in the antebellum South. By drawing on a familiarity with and observations of the animal world around them, enslaved children came to a grim realization of their enslavement.[1] The ways in which white slaveholders drew parallels between enslaved children and animals, for instance in their actions and language, contributed to children's newfound awareness. Finally, I show how this awareness would develop into a better understanding of their inferior status. An important point here is not that slaveholders appeared to treat enslaved children in a markedly different way to enslaved adults; rather, that enslaved children looked to their immediate surroundings—most importantly to the animals around them living on the plantations and farms—to try and draw conclusions about their lives and their respective social standing in a slave society.

DRAWING ANALOGIES BETWEEN OTHER SLAVES AND ANIMALS

Slaveholders often treated enslaved children as analogous to animals, from viewing young slaves as little endearing creatures to something more akin to pests. Scholars have long recognized the frequency with which travelers observed how slave owners animalized their enslaved property. In this light, seasoned traveler John Bull, speaking of a trip through the U.S. South in 1816, recounted how—notwithstanding the acutely blistering day—he witnessed a cart trundling along in which "five or six half naked black children were tumbled, like pigs, together." The witness observed how due to the cart possessing no covering, the enslaved children "seemed to have been actually broiled to sleep."[2] The term "broil" could have a dual meaning here. On the one hand, broil refers to something left to scorch in the sun. Another connotation is that of cooking meat or fish at a high temperature. The nakedness of the children and their listless demeanor give the reader the impression not only of their neglect but also of meat skinned and cooking under a high heat. Rather than focusing on travelers' perceptions of and experiences with enslaved children, this chapter centers on the extent to which Black children born into bondage were aware of such characterizations, and what they might have felt and thought in light of such analogies.

Across the U.S. South, ex-slaves recalled how they had witnessed firsthand the animalization of slaves. Formerly a slave in Dunbar, West Virginia, Eli Davison detailed in a Works Progress Administration (WPA) interview in the 1930s an encounter with a slave in chains when he was still young. The female slave in question had attempted to return to her former owners following a sale a great distance away. Her "maser" secured the enslaved woman "to his saddle leading her just like you would a dog" and at night he "chained her to the wagon wheel where she could get in the wagon and sleep that night." The woman's master recounted to Davison's master how he had "traveled about a hundred miles with her that way."[3] This must have been a terribly uncomfortable experience in both a physical and emotional sense: first, the chain would have chafed and rubbed against her neck, causing blisters, especially if this was during one of the hotter southern months, and second, she would have most likely borne great shame at being dragged along the road by a mounted rider. In this instance, even the horse perhaps appeared to have more freedom, for it was presumably only ridden with leather reins and not a metal chain. Thus, Davison remembered the woman decades later as being like a dog. Yet, unlike a dog whose fidelity sets him apart from many animals, the enslaved woman was not to be trusted even while her master rode alongside her.

The autobiographies of former slaves—freed or runaways—provide many examples of how enslaved children experienced the system of slavery. A former slave known only as Frances remembered her "first impression of slavery" as a small child when she witnessed a man "seated on horseback, brandishing a big, black whip [who] rounded up a long line of naked slaves two by two, chained to each other." The frightened girl watched as the slaves quenched their thirst from "the horse trough," which she remembered in sharp juxtaposition to the driver who "drank from the pail."[4] Frederick Douglass's earliest memory of the horrors of slavery centered on Colonel Lloyd's bloody whipping of his Aunt Hester. Concealed within a closet, Douglass witnessed his aunt, stripped to her waist and mounted on a stool, her arms tied to a hook hanging from the kitchen beams, as the Colonel dealt multiple lashes. Douglass wrote how this represented his first exposure to "the bloody scenes that often occurred on the plantation." The scene was indeed bloody as Lloyd's "heavy cowskin" whip soon brought blood "dripping to the floor."[5] The image brings forth several animalistic references. First, Hester hanging from a hook foregrounds the connotation of an animal strung up in a butcher's shop or a meat-smoking house. Second, the repeated lashing with the whip draws to mind the image of a rider incessantly whipping a horse.

These childhood recollections, penned by adult hands, illustrate two notions. First, they were memories that left an indelible imprint on the young, enslaved children's perceptions of the environments in which both children lived. In revealing the brutality of the slave system, the children's memories brought the social structures of the microcosm of the southern slave plantation into sharp relief, notably that of the distinction between enslaved and free, as well as Black and white. Both former slaves recalled how these events—*for the first time*—represented a watershed when as children, they began to see the system of slavery from which they had hitherto been shielded. For Frances, seeing the slave gang passing by was her "first impression of slavery," while Douglass later told how prior to witnessing Hester's scourging he had been "out of the way of the bloody scenes that often occurred on the plantation."[6] The lives of Frances and Douglass would not be the same in the aftermath of these traumas.

Second, the children's memories point to certain animalistic references. The whip appears in both recollections as a tool either to punish or to herd. The riding crop and its longer carriage counterpart were omnipresent tools in a world where the horse represented the primary source of transportation. Growing up in a rural setting, slave children would have been familiar with this implement and its association with animals, especially as many former slaves remembered working with their masters' mounts when they were still too young to labor in the fields.

It is worth mentioning here the differences between nineteenth-century whips, as this better illustrates this notion: the short riding crop, which might have a flat surface or end in a cord; the longer switch employed in human corporal punishment; the carriage lash that drivers secured; and finally, the bull whip. In Frances's recollections it seems most likely that the driver held a bull whip, for as the autobiography later described the driver, he was "brandishing a big, black whip" and that fits the characterization of a southern bull whip. Visualizing the whip as a bull whip and not, say, a horse crop furthers the imagery of herding. A traditional riding crop has a stock that is perhaps half the length of the lash. Generally speaking, a rider will reach behind the pommel of the saddle to whip the horse. A bull whip, in contrast, can have a lash up to six meters in length with a handle of about a third of a meter. Thus, a lash of a bull whip can measure up to twenty times the length of the stock.

Across the U.S. rural South, mounted farmers herded livestock with a bull whip. The analogy in Frances's memories cannot be more explicit: the mounted driver employed a bull whip to "herd" his slaves to his desired destination.

Furthermore, when Colonel Lloyd tied Douglass's aunt to a hook in the ceiling and stripped the clothing from her, leaving her breasts exposed, he performed an action akin to tethering a domesticated animal to impede escape and freedom of movement: he completely dehumanized her. There remains, however, the question of how enslaved children might have viewed their lives and stations through the lens of animals, especially in moments of trauma. In witnessing the degrading and animalistic treatment of fellow slaves, these children, like most children at some point or other in their psychological development, would have drawn connections to other similar instances, which might have helped them to better understand the unfolding social structure in which they found themselves—for example, the whipping of a horse and the whipping of a Black person. Frances's recollections are much more indicative in this respect: the enslaved drank from the trough, a water vessel for a four-legged creature, requiring either drinking the water with a cupped hand or bringing one's lips directly to the water's surface, an act that would have necessitated the drinker to prostrate himself on all fours *like* an animal. The slave driver, in contrast, drank from a handheld receptacle. Frances herself looked at "those poor creatures with wild staring eyes and tongues lolled out lapping the water like dumb, thirsty animals."[7] Her childhood mind perceived the slave coffle as akin to beasts, like those that she was familiar with on the plantation: for example, a dusty horse whipped by its rider, its flanks heaving and glistening with sweat from exhaustion and heat, its tongue foaming saliva, nostrils flaring, and eyes rolling. Frances's young brain, in seeking to comprehend the novelty of the situation, turned to similar visions.

Such recollections attest to Mia Bay's observations of the ways in which former slaves often drew comparisons between their infant days and the lives of domesticated animals.[8] In employing the WPA interviews, Bay convincingly argues that former slaves looked back on their childhood days as analogous to the treatment of plantation animals. Nonetheless, I propose to push her interpretations further to investigate the extent to which the enslaved children themselves might have drawn similar conclusions about their social situations, self-identifying as animals albeit without the maturity that comes in later life.

ENSLAVED CHILDREN'S EXPERIENCES AS ANALOGOUS TO ANIMALS

Former slaves' memories illustrate the connection in the minds of enslaved children with the lives of domestic animals in the antebellum South. During an interview with the WPA in the late 1930s, Lizzie Williams in North Carolina recounted how young slaves were not exempted from work tasks, and how slaves were "whupped jes like a mule iffen dey act like dey don' wanna work."[9] Speaking of his sleeping arrangements, Hal Hutson, a former slave in Tennessee, remembered in an interview how he and his siblings all "slept on the floor like hogs!"[10]

Perhaps the most frequent association between the lives of enslaved children and domesticated animals came at mealtimes. Many former slaves remembered how as children they ate in a fashion akin to that of the farmyard stock. Formerly enslaved in Arkansas, Uncle Jack Island recalled how "dey wuz six uv us chillun an dey would feed us in a big wooden tray. Dey'd po' hot pot liquor in de tray an crumble braid in hit. Den dey'd give us each a spoon an we wud all git roun an eat."[11] Another former slave recollected eating with the other enslaved children from a trough around which they stood "eating like little pigs." The only factor perhaps for these children that differentiated them from "little pigs" was that they sometimes "would go to the creek and get mussel shells for spoons."[12] But Mae Moore and her enslaved playmates had only their hands for utensils.[13]

Some enslaved children had to scrabble with their masters' animals in order to get their fill. The following recollection from George Womble provides an illustrative account of the feeding habits of enslaved children in the U.S. South, revealing how these habits were essentially animalistic in nature:

> The younger children were fed from a trough that was twenty feet in length. . . . For breakfast the milk and bread was all mixed together in the trough by the master who used his walking cane to stir it with. . . . There were times when the master's dogs and some of the pigs that ran round the yard all

come to the trough to share these meals. Mr. Womble states that they were not permitted to strike any of these animals.[14]

The master's actions demonstrate how he apparently perceived the enslaved children as somewhat akin to his domesticated livestock. In supplying the children's victuals in an animal trough, stirring the mush with a walking cane, requiring the children to await his orders to eat, and not providing utensils with which to eat the food, Womble's master underlined his animalization of enslaved children. Womble looked back on his childhood mealtimes as ones that attested to this dehumanization. But my interest lies more in how young Womble and his playmates interpreted this treatment. Eating outside and on the ground put the children on a level with the animals—indeed, perhaps even lower, since Womble remembered how the children were forbidden from striking the animals that sought to share in the meal. Womble's master appears not to have chastised the animals for attempting to take the children's fare. In addition, the children lacked utensils with which to feed themselves. This style of eating provided one framework with which enslaved children might have drawn correlations between their lives and habits and those of farmyard animals.

Another example from Frederick Douglass shows how he not only became cognizant of such similarities but began to question the slave society within which he lived. Like Womble, he spoke of having to fight with animals during mealtimes. Writing of his constant foraging for food to satiate his ever-present hunger, Douglass recalled how he would fight with "Old Nep," the house's dog, for "the smallest crumbs that fell from the kitchen table." On other occasions, he scrabbled just to get "crumbs and small bones flung out for the cats." Douglass's struggles to satisfy the nutritional needs of his growing body were, he later asserted, central motivators in his coming to interrogate the institution of slavery. He began to ask questions: "Why am I a slave? Why are some people slaves, and others masters? Was there ever a time when this was not so? How did the relation commence?" In having to scrabble in the dusty yard—presumably on all fours—young Douglass found himself in a physical situation either akin to that of a domesticated animal, or worse. Indeed, his accounts suggest that the cats and dogs of the plantation received sufficient food for their needs, whereas he often had to supplement his habitually scant portion of cornmeal with oysters and clams from the plantation's stream or a crust of bread. It was thus that Douglass began to question his social situation. The struggles for victuals with the animals represented a catalyst for Douglass's becoming aware of his inferior status—and by nature of being inferior, that of being a slave.[15]

Slaveowners' language further shows how some enslaved children began to understand their lives in bondage. In his autobiography, John Brown cited how his mistress Betty Moore "used to call us children up to the big house every morning, and give us a dose of garlic and rue to keep us 'wholesome,' as she said, and make us 'grow likely for market.'"[16] The employment of the terms "wholesome," "likely," and "market" underlines, as Brown and the editorial team probably intended, the animalization and agricultural commodification of child slaves. In a similar vein, Peter Bruner recollected how his master refused to complete a sales transaction with a so-named "Allen" because the proffered sum of $800 was too low. At around ten years of age, the prepubescent Bruner was "just growing into money" and soon would fetch $1,000.[17] Taken together, the two examples point to the notion of growth and increased *market* value.

When Isaac Johnson was sold away from his mother, this incident marked an acute change for him and his previous life with his family. As his lot was called, he "was asked if I had ever been whipped, or sick, or had had the toothache, and similar questions."[18] Scholars and abolitionists alike have long pointed to the correlations between the sale of slaves and the sale of domesticated animals, and Johnson's childhood memories of his sale are no different.[19] Perhaps the sole distinction between the sale of Johnson and that of an animal is that a child could respond to inquiries about his or her physical health and temperament. Terms such as "market" and "sale" dehumanized and commodified enslaved children. Despite their age, children both heard and retained such language, which led them to a newfound awareness of their inferior social status and even to question this revelation. These examples, moreover, foreground the role whites played in this dialectic since their language provided the stimulus for such questioning: a language that was charged with animalistic and agricultural terminology.

Threats and acts of punishment represented for many children a watershed moment in their awareness of slavery. James Williams recalled in his autobiography how one of his master's friends relayed the following warning to Williams with respect to absconding: "'You must never run away. Bad boys are the only ones that run away, and when their master gets them he will sell them to go to Georgia, where they will bore holes in your ears and plow [sic] you like a horse.' Saying this for the purpose of frightening me, thinking that I would believe such stories." In making this statement, the speaker drew a stark analogy between the working lives of slaves in Georgia and that of the domesticated horse. Furthermore, the warning spoke of the mutilation of slaves' ears in a style reminiscent of the perforation of the various body parts of farmyard animals: farmers notched the ears of pigs and cows to brand them. Contrary to the speaker's objective, the warning, rather than instilling in Williams a fear of running away, resulted in the opposite: Williams recalled later how on "seeing the difference between freedom and slavery, I made up my mind that when I was old enough I would run away."[20]

In another example, following the closure of Isaac Johnson's sale, he spoke of having to leave the auction house without bidding farewell to his mother. When William Madinglay led the young boy away with him, he gave the following command: "'Come along with me, I will train you without your mother's help." As one might do with an animal, Madinglay set about the "training" of his new slave boy, chaining the child "to a post as though I had been a horse," to which he remained till "late in the afternoon."[21] Like a chained animal Johnson was deprived of free movement and left to suffer. There is no reference to either food, water, or shelter from the natural elements. While Johnson in his adult days wrote of the experience as akin to the treatment of a horse, I believe that this event would also have awakened similar parallels in the young slave as he awaited the uncertain return of his master. I doubt, therefore, that this metaphor was used solely by abolitionist writers.

For Lewis Garrard Clarke, physical abuse served as a vicious wake-up call to the institution of slavery. When he committed the grave offence—*grave* in his mistress's eyes—of drinking from one of her children's receptacles, his mistress was furious. She

> expressed her utter abhorrence of such an act, by throwing my head violently back, and dashing into my face two dippers of water. The shower of water was followed by a heavier shower of kicks . . . but the words bitter and cutting that followed were like a storm of hail upon my young heart. "She would teach me better manners than that. . . . She would have one *slave* that *knew* his *place*; if I wanted *water*, go to the *spring*, and not drink there in the *house* [my emphasis]."[22]

The mistress's violent response acutely underlines the notion of dehumanization. Unlike the white children of the house in which Clarke was a slave, he came to see with great celerity that when *he* thirsted, *he* was to retire to the spring. First, drinking from the spring not only placed Clarke on a level inferior to his mistress's children, but it furthermore placed him in closer proximity to the drinking patterns of animals: Clarke presumably would have had to employ a cupped hand to quench his thirst or even bring his mouth to the water's edge. Drinking in this way forced Clarke to mimic the behavior of an animal. The event shaped how Clarke had hitherto viewed his life and how he would come to see his present situation. This moment signified "new times," and for a period of time he was "completely benumbed with my sorrow."[23] The mistress's response prompted this realization in Clarke and demanded a transition in the child's drinking from one that was more human to one that dripped with animalistic connotations.

Another way in which slaveholders demonstrated a dehumanization of enslaved children was treating them like pets. On the outside, this form of animalization perhaps shows a more benevolent side to slavery with respect to the paternalistic arguments of pro-slavery advocates from the nineteenth century. Slave owners who made pets of certain enslaved children demonstrated behavior not so dissimilar from that which they might bestow on a lapdog or favored hunting hound. But, by taking control of slaves' children to pet and pamper, owners—most often slave mistresses—succeeded in drawing further juxtapositions between free and enslaved, and in so doing underlined the very nature of the human-animal dyad that all too often defined the master-slave relation.

Former slaves frequently recalled masters and mistresses who treated them as "pets." Given that such a large percentage of the WPA interviewees experienced slavery as children, their memories are particularly rich in this regard. Formerly enslaved in Louisiana, Donaville Broussard spoke of being "petted" by both the white ladies and his mother alike.[24] Slave masters were not averse to such practices either. Jim Allen from Mississippi stated how "old Marster fed me so good, for I was his pet."[25] Considering examples from the antebellum South, it is difficult to fully ascertain the extent to which slave masters and mistresses viewed their "pets" as objects of charm and entertainment. I believe that former slaves' observed experiences and personal recollections of being "pets" give rise to several possible arguments. Since we cannot brand all plantation owners as one, it is therefore highly plausible that one or all of the following occurred across antebellum plantations.

First is the image of the benevolent and/or elderly grandmother/slaveholder who delighted in spoiling her Black and white pets. Jackson's mistress's adoption of "pet" may have been simply a term of endearment. Nineteenth-century dictionaries from both sides of the Anglo-Atlantic corroborate this. "Pet," arguably rooted in the French word for "little" or "petit," denoted "a little favourite" or "a fondling" and as a verb "to treat as a pet" or "to fondle."[26] In this sense masters and mistresses would have been wont to bestow both special attention and treatment, for instance biscuits, on their little "pets." For slaveholders, spoiling their little favorites most likely gave them a sense of self-gratification, like that which contemporary pet owners can similarly attest to.

The second function demonstrates the slaveholders' omnipotence vis-à-vis their chattel. When masters made pets of enslaved children, they required them to spend great amounts of time away from their mothers. Temporally speaking, this perhaps was not any different from the time spent away from working mothers if the children were under the care of an elderly slave, as was often the case.[27] For children who spent this time *not* in the care of somebody of their social caste and race, but of the "superior" white slaveholding class, this had a sharp impact on a child's cultural and social development. Living on a more permanent basis in the master's and mistress's house further exacerbated the extent to which owners shaped enslaved children's self-perceptions. Thus, former slaves recalled growing up with two mothers.[28] Such a complex dynamic had a dual psychological effect on young children, all the more formative because the early years of a child are some of the most important in both the development of self-awareness and the ways in which they come to perceive others around them.

From the enslaved parent's perspective, this quasi "fostering" of their children highlighted all too clearly their powerlessness with respect to their owners. When William Jacobs's father and mistress called for him simultaneously, the confused young child went to his mistress. This resulted in a sharp reproof from his father: "'You are my child,' replied our father, 'and when I call you, you should come immediately, if you have to pass through fire and water.'"[29] From this moment Jacobs learned that while he remained the financial property of the Flint family, he nonetheless must never forget that he was first and foremost his father's son. The reference to the father's chagrin and the emphasis on the possessive "*my*" illustrate that the incident was equally painful for the boy's father. The father likely suffered great disappointment and shame in addition to anger at his position as an enslaved parent.[30] In removing enslaved children from the slave quarters and the immediate care of their parents, slaveholders dehumanized slave parents. Bereft of the ability to reclaim their young, the repositioning of slave children in this way is reminiscent of the removal of young livestock shortly after weaning. Among mammals, parental care represents the epitome of the relationship between parent and offspring and is what separates our species as *Homo sapiens* from others. Because mammals are born in an immature state—unlike, for instance, reptiles—they have evolved to nurture and protect their offspring from outside harm. Such examples illustrated slave parents' inability to protect their children in the manner of *all* mammals.

Finally, in petting enslaved children, slaveholders—consciously or subconsciously—molded children to their legal status within the slaveholding South, and in so doing worked to preserve the institution of slavery. In this light, Coverson recalled how her mistress petted and spoiled her with biscuits at every meal even though enslaved African Americans "ain't neber eat no biscuits but missus always gimie one eber meal an' in dat way she got me interested in waitin' on de table."[31] Like Coverson, Pattillo was "considered a pet by everyone and hung around the mistress, since she did not have any children of her own." Pattillo's principal employment in this capacity was to "hand her the scissors and thread her needles."[32] As such he performed the role of both hand servant *and* pet for his mistress. Children provided a dual function to their mistresses: both as "pets" and domestic slaves in training. Such close relationships between slave owners and their young infant pets created firm emotional bonds that sometimes led ex-slaves to speak highly of their former owners decades after Emancipation.

CONCLUSION

"This is a thoroughbred boy. His teeth are good and he has good muscles and eyes. He'll live a long time."[33] This chapter has posited that instances such as the above experienced by George Womble represent moments in which enslaved children became aware of their status as slaves and, in so doing, the workings of the wider social structures in place across the Atlantic world: the system of slavery and the implicit inferiority that such a system forced on Black slaves. Such moments could be a one-off triggered event, such as the sale of young Womble and the language employed by the medical practitioners at the time of sale that created a stark correlation between enslaved child and domesticated animal. Other examples, however, were more protracted and did not necessarily require the use of such explicit language. For example, slaveowners' decisions to feed their young slaves from animal troughs, often neglecting to furnish their slaves with utensils. In such examples, the analogy between slave and animal was not simply a momentary watershed occurrence. Rather, enslaved children saw and experienced daily the dehumanization *and* commodification of slaves. Such treatment also did not escape children's knowledge. The WPA interviews demonstrate that while elderly African Americans often looked back on their slavery days as analogous to the lives of animals, enslaved children might understand their lives in a similar fashion, albeit within the limitations of a child's mind.

Some animals come to the fore more than others in slaveholders' treatment of enslaved children. Choice words such as "plough" and "thoroughbred" draw connections with horses. For centuries, Europeans had ridden horses, both breeding and domesticating them to serve their owners. Here, the word "plough" foregrounds the image of a strong horse or mule able to carry out heavy fieldwork. In contrast, "thoroughbred" brings to mind a sleek and healthy racehorse or destrier. When we read that enslaved children ate from animal troughs this brings to mind an image of smaller livestock, for instance pigs. Former slaves themselves recollected how this style of eating placed them on a level somewhat akin to pigs. Travelers also made similar connections. Finally, threats to bore holes in the ears of enslaved runaways furthers the image of notching hogs' ear flaps. All of these animals were connected through man's domestication of them, regardless of their size and temperament. Enslaved children, like horses and pigs, grew up in an environment where they were expected to live similarly domesticated lives.

The actions and words of slaveholders also stripped slave parents of their rights to comfort and provide for their children's emotional and psychological needs. This created trauma for parents who painfully had their position as slaves reinforced—a position that was much more analogous to that of a domesticated animal than a free parent with respect to parenthood and child-rearing. It was within this world—a complex blending and fusion of human and animal and free and slave—that enslaved Black children grew and developed.

NOTES

1. Pasierowska, "Up from Childhood," 94–116.
2. Paulding, *Letters from the South*, 129.
3. Rawick, *Texas Narratives*, 1100.
4. Brown, *Homespun Heroines*, 72.
5. Douglass, *Narrative of the Life*, 7–8.
6. Douglass, *Narrative of the Life*, 8.
7. Brown, *Homespun Heroines*, 72.
8. Bay, *The White Image*, 127.
9. *North Carolina Narratives*, vol. 11, part 2: 395. For another example see Brewer, *American Negro Folklore*, 235.
10. *Oklahoma Narratives*, vol. 13: 145.

11. *Arkansas Narratives*, vol. 2, part 3: 380.
12. Cited in Cade, "Out of the Mouths of Ex-Slaves," 300.
13. Cade, "Out of the Mouths of Ex-Slaves," 300.
14. *Georgia Narratives*, vol. 4, part 4: 186–87.
15. Douglass, *My Bondage and My Freedom*, 75–76, 89.
16. Chamerovzow, *Slave Life in Georgia*, 3.
17. Bruner, *A Slave's Adventures*, 14.
18. Johnson, *Slavery Days*, 10.
19. For the most comprehensive treatment of slave markets, see Johnson, *Soul by Soul*.
20. Williams, *Life and Adventures of James Williams*, 13.
21. Williams, *Life and Adventures of James Williams*, 13.
22. Clarke, *Narrative of the Sufferings of Lewis Clarke*, 15–16.
23. Clarke, *Narrative of the Sufferings of Lewis Clarke*, 16.
24. *Texas Narratives*, vol. 16, part 1: 151. See also *Georgia Narratives*, vol. 4, part 4: 51.
25. *Mississippi Narratives*, vol. 9: 2. See also *Georgia Narratives*, vol. 4, part 3: 167. Employment of Black infants in the capacity of pets was not unique to the antebellum South or indeed the broader Atlantic world. In Europe, popular culture demonstrates the popularity of little Black children as "playthings" or "pets" for wealthy white ladies, for instance as depicted in Mignard le Romain's *Portrait of Louise Renée de Kéroualle*. This seventeenth-century portrait portrays a beautiful duchess in full dress attire as the viewer's gaze is drawn immediately to the creamy tones of her skin, which balance with a number of exquisite pearls secured in a conch shell. Her tones are in sharp juxtaposition to that of the ebony hand of a young child who proffers pearls to her mistress. Adorned in pearls and silks, this child—purportedly an African servant of the duchess—bespeaks volumes about the extent of her mistress's wealth. De Kéroualle's contemporaries looking on her portrait could not have failed to see, and likely covet, what riches the king's mistress possessed. Yet, the portrait illustrates a secondary theme, that of the young child servant as a "pet," which brings us back to the enslaved child's experience in the Atlantic world. In adorning her servant child in great riches, the duchess demonstrated a trend in which wealthy white European women indulged their little Black "pets." In this light, one can see that the pearl necklace on the neck of the Black child has a dyadic function, both of wealth and as an animal collar. In contrast, the duchess sports no similar necklace; ladies and girls were wont to tie ribbons around the necks of their lapdogs and feline companions.
26. Reid, *Dictionary of the English Language*, 306.
27. *Georgia Narratives*, vol. 4, part 1: 312.
28. In her autobiography, Kate Drumgoold spoke of her "white mother," who she noted was "so kind to my dear mother." Drumgoold, *A Slave Girl's Story*, 4.
29. Jacobs, *Incidents in the Life of a Slave Girl*, 17–18
30. For another example, see Jacob Stroyer's autobiography; Stroyer, *My Life in the South*, 19–20.
31. *North Carolina Narratives*, vol. 11, part 1: 180.
32. *Georgia Narratives*, vol. 4, part 3: 167.
33. *Georgia Narratives*, vol. 4, part 4: 180.

WORKS CITED

Bay, Mia. *The White Image in the Black Mind: African-American Ideas about White People, 1830–1925.* Oxford: Oxford University Press, 2000.

Brewer, James. *American Negro Folklore.* Chicago: Quadrangle Books, 1968.

Brown, Frances. *Homespun Heroines and Other Women of Distinction.* Edited by Hallie Q. Brown. Xenia, OH: The Aldine, 1926.

Bruner, Peter. *A Slave's Adventures toward Freedom. Not Fiction, but the True Story of a Struggle.* Oxford, OH: n.p., 1918.

Cade, John B., "Out of the Mouths of Ex-Slaves." *Journal of Negro History* 20, no. 3 (1935): 294–337.

Chamerovzow, John Brown Louis Alexis. *Slave Life in Georgia: A Narrative of the Life, Sufferings, and Escape of John Brown, a Fugitive Slave.* London: W. M. Watts, 1855.

Douglass, Frederick. *Narrative of the Life of Frederick Douglass, an American Slave. Written by Himself.* Boston: The Anti-Slavery Office, 1845.

Drumgoold, Kate. *A Slave Girl's Story. Being an Autobiography of Kate Drumgoold.* Brooklyn, NY: The Author, 1898.

Johnson, Isaac. *Slavery Days in Old Kentucky. A True Story of a Father Who Sold His Wife and Four Children. By One of the Children.* Ogdensburg, NY: Republican & Journal Print, 1901.

Johnson, Walter. *Soul by Soul: Life inside the Antebellum Slave Market.* Cambridge, MA: Harvard University Press, 1999.

Garrard Clarke, Lewis. *Narrative of the Sufferings of Lewis Clarke, during a Captivity of More Than Twenty-Five Years, among the Algerines of Kentucky.* Boston: David H. Ela, Printer, 1845.

Jacobs, Harriet Ann. *Incidents in the Life of a Slave Girl. Written by Herself.* Edited by Lydia Maria Francis Child. Boston: Published for the author, 1861.

Pasierowska, Rachael L. "Up from Childhood: When African-American Enslaved Children Learned of Their Servile Status," *Slavery & Abolition* 37, no. 1 (2016): 94–116.

Paulding, James Kirke. *Letters from the South: Written during an Excursion in the Summer of 1816.* New York: James Eastburn & Co., 1817.

Rawick, George, P., ed. *Texas Narratives.* Vol. 5, Series Supplement 2, of *The American Slave: A Composite Autobiography; Part 4.* Westport, CT: Greenwood, 1979.

Reid, Alexander. *Dictionary of the English Language: Containing the Pronunciation, Etymology, and Explanation of All Words Authorized by Eminent Writers.* New York: D. Appleton & Co., 1814.

Stroyer, Jacob. *My Life in the South.* Salem: Salem Observer Book and Job Print, 1885.

US Works Progress Administration. *Slave Narratives: A Folk History of Slavery in the United States from Interviews with Former Slaves.* Washington, DC: WPA, 1941. Interviews transcribed by Library of Congress. https://www.gutenberg.org/files/13847/13847-h/13847-h.htm.

———. *Arkansas Narratives.* Vol. 2, part 3. https://www.gutenberg.org/ebooks/19446.

———. *Georgia Narratives.* Vol. 4, parts 1, 3, 4. https://www.gutenberg.org/ebooks/subject/11524.

———. *Mississippi Narratives.* Vol. 9. https://www.gutenberg.org/files/12055/12055-h/12055-h.htm.

———. *North Carolina Narratives.* Vol. 11, parts 1 and 2. https://www.gutenberg.org/files/22976/22976-h/22976-h.htm.

———. *Oklahoma Narratives.* Vol. 13. https://www.gutenberg.org/files/20785/20785-h/20785-h.htm.

———. *Texas Narratives.* Vol. 16, part 1. https://www.gutenberg.org/ebooks/30576.

Williams, James. *Life and Adventures of James Williams, a Fugitive Slave, with a Full Description of the Underground Railroad.* San Francisco: Women's Union Print, 1873.

The Double Standard

German Shepherds, Race, and Violence

Silke Hackenesch and Mieke Roscher

IN THE AFTERMATH OF THE SHOOTING OF UNARMED AFRICAN AMERICAN TEENAGER Michael Brown by a police officer in 2014, protests erupted among the residents of Ferguson, Missouri, and Ferguson residents took to the streets to voice their sorrow over the teenager's death as well as their anger and frustration about what they perceived as racially motivated and unjust treatment at the hands of the local police force. Images from these Black Lives Matter protests circulated not only in the United States, but on a global scale, and photographs of police officers with K-9 dogs patrolling the streets and keeping protesters in check revealed an uncanny resemblance to civil rights protests in Birmingham, Alabama, in 1963, and in Selma, Alabama, in 1965.[1] Indeed, German shepherds and other police dogs were widely used to control the so-called race riots of the 1960s in the United States. Pictures of dogs confronting protesters became emblematic for discourses of both white supremacy and Black liberation. In these photographs, many of them taken by Charles Moore during the Civil Rights Movement, the dogs signified weapons of white suppression aimed at nonviolent Black protestors.[2]

Watching the events unfold in Ferguson, especially the highly charged confrontations between the African American residents on the one hand, and the police officers "armed" with German shepherds on the other hand, the two of us, a human-animal studies scholar and an American cultural history scholar from Germany, began a conversation about the practice of using German shepherds as presumably effective and suitable police dogs, and the historical context of the German shepherd evolving into a signifier for police violence and white supremacy in the United States.

Rather than discussing a discourse that posits the animalization of African Americans in order to dehumanize them in racialized confrontations from the era of slavery to today, or engage in a highly problematic comparison of human enslavement and cruelty towards animals, we want to explore how processes of racialization and racial dynamics have simultaneously affected both humans and nonhumans, that is, dogs.[3] While critical race theory has insightfully shown that race is not a biological fact but a social construct, this same insight has not always been rigorously translated into human-animal studies. Posthumanist critique, one important strand of the human-animal studies line of thought, has too often been oblivious to the fact that in a world based on racial hierarchies, People of Color and the subaltern in general have been denied their humanity. While posthumanist thought is invested in deconstructing the very concept of humanity, it has not paid sufficient attention to the very fact that humanity is not granted equally and unequivocally. Yet, as Zakiyyah Iman Jackson has pointed out, human-animal studies as well as posthumanism have also laid bare the "semio-material practice of casting 'the animal' as the opposable limit to 'the human.'"[4] We therefore suggest concentrating on the racialized practices that both humans and animals are subjected to and then look at the meanings that are created through these practices.

Focusing on the German shepherd as a breed most widely used in the dynamics described above, we want to show how the trope of race is not fixed but constantly renegotiated—both with respect to humans and animals, and particularly with respect to dogs. We will therefore only briefly touch on the "creation" of the breed at the end of the nineteenth century, but will then elaborate on the racialized dog standard during the so-called Third Reich in Germany and discuss how this discourse helped to popularize the German shepherd as a police dog in the United States.

By using theoretical approaches from a variety of disciplines, such as human-animal studies, African American history, and critical race studies, as well as by reading German and American history through the lens of animal history, we hope to provide new frameworks for conceptualizing race as a historical, relational category with shifting implications. Our following discussion is intended as a think piece, adding to an ongoing conversation about a conceptual perspective we feel is largely missing: a reflection not only on the constructed character of race with regard to human beings, but also with regard to animals and breeds.

ON RACE AND BREED

Although race and racial differences are ideologically constructed—a biological fiction—the concept of race is a powerful discursive formation, which is transformed into very real inequalities and serves the legitimization of discrimination.[5] Deconstructing race as a social construct and a biological fiction, however, does not undo the psychological and physiological harms of racism—that is, the effects of believing in a hierarchical order of different races; it does not necessarily alter or impact the experiences of being a racialized subject. The insight that race is a construction, not a "truth," does not make it less immediate or relevant for the lives of those who have been traumatized by experiencing racism. But in arguing that race is a social and cultural construct, and by exposing it as an ideology, it becomes a useful and effective analytical tool. Concepts of race are historically (and falsely) inextricably linked to BIPOC (Black, Indigenous, and People of Color). The belief persists that only those who are not white have a racialized identity and belong to a certain race. Race, however, is historical and relational; it is re-created in the social and political life, and it serves the function of an ideology.[6] It is imaginary, a fraud, and a superstition, which is daily reiterated and performed. Referring to processes of racialization makes explicit the fact that Black people or white people do not constitute "races," but that Europeans participated in a historical process during which People of Color were intentionally racialized, namely, European colonialism, capitalist slavery, and the Middle Passage—out of which Blackness emerged. In this vein, Blackness is not a what, but a when, conceptualized at a specific moment, within a particular historical context.[7] From a Eurocentric perspective, whiteness often appears to be unmarked and invisible; it is regarded as the "norm," or the "standard," whereas a marker is only deemed necessary for labeling those who are deviant from this "norm." Because whites are omnipresent in representations of all kinds, they do not seem to present a certain race, but just the "human race." They are not only presented as the norm to others but are also not represented to themselves as whites. They speak from a disembodied, non-located position that marks them as neutral, "normal," and non-situated, and this enforces their cultural hegemony. Whiteness functions as the privileged signifier, and thus Blackness is characterized by a denial of recognition (or an absence of recognition).[8]

Interestingly, human-animal studies scholarship that compares the suffering of animals to the suffering of human beings and challenges the human-animal boundary rarely compares animals to humans as such, but often to one particular group, for instance, African Americans, Jews, Latinos (the list can be extended). What makes such a comparison so problematic is that both humans and animals are only connected through their sufferings and lack of agency. In *Afro-Dog*, Bénédicte Boisseron moves beyond the Blackness-animal comparison by focusing on "interspecies alliance" between People of Color and animals, and by looking for agency and defiance in both.[9] Yet, she discusses race primarily in relation to Black people. Using her groundbreaking book as our inspiration, and taking this way of thinking one step further, we propose to fully deconstruct the animal and breeds as inherently constructed categories, too.[10] It seems curious to us that the insights from critical race studies have not been fully transferred into human-animal studies (and vice versa?) as a productive way to critically interrogate the concept of breeds. It is this move beyond the metaphoric level, the dissection of power structures, the critique of essentialism, and the willingness to rely on a multiplicity of sources that is shared by both approaches. And it is the nexus between animalization and racism and its material outcome, the materialization of discourses, that interests both. Maneesha Deckha has, from a feminist posthumanist standpoint, insisted that "if the fictions of race and gender were central in humanizing some, then it is apparent how these concepts also relate to animalizing others, both human and nonhuman."[11] For us that means to bring these processes of animalization to the forefront, but also to always align them with the concept of race. However, what we don't want to do here is to conflate race with species and thereby lump together all animal species in one amorphous "the animal." Rather, we concentrate on two species, humans and dogs, and how the concept of race affects them both. We hence argue that the interrelatedness of these two categories, of species and race, produces racisms, that one category articulates itself through the other and thereby enforces it.

In his 1992 essay, Enrique Ucelay da Cal first remarked on the connection between (political) racism and breeding by identifying how genealogy was used to create certain types of animals that were then linked to a certain place, both social and spatial. To look at socio-spatial dispositions has been a major theme within human-animal studies in recent years. We want to argue alongside da Cal that the breeding of allegedly "superior" animals, as the German shepherd has been framed, in order to control allegedly "inferior" humans, those that are marked as racialized, shows an "intentional sense of dislocation on human/animal boundaries."[12] In this vein, we will try to map out a mutually constitutive relationship of breed and race that affects both humans and animals, albeit in different ways.

BREEDING DOGS TO CONTROL "SUBORDINATE" RACES: THE NAZI LEGACY

While it is generally agreed upon that different human races do not exist, different breeds of dogs are not fundamentally questioned. Here, we are following Aaron Skabelund, who suggested that "perhaps progress toward the eradication of breedism and racism can be achieved through a greater recognition of the constructed nature and artificiality of breed and race and the cruelty these ideas have inflicted—and continue to exact—on people and other animals."[13]

Such an interlocking of breedism and racism was perhaps nowhere more apparent than in the Third Reich. The racial paradigm employed by the National Socialists was connected to a notion of capability and performance. In this, they treated humans and animals alike. Dogs in particular were supposed to function in certain ways for the so-called *Volksgemeinschaft* (folk community): they were supposed to collaborate and to help shape the society not only with regard to their aesthetic value but also in the way they served as role-model soldiers—always reliable, always obedient. In this effort, dog breeders were eager to show the basic characteristics of dogs as more than just an asset. Therefore, they insisted that in the Third Reich animals were bred not primarily for sporting purposes or to satisfy the fanciers. On the contrary, performance and conduct were the only parameters that were to be applied to German dog breeding.[14] The German shepherd in particular, as his first breeder and cavalry captain Max von Stephanitz had laid out in his opus magnum *The German Shepherd in Text and Image* from 1901, was deemed to be a vanguard for racial and species superiority. In the book, he mapped out a genealogy of "worthy" dogs that were tied to a Germanic *Urheimat* of woods, heath, and sea.[15] In a later edition from 1932, he noted more bluntly:

> The bar to marriage for members of highly cultured people to women of lower races is a completely appropriate measure.... History shows time and time again how the mixing with dissimilar [*artfremd*] races, yes, even just the absorption of their other, dissimilar actions and thinking, ruins a superior people with regard to their bodily, mental, and moral constitution. This just happened to us Germans, as we are under the influence of a disseminated people [*Fremdvolk*] that has led us to unlearn how to feel and act Aryan, German, and pure. Let this be a lesson for all of us animal breeders.[16]

The German shepherd actually was quite a young breed that evolved from a local sheep dog from the Stuttgart area in the last quarter of the nineteenth century. It was von Stephanitz and the breeding society that helped to establish and encourage the reading of this dog as archetypically German.[17] Von Stephanitz not only stressed the presumably superior bodily abilities of the dogs, but also claimed that they rose to become spitting images of the Aryan race: "our cultivated breeds resemble the elite ... the elite in spirit, in arms, and in work."[18] They were in a way surrogates that helped to build the identity of the Aryan and give this identity a narrative expression.[19] All alleged virtues of the Germanic people were by this narrative act programmed into the animal body.[20] Skabelund has famously argued that by creating the shepherd dog something like a national dog ideal was to be put into effect.[21] Paul Eipper, a well-known contemporary author of animal literature, argued in 1943 that through breeding, a totally different and perfect creature was created.[22] Aligning themselves thus to the idea of the "new human," foundational to national socialist thought, breeders used these concepts and applied them to their own approaches.[23] Considering Donna Haraway's notion of material-semiotic nodes, in which the boundaries (for example between humans and animals but also between "breeds" and "races") are drawn and endowed with meaning through social and bodily interaction, breeding "Aryan" dogs is the performative tool by which the semiotic projections of racial difference were solidified and embodied.[24]

Just as with other animals, race-related issues were ostentatiously connected to breeding. It is of some importance in this context that the German term for breed is race, as the Nazis transferred many of their ideas on racial politics from the animal kingdom. Classifications and forms of social order were thus intrinsically intertwined. The ubiquitous political semantics of racialized inclusion and exclusion found in the source material on the development of the German shepherd strongly hint at the importance of these animals for the wider rhetoric of the Third Reich. The accessibility of animal bodies made them, for example, the ideal test bed for practical eugenics. These biopolitics involved not just state ambition, but the increasing role of scientific knowledge (or at least knowledge that claimed scientific status) and specialist elites in shaping policy and discourses. The flourishing so-called race science (*Rassenkunde*) was not used, however, just as a blueprint for the "art" of breeding. Rather, trying to find the perfect dog was a parallel phenomenon where both breeding and scientific racism were used to legitimize the other. What both had in common was that they were interested in the question of whether race (or breed) was a given status to be preserved or a goal to be reached. Most breeding societies tried a combination of both by referring to canine genealogies as part of a "race history" on the one hand, and by drawing attention to the potential of "hybridization" for the "refinement" of dog breeds on the other.[25]

Obviously, discourse on "racial hygiene" (*Rassenhygiene*), as eugenics was named, with regard to dogs was not purely metaphorical. Quite the contrary: The execution of the biopolitical regime on their bodies was essential for the consolidation of the ideology. That was just as true for those dogs that did not fit the ideal type. They were violently excluded by means of not getting access to food (food stamps were only issued for pure-bred or working dogs) or protection from air raids and being excluded from procreating.[26] Above all, breeding societies called for the elimination of all "mongrels." In his book, Max von Stephanitz had already contemptuously written about animals that should not be used for breeding: "Among those are the abnormal, the unhealthy, those who lack the vigor to rise above.... It is a desperate enterprise to save and to enhance all these. They are breeding garbage [*Rassenabfall*], not even usable as fertilizer."[27]

That the German shepherd enjoyed such an incredible success in Nazi Germany was also due to the fact that from as early as 1902 his purpose was defined by his guarding abilities. But it was not sheep but people who were the subjects of this guarding. In a pamphlet titled "The Use of Dogs in the Police Force," their special ability to control crowds was highlighted. As "breeding expert" Horst Anders wrote in an article on the economic value of these police dogs in 1937: "The German shepherd has left a permanent mark on the usage of dogs for the police force and will be an indispensable part of its future development."[28] To realize this, a special post for the breeding and training of police dogs was created within the government, whose duty it was to further define the breed for the job.

Moreover, under German colonial control in East and West Africa, the dog had already been used to enforce discipline and domination, and the pictures created here were to the liking of the National Socialist leadership. Additionally, the "wolf-like" appearance of the dog impressed those who were striving for the claiming of so-called Germanic animals equipped with strength and vigor.[29] The Association of the German Shepherd (Verein für Schäferhundwesen) was therefore promoting a policy of rigid eradication of all animals that did not fit the "norm," the "standard." They also stood for a training that was defined by rigorous discipline. It was especially their usage for guarding the death camps that left a permanent mark on the survivor's experience and is mentioned in nearly every eyewitness account of the prosecution of Jews and the Shoah.[30] These images of dogs in control over those the Nazis defined as "subhuman" were not created without purpose. They were just as emblematic for the alleged dominance of what was termed "Nordic races" as the images of controlling "Black insurgencies" were for "white power." The Nazis, thus, were not alone in fancying this kind of dog. The breed proved to be a sought-after export success.[31] By 1936, over 500,000 animals were registered in the international breeding book.[32]

The *Völkischer Beobachter*, the official newspaper of the Nazi Party, also embraced the German shepherd and at the same time wanted to get rid of "mongrels," the "urchin of the animal world," and "worthless dogs of undefined races."[33] With reference to breeding, social and racial exclusion was naturalized. Race as well as breed were thus used to define not only character and appearance but also the space of possibilities by falling back to seemingly biological facts. This was true for the human as well as the animal world. For the journal of the agrarian breeding societies, the *Deutsche Landwirtschaftliche Tierzucht*,[34] in dog breeding in particular, the "eternal laws of nature" would reveal themselves quite vividly.[35] The superiority of supposedly Germanic races/breeds, so they claimed in 1938, could be empirically proven with regard to both capability and appearance. Appearance as bodily beauty was granted its own merit. This was, of course, in line with a bourgeois understanding of beauty, where beauty was in itself racialized and served distinct political purposes. So even though capability, not beauty, was supposed to be the characteristic of the German dog, and particularly the German shepherd, this idea was not universally accepted. Thus, bodily beauty was coded as a prerequisite to bodily accomplishments.[36] The attempts by German anthropologists and high-ranking Nazis to create with the SS and the peasantry the breeding stock for the new "German Volk" were following similar lines.[37]

By employing such canine genealogies, questions about "human races" were made the object of both scientific and social inquiries in the Third Reich: These were published in journals ranging from the animal welfare movement, the breeding associations, and the eugenics movement to the party's papers. In these publications, people of African descent were regularly portrayed as being both physically and intellectually inferior to the German shepherd. This superior breed, it was argued, even had the ability to distinguish between humans according to the color of their skin. As one member of the *Reichstierschutzbund*, the National Animal Welfare Society, wrote in the society's journal in 1939 about her dog "Rita," who had accompanied her to Cameroon, "Though she is willing to be fed and attended to by the Colored [sic], she will always get her own way when facing members of the Black race, and even the docile houseboy must always do what Rita, the protector of the house, requires, which is, paradoxically the right thing most of the time."[38] This quote is interesting for a number of reasons. According to the owner of Rita and author of this article, this German shepherd dog was able to see, smell, and feel race and identify human beings as white/superior, or as Black/inferior. Rita was not only able to perceive different human races, but even more importantly, understood Nazi racial ideology. The dog instinctively knew who was inferior and acted accordingly towards People of Color. Rita apparently knew where to place herself in the hierarchical order of the household, namely, above the "Coloreds" [sic], and she knew better than they what was needed and what needed to be done. This dog, then, functioned as an animal extension of white supremacy towards the colonized peoples of Cameroon. Similarly, service dogs at the Western Front would instinctively only rescue people with white skin, wrote the military journal *Wissen und Wehr* in 1943.[39] On the other hand it was assumed that dog breeds of a higher quality could only be found in Germanic or Anglo-Saxon countries. Pariah dogs, those that lived in the Southern Hemisphere, would adapt to the people native to the places where all were to be said of a "lower level of civilization."[40] Moreover, it was assumed to be scientifically proven, as could be read in a 1938 edition of the *Hundewelt*, the journal of the German-shepherd breeding club, that dogs in general would only submit to Nordic peoples and would develop a natural distaste for "yellow and black races."[41] Six years later, the journal *Der Hund* added to this assumption that this was due to the allegedly "different smell of these races."[42] Such ideology was in tune with stereotypical conceptions of race not only as a visual category, but one that is grounded in other senses, too. In *How Race is Made*, Mark Smith has argued that constructions of race are not solely based on the visual, even though vision has played and continues to play a major role in calibrating definitions of Blackness, but encompass the other senses as well.[43] Given that the alleged racial inferiority of African Americans was also found in stereotypes such as smelling bad, it should not come as a surprise that dogs were seemingly capable of smelling race.

Breeding and the selection of dogs followed a line that distinguished between "mongrel" and "purebred" [*sic*] as well as between Nordic and southern dogs, while at the same time mirroring and justifying the racist ideology shown towards the human population. The historic-specific construction of the German shepherd was connected to a semiotic reading that saw the "purebred" as the better soldier, better than its "mongrel" counterparts because of its connection to its primordial being, which was assumed to have been lost in the common mutt. Naturally, the breeding societies insisted on keeping to the standards derived from eugenic theories. The killing of the weak was therefore explicitly justified with reference to the 1933 Law for the Prevention of Genetically Diseased Offspring (*Gesetz zur Verhütung erbkranken Nachwuchses*). When it came to dogs, the racial discourse obviously had more than one direction, and it involved the human as well as the dog population not only of Germany, but also of all of the occupied territories, so significantly not distinguishing between humans and nonhumans. What else becomes apparent here is that the alleged Nazi love for animals was in no way unconditional, but on the contrary followed the lines of official racial policies. The *Hundewelt* was therefore eager to stress that only with the popularizing of genetics in the Third Reich was the inbreeding of both humans and animals stopped.[44]

Breeding societies were generally founded at the turn of the century, with every new breed getting institutionalized by their own breeding club. That was not a German particularity. Indeed, Britain already had a diversified scene of dog lovers who were bonding over their expertise on how to best breed and how to establish breed standards in the nineteenth century.[45] The breeding societies organized the various dog shows, helped to connect those who wanted their bitches covered, and set the standards to which the others should, and did, adhere. All of this was communicated through a variety of magazines and books. With the Nazification of civil society, all those societies were of course "brought in line," and all people of non-Germanic descent were booted out and barred from membership.

As mentioned above, the racial quality of the German shepherd was defined by his willingness to work, which explicitly meant working for the regime. Following this line of thinking, from 1938 onwards all breeding societies were called upon to only judge the working ability and the genetic value at their dog shows and to disregard the outer appearance.[46] Henceforth, the cultivation of the dog's body was pursued with eagerness. It was assumed that one had to let the dogs work "in order for the racial assets not to wither away."[47] The aim was to make "real men" (*Kerle* in German, or "tough guys") out of dogs.[48] The breeding process was to prioritize those dogs that showed next to "unambiguous male or female characteristics, [and] a strong constitution."[49] This was important for the German shepherd in particular as it served as a stand-in for a second trope narrating the alleged superiority through power and effort vital for the Third Reich, namely, that of virility. The German shepherd was the quintessential "dog for the white man."[50] That is where the clear-cut breeding goals were established to prevent a feminization of the dog world.[51]

Dogs needed to appear to some extent manageable under the control of their owners, breeders, or handlers, but at the same time had to express a certain degree of virility that made this subordination far from natural but rather the result of the playing out of naturalized hierarchies.

Reading the classification of dogs under such categories as race, (blood) purity and impurity, bastardization, and gender from a human-animal studies perspective, the following is of importance: Animals did not function as mere images or symbols of race-related discourses targeting human societies. They themselves were subjected to similar objectives both materially and semiotically. This means that by the invention of breeds and the practice of selective breeding, bodily and aesthetic standards were established by which every single dog was measured and, depending on their matching of those standards, included or excluded. As Amir Zelinger has recently remarked, however, this has not been taken up adequately by either political history or critical race theory: "Animals are a banal metaphor in the service of racial animosity by humans against humans; they are never a substantial part of the historiography of the rise of modern racism, even though modern racism was based largely on scientific thinking that focused on them and their similarities to humans."[52] If this is true for the beginning of racist thought, as Zelinger suggests, the brutal escalation of racism in the Third Reich is only ever explicable when one looks at how it was directed at both humans and animals, but also at how they were targeted differently. Zelinger has productively differentiated between an influence narrative and a projection narrative. According to him, the influence narrative "reveals how perceptions of animal breeds and livestock-breeding practices influenced the rise of racialist and eugenic worldviews. By contrast, the second shows how conceptualizations of human racial segregation contributed to the construction of ideas about the subdivision of domestic animal species into different breeds."[53]

In line with the influence narrative, much of which the leading figures of the National Socialist eugenics movement postulated derived from their however rudimentary training in, or inspiration from, animal breeding. The adaptation of perceived biological thinking, the dividing up of mankind into specific races, and their hierarchical ordering along a value system was then again, according to the projection narrative, transferred back to the animal world. The "German Dog Society," one could argue, was subject to the same selection processes as the human population. Here, belonging to the "right" breed, being purebred, and being able to work for the cause decided how one (human or animal) could expect to be treated, and more importantly could determine the chance to survive.[54] Thus on the one hand, dogs served as the foundation for the idea of race; on the other hand, they were the material object on which this idea was forcefully exercised and put into practice.

Following Skabelund, these ideas led to stereotyping, discrimination, sterilization, and extermination, which ran parallel to the measures taken to control and shape human societies.[55] Dogs that did not conform to the deeply artificial "race standards" were not only excluded semantically from the Germanized dog world, but they were eliminated, either killed directly or not allowed to procreate.

THE DOG AS A RACIAL WEAPON?

The first German shepherd dogs came to the United States shortly after the turn of the century. Yet even before the arrival of the German shepherd, animals have been used to control, subdue, and punish Africans, Native Americans, and African Americans within the contexts of colonialism, enslavement, and the plantation economy. Based on various examples in the Americas, from colonial Saint-Domingue to late eighteenth-century Jamaica, and Florida during the Second Seminole War, Sara E. Johnson has shown that Cuban hounds were specifically used for canine warfare. These dogs were trained to perform as slave catchers, and specifically bred to track down (and devour) Black people.[56] The trade and networks that allowed these canine warfare techniques to flourish have been demonstrated, as well as the representation of animal violence towards the enslaved and indigenous population in classical texts such as Harriet Beecher Stowe's *Uncle Tom's Cabin*, and in testimonies from (formerly) enslaved individuals.[57]

In 1913, the German Shepherd Dog Club of America was founded. The early twentieth century also witnessed the popularization of the shepherd due to Hollywood productions that featured shepherds like Strongheart and Rin Tin Tin, the latter an animal celebrity of its time that was brought to the United States after World War I by an American military service member.[58] Another important figure in introducing the German shepherd to the United States and promoting this dog as a superior breed was Geraldine Rockefeller Dodge. The richest woman in her time, Dodge was also a dog lover and committed dog breeder who sat in as a judge at various dog shows and founded her winning kennel club in 1927. For her annual dog show in 1930, Max von Stephanitz came to the United States to participate as a judge.[59] Apparently, von Stephanitz's reputation as a breeder and as an expert on German shepherd dogs was recognized by American dog lovers, who were probably also receptive to the concept of the shepherd as a suitable dog for control and policing. We assume that concepts and ideas of the shepherd breed that originated in Germany thus traveled across the Atlantic with von Stephanitz and were popularized among breeders, kennel club members, and dog show participants.

What was new during the Civil Rights Movement of the 1960s, however, was that the German shepherd, already used for political purposes as a police dog, evolved into a signifier for racialized police violence that specifically targeted African Americans.[60] Two events in particular of the Birmingham Campaign—the Children's Crusade and the March from Selma to Montgomery—along with their press coverage and photographs, helped to establish the German shepherd as a tool of white oppression par excellence: "Fire hoses and police dogs were used here today to disperse Negro students protesting racial segregation," the *New York Times* reported on May 4, 1963, about the events unfolding in Birmingham, Alabama.[61] According to this headline, it was the primary purpose of the dogs, on the leashes of white police officers, to keep the young African American high school students who joined the protest against the city's segregation practices in check. Civil rights activist Martin Luther King Jr. from the Southern Christian Leadership Conference (SCLC), who had been imprisoned in Birmingham in the previous month, composed a reply to fellow clergymen critical of his activism and his involvement in the Birmingham Campaign: his now famous "Letter from Birmingham Jail."[62] Commenting on their statement, which condemned the protests, King exposes their misconception of the situation, especially with regard to who is the violent, the unruly one in the encounter.

> You warmly commended the Birmingham police force for keeping "order" and "preventing violence." I doubt that you would have so warmly commended the police force if you had seen its dogs sinking their teeth into unarmed, nonviolent Negroes. I doubt that you would so quickly commend the policemen if you were to observe their ugly and inhumane treatment of Negroes here in the city jail.[63]

According to King, it was the dogs and the police officers who behaved "inhumanely," while the protesters demanded equal and humane treatment.

Figure 1. Statue of three attack dogs, in Kelly Ingram Park, Birmingham, Alabama.

Today, sculptures in Kelly Ingram Park in Birmingham, where violent encounters between the police and protesting youth occurred during the Children's Crusade, commemorate the city's Civil Rights Movement history. Significantly, two monuments specifically commemorate the presence of violent dogs in these demonstrations, underscoring how the threat and intimidation these German shepherd dogs posed to Black protesters shaped how the movement is remembered. The statue of the three attack dogs (figure 1) shows them as aggressive animals, almost impossible to restrain were it not for the leashes their officers were holding. These dogs literally seem ready to attack the marchers, and the construction of these dogs as particularly virile, forceful, and aggressive is readily exploited and emphasized here. These dogs do not personify, but "animalify" an angry white mob who felt that African Americans demanding full citizenship was a brazen transgression. In our reading of this monument, it is crucial that the only subjects here are the dogs; those holding onto the leashes, that is, the police officers, are absent. The dogs come to be seen as the agents of racial segregation, enforcing second-class citizenship status on African Americans because of their function as police dogs. In this monument, the dogs are cast as the weapon, not the ones who hold the weapon, namely, the police officers. The police officers' racially motivated actions are thus erased, and the violence toward African Americans is depersonalized and transferred onto the dogs, in the sense that they become the agents of said violence. The German shepherd here becomes the "new white," and therefore its existence as a breed fades into the background. What is highlighted, instead, is its function as a tool for crowd control.[64] It serves as a racialized "reminder of the fragile—not to say incomplete—person status of the black."[65] In *Afro-Dog*, Boisseron aptly recounts a court case in which the mere presence of German shepherds prevented an African American woman from entering the courtroom. The dog did not attack the woman or bark at her, but its mere presence and the memory its presence triggered were forceful enough to bar that woman from entering. She was held back precisely

Figure 2. Sculpture dedicated to the Foot Soldiers of the Birmingham Civil Rights Movement, in Kelly Ingram Park, Birmingham, Alabama.

because of the pictures of oppression and racialized violence the dogs evoked. Boisseron goes on to say that even if the dogs are not present, there is something like an "invisible dog of a racially biased system."[66] We would argue, however, that it is not the dog per se that is invisible, but more precisely the *racialized dog*.

Another sculpture in Kelly Ingram Park shows a police officer with a K-9 on a leash, pushing back a young Black teenage boy while the dog barks at him and aggressively attempts to jump at him. This sculpture (figure 2) is a direct reference to a similar photograph made by Charles Moore. A quote from Richard Arrington Jr., former (and the first Black) mayor of Birmingham, is engraved on the stand of the sculpture. Part of it reads: "With gallantry, courage, and great bravery they faced the violence of attack dogs, high powered water hoses, and bombings." What is curious about this quote is that, again, the agents of this violence are dogs and things, not human beings. Both monuments encourage viewers to connect racialized state violence with German shepherds. The white supremacists are not mentioned at all, nor is the police force or segregationist politicians, but the dog. It is the animal that has to stand in for the violence the protesters were subjected to at the hands of white male police officers. In this sense, these memorials might also be read as illustrative examples of species racism or speciesism because they essentialize the German shepherd as an inherently racist breed that is used to subordinate and control nonwhite human beings.

These two memorials visualize what we have discussed in this chapter. What connects critical race theory to human-animal studies is that they both (just like posthumanist feminist studies) aim at dissecting "biological differences and naturalized bodies as social constructions."[67] It is therefore the social that includes dogs and humans and *creates* them according to cultural contexts and (highly unequal) power structures.

The "black-animal subtext," however, seems more complicated: The Nazis in a way did equate the German shepherd semantically with "Aryans," but did so in order to solidify the notion of race as such.[68] One could argue that in the context of the Civil Rights Movement this was no longer necessary, as the image of a hierarchical order based on race and involving dogs had already been imprinted on the social imagination—the dogs were a useful extension of human white supremacy in order to suppress a group of People of Color historically considered less than human. With the help of a human-animal studies approach that dissects the representational framework of animals and juxtaposes it to their material being in the world, one is encouraged to look closer at the material realities of the animals involved, and, as we would like to add, those humans that are affected by these animal representations. Critical race theory, on the other hand, helps us to disentangle the discursive formation that shapes the social existence of humans based on the alleged biological category of race, but could also be expanded in our view to include breed. Opening up a discussion between those two fields of inquiry supports an analysis of racialized practices both on the micro as well as the macro level, reveals genealogies of racialization, and uncovers what they mean not only for individuals, human and animal, but also for society at large. Especially in this current moment, with the Black Lives Matter Movement taking to the streets again to peacefully protest institutionalized racism in the police force, and with a former president who seemed willfully ignorant of white supremacy and unwilling to openly denounce racialized violence, the safety of Black lives is ever precarious. It is no coincidence, we argue, that the former president of the United States warned White House demonstrators about the "most vicious dogs" they would meet in case of taking to the streets to protest the government.[69] This was not only understood as a threat, but also a direct reference to the brutal encounters between the police force on the one hand, and civil rights protestors on the other. Making reference to this history constructs police dogs again as a declarative warning sign of white supremacy. While the German shepherd continues to be the most popular of police dogs, we would do well to pay more attention to its racialized breeding history as well as its role in acting out politics.

NOTES

1. On the Black Lives Matter movement see, for example, Taylor, *From #Black Lives Matter to Black Liberation*; Ransby, *Making All Black Lives Matter*; Lebron, *The Making of Black Lives Matter*.
2. See also Spratt, "When Dogs Attacked." On the use of police dogs to subdue African American protesters in the 1960s and 2010s, see Wall, "'For the Very Existence of Civilization.'" In the aftermath of the Ferguson protests, an investigation by the FBI also found an excessive use of police dogs in attacking African American residents. Parts from the report read: "FPD [Ferguson Police Department] engages in a pattern of deploying canines to bite individuals when the articulated

facts do not justify this significant use of force. The department's own records demonstrate that, as with other types of force, canine officers use dogs out of proportion to the threat posed by the people they encounter, leaving serious puncture wounds to nonviolent offenders, some of them children. Furthermore, in every canine bite incident for which racial information is available, the subject was African American. This disparity, in combination with the decision to deploy canines in circumstances with a seemingly low objective threat, suggests that race may play an impermissible role in officers' decisions to deploy canines." Department of Justice, "Investigation"; see also Boisseron, *Afro-Dog*, 38–39.

3. Racist stereotypes that compare African Americans to animals, or describe them in biologizing, essentializing ways, can be found from so-called scientific racism to commodity racism to popular accounts of Blacks in the United States, especially during the Reconstruction period and after. See, for example, Cassuto, *The Inhuman Race*, and Kim, "Slaying the Beast, 4; see also Glick, "Animal Instincts," and Hund, Mills, and Sebastiani, *Simianization*. On the resignification of "dog" in the African American vernacular see Ravalli, "Snoop's Devil Dogg." We perceive the comparison of animal exploitation to the enslavement of Black people, or to the Shoa, to be highly problematic, first and foremost because one is based on economic reasonings, while the others have ideological bases. On the comparison, see Spiegel, *The Dreaded Comparison*; for an overview of the ensuing debates and the current state of scholarship on the "black-animal subtext" see the introduction of Boisseron, *Afro-Dog*, ix–xxvii.
4. Jackson, "Animal," 674.
5. McClintock, *Imperial Leather*, 9.
6. Fields, "Slavery, Race, and Ideology in the USA."
7. Wright, *The Physics of Blackness*; Gilroy, *Against Race*; Roach, *Cities of the Dead*; Scott, "Was There a Time before Race?"
8. Painter, *The History of White People*; hooks, "Representing Whiteness," 167.
9. For a critique of agency as a uniquely human concept, see Pearson, "Dogs, History, and Agency."
10. Boisseron, *Afro-Dog*, xx, 33.
11. Deckha, "Toward a Postcolonial, Posthumanist Feminist Theory," 537.
12. da Cal, "The Influence of Animal Breeding," 724.
13. Skabelund, "Breeding Racism," 369; see also the discussion of pit bulls in Boisseron, *Afro-Dog*, 42–43, and Ahuja, "Postcolonial Critique," 558.
14. Fehringer, *Unser Hund*, 13.
15. *Heimat*, and even more *Urheimat* are difficult to translate. The German concepts might be understood as ideas of an "original homeland."
16. von Stephanitz, *Der Deutsche Schäferhund in Wort und Bild*, 404. Original text in German. All translations by the authors.
17. Skabelund, "Breeding Racism," 354; see also Tenner, "Constructing the German Shepherd Dog."
18. von Stephanitz, *Der Deutsche Schäferhund in Wort und Bild*, 26.
19. Bühler and Rieger, *Vom Übertier*, 136.
20. Wippermann, "Der Hund als Propaganda- und Terrorinstrument im Nationalsozialismus," 195.
21. Skabelund, "Breeding Racism," 359.
22. Eipper, *Das Haustierbuch, Vom Wesen, der Schönheit und dem Nutzen unserer Tierkameraden*, 32.
23. Bauerkämper, "Der Neue Mensch, Version: 1.0"; Burleigh, "National Socialism as a Political Religion."
24. Haraway, *When Species Meet*.
25. See for example Peters, "Breed History of the Newfoundland Dog," 141.

26. Anon., "Breeding Regulations of the Association for German Dogs (Die Bestimmungen des Reichsverbandes für Hundewesen über das Zuchtwesen)."
27. von Stephanitz, *Der Deutsche Schäferhund*, 26.
28. Anders, "Dog Breeding and Dog Keeping in Germany and Their Economic Value (Hundehaltung und Hundezucht in Deutschland und ihre volkswirtschaftliche Bedeutung)," 5.
29. For the semantic reading of animals, see Sax, *Animals in the Third Reich*.
30. Tindol, "The Best Friend of the Murderers"; for a firsthand account on Buchenwald, see Kogon, *Theory and Practice of Hell*.
31. For Japan, see Skabelund, "Breeding Racism"; for the Soviet Union, see Cherkaev and Tipikina, "Interspecies Affection and Military Aims," 30.
32. Anders, "Dog Keeping and Dog Breeding in Germany and Its Economic Significance (Hundehaltung und Hundezucht in Deutschland und ihre volkswirtschaftliche Bedeutung)," 15.
33. *Völkischer Beobachter*, 296.
34. Our translation: Society for Agrarian Livestock Breeding.
35. Luethge, "Basic Questions of German Dog Breeding (Grundfragen der Deutschen Hundezucht)," 352.
36. Anon., "Report on the Regional Meeting on Dog Sports," 99.
37. Gerhard, "Breeding Pigs and People."
38. *Reichstierschutzblatt*.
39. Berkun, "The Dog in the Wehrmacht's Service (Der Hund im Dienste der Wehrmacht)," 68.
40. von Mammen, *Der Hund in Wort und Spruch des Volkes*, 262.
41. Schultze, "Wolf and Dog in the Aryan Tradition (Wolf und Hund in den Ueberlieferungen der arischen Urzeit)," 169.
42. Anon., "Dog and Wolf in the Aryan Past (Hund und Wolf in der arischen Urzeit)," 8.
43. Smith, *How Race is Made*.
44. Anon., "In-Breeding as a Breeding Device (Von der Inzucht als Züchtungsmittel)," 1325.
45. Ritvo, "Pride and Pedigree."
46. Hentschel, "Hereditary Assessment in the Breeding of the German Shepherd Dog (Vererbungsfeststellung in der Zucht des deutschen Schäferhunds)," 749.
47. Roesbeck, "Breeding with Tough Working Dogs (Zucht mit harten Gebrauchshunden)," 105.
48. Roesbeck, "1938," 16.
49. *The Provisions of the Reich's Association for Dog Matters for Breeding (Die Bestimmungen des Reichsverbandes für Hundewesen über das Zuchtwesen)*, 10.
50. Schnippel, "Something about Our Shepherd Dog (Einiges über unseren Schäferhund)," 590.
51. Still relevant here are Gisela Bock's remarks on the connection between sexism and racism in Nazi Germany that was coupled to the idea of controlled reproduction and eugenics. See Bock, "Racism and Sexism in Nazi Germany."
52. Zelinger, "Race and Animal-Breeding," 364.
53. Zelinger, "Race and Animal-Breeding," 364.
54. However, one must also note that it was the purebred dogs that mostly ended up in the service of the Wehrmacht. Approximately 30,000 German shepherd dogs were used for war purposes. Only a few survived the war.
55. Skabelund, "Breeding Racism," 369.
56. Johnson, "'You Should Give Them Blacks to Eat,'" 66–67.
57. See, among others, Fielder, "Black Dogs, Bloodhounds, and Best Friends; see also, for instance, the searchable "North American Slave Narratives" in the digital archive "Documenting the American South."

58. Wuest, "Rin Tin Tin: Der Hund, der Niemals starb." See also Tenner, "Citizen Canine."
59. Flaim, "Rich in Tradition."
60. On the political purposes of dogs, see Skabelund, "Political History."
61. Hailey, "Dogs and Hoses Repulse Negroes at Birmingham."
62. Based on his letter, King published a book later that year: King Jr., *Why We Can't Wait*.
63. King Jr., "Letter from Birmingham Jail."
64. Skabelund, "Political History."
65. Boisseron, *Afro-Dog*, 8.
66. Boisseron, *Afro-Dog*, 9.
67. Deckha, "Toward a Postcolonial, Posthumanist Feminist Theory," 528.
68. Boisseron, *Afro-Dog*, ix.
69. Haberman, "Trump Threatens White House Protesters with 'Vicious Dogs' and 'Ominous Weapons.'"

WORKS CITED

Ahuja, Neel. "Postcolonial Critique in a Multispecies World." *PMLA* 124, no. 2 (2009): 556–63.

Alacoolwiki. 2018. Statue of Three Attack Dogs, in Kelly Ingram Park. Birmingham, AL. Photograph. Wikimedia Commons.

Anders, Horst. "Dog Breeding and Dog Keeping in Germany and Their Economic Value (Hundehaltung und Hundezucht in Deutschland und ihre volkswirtschaftliche Bedeutung)." *Zentralblatt für Kleintierkunde und Pelztierkunde "Kleintier und Pelztier"* 8, no. 3 (1937).

"Basic Questions of German Dog Breeding (Grundfragen der Deutschen Hundezucht)." *Deutsche Landwirtschaftliche Tierzucht* 18 (1938).

Bauerkämper, Arnd. "Der Neue Mensch, Version: 1.0." *Docupedia-Zeitgeschichte*, April 7, 2017.

Bock, Gisela. "Racism and Sexism in Nazi Germany: Motherhood, Compulsory Sterilization, and the State." *Signs: Journal of Women in Culture and Society* 8, no. 3 (April 1983): 400–421.

Boisseron, Bénédicte. *Afro-Dog: Blackness and the Animal Question*. New York: Columbia University Press, 2018.

"Breeding Regulations of the Association for German Dogs (Die Bestimmungen des Reichsverbandes für Hundewesen über das Zuchtwesen)." Berlin, 1941.

Bühler, Benjamin, and Stefan Rieger. *Vom Übertier: Ein Bestiarium des Wissens*. 1. Aufl. Edition Suhrkamp 2459. Frankfurt: Suhrkamp, 2006.

Burleigh, Michael. "National Socialism as a Political Religion." *Totalitarian Movements and Political Religions* 1, no. 2 (2000): 1–26.

Captain Berkun. "The Dog in the Wehrmacht's Service (Der Hund im Dienste der Wehrmacht)." *Wissen und Wehr: Monatsschrift der Deutschen Gesellschaft für Wehrpolitik und Wehrwissenschaften*. Berlin: Mittler, 1943.

Cassuto, Leonard. *The Inhuman Race: The Racial Grotesque in American Literature and Culture*. New York: Columbia University Press, 1997.

Cherkaev, Xenia, and Elena Tipikina. "Interspecies Affection and Military Aims." *Environmental Humanities* 10, no. 1 (May 1, 2018): 20–39.

Da Cal, Enrique Ucelay. "The Influence of Animal Breeding on Political Racism." *History of European Ideas* 15, no. 4–6 (December 1992): 717–25.

Deckha, Maneesha. "Toward a Postcolonial, Posthumanist Feminist Theory: Centralizing Race and

Culture in Feminist Work on Nonhuman Animals." *Hypatia* 27, no. 3 (2012): 527–45.
Department of Justice, Civil Rights Division. "Investigation of the Ferguson Police Department." April 3, 2015. Available at https://www.justice.gov.
Documenting the American South. "North American Slave Narratives." Digital archive. Available at https://docsouth.unc.edu/neh/.
"Dog and Wolf in the Aryan Past (Hund und Wolf in der arischen Urzeit)." *Der Hund* 1 (1944).
Eipper, Paul. *Das Haustierbuch, Vom Wesen, der Schönheit und dem Nutzen unserer Tierkameraden.* Berlin: Deutscher Verlag, 1943.
Fehringer, Otto. *Unser Hund.* Berlin: Dietrich Reimer, 1940.
Fielder, Brigitte. "Black Dogs, Bloodhounds, and Best Friends: African Americans and Dogs in Nineteenth-Century Abolitionist Literature." In *American Beasts: Perspectives on Animals, Animality and U.S. Culture, 1776–1920*, edited by Dominik Ohrem. Berlin: Neofelis, 2016.
Fields, Barbara J. "Slavery, Race, and Ideology in the USA." *New Left Review* 181 (June 1990): 95–118.
Flaim, Denise. "Rich in Tradition: The Legacy of Geraldine Rockefeller Dodge." American Kennel Club, January 14, 2020. Available at https://www.akc.org.
Foster, Hailey. "Dogs and Hoses Repulse Negroes at Birmingham." *New York Times*, April 5, 1963.
Gerhard, Gesine. "Breeding Pigs and People for the Third Reich: Richard Walther Darré's Agrarian Ideology." In *How Green Were the Nazis? Nature, Environment, and Nation in the Third Reich*, edited by Franz-Josef Brüggemeier, Mark Cioc, and Thomas Zeller, 1st ed., 129–46. Ohio University Press Series in Ecology and History. Athens: Ohio University Press, 2005.
Gilroy, Paul. *Against Race: Imagining Political Culture beyond the Color Line.* Cambridge, MA: Belknap Press of Harvard University Press, 2000.
Glick, Megan H. "Animal Instincts: Race, Criminality, and the Reversal of the 'Human.'" *American Quarterly* 65, no. 3 (2013): 639–59.
Haberman, Maggie. "Trump Threatens White House Protesters with 'Vicious Dogs' and 'Ominous Weapons.'" *New York Times*, May 30, 2020.
Haraway, Donna Jeanne. *When Species Meet.* Posthumanities 3. Minneapolis: University of Minnesota Press, 2008.
Hentschel, Herbert. "Hereditary Assessment in the Breeding of the German Shepherd Dog (Vererbungsfeststellung in der Zucht des Deutschen Schäferhunds)." *Zeitung der Fachschaft für Deutsche Schäferhunde* 37, no. 17 (1939).
Highsmith, Carol M. 2010. *Sculpture Dedicated to the Foot Soldiers of the Birmingham Civil Rights Movement.* Kelly Ingram Park, Birmingham, Alabama. Photograph. Wikimedia Commons.
hooks, bell. "Representing Whiteness in the Black Imagination." In *Displacing Whiteness: Essays in Social and Cultural Criticism*, edited by Ruth Frankenberg, 165–79. Durham, NC: Duke University Press, 1997.
Hund, Wulf D. (Wulf Dietmar), Charles W. (Charles Wade) Mills, and Silvia Sebastiani, eds. *Simianization: Apes, Gender, Class, and Race.* Racism Analysis. Volume 6. Zürich: Lit Verlag, 2015.
"In-Breeding as a Breeding Device (Von der Inzucht als Züchtungsmittel)." *Die Hundewelt* 18, no. 12 (1942).
Jackson, Zakiyyah Iman. "Animal: New Directions in the Theorization of Race and Posthumanism." *Feminist Studies* 39, no. 3 (2013): 669–85.
Johnson, Sara E. "'You Should Give Them Blacks to Eat': Waging Inter-American Wars of Torture and Terror." *American Quarterly* 61, no. 1 (2009): 65–92.
Kim, Claire Jean. "Slaying the Beast: Reflections on Race, Culture, and Species." *Kalfou* 1, no. 1 (2009).
King, Martin Luther, Jr. "Letter from Birmingham Jail," April 16, 1963. African Studies Center at the

University of Pennsylvania. Available at https://www.africa.upenn.edu.

———. *Why We Can't Wait*. New York: New American Library (New York: Harper & Row, 1964).

Kogon, Eugen. *The Theory and Practice of Hell: The German Concentration Camps and the System behind Them*. 1st rev. ed. New York: Farrar, Straus and Giroux, 2006.

Lebron, Christopher. *The Making of Black Lives Matter: A Brief History of an Idea*. Oxford: Oxford University Press, 2018.

Luethge, H. "Basic Questions of German Dog Breeding (Grundfragen der Deutschen Hundezucht)" *Deutsche Landwirtschaftliche Tierzucht* 18 (1938): 352.

Mammen, Franz von. *Der Hund in Wort und Spruch des Volkes*. Dresden: Piersons Verlag, 1936.

McClintock, Anne. *Imperial Leather: Race, Gender, and Sexuality in the Colonial Contest*. New York: Routledge, 1995.

Painter, Nell Irvin. *The History of White People*. New York: Norton, 2011.

Pearson, Chris. "Dogs, History, and Agency." *History and Theory* 52, no. 4 (December 2013): 128–45.

Peters, H. "Breed History of the Newfoundland Dog (Zur Rassegeschichte der Neufundlandhunde)." *Deutsche Kynologen-Zeitung* 22, no. 9 (1940).

"The Provisions of the Reich's Association for Dog Matters for Breeding (Die Bestimmungen des Reichsverbandes für Hundewesen über das Zuchtwesen." Berlin, 1941.

Ransby, Barbara. *Making All Black Lives Matter: Reimagining Freedom in the Twenty-First Century*. Berkeley: University of California Press, 2018.

Ravalli, Richard. "Snoop's Devil Dogg: African American Ghostlore and Bones." *Journal of American Culture* 30, no. 3 (September 2007): 285–92.

Reichstierschutzblatt 3 (1939).

"Report on the Regional Meeting on Dog Sports in the Districts of Auerbach i:B in the Gau of Saxony and Centre within the Association for German Dogs (Bericht über die Hundesport-Kreistagung des Kreises Auerba i.B. im Gau Sachsen und Mitte im Reichsverband für Das Deutsche Hundewesen)." *Rundschau für Jagd und Hundesport* (1935).

Ritvo, Harriet. "Pride and Pedigree: The Evolution of the Victorian Dog Fancy." *Victorian Studies* 29, no. 2 (1986): 227–53.

Roach, Joseph R. *Cities of the Dead: Circum-Atlantic Performance*. The Social Foundations of Aesthetic Forms. New York: Columbia University Press, 1996.

Roesbeck, Kurt. "1938." *Zeitung der Fachschaft für Deutsche Schäferhunde* 38, no. 1 (1939).

———. "Breeding with Tough Working Dogs (Zucht mit harten Gebrauchshunden)." *Zeitung der Fachschaft für Deutsche Schäferhunde* 37, no. 3 (1938).

Sax, Boria. *Animals in the Third Reich: Pets, Scapegoats, and the Holocaust*. New York: Continuum, 2000.

Schnippel, K. H. "Something about Our Shepherd Dog (Einiges über unseren Schäferhund)." *Zeitung der Fachschaft für Deutsche Schäferhunde* 34, no. 13 (1935).

Schultze, E. "Wolf and Dog in the Aryan Tradition (Wolf und Hund in den Ueberlieferungen der arischen Urzeit)." *Die Hundewelt* 14, no. 8 (1938).

Scott, Helen. "Was There a Time before Race? Capitalist Modernity and the Origins of Racism." In *Marxism, Modernity and Postcolonial Studies*, edited by Crystal Bartolovich and Neil Lazarus, 1st ed., 167–82. Cambridge: Cambridge University Press, 2002.

Skabelund, Aaron. "Breeding Racism: The Imperial Battlefields of the 'German' Shepherd Dog." *Society & Animals* 16, no. 4 (2008): 354–71.

———. "Political History." In *Handbook of Historical Animal Studies*, edited by Mieke Roscher, André Krebber, and Brett Mizelle. Boston: DeGruyter, 2021.

Smith, Mark M. *How Race Is Made: Slavery, Segregation, and the Senses*. Chapel Hill: University of

North Carolina Press, 2006.

Spiegel, Marjorie. *The Dreaded Comparison: Human and Animal Slavery*. Rev. and expanded ed. New York: Mirror Books, 1996.

Spratt, Meg. "When Dogs Attacked: Iconic News Photographs and Construction of History, Mythology, and Political Discourse." *American Journalism* 25, no. 2 (Spring 2008): 85–102.

Taylor, Keeanga-Yamahtta. *From #Black Lives Matter to Black Liberation*. Chicago: Haymarket Books, 2016.

Tenner, Edward. "Citizen Canine." *Wilson Quarterly* 22, no. 3 (1998): 71–79.

———. "Constructing the German Shepherd Dog." *Raritan: A Quarterly Review* 36, no. 3 (2017): 90–115.

Tindol, Robert. "The Best Friend of the Murderers: Guard Dogs and the Nazi Holocaust." In *Animals and War. Studies of Europe and North America*, edited by Ryan Hediger. Human-Animal Studies 15. Boston: Brill, 2013.

Völkischer Beobachter 296 (1935).

von Stephanitz, Max. *Der Deutsche Schäferhund in Wort und Bild*. Munich, 1901.

———. *Der Deutsche Schäferhund in Wort und Bild*. Jena, 1932.

Wall, Tyler. "'For the Very Existence of Civilization': The Police Dog and Racial Terror." *American Quarterly* 68, no. 4 (2016): 861–82.

Wippermann, Wolfgang. "Der Hund als Propaganda- und Terrorinstrument im Nationalsozialismus." In *Veterinärmedizin Im Dritten Reich*, edited by Johann Schäffer. Tagung/Deutsche Veterinärmedizinische Gesellschaft e.V., Fachgruppe Geschichte der Veterinärmedizin am 14. und 15. November 1997 in Hannover, 5. Giessen: DVG, 1998.

Wright, Michelle M. *Physics of Blackness: Beyond the Middle Passage Epistemology*. Minneapolis: University of Minnesota Press, 2015.

Wuest, Markus. "Rin Tin: Der Hund, der Niemals starb." *Basler Zeitung*, December 25, 2020. Available at https://www.bazonline.ch.

Zelinger, Amir. "Race and Animal-Breeding: A Hybridized Historiography." *History and Theory* 58, no. 3 (September 2019): 360–84.

Sheep Trouble on Clifton Beach
Sacrificial Sheep Exorcising the Demon of Racism?

Benita de Robillard

Illuminated by the Instagram-ready glamour of Clifton's Fourth Beach, Cape Town's denizens and holidaymakers congregated for picnics, cocktails, and icy swims on a balmy late December afternoon in 2018. This littoral scene was transformed into a political protest that involved the sacrifice of a sheep when a coalition of social movements and political parties assembled on the beach to contest the racist spatial politics that continues to structure the city. The protest sparked frenzied disputes about the shape of racism in South Africa and how the animal figures in the production of a racist ontological imaginary.

Through reading the animalizing politics at work in the spectacle of a sheep being slaughtered on Clifton's Fourth, this chapter addresses how the ongoing interconnections of race and animality are implicated in the post/apartheid national symbolic.[1] The sheep's slaughter, provoked by a racist incident on the beach, was conceived as a sacrifice that should purge the site, and South Africa itself, of the racist structures through which the Republic was formed. Bringing into focus what was sublimated in the controversy the sheep's slaughter instigated, the discussion that follows tracks how cultural practices and anti-racist politics were pitted against animal welfare and rights imperatives to argue that this way of framing the race and animal questions fails to come to terms with the long and persistent history of interspecies entanglement—a history that has produced, and been hounded by, logics and techniques of animalization, a term that describes ways of thinking and doing that make certain forms of life "animal" and therefore not "human." Animalization has been integral to the complex machinery of racialization, which degrades Black life so that race can materialize.[2] The "fallacy of race as a biologically traceable marker of difference" is, of course, the basis for enduring racist hierarchies.[3] Race-making technologies conjure the intricate and mobile interconnections of animalization and racialization to delineate which forms of life personhood can be attached to and which lives are not permitted to attain this status.[4] The terms and effects of these interconnected logics organized the sacrificial scene in question. In South Africa, "racializing technologies have always instrumentalised an animalising apparatus."[5] For this reason, an ethics and politics of futurity that sets out to undo white supremacy must dismantle animalization. Such an ethico-politics, in turn, cannot materialize if the animal is unseen.[6] None of this is to say that the histories of racial and animal oppressions are identical. It is also not to invite a simple comparison of these histories. This discussion begins at a different analytical juncture.[7] It is one that eschews analogical terms for this examination in favor of analysis, which addresses the plastic and vexed interconstitution of race and animality that in turn fabricates "the discourse of species" and the "zoologo-racial order" it secures.[8]

BEACH POLITICS

Beaches are places where many who live in South Africa spend the languorous (for some) interstitial time between the official Christmas and New Year's Day public holidays. As one would expect, the post/apartheid Republic's white-sanded beaches are streaked with its histories of colonial and apartheid violence, both of which were, among other things, engine rooms of racial capitalism.[9] During the apartheid period, beaches were one of the many racially segregated spaces through which the state's biopolitical procedures and effects were organized.[10] Of late, the now ostensibly desegregated beach has become a potent site of national psychic drama and purgation.

In what has become something of a tradition, 2018's end-of-year languor was disturbed by reports about an incident that had unfolded on one of the country's most famous beaches.[11] As media accounts had it,[12] on December 23, a private security company, Professional Protection Alternatives (PPA), whose personnel are styled in the manner of a "paramilitary" unit, removed from Clifton's Fourth groups of beachgoers who had congregated to picnic and view the sunset.[13] According to these reports, PPA told people who were on the beach that it closed at 8 p.m. While the incident was widely condemned, disputes about the sequence of events on the evening in question, as well as what the affair revealed about the post/apartheid racial order, dominated national headlines for over a week. One of the sources of disquiet was the allegation that the City of Cape Town had authorized PPA's conduct when they illegally restricted access to—and in effect privatized—public space. Dan Plato, City of Cape Town mayor, rejected these claims and stated that PPA was not working in concert with the city's police department, while noting that the company had removed everyone who was on the beach at the time without discriminating on the grounds of race.[14] Plato also tried to refute allegations that his administration was "fostering racial segregation reminiscent of the apartheid era"[15] when stating that "the City of Cape Town is an inclusive city and will always encourage everyone of all demographics to enjoy our public spaces . . . we will not allow any private organisations to limit access to our public spaces. . . . Even though some political organisations will exploit any opportunity to drive a racial wedge in our society, this is something we must never allow."[16] Plato's claims were challenged on a number of grounds. One political commentator scoffed at the assumptions that underpinned the mayor's comments when writing, "Obviously, a white supremacist who hires black security guards to ask black and white people to leave a public beach is well aware that they should not be seen as racist. They achieve this aim by asking the hired goons to ask everyone on the beach to leave the area. . . . That is covert racism. The aim is to get black residents of Cape Town away from Clifton."[17] The details of what transpired and whether or not the incident was precipitated by a sexual assault involving a fifteen-year-old beachgoer were, and remain, contested. In March 2019, a parliamentary inquiry concluded that the alleged rape had not taken place and that "a private security company should never be allowed to curtail people's freedom in the manner that PPA had mismanaged beachgoers on 23rd December 2018."[18] The event, and the inquiry that ensued from it, were mired in the expediencies of the African National Congress's (ANC) and the Democratic Alliance's (DA) respective national election campaigns in 2019.

Insofar as its record of governing in Cape Town is concerned, the DA has been accused of privileging the interests of property developers, some of whom are said to be among its donors, and thereby perpetuating the spatial and economic injustices born of apartheid racial segregation.[19] Cape Town illustrates in the starkest terms possible South Africa's ignominious status as the world's "most unequal society."[20] Moreover, Clifton itself is an index of South Africa's yawning and widening economic inequalities. According to de Villiers, "There are some 2,200 residential properties in South Africa valued at R20 million or more," and "the ten most expensive streets in South Africa are all located in Cape Town"; five of those streets are located in Clifton.[21]

After the sheep protest, intense contestation on social media revealed a hidden aspect of the Clifton beaches' imbrications with slavery. Previously submerged dimensions of Clifton's place in the "pelagic" history of slavery surfaced with the discovery and documentation in the period between 2011 and 2014 of a shipwreck off the Clifton Beaches.[22] Tracking the "ReclaimClifton" hashtag brought to my attention an article about the wreck of the *São José Paquete d'Africa* slave ship that lay "undiscovered" along Clifton's shores "for more than 200 years."[23] The ship carrying "512 enslaved Mozambicans" was destined for Brazil but sank on December 27 in 1794.[24] Two hundred slaves drowned, and the "survivors were sold into slavery in Cape Town."[25]

Gabeba Baderoon reminds us that, for "176 years," slavery was "the central form of social and economic organization in the territories that would form South Africa."[26] Slavery, Baderoon adds, "generated foundational notions of race and sex in South Africa, yet we have largely forgotten its role in our history."[27] All of this is to say that the Clifton incident was a case of colonial, apartheid, and post/apartheid realities colluding with an up-to-the-minute neoliberal "spatial register" that mobilizes techniques of privatization and securitization.[28] Put differently, the event provided a caesural opening onto the techno-politics of racial capitalism at the tip of the African continent.[29] As Brawley, drawing on Wendy Brown, puts it, neoliberalism "is a specific form of 'political rationality'"; it is a "constructivist project" that "endeavors to create the world it claims already exists."[30] Neoliberalism is characterized by extensive securitization, "the intensification of spatial division, and the emergence of the 'quartered' or 'layered city' in which we can chart 'fortified enclaves, ghettoes of exclusion, and center-city citadels of capital.' This ordering of 'the built environment . . . and of the spatial scale of lived experience' constructs 'the truth-effects of this 'new political form.'"[31]

Housing activists and the unhoused are working to undo Cape Town's spatial apartheid at multiple sites of resistance—for instance, through the occupation in 2017 of the Helen Bowden nursing home and the different forms of protest that the Clifton beach incident provoked.[32] One group of beachgoers who were removed from Clifton's Fourth used the well-known anti-apartheid slogan #God'sbeachesforallGod'speople in a hashtag to organize a "protest picnic" at sunset on December 29. Using the hashtags #OccupyClifton, #ReclaimClifton, and #EFFPicnicAgainstRacism, the Economic Freedom Fighters (EFF), another opposition party represented in the South African parliament, marched from the city's center to Clifton, where they planned to occupy the beach from 6 p.m. to 6 a.m. On December 28, several groups, including some of the leaders of the Rhodes Must Fall and Fees Must Fall protest movements, organized under the umbrella of what they called the Black People's National Crisis Committee (BPNCC) and gathered on the beach to slaughter a sheep in what they described as a "traditional ceremony."[33]

The event was staged for, and disseminated by, national media.[34] Reporting about the event, Philani Nombembe and Aaron Hyman wrote that the beach "was stained with the blood of a sheep whose throat was cut by protestors" in a "cleansing ceremony" that was meant to "exorcise the demon of racism."[35] The discussion that follows considers the politico-ethical dimensions and effects of this sacrificial scene. To use a formulation Gossett borrows from Hartman and Wilderson, I want to think what was "unthought" in both the event and the ways in which it was read.[36] Thinking the unthought here requires squaring up to the profound interconnections of colonialism, racial slavery, species, racism, racial capitalism, and animality—the afterlives and stains of which were all contained in this scene. Although this was not acknowledged at the time, the spectacle of animal sacrifice on Clifton Beach became a highly visible staging ground for what

Gossett, and others, have charted as the "co-constitutive"—or "interconstitutive"—history of "racialized and animal oppressions."[37] While symbolically disrupting the racist spatial politics at work in the city, the sheep's slaughter did not adequately confront this history. As Bénédicte Boisseron notes, "The intersection of race and animality is based on a shared status of nonrelevance as nonhuman and nonwhite. To grapple with colonialism means to first acknowledge and embrace the inextricable compoundedness of race and animality in order to then defiantly inhabit or transcend it."[38]

SACRIFICIAL SHEEP

Chumani Maxwele, a co-organizer of the BPNCC, said that he was one of the beachgoers who was driven off the beach by PPA.[39] Maxwele is reported to have said that "wealthy homeowners thought they were entitled to the beach.... We know white people are offended by black people on the beach. If you visit the First to the Fourth beaches you will find that the beaches are personalised. The discrimination of black people in these areas is so deep."[40] In accounting for why the BPNCC intended to slaughter a sheep on the beach, Maxwele said that "The offering of the sheep is calling on our ancestors to respond to our trauma at the hands of white people over the years."[41] On the day in question, one of the protestors addressed and rallied the group of protestors who had gathered at the beach for the ceremony in the following terms: "White settlers cannot come and tell us what to do in our country. White settlers cannot tell us what to do in our native lands. I am saying their days are numbered.... Roets of Afriforum, all of them, they must go to hell. The sea belongs to us. The beach belongs to us."[42] Holding the tethered sheep, who had been dragged across the beach, Maxwele directed the ceremony, announcing, "We are going to untie the sheep and walk it to waken Nxele's spirit, Nxele's spirit is along this ocean. Down with racists down."[43] Nombembe described the sacrificial scene thus: "Maxwele then cut the sheep's throat as other protestors burned incense. He declared: Today the dignity of the black people has been restored. This is an offering to our ancestors. The sheep will be slaughtered here and eaten here."[44] In video footage of the slaughter, Maxwele is seen to burn *imphepho* (incense) while proclaiming, "Here is the sacrifice Nxele," as the mortally wounded sheep's blood pumped into the sand.[45]

The scene was also witnessed by a small group of residents from the area, one of whom became involved in an altercation with some of the protestors. A group of animal rights activists who articulated what they took be both an anti-racist and anti-speciesist position also attended the protest with a view to imploring the protestors not to slaughter the sheep. One of these activists, identified in media reports as Chloe Kingdom, approached the organizers and said, "As a vegan animal rights activist we use a concept of speciesism and we say that there is an interlocking system throughout the world and throughout society and we think it's the root cause of discrimination and oppression and we feel from speciesism stems racism.... Sir... we are not here to disrespect or undermine or oppress any of your cultural practices and traditions. However, we wanted to ask a question, is there ways [*sic*] to reach your ancestors and communicate with them and preserve those traditions and practices without exploiting and killing animals and taking their lives?"[46] The person to whom Kingdom was speaking retorted, "That is the culture. There's a difference between killing and slaughtering."[47] Kingdom's response was to say, "Okay, but you're still killing an animal." At this point, Maxwele pushed the animal rights activists out of his way and was reported to have subsequently dismissed their objections, saying, "Let them go and lay a complaint with the commission for cultural rights . . . and other platforms."[48] In the context of a previous controversy involving the ritual slaughter of a bull, the chairperson of the Cultural and Linguistic Rights Commission, Mongezi Guma, "acknowledged that the furore had led to discussion and more understanding between 'different cultures'" and "committed himself to the principles of animal welfare, promising to investigate how 'to do cultural slaughtering in a way that will promote and protect the welfare of animals.'"[49] In media reports about, and footage of, the slaughter at Clifton, these were questions that the BPNCC were not prepared to consider.

The DA-led administration in Cape Town laid charges against three of the protestors "in terms of the city's by-laws" while the Society for the Prevention of Cruelty to Animals (SPCA) brought charges of animal cruelty against those who had conducted the ritual slaughter.[50] Not unpredictably, the protest and the differently focused interventions by a Clifton resident, the vegan-identified animal rights activists, the SPCA, and the DA administration generated fierce debates in the media.[51] These debates constituted what Claire Jean Kim would call an "impassioned dispute" that pitted cultural practices and anti-racist politics against animal welfare and rights, the latter of which were coded as white concerns.[52] While there is much to consider in respect of this dispute and the profound limits to pitting one injury against another, that discussion must be pursued elsewhere. My focus here is on the #ReclaimClifton protestors' aims and procedures with regard to their objectives, which were to purge South Africa of racists and racism and help it recuperate from the traumatic afterlives of slavery, colonialism, and apartheid.

In a discussion of how southern African novelists have represented animal subjectivities, Wendy Woodward reflects on the metaphysical significance ritual sacrifice holds in Xhosa systems of knowing. Woodward comments on the ways in which these writers "foreground traditional knowledges, or the lacunae left by their obliteration, in their representations of animals" to highlight that "In Xhosa creation myths both humans and cattle emerge together from dark, fertile caves. Spirituality is of and below the earth; it exists in the everyday and because it is embodied rather than transcendent, it is part of nature." Woodward emphasizes that these novels "contradict colonial discourses about nature" to "imagine kinship between humans and animals so that their knowledge productions become 'relational epistemologies.'" These "relational epistemologies," Woodward argues, "implicitly question the dualistic episteme of western metaphysics which categorises humans and other animals hierarchically."[53] One of the striking features of the sacrificial scene staged on Clifton Beach was that the kinship among human and nonhuman animals to which Woodward refers was neither foregrounded nor described.[54] The Xhosa metaphysical imaginary was conveyed in very limited terms, and the ritual was conducted in a manner that demonstrated masculine control over the nonhuman animal.[55]

A number of commentators expressed disquiet about what they took to be material breaches of custom. For instance, Zuko Mnukwa, a *sangoma* (traditional healer), was asked by the national broadcaster to comment on complaints to the effect that the Clifton ceremony was "too short," that "proper steps and processes weren't followed," and that "a sheep was not the right animal to use."[56] Mnukwa said that while they thought that

> the intention behind the slaughtering of the sheep [was] to heal and to dispel all of the bad evil that includes racism . . . rituals are done by people who know how to conduct them because there's a way of doing rituals, especially if you are coming to the beach which we regard as a very sacred place in our practice . . . the sheep may not necessarily be the right animal but the people were too excited, they found what will help them in their cause but yes how they did it was wrong, the way they burned

imphepho and the way they took the sheep to the sea and after they lit *imphepho* they were like viva, there's a way of doing things and even though I understand the intent and the cause, the way they did it was wrong because you will invoke the spirits then who will appease them ... the atmosphere is ... tense because of instabilities in the air after what has been done here, so to correct it, so I think healing from racism, we need as a collective not just certain people coming to the sea and doing it on behalf of the nation.[57]

To be clear, Mnukwa did not object to traditional ceremonies in which animals are slaughtered, but rather to the manner in which Maxwele et al. deviated from the traditional repertoire. Now, while the ceremony conducted at Clifton can be read in terms of the significance that is ascribed to the ritual slaughter of animals, this was not the only interpretive frame within which the affair was formulated. The sacrificial scene was also devised as a political spectacle at the scale of the nation. In effect, the BPCC conceived of the event as an instrument that was meant to unmake Clifton's whiteness and challenge techniques of privatization and securitization that entrench racial capitalism. Although the BPNCC claimed that it was not representing a political party, Black First Land First, a political party that contested the national elections a few months later,[58] was one of the organizations that formed the group, as the following statement on their website attested:

> It has come to the attention of Black First Land First (BLF) that an entity known as the Cape of Good Hope Society for the Prevention of Cruelty to Animals (SPCA) plans to criminalize the Reclaim Clifton protesters. The racist entity plans to harass black people who are fighting racism. The racist organization shall try and use the claim of fighting cruelty against animals as a pretext to unleashing the police against those blacks who performed the sacred duty of cleansing Clifton beach of the evil spirits inhabiting it. BLF warns the SPCA that should it continue with its racist agenda, we shall slaughter five sheep at its different outlets including its head office. We are tired of being insulted by whites in our own country.[59]

This statement demonstrates how animal rights and welfare positions are construed by many in South Africa to be white supremacist practices that are inherently racist. The view taken is that white South Africans are more concerned with animal suffering than they are with the material and existential circumstances of Black people.[60] Reading the situation in these terms has much to do with how animal practices that involve the ritual slaughter of animals have become especially intense flashpoints in the post/apartheid setting. Notwithstanding the attempt at articulating an animal rights position with an anti-racist one, there was little evidence in the mediatized framing of the Clifton event to indicate that the vegan animal-rights advocates had done the work of accounting for the ways in which practices that are thought to be "cultural" have been figured within much anti-cruelty discourse and legalization.[61]

Maneesha Deckha points out that "how racially minoritized cultures use animals ... continues to come under dominant legal scrutiny through anticruelty legislation as evidence of cultural and racial backwardness and inferiority despite the gross exploitation that dominant cultural practices—unmarked as cultural but rather normalized as mainstream—entail."[62] Returning to the question of how to interpret the affair, despite the BPNCC's assertion to the contrary, BLF's participation in the event showed that the ceremony was entwined with national electoral party politics. In fact, BLF was not the only party who attended the event. Members of the ANC, DA, and EFF jostled to make political capital from the episode. It would not be overstating matters to say that the protest's symbolic politics reeked of electoral opportunism. Furthermore, in its communications on the day before the event, the Fees Must Fall Western Cape group, a formation that was located at the organizational pivot of the protest action, addressed its membership as follows:

> We are calling on all self-respecting Blacks (Indian, Coloured and Africans) to descend at Clifton 4th Beach on Friday 28 December 2018 at 18h00 for a political protest. We must be clear that this is a political protest after some of our people were illegally removed by a private security company called Professional Protection Alternatives (PPA). In justifying its illegal actions, the company claimed that the patrons were not allowed to be at the beach after 20h00. This is illegal as only the City of Cape Town can enforce such by-laws, even then, such by-laws need to be fair and just taking into consideration the needs of the public at large.[63]

In one sense this instruction had to do with the municipal bylaws governing where sheep might be slaughtered. In another sense it wanted the membership to understand the protest as a political event and to act accordingly. For all of the reasons just enumerated, the sacrificial scene must therefore also be evaluated in terms of its political instrumentality. It is in reading the event in these terms that I would say that the sacrificial scene could not "exorcise the demon of racism." This is because the spectacle of animal sacrifice neither acknowledged nor reckoned with the co-constitutive history of racialized and animal oppression. Eliding this linkage is, as Boisseron explains, to fail to deconstruct the racialization of Blackness as animalization.[64] Instead of trying to ignore or erase this history, the task is to "expose a system that compulsively conjures up blackness and animality together to measure the value of existence."[65] Anti-racist praxis therefore must confront the history of interspecies entanglement.

SHEEP'S BLOOD AND MEAT MAKING THE ANIMALIZATION-KILLABILITY NEXUS

Looking at the bloody Clifton scene through the prism of other histories of slavery, those of the Americas that Boisseron traces, one encounters an archive of sacrificial scenes that recasts the drama of blood, sand, and ancestors as a spectacle through which those conducting the sacrifice could distinguish themselves from the animal; through which they could distinguish themselves from the meat that they made from the sheep. Boisseron describes how General Donatien de Rochambeau, leader of the French expeditionary force in Saint-Domingue (Haiti), arranged public executions in which dogs were forced to eat enslaved persons, noting that "sacrificing blacks to dogs reveal[ed] a need for whites to bond among themselves and to dissociate themselves from blacks as a distinct group." Rochambeau, Boisseron adds, "organised the sacrificial scene in the name of the collective French in order to assert their superiority and distinguish themselves as more human than food." Arguing that the canines were used as "proxies" for the "French body in combat with the blacks," Boisseron says that the objective was to "distinguish" the French from "the animalized men" that the bloodhounds were trained to "hunt." In effect, the French colonizers instrumentalized dogs to manufacture racial difference. On the question of flesh and meat, Boisseron points out that "the slave [was] defined not only by his or her chattel status but also by his or her edibility." So, "using dogs ... to punish the slave ... enact[ed] a strategy of domination through a rhetoric of edibility," which was "a racially invested kind of carnophallogocentrism."[66]

Returning to the Clifton event with this sacrificial archive in mind, one is struck by the repetitive quality to the scene of the sheep's slaughter. The sacrificial logic at work in the BPNCC's ceremony effected a repetition of Rochambeau's scene with a very significant difference. If colonization is viewed "as a sublimated form of cannibalism,"[67] then, unlike the enslaved people on the *São José Paquete d'Africa* who were swallowed whole, and unlike the slave in Rochambeau's gruesome spectacle, Maxwele et al. assumed the role of the political subject who can kill and eat. Within this sacrificial economy, assuming the position of the one who kills and eats has the effect of removing that subject from the zone of edibility.

In symbolic terms, the Clifton event enacted the domination of the animal through the ritualized performance of making blood and meat—to wit, BLF's reiterative statement about killing sheep. Whatever else it was, invoking and producing blood, to use Achille Mbembe's terms, became a spectacle of bio-necropolitical force. This bio-necropolitical theater was both predicated on and asserted what Mbembe calls "the law of blood," which, he argues, must be repudiated. Mbembe has written that he "profoundly disagrees with those who confuse radical and future-oriented politics with the continuous invocation of blood and burning," adding, "there can be no sustained project of freedom without a voluntary renunciation of the law of blood."[68] As Cary Wolfe reminds us, that "the law" is grounded in a sacrificial structure is, of course, something that Jacques Derrida addressed when highlighting that "Freud addresses the problem of the origin of law . . . he resorts to what amounts to a sacrifice of the animal, and more broadly, of animality, as the means by which both the human and the basis of the law are secured." For Derrida, this sacrificial structure is a purificatory "schema" marked by the "purification of the animal in 'man.'" Evaluating the significance of Derrida's insight here for biopolitical thought, Wolfe draws our attention to what is at stake if we proceed from the understanding that Derrida is correct to say that "this sacrificial structure is fundamental to the entire canonical discourse of 'Western metaphysics or religions.'" For Wolfe, the necessary implication of Derrida's thesis is that "to live under biopolitics is to live in a situation in which we are all always already (potential) 'animals' before the law—not just nonhuman animals according to zoological classification, but any group of living beings that is so framed. Here, the distinction 'human/animal'—as the history of slavery, colonialism, and imperialism well shows—is a discursive resource, not a zoological designation . . . it is . . . a kind of *dispositif.*"[69] Making blood and meat, then, is to reenact the purificatory scheme Derrida describes. This sacrificial structure, which is a bio-necropolitical apparatus, was authorized through the slaughter of the sheep at Clifton Beach. Thus, invoking blood, and producing meat, sanctioned the animalization of life.

It is well established that animalization is a *techné* that makes racial difference.[70] Slaughtering the sheep was an attempt to expurgate racism by creating a distinction between the human political subject doing the bloodletting and the animal whose death secures the contours of that subjectivity in virtue of their animality, and hence killability. Killability has been both an instrument and effect of race-making. As Wolfe points out, "racial marking becomes the means by which the subject is deemed, not automatically animal, but killable." Killability, Wolfe elaborates, rather than "murderability," is a "condition that overlaps with the designation animal."[71] So, authorizing and performing animalization and killability cannot "exorcise the demon of racism" since these biopolitical procedures loop back into the sacrificial scheme that undergirds race-making. Anti-racist politics, therefore, should not be anchored in the animalization-killability nexus. The corollary is, as Boisseron commenting on Gossett's thesis notes, that "blackness should constitute the primary matrix in which we think about animal rights."[72] All of this is to say that a different scheme is required, one that is located in "anthro-decentric thought" and praxis.[73] Such a scheme should be grounded in what Kim has described as an "ethics of avowal" and a "multi-optic vision" through which both racial and animal oppression—and their interconstitution—are addressed together and simultaneously.[74] We need to do more to investigate the extent to which resources for dismantling racism's animalizing violence might be located in Xhosa, or other, knowledge schemes that do not rely on the human/nonhuman framework, in which "animal personhood" and mutual kinship can be avowed rather than effaced.[75]

NOTES

1. From this point on, I will refer to Clifton Fourth Beach as Clifton's Fourth.
2. Weheliye describes this complexity as follows: "I construe race, racialization, and racial identities as ongoing sets of political relations that require, through constant perpetuation via institutions, discourses, practices, desires, infrastructures, languages, technologies, sciences, economies, dreams, and cultural artifacts, the barring of nonwhite subjects from the category of human as it is performed in the modern west"; *Habeus Viscus*, 3.
3. Boisseron, *Afro-Dog*, 62.
4. While the contours and strata of Jackson's arguments cannot be excavated here, it is important to note that they set out to reframe accounts of how animalization and racialization are related. Orienting the discussion of the mutual constitution of Blackness and animality away from the idea that animalization translates into the dehumanization of Blackness, Jackson reinterprets a particular strand of racist Enlightenment thought by replacing "the notion of 'denied humanity' and 'exclusion' with bestialized humanization, because *the African's humanity is not denied but appropriated, inverted, and ultimately plasticized in the methodology of abjecting animality*," "Becoming Human," 2.
5. De Robillard and Lipschitz, "Race and 'the Animal,'" 74.
6. Space constraints preclude a discussion of the sheep at the center of the sacrificial scene. This crucial aspect of the event will be pursued in another forum.
7. For analysis of the problems associated with analogizing racial and animal oppressions refer to Boisseron, *Afro-Dog*, Kim, *Dangerous Crossings*, and Jackson, "Animal."
8. Wolfe, *Animal Rites*. Kim, "Murder and Mattering."
9. Mbembe describes this formation in the following terms, "Racial capitalism is the equivalent of a giant necropolis. It rests on the traffic of the dead and human bones," *Critique of Black Reason*, 136–37. See also Goldberg, "The Reason," and Melamed, "Racial Capitalism."
10. It is well understood that these effects are ongoing.
11. In recent times numerous instances of racist hate speech about—and conduct on—South African beaches have disturbed the polity.
12. See Adriaanse, "Resident Hired Beach Guards"; Fokazi, "Clifton All Sun, Sand and Sizzle as Beachgoers Chill—For Now"; Jacobs, "Cape Town Beach Dispute Unearths the Spectre of Unrepentant Apartheid"; Kiewiet, "Clifton's New Year Baa-Baa-Las"; Makinana, "Why Police Did Not Stop the Sheep Slaughter on Clifton Fourth Beach"; Nombembe and Hyman, "Beach Bust-Up"; Sunday Times, "The Ugly Ghosts Trying to Keep Clifton White by Night"; Swart, "Drawing a Line in the Sand on Racism."
13. The Clifton beaches are jewels in the crown of Cape Town's lucrative tourism industries. In 2015, *Traveller24* reported that "Cape Town's sandy shores" were "ranked 2nd best in the world on

National Geographic's new Best Beach Cities list... the magazine specifically mentions the Clifton beaches, saying they're known for the posh homes that overlook them. These beaches are also praised for their 'stellar sunset-viewing'"; "Clifton Beaches Rank 2nd on NatGeo's Best Beach List."

14. Plato, "Race-Baiting and Political Opportunism at the Heart of Clifton Drama." Cape Town's city council is run by the Democratic Alliance (DA). The DA, which in recent times has moved even further rightward, is South Africa's official opposition in parliament. Cape Town is the first major metropolitan city it governed after ousting the governing African National Congress (ANC) during the 2006 elections. In the 2009 elections, the DA secured a narrow majority and formed the provincial government in the Western Cape, the first and only province it has governed to date; see South African History Online, "Democratic Alliance." Cape Town is this province's major city and it is where South Africa's parliament is located.
15. Africa News Agency, "Three Protestors to Face Charges over Clifton Beach Sheep."
16. Plato, "Cape Town Beaches Open for ALL to Enjoy."
17. Mckaiser, "A Racism Lesson for Mayor Plato."
18. A report on the inquiry's findings is available on the Parliamentary Monitoring Group's website, "ATC190320: Report of the Portfolio Committee on Environmental Affairs on the Parliamentary Inquiry into the Alleged Eviction of Beach Goers at Clifton Fourth Beach on 23 December."
19. See McCool, "'End Spatial Apartheid': Why Housing Activists Are Occupying Cape Town," for a report about gentrification in Cape Town and the social movements that have been organizing against the practice with their demands for social housing. Wittles, "Crooks, Cons among Party Donors," reports on a controversial link between Patricia De Lille, Cape Town's former DA mayor, and property developers who were said to be DA funders that were also involved with a 1.5 billion Rand property development in Clifton.
20. This is according to a 2018 World Bank report. According to Baker, "South Africa's Dividing Line," 36–37, the bank "estimat[ed] that the top 10% owned 70% of the nation's assets in 2015. And the split is still largely along racial lines; the bottom 60%, largely comprising blacks—which, for the purposes of this story, includes mixed-race people and Asians descended from a period of slavery and colonial rule—controls 7% of the country's net wealth." Noting that the inequalities that mark South Africa are "multifaceted," Baker also highlights that the "largest dividing line is land, where the legacy of apartheid meets the failures and broken promises of the current government. It's manifested most plainly in the lack of affordable housing, particularly in urban areas. The number of decaying slums... has gone from 300 in 1994 to 2,700 today. Nowhere is this more obvious than in Cape Town, where 60% of the population, almost all black, lives in townships and informal settlements far from the city center. There, government services are limited, schools and health care are underfunded, insecurity is rife, and jobs almost nonexistent. Transport into the center is expensive, dangerous and unreliable. In an almost exact replica of apartheid-era urban planning, wealthy and middle-class whites are concentrated in the city center and in well-connected suburbs. Between the townships and the well-appointed central business district are vast tracts of unused land that, if developed correctly, could work to reverse the city's apartheid legacy by providing affordable urban housing and breaking up racial segregation. However, as is often the case when it comes to public land, history, politics, funding, government incompetence and prejudice are getting in the way."
21. De Villiers, "These South African Towns Could Be the Hotspots for R20 Million Homes."
22. This is Paul Gilroy's term for thinking the oceanic dimensions of slavery. See van Schalkwyk, "'Imagination Is Everything.'"
23. Sarah Crowe, "Deeply ironic, poignant piece of South African history hidden off shore of the very

beach that has seen #reclaimClifton race row over sheep slaughtering. Beach should be renamed February after surviving slaves @nkosi_milton @Bruceps @TimModise @BBCWorld," Twitter, December 30, 2018, 2:33 p.m. See also van Niekerk and Hoffmann, "Cape Town's Slave Ship Secret."
24. Parts of the wreckage have been "on loan and exhibited at the Smithsonian National Museum of African American history and Culture in Washington DC." A "founding director" of the museum characterized the discovery's significance thus: "There has never been archeological documentation of a vessel that foundered and was lost while carrying a cargo of enslaved persons," Van Niekerk and Hoffmann, "Cape Town's Slave Ship Secret."
25. Van Niekerk and Hoffmann, "Cape Town's Slave Ship Secret."
26. Baderoon, "Remembering Slavery in South Africa."
27. Baderoon, "Remembering Slavery in South Africa." See also Baderoon, *Regarding Muslims*.
28. Although differently inflected, both the ANC and DA advance neoliberal policies. See Bond, *Elite Transition*; Brawley, "The Practice of Spatial Justice in Crisis," 2.
29. Jodi Melamed, "Racial Capitalism."
30. Brawley, "The Practice of Spatial Justice in Crisis," 5.
31. Brawley, "The Practice of Spatial Justice in Crisis," 2.
32. McCool, "'End Spatial Apartheid.'"
33. Rhodes Must Fall originated in March 2015 as a protest movement at the University of Cape Town (UCT). The movement's objective was to force the university to remove from the campus a statue of Cecil John Rhodes. Rhodes Must Fall instigated the wider Fees Must Fall protests. As I have written elsewhere with Ruth Lipschitz, in 2015 and 2016 a student-led protest movement using the Fees Must Fall hashtag disrupted the South African higher-education sector with demands for "free, quality, and decolonised education." Rhodes Must Fall continues to resonate in other transnational struggles, for instance efforts to decolonize Oxford University and the toppling by Black Lives Matter protestors of a statue in Bristol of slave trader Edward Colston. See Mhodin, "Fall of Bristol's Colston Statue Revives Rhodes Campaign in Oxford."
34. Cloete, "From Clifton to Chief Makanda Beach"; Kiewit, "Clifton's New Year Baa-Baa-Las"; Makinana, "Why Police Did Not Stop the Sheep Slaughter on Clifton Fourth Beach"; Maphanga, "Protest to 'Reclaim' Clifton Beach with Ancestral Cleansing Ceremony"; News24, "WATCH: Residents Clash with Protesters"; Nombembe, "Sheep Slaughtered on Clifton Beach as Animal Rights Activists Protest"; Thamm, "Clifton 4th Beach: Of Slaughtered Sheep, Drowned Slaves and Collective Rituals."
35. Nombembe and Hyman, "Beach Bust-Up."
36. Gossett, "Blackness, Animality, and the Unsovereign."
37. See Deckha, "Postcolonial"; Kim, "Slaying the Beast"; Kim, *Dangerous Crossings*; Kim, "Murder and Mattering"; Kim and Freccero, "Introduction"; Gossett, "Blackness, Animality,"; De Robillard, "In/On the Bones," de Robillard and Lipschitz, "Race and 'the Animal.'"
38. Boisseron, *Afro-Dog*, 108.
39. Maxwele was a prominent figure in the Rhodes Must Fall and Fees Must Fall campaigns. In 2015 he covered in human excrement the Cecil John Rhodes statue on the UCT campus and faced criminal charges for this protest; Bester, "Protesters Throw Poo on Rhodes Statue." Maxwele also came to national attention following his involvement in a Fees Must Fall protest at the University of Witwatersrand in April 2016. As a consequence of an incident that occurred during this protest, Maxwele was embroiled in a controversy and heated discussion with Thenjiwe Mswane, a feminist and queer-identified student, on a radio call-in program. Mswane was one of the Black female

student activists who, according to the show's presenter, Redi Tlhabi, was "accussing [sic] their black male counterparts of sexual assault and misogyny"; News24, "UCT's Maxwele Slammed over Physical Altercation with Female Student." For further context about the episode that the radio program investigated, see TMG Digital, "#NotMyFMF—Sjamboks and Muscles in Wits Gender Showdown."

40. Philani Nombembe, "Protesters Aim for Clifton Beach as Cops Deny Security Firm 'Rape' Claim." A feature of post/apartheid economic realities that should be noted is the changing face of the capitalist class and patterns of property ownership. Without overstating these changes, it would be remiss not to mention that the current president, Cyril Ramaphosa, amassed a fortune in the post/apartheid period and that he owns one of the more expensive properties in Cape Town in Fresnaye, a suburb that is not far from Clifton. It is also worth noting that a few months after the protests at Clifton's Fourth, members of the EFF rented, and damaged during a house party, lavish accommodation in Camps Bay, a suburb that is adjacent to Clifton.
41. Canny Maphanga, "Protest to 'Reclaim' Clifton Beach with Ancestral Cleansing Ceremony."
42. These comments were made by a person I have not been able to identify in a video taken at the beach and posted on Twitter by David Chambers @daveincapetown, 7:33 p.m., December 28, 2018. The tweet and the video are embedded in Nombembe, "Sheep Slaughtered on Clifton Beach."
43. "Maxwele was referring to the Xhosa warrior who died on Christmas Day in 1819. He instigated an attack against the British garrison at Grahamstown"; Nombembe, "Sheep Slaughtered on Clifton Beach."
44. Nombembe, "Sheep Slaughtered on Clifton Beach."
45. News24, "WATCH: Residents Clash with Protesters."
46. News24, "WATCH: Residents Clash with Protesters."
47. In *Animals and Society*, deMello demonstrates that this distinction obtains in many practices of ritual animal sacrifice.
48. Nombembe and Hyman, "Beach Bust-Up."
49. Tony Yengeni, an erstwhile ANC MP, slaughtered the bull in a cleansing ceremony following his release from prison. Yengeni had served four months of a four-year sentence for fraud. In *The Animal Gaze*, Wendy Woodward notes that the "much publicized killing of the bull by Yengeni transgressed expectations that animals slaughtered should die orderly and invisible deaths in which the killers are not emotionally involved." While Guma was prepared to consider animal welfare in the context of cultural practices that involve the slaughter of animals, the chairperson, as Woodward highlights, continued to "cast culture in stone"; Woodward, *The Animal Gaze*, 9, 11.
50. Africa News Agency, "#ReclaimClifton: Three to Face Charges over Sheep Slaughter"; Africa News Agency, "CT Mayor to Take Steps over Sheep Slaughter."
51. Animal rights and animal welfare perspectives are, of course, not equivalent and are frequently in tension with one another.
52. Kim, *Dangerous Crossings*.
53. Woodward, *The Animal Gaze*, 3, 19.
54. Here I am referring to the terms in which Maxwele and other protestors were reported to have spoken about the ceremony.
55. An analog of which can be found in the performance of the social ritual of the *braaivleis* or barbecue, a practice that is coded as masculine. For reasons I cannot elucidate here, the *braai* is not considered to be somehow retrograde. The sheep was prepared and eaten on the beach after the cleansing ceremony, a feature of the protest to be considered in another forum.
56. SABC News, "Sangoma Explains Sheep Slaughtering."

57. SABC News, "Sangoma Explains Sheep Slaughtering."
58. BLF has been implicated in ongoing investigations into the activities of the Gupta family, who are suspected of corruption on a scale that is tantamount to the capture of the South African state. Email correspondence in the Gupta Leaks documents revealed that BLF's leader, Andile Mngxitama, received an instruction from the Guptas to write an adverse article about a journalist who had been reporting on the family's allegedly corrupt practices. In the subsequent period, BLF has become one of the Gupta family's most ardent defenders. In 2019 the Independent Electoral Commission annulled the party's registration because, the commission said, BLF limited its membership on the basis of race and was therefore acting in violation of the Electoral Act. See Barry Bateman, "#Guptaleaks Expose BLF Leader's Role in Campaign against Gupta Critic"; Rebecca Davis, "End of an Error: BLF Officially Deregistered as Political Party."
59. Black First Land First, "BLF Warns the SPCA."
60. Sorting and codifying animal rights and welfare positions in these terms is not peculiar to the South African context. For an overview of debates about race, species, and veganism refer to Deckha, "Toward a Postcolonial, Posthumanist Feminist Theory"; Deckha, "Welfarist and Imperial"; Deckha, "Postcolonial." There is much to consider in the BLF's statement and the discursive positions that were evident in public debates about the affair. Constraints require that these are taken up in another venue.
61. This might well be something that they have considered in other fora. Media coverage of the animal rights position was both scant and facile.
62. Deckha, "Postcolonial," 282.
63. Cilliers, "Sheep-Loving Protesters Raise the Ire of EFF."
64. Boisseron, *Afro-Dog*.
65. Boisseron, *Afro-Dog*, xx.
66. Boisseron, *Afro-Dog*, 53, 54, 58, 59, 60, 61.
67. Boisseron, *Afro-Dog*, 61.
68. Mbembe, "If We Don't Rehabilitate Reason, We Will Not Be Able to Fix Our Broken World."
69. Wolfe, *Before the Law*, 9, 10.
70. For instance Gossett, in "Blackness, Animality," notes that "blackness has . . . been racialized through animalization."
71. UC Berkeley Events, "Cary Wolfe: 'Life': Neovitalism and Biopolitical Thought."
72. Boisseron, *Afro-Dog*, 13.
73. Dana Luciano and Mel. Y. Chen, "Has the Queer Ever Been Human?," 192.
74. Kim, *Dangerous Crossings*.
75. See Tallbear, "Why the Animal? Queer Animalities, Indigenous Naturecultures, and Critical Race Approaches to Animal Studies"; Tallbear, "Why Interspecies Thinking Needs Indigenous Standpoints"; Tallbear, "An Indigenous Reflection on Working beyond the Human/Not Human."

WORKS CITED

Adriaanse, Dominic. "Resident Hired Beach Guards." *The Star*, December 31, 2018. Available at https://www.Security.co.za.

Africa News Agency. "CT Mayor to Take Steps over Sheep Slaughter." *The Citizen*, January 2, 2019. Available at https://www.PressReader.com.

———. "#ReclaimClifton: Three to Face Charges over Sheep Slaughter." *Independent Online*, December 31, 2018. Available at https://www.IOL.co.za.

———. "Three Protestors to Face Charges over Clifton Beach Sheep." *The Citizen*, December 30, 2018. Available at https://www.Citizen.co.za.

Baderoon, Gabeba. *Regarding Muslims: From Slavery to Post-Apartheid*. Johannesburg: Wits University Press, 2014.

———. "Remembering Slavery in South Africa." *Africa Is a Country*. September 4, 2020. Available at Africasacountry.com.

Baker, Aryn. "South Africa's Dividing Line." *Time* magazine, May 13, 2019.

Bateman, Barry. "#Guptaleaks Expose BLF Leader's Role in Campaign against Gupta Critic." *Eyewitness News*, July 24, 2017. Available at https://EWN.co.za.

Bester, Junior. "Protesters Throw Poo on Rhodes Statue." *Independent Online*, March 10, 2015. Available at https://www.IOL.co.za.

Black First Land First. "BLF Warns the SPCA." Black First Land First [website], December 30, 2018. Available at http://BLF.org.za.

Boisseron, Bénédicte. *Afro-Dog: Blackness and the Animal Question*. New York: Columbia University Press, 2018.

Bond, Patrick. *Elite Transition: From Apartheid to Neoliberalism in South Africa*. Rev. and expanded edition. London: Pluto Press, 2014.

Booysen, Susan, ed. *Fees Must Fall: Student Revolt, Decolonisation and Governance in South Africa*. Johannesburg: Wits University Press, 2016.

Braidotti, Rosi. "The Posthuman." Cambridge: Polity Press, 2013.

Brawley, Lisa. "The Practice of Spatial Justice in Crisis" ("La Pratique de la justice spatiale en crise"). Translated by Ninon Vinsonneau and Bernard Bret. *Justice Spatiale/Spatial Justice*, no. 1 (September 2009).

Chen, Mel Y. *Animacies: Biopolitics, Racial Mattering, and Queer Affect*. Durham, NC: Duke University Press, 2012.

Cilliers, Charles. "Sheep-Loving Protesters Raise the Ire of EFF." *The Citizen*, December 29, 2018. Available at https://www.Citizen.co.za.

Cloete, Norman. "From Clifton to Chief Makanda Beach." *Saturday Star*, December 29, 2018. Available at https://www.Security.co.za.

Davis, Rebecca. "End of an Error: BLF Officially Deregistered as Political Party." *Daily Maverick*, November 6, 2019. Available at https://www.Dailymaverick.co.za.

Deckha, Maneesha, "Postcolonial." In *Critical Terms for Animal Studies*, edited by Lori Gruen, 280–93. London: University of Chicago Press, 2018.

———. "Toward a Postcolonial, Posthumanist Feminist Theory: Centralizing Race and Culture in Feminist Work on Nonhuman Animals." *Hypatia* 27, no. 3, special issue: Animal Others (Summer 2012): 527–45.

———. "Welfarist and Imperial: The Contributions of Anticruelty Laws to Civilizational Discourse." *American Quarterly* 65, no. 3 (2013): 515–48.

de Robillard, Benita. "In/On the Bones: Species Meanings and the Racialising Discourse of Animality in the *Homo naledi* Controversy." *Image & Text* 32, no. 1 (2018): 1–26.

de Robillard, Benita, and Ruth Lipschitz. "Race and 'the Animal' in the Post-Apartheid 'National Symbolic.'" *Image & Text* 30, no. 1 (2017): 73–93.

deMello, Margo. *Animals and Society: An Introduction to Human-Animal Studies*. New York: Columbia University Press, 2012.

Derrida, Jacques. *The Animal That Therefore I Am*. Edited by Marie-Louise Mallet. Translated by David Wills. New York: Fordham University Press, 2008.

de Villiers, James. "These South African Towns Could Be the Hotspots for R20 Million Homes." *Business Insider*, June 27, 2019. Available at https://www.Businessinsider.co.za.

Felix, Jason. "Plato to Act Against Clifton Beach Security Company." *The Star*, January 2, 2019. Available at https://www.Security.co.za.

Fokazi, Sipokazi. "Clifton All Sun, Sand and Sizzle as Beachgoers Chill—for Now." *Sowetan*, January 1, 2019. Available at https://www.Sowetanlive.co.za.

Goldberg, David Theo. "'The Reason of Unreason': Achille Mbembe and David Theo Goldberg in Conversation about *Critique of Black Reason*." *Theory, Culture & Society* 35, no. 7/8 (December 2018): 205–27.

Gossett, Che. "Blackness, Animality, and the Unsovereign." *Verso* [blog], September 8, 2015. Available at Versobooks.org.

Gruen, Lori. "Samuel Dubose, Cecil the Lion and the Ethics of Avowal." *Aljazeera America*, July 31, 2015. Available at https://www.aljazeera.com.

Haraway, Donna J., and Cary Wolfe. *Manifestly Haraway*. Minneapolis: University of Minnesota Press, 2016.

Jackson, Zakiyyah Iman. "Animal: New Directions in the Theorization of Race and Posthumanism." *Feminist Studies* 39, no. 3 (2013): 669–85.

———. "Becoming Human: Matter and Meaning in an Antiblack World." *Philosophy World Democracy*, January 9, 2021. Available at https://www.Philosophy-world-democracy.org.

Jacobs, Faiez. "Cape Town Beach Dispute Unearths the Spectre of Unrepentant Apartheid." *Sunday Times*, January 6, 2019. Available at https://www.Timeslive.co.za.

Kiewit, Lester. "Clifton's New Year Baa-baa-las." *Mail and Guardian*, January 4–10, 2019. Available at https://www.Pressreader.com.

Kim, Claire Jean. *Dangerous Crossings: Race, Species, and Nature in a Multicultural Age*. New York: Cambridge University Press, 2015.

———. "Murder and Mattering in Harambe's House." *Politics and Animals* 3 (Fall 2016): 37–57.

———. "Slaying the Beast: Reflections on Race, Culture, and Species." *Kalfou*, inaugural issue (Spring 2010): 57–74.

Kim, Claire Jean, and Carla Freccero. "Introduction: A Dialogue." *American Quarterly* 65, no. 3 (2013): 461–79.

Lipschitz, Ruth Adele. "Abjection." In *Edinburgh Companion to Animal Studies*, edited by Lynn Turner, Undine Sellbach, and Ron Broglio, 13–29. Edinburgh: Edinburgh University Press, 2018.

———. *Animality and Alterity: Species Discourse and the Limits of "the Human" in Contemporary South African Art*. PhD diss., University of London. Goldsmiths, University of London, 2014.

Luciano, Dana, and Mel Y. Chen. "Has the Queer Ever Been Human?" *GLQ: A Journal of Lesbian and Gay Studies* 21, no. 2 (2015): 183–207.

———. "Queer Inhumanisms." *GLQ: A Journal of Lesbian and Gay Studies* 21, no. 2 (2015): 113–17.

Lundblad, Michael. *The Birth of a Jungle: Animality in Progressive-Era U.S. Literature and Culture*. New York: Oxford University Press, 2013.

Makinana, Andisiwe. "Why Police Did Not Stop the Sheep Slaughter on Clifton Fourth Beach." *Times Live*, February 5, 2019. Available at https://www.Timeslive.co.za.

Maphanga, Canny. "Protest to 'Reclaim' Clifton Beach with Ancestral Cleansing Ceremony." *News24*, December 28, 2018. Available at https://www.News24.com.

Mbembe, Achille. *Critique of Black Reason*. Translated by Laurent Dubois. Durham, NC: Duke

University Press, 2017.

———. "'If We Don't Rehabilitate Reason, We Will Not Be Able to Fix Our Broken World.'" *Mail and Guardian*, May 9, 2019. Available at https://MG.co.za.

Mbembe, J.-A., and Libby Meintjes. "Necropolitics." *Public Culture* 15, no. 1 (2003): 11–40.

McCool, Alice. "'End Spatial Apartheid': Why Housing Activists Are Occupying Cape Town." *The Guardian*, May 25, 2017.

McKaiser, Eusebius. "A Racism Lesson for Mayor Plato." *Mail and Guardian*, January 4–10, 2019.

Melamed, Jodi. "Racial Capitalism." *Critical Ethnic Studies* 1, no. 1 (Spring 2015): 76–85.

Mohdin, Aamna. "Fall of Bristol's Colston Statue Revives Rhodes Campaign in Oxford." *The Guardian*, June 8, 2020.

News24. "UCT's Maxwele Slammed over Physical Altercation with Female Wits Student." *News24*, April 5, 2016.

———. "WATCH: Residents Clash with Protesters over Slaughter of Sheep at Clifton Beach." YouTube video, 3:00, December 28, 2018. Available at https://www.YouTube.com.

Nombembe, Philani. "Protesters Aim for Clifton Beach as Cops Deny Security Firm 'Rape' Claim." *Times Live*, December 27, 2018.

———. "Sheep Slaughtered on Clifton Beach as Animal Rights Activists Protest." *Times Live*, December 28, 2018.

Nombembe, Philani, and Aron Hyman. "Beach Bust-Up." *Sunday Times*, December 30, 2018. Available at https://www.Pressreader.com.

Parliamentary Monitoring Group. "ATC190320: Report of the Portfolio Committee on Environmental Affairs on the Parliamentary Inquiry into the Alleged Eviction of Beach Goers at Clifton Fourth Beach on 23 December." *Parliamentary Monitoring Group*, March 20, 2019. Available at https://Pmg.org.za.

Plato, Dan. "Cape Town Beaches Open for ALL to Enjoy." *Politicsweb*, December 28, 2018.

———. "Race-Baiting and Political Opportunism at the Heart of Clifton Drama." *Sunday Times*, January 6, 2019. Available at https://www.Timeslive.co.za.

Prasad, Pritha. "Beyond Rights as Recognition: Black Twitter and Posthuman Coalitional Possibilities." *Prose Studies* 38, no. 1 (2016): 50–73.

Probyn-Rapsey, Fiona. "Stunning Australia." *Humanimalia: A Journal of Human/Animal Interface Studies* 4, no. 2 (2013).

SABC News. "Sangoma Explains Sheep Slaughtering, Cleansing at Clifton Beach." YouTube video, 15:35, December 29, 2018.

South African History Online. "Democratic Alliance (DA)." *South African History Online*. Available at https://SAhistory.org.za.

Sunday Times. "The Ugly Ghosts Trying to Keep Clifton White by Night." https://*TimesLive*, December 30, 2018.

Swart, Mia. "Drawing a Line in the Sand on Racism." *Mail and Guardian*, January 3, 2019. Available at https://MG.co.za.

TallBear, Kim. "An Indigenous Reflection on Working beyond the Human/Not Human." *GLQ: A Journal of Lesbian and Gay Studies* 21, no. 2 (2015): 230–35.

———. "Why Interspecies Thinking Needs Indigenous Standpoints." *Fieldsights*, November 18, 2011. Available at https://Culanth.org/fieldsights.

———. "Why the Animal? Queer Animalities, Indigenous Naturecultures, and Critical Race Approaches to Animal Studies." Opening Comments [Symposium], April 12, 2011. Available at https://Indigenoussts.com.

Thamm, Marianne. "Clifton 4th Beach: Of Slaughtered Sheep, Drowned Slaves and Collective Rituals." *Daily Maverick*, December 30, 2018.

TMG Digital. "#NotMyFMF—Sjamboks and Muscles in Wits Gender Showdown." *Times Live*, April 5, 2016.

Traveller24. "Clifton's Beaches Rank 2nd on NatGeo's Best Beach list." *Traveller24*, January 29, 2015.

"2019 National and Provincial Elections: Results Dashboard National Assembly 2019." International Electoral Commission [website]. Last modified November 1, 2019, 10:24:59. Available at https://Elections.org.za.

UC Berkeley Events. "Cary Wolfe: 'Life': Neovitalism and Biopolitical Thought." YouTube video, 1:25:30, September 15, 2011.

van Niekerk, Piet, and Werner Hoffmann. "Cape Town's Slave Ship Secret." *BBC Travel*, October 23, 2018.

van Schalkwyk, Simon. "'Imagination Is Everything': Paul Gilroy Chats to the JRB about Race, Land and South Africa's Role in Overthrowing the Racial Order." *Johannesburg Review of Books*, April 4, 2018.

Weheliye, A. G. *Habeus Viscus: Racializing Assemblages, Biopolitics, and Black Feminist Theories of the Human*." Durham, NC: Duke University Press, 2014.

Wittles, Govan. "Crooks, Cons among Party Donors." *Mail and Guardian Online*, August 4, 2017. Available at https://MG.co.za.

Wolfe, Cary. *Animal Rites: American Culture, the Discourse of Species and Posthumanist Theory*. Chicago: University of Chicago Press, 2003.

———. *Before the Law: Humans and Other Animals in a Biopolitical Frame*. Minneapolis: University of Minnesota Press, 2012.

———. "Flesh and Finitude: Thinking Animals in (Post) Humanist Philosophy." *SubStance* 37, no. 3, Issue 117: The Political Animal (2008).

Woodward, Wendy. *The Animal Gaze: Animal Subjectivities in Southern African Narratives*. Johannesburg: Wits University Press, 2008.

Of Menageries and Empires

Llamas, Snakes, and Indigenous Colonial Equivalency in the Andes

Rachel Sarah O'Toole

IN 1656, HERNANDO CARUACHIN TOLD A CATHOLIC CLERIC THAT, IN A DREAM, A DONKEY had told him to come to the Spanish colonial capital of the Peruvian viceroyalty, Lima. Instantly transporting him from the rural highlands to the cosmopolitan coast, the animal escorted Caruachin on a tour of "all the churches of the city."[1] Caruachin confessed his dream, his demonic communication, and his idolatrous activity. Fittingly, the animal with European origins facilitated Caruachin's entry into the lettered city, the center of colonial Catholic governance.[2] The animal all but forced the Indigenous man's participation. The evangelizing Catholic Church required the neophyte status of Indigenous Andeans to secure its ongoing mission.[3] Some Spanish colonizers speculated that those called "Indians" were suspect Catholics who might not have the intellectual and spiritual capabilities to understand the mysteries of the faith.[4] Caruachin's invocation of his dream donkey, however, articulated a colonial indigenous Christianity that defied the racial ideologies of clerics and colonial authorities. Caruachin's dream provided evidence of his knowledge and his confidence with colonizing institutions that radiated from the viceregal city. Caruachin was a known ritual specialist who, in addition to worshipping local and regional deities, claimed equivalency, as an Indigenous Andean, with European colonizers.

Throughout the seventeenth century, as Spanish missionaries and colonial authorities institutionalized Catholic practices and expanded resource extraction throughout the Americas, Indigenous Andeans talked with animals. Speaking directly to donkeys as peer beings with souls in a shared universe, Indigenous Andeans challenged European ontologies that separated humans from beasts.[5] Simultaneously, Indigenous Andeans adapted European animals voraciously and vigorously, quickly integrating sheep into llama herds while adding pigs and chickens to household corrals of guinea pigs.[6] Scholars of Indigenous Andeans, however, have primarily approached animals, and their representations, as symbols of political and cultural practices.[7] In this chapter, I take a more materialist approach to cultural actions. As pastoralists and agriculturalists engaged in a dynamic colonial market economy, Indigenous Andeans spoke in seventeenth-century animal speech acts or did something with the words about and with animals.[8] A shared language did not ensure understanding. Ontologically unattuned to Indigenous Andean speech acts, Spanish clerics and colonial officials often missed their challenging messages. In this chapter, I examine communications with and about animals, or how Andean speakers did things with words.[9] I reveal how Andean speakers affirmed Indigenous authority while simultaneously noting their current colonial status.

Andean animal speech acts confronted and conformed to seventeenth-century Spanish colonial attempts to reduce indigenous communities into a singular racial category of Indian. Indigenous Andeans, as Indians, were depicted as unable to fulfill their Christian devotions, perpetually consigned to the legal status of minor, and repeatedly required to pay tribute while serving *mita,* the Spanish colonial labor requirement. At the same time, Indigenous people of the seventeenth-century Andes adapted colonial structures and reinscribed themselves within imperial culture on their own terms.[10] The juxtaposition, and boundary, between Indian pagan others and Christianized Andeans deeply troubled Spanish colonizers. As Catholic clerics searched for a Christian Satan among the animal manifestations of local, regional, and Inca deities, Indigenous Andeans, through their animal speech acts, expressed epistemological disconnects caused by Iberian domination. In other words, Indigenous Andean people looked for solutions to the problems erupting from colonization. Hernando Caruachin elaborated on how the Indigenous religious practices of sacrificing llamas could be repurposed, while inhabitants of Huarochirí named a vengeful serpent who would remake the world. Colonizing clerics and Spanish authorities interpreted the animal speech acts of Indigenous Andeans as proof of Indian otherness, indications of a shared lack of civilization, and a reason for Iberian colonization of the Americas.[11] In contrast, speech practices, or acts, regarding specific animal species illuminate how Indigenous Andeans saw themselves as full participants, not marginal Indians, in colonial Christian Peru.[12] By speaking with and about animals, colonial Indigenous Andeans such as Hernando Caruachin defined their place within coloniality as well as articulated their own paradigms of value and change.

THE VALUE OF LLAMAS AND DONKEYS

For colonial Indigenous Andeans, the voices and the bodies of domestic animals communicated a strategic blending of known and new practices. Llamas provided Indigenous Andeans with life's most basic necessities, including wool for textiles, dung for fertilizer and fuel, and meat to consume. At a smaller scale and raised literally in one's home, guinea pigs were a ready source of protein. Sacrifices of these animals punctuated life cycles of birth, the growth of children, marriage, and death. By the mid-seventeenth century, the domestic livestock originating in Europe were also integral to the Andean world. As skilled pastoralists, practiced agriculturalists, and expert hydrologists, Indigenous Andeans celebrated the fecundity of chickens and pigs along with the strength of oxen and donkeys. Animals, new and old, fit into desired tasks so that Indigenous Andeans instilled value into colonial livestock.[13] Speaking with and through animals, Indigenous Andeans chose among European and American species based on the task, the market, and the outcome.

Nonetheless, after a century of Christian evangelization, Indigenous Andeans continued to prefer llamas and guinea pigs in their communications with local deities. Colonial Andeans thanked *huacas* (deities) or ancestors with a llama or guinea pig sacrifice in May or June during Catholic Corpus Christi celebrations and while maize matured.[14] Ancestors and local deities who fed on llamas protected the well-being of communities and people's herds from predators.[15] Guinea pigs, sacrificed in pastures and corrals, would generate productive llama herds and ensured the flow of water in irrigation canals.[16] Explaining to missionaries in anti-idolatry trials, Andean Indigenous witnesses elaborated how they and their neighbors sacrificed the blood, bodies, or fat of these Andean animals to community deities in order to ensure good weather and a good harvest.[17] Having been fed, deities released water from mountain springs or diverted torrents from glacier lakes that could flood fields.[18] Llama and guinea pig sacrifices marked life-cycle events, including when a child was old enough for their first haircut.[19] Clearly, Indigenous Andeans spoke to their deities in the animal speech acts that had previously worked before colonization to generate fecundity and prosperity.

Animal speech acts also worked within colonial Christian religious practices. As Kenneth Mills has deftly argued, Indigenous Andeans conjoined their own rites with Catholic feast days.[20] Indigenous Andeans also respected religious specialists who employed Catholic rituals and symbols. In fact, Indigenous Andean assistants to Catholic clerics and idolatry inspectors such as sacristans and interpreters, key figures in the evangelization process, continued to engage in local and regional religious practices. For example, leaders of rural indigenous confraternities devoted to Catholic saints performed animal sacrifices to local Andean deities.[21] Indigenous people also relied on the potency of Andean animals when practicing Christianity. In the early 1740s, Domingo García testified to Catholic inspectors that "he planned to smear llama's blood on the foundation and adobe walls of a new local church 'to make it strong.'"[22] Indigenous Andean people had been drenching new houses and buildings with the blood of llamas and guinea pigs throughout (and before) the seventeenth century.[23] As a parish church became the site of community gatherings, a display for local lineages, and where people buried their dead, why not ensure its longevity with a well-known sacred communication?

With their encompassing and ever-present power, protective llamas reminded colonial Indigenous Andeans of their religious obligations. Indigenous Andeans sacrificed llamas to divine the future and diagnosis illness.[24] In turn, llama deities demanded payment. A converted Catholic Andean testified that despite his best efforts to rid himself of "idolatry," local deities continued to seek him out. Don Cristóbal Choque Casa worked for the religious inspector of Huarochirí and, according to historian Alan Durston, was one of the few indigenous people to have produced a colonial written text in Quechua.[25] In a remarkable account of his personal spiritual struggle, Don Cristóbal explained that the "demon" appeared to him in a colonial form with decidedly Andean imagery. The indigenous assistant of the Catholic anti-idolatry campaigns described a painting of a small black demon with silver eyes holding a staff, including floating images of a llama head, the small demon, and another llama head. Frightened by a clear manifestation of an Andean deity, whose worship he had publicly abandoned and famously disparaged, Don Cristóbal confronted his vision with a declaration of his Christian faith.[26] In response, the llama-head deity spoke in the language of indigenous Andean deities. By eating or being fed, the deity received reciprocal nourishment from Don Cristóbal, and then expanded from a singular form "into a twofold pattern," to manifest as an Andean woven textile that "encircled the whole house."[27] While Don Cristóbal recalled the dream as an attack on his Christian credentials, in many ways the llama-head deity demanded that the proselytizing Christian Andean reengage and speak again to Huarochirí's animal sacred.

Andean deities employed animal speech acts to call attention to the exceptional value of their esteemed sacred beasts. In 1656, the elderly widow Leonor Rimay declared to a priest in the Canta region that the "demon" had appeared to her as a black llama. Missionizing clerics clearly took animalistic devotions as disparaging proof of Indian domestic idolatry and the abominable imperviousness of Indigenous Andeans to Christian conversion. Indeed, while the elderly Indigenous woman was not specific about the season, the former rulers of the Andes, the Incas, had sacrificed black llamas in March in order to encourage crops to mature.[28] The animal

Figure 1. A black llama conopa. Hamilton, *Scale & the Incas*, 61–62.

manifestations communicated clear economic value well into the seventeenth century. Using black stone (commonly basalt) prized for its rare color, colonial Indigenous Andeans employed figures of black llamas, or *conopas*, like the one pictured in figure 1, to petition for the good health and increase of their herds.[29]

Small in size, easy to transport, and incorporated into individual or household shrines, black llama *conopas* were rarely found by idolatry inspectors, except if revealed by community members.[30] Leonor Rimay's confession, therefore, was rare. She explained that, when she was a young unmarried woman, she had gone to a nearby stream when the black llama appeared and spoke to her directly, asking "what she was doing here."[31] When she replied that she had come to drink (or take) its water, the llama followed her home, perhaps demanding its required offering, which she did not provide. The llama deity was right to ask. Throughout the seventeenth century, sacred beings throughout the Andes lamented their hunger and poverty since their abandonment by their former followers.[32] Coming empty-handed to the stream, Leonor Rimay had insulted the black llama deity, who she suggested caused her subsequent illness, or the costs of Catholic conversion.

Llamas and guinea pigs remained steadfast currencies of Andean livelihoods. Andeans measured their own wealth and the wealth of others based on the size and diversity of llama herds.[33] Likewise, Indigenous Andeans relied on old ways of increasing their herds and flocks. Despite the attempts of Catholic clerics, colonial Indigenous Andeans continued to place small llama *conopas* (as pictured in figure 1) in pastures in order to increase the fertility of herds.[34] In dense animal speech acts, Indigenous Andeans activated these llama figures with llama fat, inserted in a hole on the top, to encourage fertility, multiplication, and prosperity.[35] As measles, smallpox, and other new illnesses rolled through the Andes, indigenous people petitioned for relief from their deities with the previous practices of sacrifices of llamas and guinea pigs.[36] Notably, European animals could not communicate with Andean deities in these moments of need. During annual purification events, local deities were petitioned for health, prosperity, and productivity in the fields and herds. In particular, local deities demanded that their followers eat only llamas and guinea pigs, avoiding European animals such as pigs in a complete separation from Spanish elements, reminiscent of the late sixteenth-century resistance movement Taki Onqoy.[37] Speaking with llamas and guinea pigs, Indigenous Andeans of the seventeenth century declared their authority as well as that of local deities to determine a healthy future.

At the same time, by actively adapting new animal species, Indigenous Andean people communicated an equivalency with Europeans. By the seventeenth century, European livestock were abundantly interchangeable in the animal speech acts of Indigenous Andeans. The colonial indigenous chronicler Felipe Guaman Poma de Ayala explained that inhabitants tended herds of sheep, goats, and alpaca with llamas and depicted successful Andean households with their pigs, cattle, and chickens.[38] Familiar animals of the Andes did not disappear from the colonial landscape or conversation, but were called on to solve new problems. With guinea pig sacrifices, colonial Indigenous Andeans asked deities for laborers to work in their fields and corrals that had been previously maintained by kin who had migrated, disappeared, or now worked on Spanish colonial enterprises.[39] As Andean religious practices merged with Catholicism, the goods of local deities included herds of sheep and goats as well as llamas and guinea pigs.[40] Indigenous witnesses accused local ritual specialists of endangering camelid herds and mules along with cattle.[41] Others testified that local ritual specialists employed their skills to locate missing horses and mules, ensure the health of sheep, and maintain the production of hens.[42] The species of animals had clearly changed, but not the sacred use of livestock among Andean pastoralists.

Llamas and guinea pigs, nevertheless, retained potency. In 1657, an indigenous leader of San Pedro de Hacas explained to the inspecting Catholic cleric that he had sacrificed a llama and guinea pigs to local deities. In order to serve his community well, he had petitioned for assistance to govern peacefully, be respected by his subjects, and be recognized by other Indigenous leaders.[43] Familiar animals, therefore, were required for the political work of Indigenous leaders who collected tribute, organized labor demands, and oversaw their community's obligations to the Spanish colonial state. Similarly, an Indigenous *cacique* or leader from Cajatambo asked a religious specialist to sacrifice a llama and guinea pigs in order to ensure his son's success at the Jesuit boarding school in the Cercado, Lima's official Indian ward. Don Juan de Mendosa asked that his son, Don Alonso, learn how "to read and to write, coming out as a good, lettered man."[44] With the skills of literacy, the young leader would be able to compose legal writs in colonial courts, keep the community's archives, and read the orders issued by colonial authorities.[45] Don Juan wished to ensure that his son had the necessary skills to assume the mediating role of a colonial Indigenous leader, as he petitioned the ancestral deities with additional sacrifices.[46] Animals, therefore, communicated how Indigenous Andean men meant to level the playing field with Spanish colonizers.

In animal speech acts, Indigenous Andeans articulated their versions of colonial hierarchies. According to Felipe Guaman Poma de Ayala, the first inhabitants of the Andes were descendants of Adam, and therefore Christians, long before the arrival of the Spanish.[47] In his retelling of the past, llamas coexisted with sheep in an ancient Andean world that was co-equivalent with the Biblical landscape. Equal to European animals, a llama climbed aboard Noah's Ark along with sheep, goals, and cattle as pictured in figure 2.

Speaking through the value of animals, indigenous intellectuals such as Guaman Poma argued for the religious and cultural equivalency of Andean people with Spanish Christians.

Figure 2. Felipe Guaman Poma de Ayala, "The Second Epoch of the World: Noah," *Nueva corónica y buen gobierno* (c. 1615), page 24. Royal Danish Library, GKS 2232 kvart.

According to Guaman Poma, even ancient Indigenous Andeans raised livestock such as alpacas and llamas, and therefore were not "savage animals" as colonizing Europeans might suggest.[48] Other Indians, however, were more suspect. Repeatedly, Guaman Poma demoted Incas (who he blamed for Andean idolatry) by depicting their households as filled with monkeys and birds, animals that Indigenous highland Andeans categorically associated with the uncivilized Amazon.[49] Contemporary rivals were also worthy of animalistic devaluation. According to the colonial Indigenous chronicler, Colla people were "the biggest animals" due to their wealth, their size, and their tendency to only eat and sleep.[50] With animal speech acts, Guaman Poma put himself on par as a Christian Indigenous man with the Spanish to demonstrate how literate Andeans shared origins as well as histories with the colonizers.

European animals, still, were coveted. Guaman Poma repeatedly depicted the Spanish conquerors "on top of their horses," furiously, armed and angry, riding into battle.[51] More than fear of horses, Guaman Poma communicated the expense of horses and the privilege of nobility who rode on horseback while Incas and Indigenous Andeans suffered colonial abuses from the ground.[52] Judgmental and envious, Guaman Poma constructed colonial gender and racial hierarchies when describing who had access to horses. The Indigenous chronicler accused acculturated Indigenous men who served Spaniards and who associated with Black men of stealing horses as well as llamas, patronizing Indigenous "whores," and encouraging the proliferation of mixed-race children. In his racist and misogynist version of the colonial Andean world, a Black man, in service to a Spaniard, mounts a horse while Guaman Poma portrays himself walking beside his own trusty steed.[53] Notorious for his disparagement of independent Black men, Guaman Poma clearly could not recognize Afro-Andean men as equal to or superior to Indigenous men.[54] Still beholden to colonial hierarchies, Guaman Poma avoided showing himself astride the horse, the paramount symbol of Spanish conquest. Speaking with animals, the colonial Indigenous chronicler sadly placed himself below the Spanish yet above Africans and Afro-Andeans.

By the seventeenth century, Indigenous Andeans understood that the Spanish invasion had irrevocably changed their sacred and economic landscape. Famine and epidemics combined with excessive tribute collection, colonial demands for labor, and repeated assaults on Indigenous sacred environments had ruptured Andean community connections. In their animal speech acts, Indigenous Andeans nonetheless revealed their creative adaptation to the possibilities of the new colonial world. Explaining a dream or vision to the clerical inspectors, Hernando Caruachin of Guamantanga confessed that a donkey appeared, wanting to take him to Lima's San Sebastián church.[55] Located at the edge of the viceregal capital, the multiracial urban neighborhood was home to urban Indigenous migrants as well as enslaved and free Africans.[56] Relocating to this urban environment would have allowed an Indigenous person to take advantage of the teeming markets of labor and trade of the vibrant colonial city. The European animal facilitated Caruachin's fantastical, but also mystical, tour of Lima's churches, then returning the religious specialist to his home in the rural highlands.[57] By expertly naming the donkey as his spiritual guide, Caruachin, like many colonial Indigenous Andeans, inserted himself as a protagonist in the ruptures and opportunities of Spanish colonialism.

SERPENTINE CHANGE

The Andes, even in ancient times, were an uneven terrain where wealthy lords suffered from their disastrous boasting and poor beggars were revealed as deities. Colonial authorities, however, communicated a binary worldview of sin and redemption where crimes were punished according to a person's categorization as Indian, Spanish, or Black. Countering their new rulers, Indigenous Andeans spoke in puma speech acts to disparage how the Spanish ruled. Instead of acting as predator protectors like the Incas, Guaman Poma explained how Spanish soldiers and other private colonizers were pumas who caught and devoured Indigenous people of colonial towns without giving back.[58] Indeed, the reciprocity among subjects and leaders or between prey and predators had eroded in the colonial era. According to the Indigenous chronicler, the Spanish *encomendero* entered Indigenous Andean towns and, with his claws, caught and did not pardon his Indigenous subjects.[59] In puma speech acts, Guaman Poma explained that the Spanish rulers were at the greatest fault since "these said animals do not fear God, skinning the Indian poor of this kingdom."[60] As a result, the prey or the Indigenous Andean subjects feared a colonial puma sovereign in his manifestation as a Spaniard, who demanded excessive tribute payments and labor obligations that included horrific and denigrating sexual assaults.

Responding to colonial violence, Indigenous Andean parishioners heard the Biblical snake speech acts of Spanish priests as a sign of change. Catholic clerics unequivocally employed serpents to represent the devil, the presence of evil, and the manifestation of Satan.[61] Yet, Indigenous Andeans came to adapt European snake speech acts but did not imagine their serpentine sacred beings as categorically diabolic. Indigenous Andeans worked with a wider serpentine vocabulary. Snake talk included alternative names and metaphors for the poisonous snake of the highlands, the large boa of the lowlands, and the celestial rainbow deity, including a warning of an *amaru* who would destroy as well as remake the world.

Unsurprisingly, snake speech acts were entangled with a process of remedy and healing for Indigenous Andeans. Elderly ritual specialists, both men and women, were reported to have removed snakes as well as spiders, worms, toads, and stones from sick people.[62] Ontologically, worms and toads meant sickness, evil, and maleficence to the Spanish just as Indigenous Andean witnesses, by the seventeenth century, associated these and other witchcraft practices with women's sexual misconduct, such as a wife's adultery, another common European association. Simultaneously, snakes and toads were part of a potent community of inanimate and animate actors for Indigenous Andeans.[63] According to the informants in Huarochirí, a local deity cured a local lord by removing two snakes and a two-headed toad from his house.[64] The elite man regained his health once the animals were dislodged. Andeans worked to coordinate with animals and work with their possibilities. Witnesses explained to missionizing clerics that ritual specialist Isabel Poma Corua took out snakes and spiders as well as dispensed remedies to women in order to encourage men's love.[65] The inspecting Catholic clerics framed Poma Corua as a witch engaged in love magic. But, ritual Andean specialists did not attend to an evil that lay, fixed, within a human body as understood within an early modern Iberian framework. According to colonial Indigenous Andeans, ordinary humans could not bodily hold snakes as the serpentine destabilized only the most able religious practitioner.[66] To Europeans, these animals were always vile, but to Indigenous Andeans, their power to harm resided in their location—remove them from the "wrong" place, and their existence was no longer objectionable.

Snake talk, then, appeared when Indigenous Andeans engaged in anxious conversations over the consequences of colonialism. When questioned by Catholic missionaries, Indigenous Andeans denounced witchcraft practitioners in their communities, but also confessed their own sins or Andean religious practices. In animal speech acts, misunderstood by Spanish colonizers, Indigenous Andeans explained that their bodies were filled with spiders and snakes that, with the assistance of local healers, they vomited into their hands.[67] Hardly markers of inherent evil,

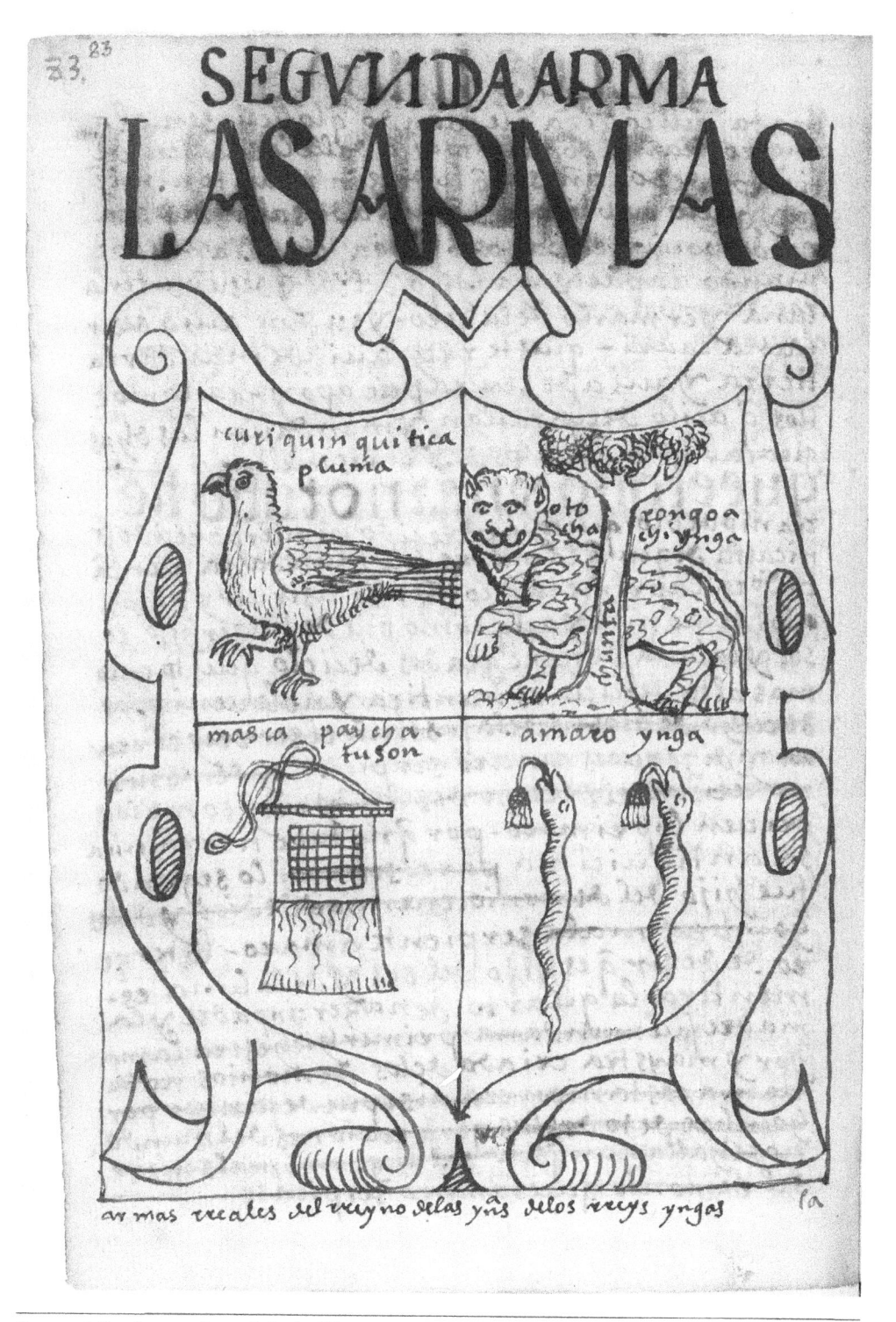

Figure 3. Felipe Guaman Poma de Ayala, "The Second Coat of Arms of the Inka," *Nueva corónica y buen gobierno* (c. 1615), page 83. Royal Danish Library, GKS 2232 kvart.

these Andean animals brought messages to the present world that included "a broad framework of assumptions" mediated through the punishing inquiries of the inspecting Catholic clerics, but also filtered within the process of physical and spiritual Andean cures.[68] If taken as "a framework of metaphysical ideas," then Indigenous Andeans wondered, through the creatures of the underground, what they were paying for in their sacrifices.[69] Were local deities hungry or disappointed with their Catholic conversion or migrations away from places of origin?[70] What was the sickness or misfortune that Indigenous Andeans needed to expel?[71] In the mid-seventeenth century, Indigenous Andeans contemplated the effects of their consumption and adaptation of Spanish colonialism.

Sacred and timely messages of current colonial predicaments often arrived through snakes and birds. Indigenous witnesses explained to inspecting clerics that ritual specialists would predict coming disasters such as sickness by observing the movement of snakes, or listening to the songs of small owls (as well as other birds).[72] According to one Indigenous colonial litigator, two elderly brothers near Otuco (in Cajatambo) were able to predict deaths in the community by their close attention to snakes and birds.[73] Animals warned rather than judged. If Catholic clerics feared the appearance of snakes as signs of the devil, Indigenous Andeans sought out the serpentine. As Juan Huaraz and Juan Chuchu confessed to missionizing clerics, listening to snake and bird speech acts allowed them to warn people of a future that included loss of property, bad harvests, lack of food, or other disasters associated with Spanish colonialism.[74] More critically, snake speech acts elaborated on the protection that Indigenous Andeans required to survive the illnesses that wiped out their communities, along with the tribute and debt obligations that could cause families to migrate. With the assistance of these animal translators, Indigenous Andeans could be forewarned and take action.

The *amaru*, most of all, was a just ruler of the Andes. Whether Inca royalty or local nobility, colonial Andean lords represented their claims to sovereignty with the visual rhetoric of two straight snakes.[75] Most notably on their newly Spanish-sanctioned coat of arms, petitioners in Spanish courts, Indigenous nobles in Cuzco, and other political actors in the transitional sixteenth and seventeenth centuries demonstrated their nobility by creating new colonial visual representations that included pairs of snakes with gold crowns or sprouting rainbows.[76] As illustrated in figure 3, Guaman Poma represents a colonial Inca herald with two vertical snakes holding tassels in their mouths in the lower right corner, labeled as Amaru Inca.[77] The colonial chronicler associated the paired vertical snakes with the headdress fringe (pictured to the left in the herald) that connoted Inca rulers before and immediately following the Spanish conquest, as well as into the colonial period.[78] Elevated from the everyday snake talk, the *amaru* speech act allowed Guaman Poma to amplify the Inca's claim of lineage and right to rule.[79] In the colonial media of royal heraldry, the vertical paired *amaru*, however rendered, communicated how Incas claimed sovereignty of the Andes even under Spanish dominion.

Colonial Indigenous Andeans, then, heard snake speech acts much like governmental mandates. For one thing, unlike an early modern European condemnation of the serpentine, people of the Andes understood particular types of snakes as ancestral providers. The Incas had appropriated a widely shared Indigenous Andean belief in an ancestral snake, or *amaru*, that Guaman Poma explained existed in the period before humans learned how to make clothing and build houses.[80] Taking multiple forms, the ancestral serpent included the Snake-belt deity who was known to have taught northern coastal Indigenous Andeans how to fish as well as hunt, and even defended the Moche people against threatening monsters.[81] An ancestor as well as a creator, the Moche snake deity suggests what colonial Indigenous Andeans could have expected from the

Figure 4. Moche stirrup spout vessel. Penn Museum, object number 51-14-2.

serpentine. According to the early seventeenth-century testimonies from Huarochirí, snakes directed the making of critical irrigation canals, leaving their names to these essential technologies of the arid Andean landscape.[82] Most potently, twentieth-century residents recounted, a snake with golden braids emerged when their regional irrigation canal flowed with water.[83] The snake, then, was an overseeing, regional, and ancestral unifying force who, however potent and dangerous, was welcomed by past and present Indigenous Andeans.

Serpentine speech acts were multivocal in the Andes. As Juan Carlos Estenssoro and other scholars have suggested, a snake was also a dragonlike beast with arms, ears, wings, fangs, and whiskers or a beard.[84] In this manifestation, the snake or *amaru* could not be rendered in a straight line as in figure 3, but more as a serpentine lizard or uncontained beast as suggested by the Moche depiction in figure 4.

This *amaru*—perhaps an anaconda or a boa—would have been simultaneously monstrous and glorious, a foe worthy of the Incas and additional to the signifiers of straight paired snakes.[85] The *amaru* continued to be a challenging signifier into the eighteenth century with the rebellion of the colonial Inca José Gabriel Condorcanqui. His chosen revolutionary name of Tupac Amaru invoked the last legitimate Inca ruler assassinated by the Spanish in the sixteenth century, but also signaled a claim to the returning rule of the Royal Serpent.[86] Therefore, when Indigenous Andeans engaged in *amaru* speech acts, they discussed the Inca right to rule, but also anticipated political challenges that could exceed the current state sovereignty.

In the seventeenth century, Indigenous Andeans invoked the *amaru*, then, to clear a way for transformation. When Domingo Rimachim confessed his idolatrous practices to missioning clerics in 1656, he described a regional deity who could appear in a snake-like form and came to eat people.[87] Rimachim, like other Indigenous Andeans, may have thought that their betrayal of local deities had caused the spiritual threat that included deadly epidemics and religious persecution.[88] Yet, the appearance of a consuming and threatening *amaru* did not portend sinful punishment. Accused by the inspecting clerics, elderly Indigenous Andean woman Francisca Carguachuqui explained that she was terrified by the demands made by the *amaru*. The "deformed serpent ... with a beard that seemed like fire" demanded white and black corn to eat, or he would eat her.[89] Indeed, the *amaru* was a creature or fire-monster that the people of Huarochirí warned would "bring misfortune."[90] Yet, Carguachuqui had appeased the *amaru* by feeding the demanding deity.[91] Sacrifice to the *amaru*, she anticipated, would facilitate, or allow the necessary change that she and other Indigenous Andeans expected the serpentine would bring.

Indigenous Andeans then imagined their *amaru* conversations could bring salvation. Indeed, the *amaru* of Cajatambo had been tamed because a ritual specialist had appeared and prayed to the regional deity.[92] When examined from an Indigenous Andean ontology, *amaru* speech acts were filled with sensations of physical transformation and shifting futures. As the elderly man Chaupis Condor recalled to inspecting clerics, a big snake was known to his community as Guayaura, "who walked under the earth and made the mountains shake."[93] Hardly an idol or a demon to Indigenous Andeans, this *amaru* was powerful and tremendous, but familiar and named. Likewise, informants of Huarochirí recounted how a former huge snake was now known as a stone called Amaru. In the early seventeenth century, Indigenous Andeans struck chips off the rock to carry as protection against disease.[94] For Indigenous Andean people, the *amaru*—on the ground in everyday life—was a threatening and fierce protector.

Through *amaru* speech acts, Indigenous Andean people articulated their desires for responsible higher-level authority. Hernando Chaupis Condor explained to seventeenth-century missionizing clerics that in the past a big snake, or *culebrón*, went about eating community members and tearing them to shreds.[95] Likewise, the informants in early seventeenth-century Huarochirí recounted how a lowlands fire-monster unleashed a huge two-headed snake "called the Amaru" in order to defeat his sacred rival.[96] In both cases, the regional deity thankfully intervened, and changed the threatening snake into a local *huaca* or sacred stone. Colonial Indigenous Andeans were well aware of their need for protection from similar threats. They remarked that in contrast to the *amaru*'s power, potential, and promise, Spanish authorities could not contain the current poverty, labor demands, and diseases of the seventeenth century. According to Guaman Poma, as a serpent, the colonial Spanish magistrate ate people and ate life, including the insides of a person, "taking him like a fierce animal."[97] Indigenous Andeans clearly did not equate the Spanish authority with a ritual specialist who could appeal to a serpentine deity. Rather, in their *amaru* speech acts, Indigenous Andeans suggested that the colonial Spanish magistrate *was* a consumptive deity who required management, sacrifice, and transformation. Yet, as Guaman Poma explained, the serpent colonial magistrate only destroyed indigenous resources with excessive consumption.[98] How could he be stopped if the Spanish did not believe or did not understand? Guaman Poma appears to frame the magistrate as a European serpent let loose in the Andean Garden of Eden, hardly capable of *amaru* transformation.

Colonial Indigenous Andeans saw themselves, through their *amaru* speech acts, as capable of bringing about the next version of the world. In its abstract form of the rainbow or geometric design, the serpentine provided a means of transition for Indigenous Andean people.[99] In Cajatambo, Indigenous Andeans testified to missionizing clerics of their dreams or visions that a snake with tail feathers came from the high plateaus to drink river waters, while Francisca Carguachuqui explained that the *amaru* approached her at a mountain spring.[100] The result of such a rainbow appearance would be agricultural prosperity, procreative energy, reproduction, and regulated irrigation.[101] Inquiring clerics associated snakes with the demonic, and Indigenous Andeans responded to explain that snakes came with messages of death.[102] Spanish clerics, it would seem, could not understand the radically incommensurable snake discourse of Indigenous Andeans.[103] In *amaru* speech acts, snakes returned to the surface to foretell the shifting of the current world, and perhaps the coming of the next.[104] In the process, some, but not all, Indigenous Andeans would perish; but most importantly the Spanish occupation and their demotion as idolatrous Indians would be wiped away.

CONCLUSIONS

In the seventeenth century, Spanish clerics and colonial administrators throughout predominately rural communities turned Indigenous Andeans into colonial Indians. Indigenous Andeans who spoke multiple languages and identified according to regional polities were "reduced" by Catholic clerics and colonial authorities into colonial villages to pay tribute, serve the colonial labor demand of *mita*, and practice Christianity. Designated as legal minors, targeted as laborers for colonial enterprises, and questioned as members of humanity, Spanish colonizers created the early modern racial category of Indian throughout the Americas by imposing uniform expectations onto heterogenous populations.[105] Colonial Indigenous Andeans, though, were agential within colonial processes through their animal speech acts. Llamas, like Andean economies, were still valuable, even if pigs and chickens presented new possibilities. Supernatural serpents, whether embodied in ceramics, stone, or irrigation canals, provided the means to employ colonial litigation as well as Andean religiosity.[106] Indigenous Andeans adapted to colonial impositions, demanding wages as laborers in silver mines and exploiting the vast markets in textiles and foodstuffs fueled by Iberian extraction.[107] Indigenous Andeans employed colonial courts to secure hereditary lands, appealed to the Spanish crown in order to reduce tribute demands, and integrated beliefs into everyday Catholicism.[108] Indigenous Andeans, most critically, engaged in animal speech acts in ways that could not be absorbed or comprehended by European colonizers. Animals and actions allowed Indigenous Andeans to encourage rescue from epidemics, famine, and sacred destruction within Spanish colonialism. Most critically, Indigenous Andeans spoke to each other through animal speech acts regarding how to worship, what to expect, and what to envision for the future.

NOTES

I thank Kristen Block, Robin (Lauren) Derby, Ann Kakaliouras, Jonathan Thurston-Torres, and Tamara Walker for their excellent suggestions. I thank Tamara Beauchamp, Giovanna Fogli, and Sharareh Fourzesh for their provocative comments. The University of California, Irvine Humanities Center Publication Support Grant provided funding for the image reproduction and rights.

1. "Visitas y procesos," 238.
2. Rama, *Lettered City*, 19.
3. Durston, *Pastoral Quechua*, 175.

4. Mills, *Idolatry and Its Enemies*, 102, 161.
5. Costa, "Making Animals," 96–97; Kohn, *How Forests*, 9; Norton, "Chicken or the *Iegue*," 24; Viveiros de Castro, "Cosmological Deixis," 470, 472, 479.
6. Donkin, "Peccary: With Observations," 43; Flores Ochoa, *Pastoralists of the Andes*, 26.
7. For example, see Urton, *Animal Myths*.
8. For speech acts, see Austin, *Works of J.L. Austin*, 13.
9. Taylor, "How to Do Things," 529, 531, 535; Vourloumis, "Doing Things," 53.
10. By obeying European frameworks, Andean leaders created a distinct Indigenous literacy, negotiated the location of colonial *reducciones*, and adapted Catholic iconography to fit local needs. Cohen Suarez, *Heaven, Hell*, 11, 73; De la Puente Luna, *Andean Cosmopolitans*, 11; Mumford, *Vertical Empire*, 132; Rappaport and Cummins, *Beyond the Lettered*, 149, 153.
11. Mills, *Idolatry and Its Enemies*, 189, 211.
12. Indigenous Andeans negotiated their cosmopolitan vassalage in colonial courts, translated Inca authority into Catholic festivities, and embedded their pre-Hispanic values into colonial property holdings. De la Puente Luna, *Andean Cosmopolitans*, 124–25; Dean, *Inka Bodies*, 95; Graubart, "Shifting Landscapes," 68; Rappaport, *Disappearing Mestizo*, 202–3.
13. Anderson, *Creatures of Empire*, 218, 237; De la Puente Luna, *Andean Cosmopolitans*, 50; Rappaport and Cummins, *Beyond the Lettered*, 153.
14. "Visitas y procesos," 332; *Huarochirí Manuscript*, 84. For a contemporary association, see Platt, "From the Island's Point of View," 39.
15. "Visitas y procesos," 265, 299, 301, 503; *Huarochirí Manuscript*, 100.
16. "Visitas y procesos," 411, 418, 421, 464, 515, 519, 739; *Huarochirí Manuscript*, 142, 143.
17. "Visitas y procesos," 226, 237, 297, 327, 338, 389, 390, 392, 395, 409, 416, 420, 429, 430, 435, 449, 452, 453, 454, 459, 481, 504; Guaman Poma, "Nueva corónica," 267.
18. "Visitas y procesos," 171, 217, 269, 329, 345, 369, 416, 429, 430, 431, 433, 445, 446, 448, 449, 451, 454, 484, 628.
19. "Visitas y procesos," 449.
20. Mills, *Idolatry and Its Enemies*, 254; "Visitas y procesos," 175, 202, 205, 208.
21. "Visitas y procesos," 426, 451.
22. Mills, *Idolatry and Its Enemies*, 263.
23. "Visitas y procesos," 209, 253, 255, 257, 276, 279.
24. Guaman Poma, "Nueva corónica," 881. Cobo cited in Cowie, *Llama*, 43.
25. Durston, "Cristóbal Choquecasa," 151, 153.
26. Mills, *Idolatry and Its Enemies*, 228.
27. *Huarochirí Manuscript*, 109. For a discussion of how textile patterns work in Andean sacred spaces, see Cohen Suarez, *Heaven, Hell*, 117. For discussion of eating, feeding, and offering to Indigenous Andean deities, see Brosseder, *Power of Huacas*, 185; Salomon, "Introductory Essay," 17.
28. Guaman Poma, "Nueva corónica," 241.
29. Mills, *Idolatry and Its Enemies*, 94; Hamilton, *Scale and the Incas*, 61.
30. "Visitas y procesos," 685, 701.
31. "Apéndice documental," 249.
32. Silverblatt, *Moon, Sun*, 184–85.
33. *Huarochirí Manuscript*, 55, 102, 138, 139, 140, 147, 152.
34. "Visitas y procesos," 111, 496, 503, 505; Cowie, *Llama*, 45.
35. Hamilton, *Scale and the Incas*, 69.
36. "Visitas y procesos," 267, 297, 405, 454, 484, 504, 799; "Apéndice documental," 248; Mills, *Idolatry*

and Its Enemies, 64–65. Guinea pigs were acceptable, but deities preferred the more generous gift of llamas. Brosseder, *Power of Huacas*, 175, 183. The main mountain deity of Huarochirí named and loved the first llama to reach his summit during the annual fiesta, accepting llama sacrifices in protection of the deceased. *Huarochirí Manuscript*, 72–74.

37. "Visitas y procesos," 359, 399, 412, 419, 444, 600; Mills, *Idolatry and Its Enemies*, 177.
38. Guaman Poma, "Nueva corónica," 11, 40, 1149, 1150, 1158.
39. "Visitas y procesos," 411.
40. "Apéndice documental," 241, 249; Mills, *Idolatry and Its Enemies*, 43.
41. Archivo Arzobispal de Lima, Visitas de Hechicerías e Idolatrías. Legajo 3. Exp. 1 (1650), 1, 3.
42. Apéndice documental," 244.
43. "Visitas y procesos," 452, 454.
44. "Visitas y procesos," 383.
45. De la Puente Luna, *Andean Cosmopolitans*, 105; Rappaport and Cummins, *Beyond the Lettered*, 114, 171.
46. "Visitas y procesos," 390.
47. Adorno, *Guaman Poma*, 100; Ossio A., *En busca del orden*, 26.
48. Guaman Poma, "Nueva corónica," 60.
49. Guaman Poma, "Nueva corónica," 133, 143; Norton, "The Chicken or the *Iegue*," 44.
50. Guaman Poma, "Nueva corónica," 178.
51. Guaman Poma, "Nueva corónica," 383, 163, 169, 170.
52. Guaman Poma, "Nueva corónica," 174, 209, 524, 527, 531, 606, 676, 681, 684, 693; De la Puente Luna, *Andean Cosmopolitans*, 116; Lamana, *Domination without Dominance*, 104–5.
53. Guaman Poma, "Nueva corónica," 929, 1083, 1095.
54. O'Toole, *Bound Lives*, 160.
55. "Visitas y procesos," 238, 458.
56. Bell and Ramón, "Making Urban Colonial Lima," 110; Gómez, "*Nuestra Señora*," 85; Lowry, "Forging an Indian Nation," 80, 234.
57. Charles, *Allies at Odds*, 146; Mills, *Idolatry and Its Enemies*, 241.
58. Indigenous Andean men and women confessed visitations from pumas who, though named as demons by missionizing priests, delivered messages of escape. As María Ticllaguacho, an Indigenous Andean widow of Guamantanga, explained, a black puma appeared to her, telling her to live with him and never return to the colonial settlement. "Apéndice documental," 255; Guaman Poma, "Nueva corónica," 899; Zuidema, "Lion in the City," 62.
59. Guaman Poma, "Nueva corónica," 695, 899.
60. Guaman Poma, "Nueva corónica," 272.
61. Mills, *Idolatry and Its Enemies*, 252; Silverblatt, *Moon, Sun*, 193, 194.
62. "Visitas y procesos," 333, 394; Silverblatt, *Moon, Sun*, 193.
63. For toads, see Brosseder, *Power of Huacas*, 215, 218.
64. *Huarochirí Manuscript*, 56–57.
65. "Visitas y procesos," 202, 206.
66. Guaman Poma reported how Indigenous Andean specialists accused of witchcraft extracted snake venom in order to poison enemies, or burned snakes (or their fat) in offerings to Andean deities. Guaman Poma, "Nueva corónica," 275, 278.
67. "Visitas y procesos," 221, 225.
68. Mills, *Idolatry and Its Enemies*, 132.
69. Douglas, "Animals in Lele," 47.

70. Silverblatt, "Political Memories," 189.
71. Brosseder, *Power of Huacas*, 220.
72. "Visitas y procesos," 357.
73. "Visitas y procesos," 233. Guaman Poma explained how Indigenous Andeans believed that if a bat, butterfly, or snake entered a house, death was to follow. Guaman Poma, "Nueva corónica," 282.
74. "Visitas y procesos," 271, 276, 305.
75. De la Puente Luna, *Andean Cosmopolitans*, 22.
76. Dean, *Inka Bodies*, 147; Rowe, "Colonial Portraits," 263, 267; Pillsbury, "Inca-Colonial Tunics," 166.
77. Lizárraga Ibáñez, "Del *Amaru* al Dragón," 77.
78. Dean, *Inka Bodies*, 100; Lizárraga Ibáñez, "Del *Amaru* al Dragón," 77.
79. Rowe, "Colonial Portraits," 263.
80. Guaman Poma, "Nueva corónica," 50. Described as distinct from the snake or the serpent, the *amaru* existed along with the ancestors of Guaman Poma's early seventeenth-century Indigenous Andean contemporaries. Guaman Poma, "Nueva corónica," 65.
81. Benson, *Worlds of the Moche*, 67. Guaman Poma also describes the snake ancestor of an Aymara community. See Guaman Poma, "Nueva corónica," 74.
82. *Huarochirí Manuscript*, 63; Allen, "Incas Have Gone," 193.
83. Bunker, *Snake with Golden Braids*, 95, 96, 102.
84. Estenssoro, "Plástica colonial," 429; Gisbert, "*Amaru* in the Iconography," 231.
85. Gisbert, "*Amaru* in the Iconography," 229, 231.
86. Campbell, "Ideology and Factionalism," 118; Gisbert, "*Amaru* in the Iconography," 229; Estenssoro, "Plástica colonial," 420, 428.
87. "Visitas y procesos," 305.
88. Silverblatt, *Moon, Sun*, 193–94.
89. Archivo Arzobispal de Lima, Leg. 1, Exp. 12, as cited in Silverblatt, *Moon, Sun*, 192.
90. *Huarochirí Manuscript*, 93.
91. Silverblatt, *Moon, Sun*, 192.
92. "Visitas y procesos," 356.
93. "Visitas y procesos," 356.
94. *Huarochirí Manuscript*, 93.
95. Visitas y procesos," 356.
96. *Huarochirí Manuscript*, 93.
97. Guaman Poma, "Nueva corónica," 695.
98. Guaman Poma, "Nueva corónica," 899.
99. Gisbert, "*Amaru* in the Iconography," 221; Lizárraga Ibáñez, "Del *Amaru* al Dragón," 75.
100. "Visitas y procesos," 232; Silverblatt, *Moon, Sun*, 191.
101. Allen, "Incas Have Gone," 196, 197, 199.
102. "Visitas y procesos," 233, 234.
103. Armstrong, "Postcolonial Animal," 414.
104. Campbell, "Ideology and Factionalism," 118.
105. Martínez, *Genealogical Fictions*, 99, 105.
106. Allen, "Incas Have Gone," 192, 193.
107. Bakewell, *Miners of the Red Mountain*, 49; Mangan, *Trading Roles*, 179.
108. Cohen Suarez, *Heaven, Hell*, 137; De la Puente Luna, *Andean Cosmopolitans*, 125; Stern, *Peru's Indian Peoples*, 117–18.

WORKS CITED

Adorno, Rolena. *Guaman Poma: Writing and Resistance in Colonial Peru*. Austin: University of Texas Press, [1986] 2000.

Allen, Catherine J. "The Incas Have Gone Inside: Pattern and Persistence in Andean Iconography." *RES: Anthropology and Aesthetics* 42 (2002): 180–203.

Anderson, Virginia DeJohn. *Creatures of Empire: How Domestic Animals Transformed Early Virginia*. Oxford: Oxford University Press, 2004.

"Apéndice documental." In Dino León Fernández, *Evangelización y control social a la doctrina de Nuestra Señora de La Limpia, Purísima e Inmaculada Concepción de Canta. Siglos XVI y XVII*. Lima: Universidad Nacional Mayor de San Marcos. Fondo Editorial de la Facultad de Ciencias Social—Unidad de Post Grado, 2009.

Archivo Arzobispal de Lima. *Visitas de Hechicerías e Idolatrías*. Legajo 3. Exp. 1 "Causa criminal contra una yndia llamada Juana Ycha, viuda, de echizos y pactos expresos con un demonio llamado Apo Parato, y de otros maestros que la dicha conosce, y de mingadores que la ha mingado para que hiciese muchos echizos para diversos intentos, por don Antonio de Cazeres sustanciada" (1650).

Armstrong, Philip. "The Postcolonial Animal." *Society and Animals* 10, no. 4 (2002): 413–20.

Austin, J. L. *The Works of J.L. Austin*. Charlottesville: University of Virginia Press, 2000.

Bakewell, Peter. *Miners of the Red Mountain*. Albuquerque: University of New Mexico Press, 1984.

Bell, Martha G., and Gabriel Ramón. "Making Urban Colonial Lima (1535–1650): Pipelines and Plazas." In *A Companion to Early Modern Lima*, 103–26. Leiden: Brill, 2019.

Benson, Elizabeth P. *The Worlds of the Moche on the North Coast of Peru*. Austin: University of Texas Press, 2012.

Brosseder, Claudia. *The Power of Huacas: Change and Resistance in the Andean World of Colonial Peru*. Austin: University of Texas Press, 2014.

Bunker, Stephen G. *The Snake with Golden Braids: Society, Nature, and Technology in Andean Irrigation*. Lanham, MD: Lexington Books, 2006.

Campbell, Leon. "Ideology and Factionalism during the Great Rebellion, 1780–1782." In *Resistance, Rebellion, and Consciousness in the Andean Peasant World, 18th to 20th Centuries*, edited by Steve Stern. Madison: University of Wisconsin Press, 1987.

Charles, John. *Allies at Odds: The Andean Church and Its Indigenous Agents, 1583–1671*. Albuquerque: University of New Mexico Press, 2010.

Cohen Suarez, Ananda. *Heaven, Hell, and Everything in Between: Murals of the Colonial Andes*. Austin: University of Texas Press, 2016.

Costa, Luiz. "Making Animals into Food among the Kanamari of Western Amazonia." In *Animism in Rainforest and Tundra: Personhood, Animals, Plants and Things in Contemporary Amazonia and Siberia*, edited by Marc Brightman, Vanessa Elisa Grotti, and Olga Ultugasheva, 96–112. New York: Berghahn Books, 2012.

Cowie, Helen. *Llama*. London: Reaktion Books, 2017.

Dean, Carolyn. *Inka Bodies and the Body of Christ: Corpus Christi in Colonial Cuzco, Peru*. Durham, NC: Duke University Press, 1999.

De la Puente Luna, José Carlos. *Andean Cosmopolitans: Seeking Justice and Reward at the Spanish Royal Court*. Austin: University of Texas Press, 2018.

Donkin, R. A. "The Peccary: With Observations on the Introduction of Pigs to the New World." *Transactions of the American Philosophical Society* 75, no. 5 (1985): 1–152.

Douglas, M. "Animals in Lele Religious Symbolism." *Africa* 27, no. 1 (January 1957): 46–58.

Durston, Alan. "Cristóbal Choquecasa and the Making of the Huarochirí Manuscript." In *Indigenous*

Intellectuals: Knowledge, Power, and Colonial Culture in Mexico and the Andes, edited by Gabriela Ramos and Yanna Yannakakis, 151–69. Durham, NC: Duke University Press, 2014.

———. *Pastoral Quechua: The History of Christian Translation in Colonial Peru, 1550–1650.* Notre Dame, IN: University of Notre Dame Press, 2007.

Estenssoro, Juan Carlos. "La plástica colonial y sus relaciones con la gran rebelión." *Revista Andina* 9, no. 2 (1991): 415–39.

Flores Ochoa, Jorge A. *Pastoralists of the Andes: The Alpaca Herders of Paratía*. Philadelphia: Institute for the Study of Human Issues, 1979.

Gisbert, Teresa. "The *Amaru* in the Iconography of the *Keros*." *Journal of the Steward Anthropological Society* 25, no. 1/2 (1997): 219–36.

Gómez, Ximena. "*Nuestra Señora*: Confraternal Art and Identity in Early Colonial Lima." PhD diss., University of Michigan, 2019.

Graubart, Karen. "Shifting Landscapes: Heterogeneous Conceptions of Land Use and Tenure in the Lima Valley." *Colonial Latin American Review* 26, no. 1 (January 2017): 62–84.

Guaman Poma de Ayala, Felipe. "Nueva corónica y buen gobierno (c. 1615)." Royal Danish Library, GKS 2232 kvart. (c. 1615). Available at https://www.kb.dk.

Hamilton, Andrew. *Scale and the Incas.* Princeton, NJ: Princeton University Press, 2018.

The Huarochirí Manuscript: A Testament of Ancient and Colonial Andean Religion. Edited by Frank Salomon and George Urioste. Austin: University of Texas Press, 1991.

Kohn, Eduardo. *How Forests Think: Toward an Anthropology beyond the Human*. Berkeley: University of California Press, 2013.

Lamana, Gonzalo. *Domination without Dominance: Inca-Spanish Encounters in Early Colonial Peru*. Durham, NC: Duke University Press, 2008.

Lizárraga Ibáñez, Manuel Antonio. "Del *Amaru* al Dragón. El componente clásico y renacentista en la construcción del imaginario Andino colonial puesto en los *limpisccaqueros* (vasos pintados de madera de los siglos XVI al XVII d.C.)." *Inka Llaqta* 4, no. 4 (2016): 53–84.

Lowry, Lyn. "Forging an Indian Nation: Urban Indians under Spanish Colonial Control, Lima, Peru, 1535–1765." PhD diss., University of California, Berkeley, 1991.

Mangan, Jane. *Trading Roles: Gender, Ethnicity, and the Urban Economy in Colonial Potosí*. Durham, NC: Duke University Press, 2005.

Martínez, María Elena. *Genealogical Fictions: Limpieza de Sangre, Religion, and Gender in Colonial Mexico*. Stanford, CA: Stanford University Press, 2008.

Mills, Kenneth. *Idolatry and Its Enemies: Colonial Andean Religion and Extirpation, 1640–1750*. Princeton, NJ: Princeton University Press, 1997.

Mumford, Jeremy. *Vertical Empire: The General Resettlement of Indians in the Colonial Andes*. Durham, NC: Duke University Press, 2012.

Norton, Marcy. "The Chicken or the *Iegue*: Human-Animal Relationships and the Columbian Exchange." *American Historical Review* 120, no. 1 (2015): 28–60.

O'Toole, Rachel Sarah. *Bound Lives: Africans, Indians, and the Making of Race in Colonial Peru*. Pittsburgh, PA: University of Pittsburgh Press, 2012.

Ossio A., Juan. *En busca del orden perdido. La idea de la historia en Felipe Guaman Poma de Ayala*. Lima: Fondo Editorial PUCP, 2008.

Pillsbury, Joanne. "Inca-Colonial Tunics: A Case Study of the Bandelier Set." In *Andean Textile Traditions: Papers from the 2001 Mayer Center Symposium*, edited by M. Young Sánchez and F. W. Simpson, 123–68. Denver: Denver Art Museum, 2006.

Platt, Tristan. "From the Island's Point of View: Warfare and Transformation in an Andean Vertical

Archipelago." *Journal de la Société des américanistes* 95, no. 2 (2009): 33–70.

Rama, Angel. *The Lettered City*. Durham, NC: Duke University Press, [1984] 1996.

Rappaport, Joanne. *The Disappearing Mestizo: Configuring Difference in the Colonial New Kingdom of Granada*. Durham, NC: Duke University Press, 2014.

Rappaport, Joanne, and Tom Cummins. *Beyond the Lettered City: Indigenous Literacies in the Andes*. Durham, NC: Duke University Press, 2012.

Rowe, John. "Colonial Portraits of Inca Nobles." *Congrès International des Américanistes* 29, no. 1 (1948): 258–68.

Salomon, Frank. "Introductory Essay: The Huarochirí Manuscript." In *The Huarochirí Manuscript: A Testament of Ancient and Colonial Andean Religion*, edited by Frank Salomon and George Urioste, 1–38. Austin: University of Texas Press, 1991.

Silverblatt, Irene. *Moon, Sun, and Witches: Gender Ideologies and Class in Inca and Colonial Peru*. Princeton, NJ: Princeton University Press, 1987.

———. "Political Memories and Colonizing Symbols: Santiago and the Mountain Gods of Colonial Peru." In *Rethinking History and Myth: Indigenous South American Perspectives on the Past*, edited by Jonathan Hill, 174–94. Urbana: University of Illinois Press, 1988.

Stern, Steve. *Peru's Indian Peoples and the Challenge of Spanish Conquest: Huamanga to 1640*. Madison: University of Wisconsin Press, 1982.

Taylor, M. "How to Do Things with Sanskrit: Speech Act Theory and the Oral Performance of Sacred Texts." *Numen* 62, no. 5–6 (2015): 519–37.

Urton, Gary. "Animal Metaphors and the Life Cycle in an Andean Community." In *Animal Myths and Metaphors in South America*, edited by Gary Urton, 251–84. Salt Lake City: University of Utah Press, 1985.

"Visitas y procesos de Bernardo de Noboa." In *Procesos y visitas de idolatrías: Cajatambo, siglo XVII*, edited by Pierre Duviols. Lima: Instituto Francés de Estudios Andinos, Pontificia Universidad Católica del Perú Fondo Editorial, 2003.

Viveiros de Castro, Eduardo. "Cosmological Deixis and Amerindian Perspectivism." *Journal of the Royal Anthropological Institute* 4 (2000): 469–88.

Vourloumis, Hypatia. "Doing Things with Words: Indonesian Paralanguage and Performance." In *Theatrical Speech Acts: Performing Language: Politics, Translations, Embodiments*, edited by Erika Fischer-Lichte, Torsten Jost, Saskya Iris Jain, 48–64. London: Routledge, 2020.

Zuidema, R. Tom. "The Lion in the City: Royal Symbols of Transition in Cuzco." *Journal of Latin American Lore* 9, no. 1 (1983): 39–100.

Disguise Hunting and Indian Otherness in Theodor de Bry's *Brief Narration of What Befell the French in Florida* (1591)

Thomas Balfe

Long before the emergence of racial theories supposedly grounded in Darwinian science, animals and race coincided in sixteenth- and seventeenth-century European debates about the humanity, civility, and moral character of the American Indian.[1] An important point of reference in these debates was indigenous peoples' proficiency in hunting. Period texts including travel books, philosophical works, and natural history treatises consistently praise Indian hunters' ability to track wild animals and their knowledge of the physical environment, often by aligning these capacities with European conceptions of hunting as an expression of human dominion over nature, an indicator of technological or social development, a valuable embodied skill, or a marker of noble status.[2] A more controversial aspect of Indian hunting, at least from a European perspective, was the range of techniques that involved close imitation of the quarry, such as the use of masks, disguises, or other mimetic devices to simulate its appearance in the field. These not only cast doubt on the Indian's ability to resist identification with the quarry; insofar as they evoked, in striking and visually overt form, the affective and bodily ties with animals that were also part of hunting in the Old World, they raised the troubling question of whether any clear divisions could be drawn between indigenous and European cultural practices.

Building on these ideas, my chapter focuses on a remarkable engraving that depicts three Indian hunters using deerskin disguises to stalk a group of stags (figure 1). *Hunting of Deer* (*Cervorum Venatio*) comes from a series of forty-two text-image pairs in the *Brief narration of what befell the French in the Province of Florida in America*, a luxury work of travel literature published in 1591, in Latin and German editions, by the Flemish printer Theodor de Bry.[3] The *Brief narration*, as de Bry's book will be called from now on, describes four expeditions to "Florida" (present-day Peninsular Florida and parts of Georgia and the Carolinas) undertaken by French travelers in the period 1562–68. Instigated by Huguenot Protestant factions at the French court, the original purpose of the venture was to establish a viable settlement in Florida to compete with the Iberian commercial and missionary groups that had dominated European exploration of the area since 1513.[4] The book's images, proudly described on de Bry's title page as *ad vivum expressae* ("engraved in a lifelike way"), are based on a set of watercolor drawings, now largely lost, by the French artist Jacques Le Moyne de Morgue. Le Moyne sailed on the second voyage of 1564, and his narrative about the expeditions and his descriptions of his own images are the main textual elements in the *Brief narration*.[5] Other important sources for the voyages are the accounts by Le Moyne's colleagues Jean Ribault, captain of the first expedition, and his deputy, René Goulaine de Laudonnière.[6] Published in 1563 and 1586 respectively, these works might well

Figure 1. Theodor de Bry, *Hunting of Deer*, *Brevis narratio*, no. 25, engraving. Rijksmuseum, Amsterdam.

have been available to de Bry, the head of a leading European printing firm, when he was compiling his own travel book.

The *Brief narration* contains a great deal of information about the Timucua, the now-extinct group of Indian nations, defined by their shared language, that Iberian, French, and English explorers encountered during their initial forays into Florida.[7] Timucuan hunting methods and linked social practices, such as the expert processing of deerskins, feature prominently in the book. In this chapter, I explore how *Hunting of Deer*, along with its accompanying text, would have shaped period readers' perceptions of the Timucua hunters, given the links that existed between nascent European racial thinking and ideas about animals and the human-animal boundary. The starting point for my discussion is an association, current in the sixteenth century but largely forgotten today, between race, nobility, and innate disposition. Just as certain animals were regarded as having an incorrigibly noble or ignoble nature, so human groups were thought to be distinguishable by their intrinsic quality, with the noblest human "races" enjoying an innate disposition towards excellence or virtue that set them apart from lower (human or nonhuman) living beings. Bringing this and related period discourses to bear on the engraving, I argue that *Hunting of Deer* offers a complex and ambivalent view of the Timucua. It underlines the hunters' ingenuity and skill, but also hints at continuities between the three men, the natural environment in which they operate, and the quarry animal, casting doubt on whether they possess the full humanity that European elites attributed to themselves.[8]

This approach takes its lead from the work of Karl Jacoby, Anthony Pagden, Virginia DeJohn Anderson, and Andreas Höfele, who have investigated the role of the animal in the construction of American Indian and African-American identities before 1900.[9] It also draws on recent studies of the *Brief narration* by Frank Lestringant, Todd Olson, Heather Martel, and Michiel van Groesen, which have explored its articulation of French colonial or religious (especially Huguenot) identity, how it served the commercial agenda of the de Bry firm, and its usefulness for understanding the historical Timucua.[10] The human-animal interactions in the book have received less attention, despite the fact that they are one of its most prominent themes, appearing in fourteen of its forty-two text-image pairs.[11] An exception is Martel's 2013 essay, which includes a detailed analysis of *Hunting of Deer*. Martel reads the hunters' act of imitation as a projection of tensions within the French colonists' political and religious imperatives in the New World, where deception of the Indian was periodically necessary but also, from a Christian perspective, suspect because it involved the same kind of deliberate trickery that Europeans regularly attributed to indigenous groups. While anxieties over cultural assimilation (the danger of "going native") are clearly at play in the engraving, my interpretation frames the deerskin differently than Martel: as an integral constituent of the hunter's selfhood when pursuing deer rather than as a "covering" that hides an authentic subjectivity allegedly inside or behind it.[12] This stance resonates with the Timucuan belief, which Europeans knew of and which will be discussed later, that assuming the quarry's identity is what enabled mastery over it, and it also takes account of the fact that early modern Europeans would have regarded clothing as actively producing the self, instead of merely ornamenting or concealing it.[13]

Underlying the central issues raised by *Hunting of Deer*—French fears about assimilation, the possibility of the hunter becoming animal-like, the effect of disguise stalking on human identity, and, more broadly, the promise of lifelike depiction offered by the engravings in the *Brief narration*—is a concern over the potency, and potential dangers, of imitation. Nandini Das has highlighted the importance of different models of imitation in early modern constructions of the non-European subject, identifying a fundamental distinction between useful, transformative imitation of the kind achieved by the ideal traveler who was able to turn their experience of foreign customs into valuable social capital, and mechanical imitation, which fails to rise above its materials.[14] This second, disparaged form of imitation was associated with the indigenous subject as well as with the traveler who succumbs to foreign influence, and was often represented by the ape, "an image of the inept imitator's passive submission to the model and resulting loss of identity."[15] At the heart of the interpretative problems posed by *Hunting of Deer* is the question of how to characterize the hunters' act of imitation—as active and transformative, or as passive and "apish." Equally, imitation would seem to be where its deeper concerns with the difference between the human and the animal, and between European and Indian cultures, intersect. Accordingly, the main part of my chapter explores three aspects of the hunters' cunning imposture: the men's coordinated bodily mimicry of the deer's behavior, their simulation of animal perceptions, and their use of the deerskin disguise. I begin, however, with a more detailed examination of the association between hunting, human nature, and early vocabularies of race, drawing particularly on French sources that were in circulation by the time the Florida voyages were launched.

HUNTING, HUMAN NATURE, AND "NOBLE RACE"

In premodern Europe, hunting was a defining activity of the nobility, one that was connected to their ownership of land and, in the case of more valuable quarries like deer, usually restricted to them by law.[16] The stag or hart (a mature male deer) was considered by most authorities to be the most prestigious of the "beasts of venery" pursued in the highest forms of hunting. Deer hunting as practiced by elites was an elaborate ritual system that assigned distinct grades of status to the dogs and horses used as human assistants and to the animals that were hunted; it manifested a "natural" hierarchy with the human hunter at its head.[17] Nonparticipants in the sport could have learned about its ritual and hierarchical aspects from practical hunting manuals and poetic and artistic representations, which were abundant by the sixteenth century.[18] Unlike many of the cultural practices shown in the *Brief narration*, then, the activity depicted in *Hunting of Deer* was one that many of de Bry's readers would have had some familiarity with (through books and pictures if not in reality), and which invited comparison with their own knowledge and experience.

Perhaps because hunting discourse was saturated with categories and distinctions, cynegetic vocabularies became intwined with early ideas of race. While the post-Classical Latin lexicon contained a wide range of terms encompassing what we would now call racial, ethnic, religious, legal, and political human collectives, the word "race" itself seems to have emerged in the late medieval Romance languages and does not have a precise Latin equivalent.[19] As Charles de Miramon has shown, it may derive from the Old Norman word *haraz* or *haras* (type, breed), which was applied to dog and horse breeds or the stud farm, and which is cognate with the early modern Italian *razza*, the first usage of race in something like our modern sense.[20] By the late fifteenth century, the word had also begun to appear in descriptions of hunting.[21] The emergence of the neologism "race" represented an important shift in European thinking about group identity; in the words of Justin Smith, "the appearance of a new term, as if out of nowhere, suggests that there was a new preoccupation in the early modern period with the practices and techniques that 'race,' as applied to animal breeding, initially described."[22]

The extensive scholarship dealing with the history of race has shown that the meanings that premodern Europeans gave to the term were extremely varied, that they changed over time, and that many of them depart from current usage. For example, while race (unlike its more innocuous cousin ethnicity) now calls to mind the controversial notion of biological essentialism, premodern views of race were generally more receptive to the shaping role of cultural, environmental, climatic, astrological, and even supernatural factors, such as the unequal distribution of divine grace among the world's populations.[23] Another important difference, one that is particularly relevant to my discussion, is that whereas we now tend to use race to distinguish between people from different places, prior to the nineteenth century it often referred to elite lineages, filiations, families, or the nobility in general, as in an early sixteenth-century description of the French nobility as a "noble and ancient [i.e., time-honored] race."[24]

The strand of premodern racial discourse that connected race and nobility drew on tropes involving animals and hunting. In line with its possible derivation from *haras*, the word "race" was used to designate animal as well as human types and often occurs in analogies linking the two. In the 1533 French edition of theologian Josse Clichtove's treatise on nobility, the inequality between noble and ignoble men is explained via a comparison with nonrational animals, some of which (like the lion, elephant, horse, and dog) are "not wanting in generosity and nobility of spirit, proceeding from nature," while others "have, inherently, an ignoble nature, such as the wolf, bear and ass."[25] In 1581, the Burgundian historian Pierre de Saint-Julien defended the concept of nobility against its egalitarian critics by noting that nature itself is riven by inequality: in every land "particular breeds [*haraz particuliers*] of horses are more noble and estimable than others," and "among dogs there are varieties [*races*] so sought after" that experienced hunters are keen to acquire them.[26] An extension of this argument was that the maintenance of breed animals offered a model for sovereign rule. A 1559 princely advice poem by Joachim du Bellay counsels:

> For if we are so careful to preserve the race
> Of good horses and good hounds for chase,
> How much more should a king carefully provide
> For the race, which is his principal power?[27]

By the early seventeenth century, the link between animal and human "races" was sufficiently well established for it to appear in the 1606 edition of Jean Nicot's dictionary, *Thresor de la Langue Françoyse*, where race is defined as "ancestry [*extraction*], thus one speaks of a man, horse, dog or other animal of good or ill race."[28]

A key justification for the idea that different living entities, whether human or animal, had an inherently noble or ignoble nature was provided by the concept of innate disposition, which was widely debated by European humanists. In discussions of how far natural tendencies could be shaped by education and good habits, animals were often contrasted with (elite) human beings as creatures that could not change their inclinations, or—to make the opposite point—held up as examples of the efficacy of training.[29] Philosophical backing for the differentiation of human groups according to innate disposition came from the political works of Aristotle, which identified an ideal humanity with the rational soul. For Aristotle, the most important manifestations of rationality were its social applications: the ideal human being was distinguished from other animals by his ability to found cities and to produce intelligible speech with his unusually broad, loose, and soft tongue.[30] While in theory rationality was not exclusive to any one human group, Aristotle associated it mainly with the male citizens of Athens. The distinction between rational and nonrational (or quasi-rational) human beings thus came to be associated with further oppositions between Greek and foreigner, civilized and uncivilized cultures, and the human and the animal. Athenian citizens are contrasted in Aristotle's writings with the barbarian (literally, a babbler), who lacks full rationality, whose speech is incoherent, and whose character and dispositions seemed to the philosopher to be inherently defective, approaching those of the natural slave for whom like "tame animals there is an advantage in being under human control."[31] In the post-Classical era, this view existed in parallel, and often in tension, with the emphasis in orthodox Christianity on monogenesis: the belief that all the world's races had descended from Adam and Eve and were thus essentially alike in their bodily nature and spiritual and intellectual potential.[32] Nevertheless, Aristotle's views had great influence on later European discussions of human nature, and figured centrally in debates about the humanity of non-European peoples, including among French thinkers.[33]

The corollary of the idea that the ideal human being's reason distinguished him from animals was that mastery over animals, whether achieved through domestication, hunting, or other means, could be viewed as a form of embodied knowledge or rationality.[34] In Jacques du Fouilloux's influential hunting manual *La Vénerie* (1561), published one year before the first Florida expedition, the author develops a rich vocabulary of the tokens, signs, and "marks" left by quarries like deer (such as broken branches and hoofprints) that demand the hunter's "judgment and knowledge" (*jugement et cognoissance*) in the early stages of the chase.[35] Elsewhere, du Fouilloux offers many recommendations on how to produce hunting dogs "de bonne race"—that is, of good physical and behavioral character.[36] "Race" is implicitly understood here as an innate attribute that can be developed (or drawn out) through breeding, training, diet, grooming, and other human interventions. A connection operates throughout the *Vénerie* between breeding techniques, the quality of the animals these techniques produce, and the noble status of the hunter, as when du Fouilloux notes of the scent hound called the limer (*limier*) that "today princes have mingled the breeds [*races*] of the fawn dogs, [so] they are now the strongest and best for hunting the stag."[37]

Hunting, then, required forms of judgment and embodied knowledge that were thought to reveal the gap between an ideal humanity and the rest of nature. This logic was frequently transferred to the New World context, where it was used to characterize the Indian as fully or potentially human, as partially or wholly distinct from animals, or *as* an animal, to mention only some of the possibilities. Among the positive descriptions, Louis Nicholas, a French Jesuit missionary based in New France, highlighted the local Algonquians' inclination toward war and hunting as "the most veritable and unique characteristics of the highest and most ancient nobility."[38] By contrast, Samuel Purchas dismissively described the Powhatan force responsible for the so-called Jamestown Massacre of 1622 as "more brutish than the beasts they hunt," and Richard Hakluyt made a similar statement about the Indians of the Meta Incognita Peninsula, who, according to him, "live in Caves of the earth, and hunt for their dinners or praye, even as the beare or other wild beasts do."[39]

Set against these remarks, and the derisive comments of Nicholas and Purchas in particular, *Hunting of Deer* resists interpretation as a categorically positive or negative response to the Timucua. While it underscores the Indians' ability to extract value from their environment, in ways that recall the judgment and knowledge endorsed by du Fouilloux, the use of the deerskin disguises also raises the suspicion that the hunters may not possess the kind of stable selfhood constitutive of period conceptions of "noble race." Recalling Das's distinction between active and passive imitation, the question seems to turn on whether, or to what degree, impersonation of the animal entails identification with it.

PERFORMING THE QUARRY

The text accompanying *Hunting of Deer* informs us that

> The Indians, when hunting deer, use a method [*industria*] such as we have never seen before. They fitted the skins of the largest deer that they were able to catch over their bodies so that the deer's head covered their own and they were able to look through the eye holes like a mask. Having noted the time when the deer came down to the river to drink, the Indians, dressed like this, were able to approach and get close to them without arousing their suspicions. There were a lot of deer in that region so they were easily able to shoot them with their bows and arrows. In doing this they had learnt to protect their left arm with tree bark from the string of the bow, as they were taught by nature [*ad natura ita edocti*]. They were able to remove the deer skin and prepare it without any metal knife, just shells, with such skill [*arte*] that I doubt there was anyone in the whole of Europe who could do it better.[40]

While this passage clearly views its subject through a European lens, it nevertheless refers to an actual social practice.[41] Variations on the stalking method described here were used by many Indian groups in present-day North America: the Sioux, Natchez, Chickasaw, and Choctaw tribes, and the Powhatan Indians, as well as the Timucua. De Bry's text-image pair may be the earliest detailed European representation of the technique, and is to my knowledge the only visual depiction of it in a printed source prior to the nineteenth century. Several later accounts exist, mostly written between the seventeenth and nineteenth centuries; in addition, archaeological evidence, in the form of pottery fragments, cave paintings, and petroglyphs (rock engravings), demonstrates that disguise stalking was practiced by Indian groups continuously from prehistoric times.[42] Certain indigenous images that show antlered, theriomorphic figures reveal, furthermore, that deerskin coverings were used in propitiatory ceremonies where hunters or the shaman took on the role of deer or of human-animal spirit creatures in an attempt to ensure future success in the hunt.[43]

Certainly by the late sixteenth century, Europeans in North America were aware of the ongoing use of disguise stalking among Indian groups. An important piece of evidence for this is the *Confessionario* (Confessional) of the Spanish missionary Francisco de Pareja, which circulated in manuscript before being printed in the early seventeenth century.[44] Pareja's book, written in Spanish and the Timucuan language, describes a ceremony in which Floridian hunters kick their legs in imitation of a deer struck by an arrow, as well as charms that were spoken over the deerskin disguise and the hunters' arrows.[45] The reason these practices are mentioned in bilingual sources like the *Confessionario* was, of course, to help missionaries establish whether recently Christianized Indians had reverted to their original religious practices or lapsed into syncretism. References to disguise stalking in confessionals thus reveal an uncertainty felt by clerics like Pareja about whether the Timucua could refrain from attributing agency and talismanic force to animals and inanimate objects like arrows and masks, a tendency also seen in their worship of idols.[46] Important though they were, concerns over correct religious observance were only one aspect of Europeans' more general skepticism about Indian societies' ability to transcend nature, to perceive and maintain the boundary between themselves and their environment. Readers of the *Brief narration* living before the advent of a modern, Cartesian conception of the subject-object opposition are likely to have regarded this aspect of indigenous "nature" equivocally: as a challenge to the Indians' full humanity, but also as a sign of their connection to a tangible living world that was a source of knowledge and material plenitude.

Exhibiting a similar doubleness, *Hunting of Deer* highlights both the hunters' control over their environment and their immersion in a variegated, fertile landscape where they operate with assurance. The two hunters in the foreground deftly bear the deerskin disguise, maintaining a low stance so that the hooves of the deerskin bob above the ground in imitation of a stag's natural gait. They move in unhurried synchrony, the stepped profiles of their bodies evoking the quiet, coordinated footfalls that have brought them close to the edge of the water. The shadows indicate that the men have approached the deer with the sun behind them, exploiting the glare that will render their quarries unsighted. As they close in, the hunters mimic each other imitating deer while preparing to release their arrows at the same moment to increase their chances of a double killing.

The hunter in the background, who follows half a step behind and whose upper body is slightly elevated, seems to be setting himself into the same crouching stance his companions have adopted. Whereas the deer display varied movements and behaviors, the coordinated postures of the three human figures, and the parallel lines of the foreground hunters' arrows, suggest their ability to act in unison. In a departure from written accounts of disguise stalking, which repeatedly describe it as a method used by Indians when hunting alone, the engraving underscores the fact that the men are working collaboratively.[47] Readers familiar with the Aristotelian ideal of

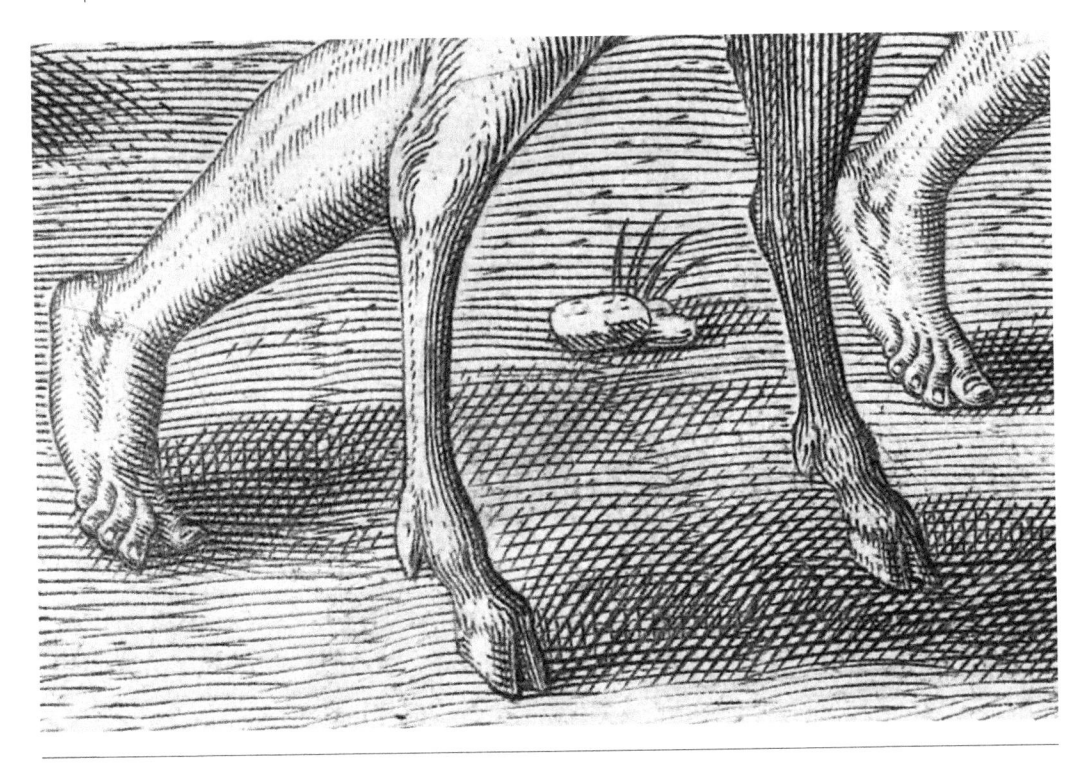

Figure 2. Detail of figure 1.

man as a socially oriented, cooperative creature might well have interpreted this as evidence of the hunters' relatively advanced level of cultural development—or at the very least as a challenge to the type of attitude expressed by Hakluyt, cited in the previous section, which likened Indian hunting practices to the scavenging of wild animals.

At odds with the engraving's positive emphasis on the hunters' acumen and ability to collaborate is the fact that their deceptive stratagem involves emulating an animal—in effect, overcoming the quarry by becoming like the quarry. As Shannon Lambert has argued, this aspect of hunting, which was also part of European traditions like the one codified in du Fouilloux's *Vénerie*, put pressure on human essentialism since it required the hunter to "perform" the animal, miming it in ways that induced identification with its embodiment, vulnerability, and sensory faculties.[48] This recalls the process of merging with the model that Das has identified as a sign of defective, "apish" imitation, though in Lambert's analysis the threat to the hunter's identity arises when their act of imitation becomes (from a certain point of view) *too* successful or comprehensive. Effectively mimicking the animal's behavior leads to "ontological blurriness": a destabilization of the human that occurs because the hunter's performance is no mere *replication*, yielding a lifeless copy, but an authentic *imitation* that has its own "decisively corporal, physical and tangible quality."[49] In *Hunting of Deer*, the active, embodied character of the imitation reveals itself primarily in the zoomorphic effect of the disguises, but also in details such as the rhyme between the hunters' splayed toes and the cleft hooves of the deer (figure 2), hinting at a deep, involuntary process of identification with the quarry that occurs during disguise stalking.

Visual echoes of this kind call to mind moments in the *Brief narration*'s text when animal comparisons are used to describe indigenous customs that conspicuously depart from European norms. We are told, for example, that the Indian chief Satouriona "sat on the ground in Indian fashion like a monkey or other animal," that the scouts in a Timucuan military force "detect the enemy's tracks like a dog scents out wild game," and that the caste of hermaphrodites, noted for their physical strength, serve as the "oxen" of higher-status citizens.[50] Although not explicitly pejorative, what is insidious about these remarks is that it is unclear whether they should be taken merely as metaphors intended to make unfamiliar aspects of Indian life vivid for a European audience, or, more literally, as assertions of the essential otherness of the Indian, an otherness that verges on animality. The drift between these possibilities finds its visual analog in the elevated viewpoint and vertically divided pictorial space of *Hunting of Deer*, which encourage detached contemplation and a weighing-up of what is shown. While conveying admiration for the hunters' skill, the engraving thus also submits their mimicry of the deer to the judgment of the *Brief narration*'s reader, who is positioned as the ultimate arbiter of its value and meaning.

READING ANIMAL MINDS

Alongside its interest in the bodily choreography of stalking, considered in the previous section, *Hunting of Deer* explores animal perceptions and what is at stake in deciphering them.[51] This aspect of the image presents difficult issues of interpretation, even when compared to other engravings in the *Brief narration* that set humans and animals in parallel. The next text-image pair in the book, for example, which describes alligator hunting (figure 3), fits more easily into an older tradition of the marvelous "exotic" in which the oddities of foreign bodies—here the outlandish size of the reptile and the Indians' nakedness—are exhibited for the European gaze. In *Hunting of Deer*, by contrast, the animal is no passive object of vision. Complementing the hunters' cunning simulation of animal thought processes, the engraving itself seems to internalize, and then to articulate visually, the quarries' varied impressions of the situation unfolding around them. The double reflection of antlered heads in the water encapsulates the two foreground stags' misperception that the creatures on the opposite bank are deer like themselves. Tellingly, the hunters' bows and arrows do not appear in the reflection. The innocent curiosity of these animals is further suggested by the directed gaze and cantering legs of the stag nearest to us, which has evidently just entered the clearing, intrigued at something amiss about these strange new arrivals.[52] By contrast, the female deer in the background, who bounds away into the forest, takes a more cautious (and more accurate) view of what is about to happen. While offering a less complex view of animal psychology, the text accompanying the engraving also notes the deer's capacity for suspicion or apprehension, which the Indians were evidently able to circumvent when the narrator witnessed them hunting.

Readers would have been attuned to the sensitive way the engraving evokes the deer's diverse perceptions from having encountered thinking, sensing, and even interpreting animals in other literary contexts. One example is the beast fable, a hugely popular genre that would certainly have been known to de Bry and his audiences. The reflection in *Hunting of Deer* recalls illustrations of the fable called "The Hart and Its Antlers" (figure 4) in Aesopic works deriving from the influential 1567 Flemish collection *De warachtighe fabulen der dieren* (The Truthful Fables of the Animals). In the fable, the hart catches sight of its reflection in a pool. It admires the beauty of its antlers and despairs at the ugliness of its legs, but then is undone when a hunter appears on the scene and it tries to escape: "When he came to the thick and bushy groves, he was hampered by the horns [antlers] and made a prey to the hounds. In whose rending of him in pieces, he blamed

Figure 3. Theodor de Bry, *Their Way of Killing Crocodiles*, *Brevis narratio*, no. 26, engraving. Rijksmuseum, Amsterdam.

Figure 4. Marcus Gheeraerts, *The Hart and Its Antlers*, *Warachtighe fabulen*, 122, etching. Bibliothèque nationale de France.

his former preposterous praisings, lamenting that he had found fault with his feet which had so often saved him afore."[53] Whereas the hart deludes itself about the value of its bodily beauty, the "greedy" dog in another fable fails to recognize its own reflection in a stream (figure 5), dropping the meat in its mouth when it tries to snatch up another piece in the water; "disappointed of his fat morsel, he bewailed too late *his deceiving of himself,* imputing his loss ... only to his own covetousness."[54] In both fables, the animal's reflexive misreading of its own likeness blends with a more active propensity for self-deception, undermining the boundary between animal instinct and the fully volitional acts of fallible human beings.

The captioned hunting print is another genre that explores animals' perceptions and their ability to tell images and reality apart. In the expanded version of Jan van der Straet's series of captioned engravings, *Venationes Ferarum, Avium, Piscium* (Hunts for Wild Beasts, Birds, and Fishes), which was reissued many times after its first printing in around 1600, hunting is repeatedly presented as a contest in which the animal is tricked by superior human intelligence. Van der Straet's series includes prints in which the hunter, working with an accomplice, uses an artificial ox to stalk deer gathered near water (figure 6) or "greedy starlings" (figure 7), as well as prints depicting the use of artificial decoys and living animals as baits.[55] Non-European animals are also cast as the victims of technologically assisted forms of hunting, as in the plate that depicts tigers being lured into traps with mirrors: the animal "unfamiliar with this trick thinks that its reflections are real [and] jumps into the nets" (figure 8).[56]

The decoys in the *Venationes* series, which appear in practical hunting manuals too (figure 9), have clear resonances with *Hunting of Deer*. Where de Bry's image differs is in placing less emphasis on the separation between the ingenious hunter and the guileless quarry. Not only do the Indians wear their imitative device like a second skin rather than using a stalking horse from which they can remain physically separate, they are also shown mimicking the same animal they are stalking—and would even *see* themselves as deer if they were to glimpse their masked reflections in the water. Developing the latter point, Martel has argued that the motif of the reflection, which shows a human being whose identity has been decisively transformed, "echoes the sixteenth-century European fear that 'constant communication' with the Timucua might also destabilize [the travelers'] French identities as they were assimilated into Timucuan Florida instead of colonizing it." While this is a plausible interpretation, the assimilation that the image contemplates, and in a sense warns against, is not only a cultural and physical blending with the Indian but a merging with the animal. Indeed, these concerns are probably best thought of as mutually reinforcing: surrender to non-European standards and cultural norms means becoming beastlike.[57]

From the hunter's perspective, on the other hand, it is precisely the ability to model the deer's intentions that will lead to a favorable outcome. Even so, what *Hunting of Deer* implies, and what the fable and hunting prints seem to confirm, is that the quarry's impressions cannot be grasped directly. The hunter needs to project onto the animal human traits like vanity, greed, curiosity, gullibility, or the feelings of suspicion or apprehension mentioned in the text accompanying the engraving, which allow its defensive responses to be predicted and, at the crucial moment, nullified. While the ability to perform this projection is presented by de Bry as a potent form of hunting knowledge, it also involves a temporary weakening of human identity—one that *Hunting of Deer* displaces onto the Indian through the text's claim that the image shows something "we have never seen before," even though (as van der Straet's series reveals) similar techniques were known in Europe. In presenting the Timucuan method as exceptional, the text guards against the thought that all forms of large game hunting, foreign or not, involve entering the quarry's

Figure 5. Marcus Gheeraerts, *The Dog and Its Reflection*, *Warachtighe fabulen*, 22, etching. Bibliothèque nationale de France.

Figure 6. Hunter, working with an accomplice, uses an artificial ox to stalk deer gathered near water. Engraving after drawn design by Jan van der Straet, *Venationes Ferarum*, no. 32. Bibliothèque nationale de France.

Figure 7. Hunters use an ox disguise to catch starlings. Engraving after drawn design by Jan van der Straet, *Venationes Ferarum*, no. 73. Bibliothèque nationale de France.

Figure 8. Tigers being captured in traps. Engraving after drawn design by Jan van der Straet, *Venationes Ferarum*, no. 16. Bibliothèque nationale de France.

Figure 9. Deer hunter using a decoy. Gaston Phoebus, *Livre de chasse*, BNF ms. fr. 616, fol. 115v, illumination on velum. Bibliothèque nationale de France.

perceptual world. Further implications of this type of identification are raised by the mimetic technology that the Timucua use to overcome the animal: the deerskin disguise.

FASHIONING THE STAG

The *Brief narration* abounds with references to Timucuan items made from deerskins: clothes, hides for trade, and cultic and ornamental objects, as well as hunting disguises.[58] Indian expertise in preparing skins is highlighted in the first of the book's text-image pairs, when Ribault accepts from the Indian leader Satouriona "a large skin decorated all over with pictures of various kinds of wild animals depicted in a lifelike way [*ad vivum expressorum*]"—a claim that reprises the statement on the *Brief narration*'s title page that its own engravings are *ad vivum expressae*.[59] At the outset, European and indigenous image-making are placed on a par, and later the book makes an even stronger claim along these lines when we are told that during his recreational walks, Satouriona wore "a deerskin so elegantly prepared and painted in various colors that nothing more beautifully decorated is to be seen."[60]

Viewed in light of these remarks, the disguise depicted in *Hunting of Deer* can also be thought of as a skillfully made visual artifact, though one different in kind to the garment gifted to Ribault. In a disguise, the deerskin is not a substrate for hand-drawn images, but a raw material used to create a model of the animal itself, which is then brought to life by the impress of the hunter's body. The craftsmanship required to make these disguises is stressed in the text accompanying *Hunting of Deer*, which notes that Timucuan skill (*arte*) in skinning deer is so remarkable that perhaps no one "in the whole of Europe . . . could do it better." Other commentators expressed similarly positive opinions. The English explorer John Smith noted approvingly "the horns, head, eies, and every part as arteficially counterfeited as they can devise," in his description of the disguises used by Algonquian hunters.[61] Period descriptions also mention sophisticated fabrication methods, such as using wooden splints to keep the head in shape, filling the hollowed-out skull and antlers with lightweight material, and fixing bright seeds to the face to mimic eyes.[62] On occasion, Indian disguises even inspired Europeans to change their own hunting methods. Praising the "pretty Inventions" used by Indians in Virginia, Robert Beverley reported that having seen their "Stalking-Head," "many People have taught their Horses . . . to walk gently by the Huntsman's side, to cover him from the sight of the Deer."[63] Notable here is that the Europeans turn the stalking head into a stalking horse, introducing a greater degree of separation between the hunter and the animal hunting aid.[64]

While Europeans were clearly fascinated by the disguise, its role as a convincing replication of a natural entity may have carried deeper significance. The ability to create mimetic images was a central issue in discussions of the status of Indian peoples, especially after the debate of 1550–51 in Valladolid, sponsored by the Spanish court, on the rights of colonized populations in present-day Latin America. Indigenous artistic or mimetic ability was adduced to support the claim that the Indian was, in all essential respects, the equal of the European. This argument appears frequently in the works of Bartolomé de Las Casas, the Spanish missionary who attacked the exploitation of New World peoples by his own countrymen and whose shorter works had been translated from Spanish into English, Dutch, French, and German by the mid-1580s.[65] Las Casas's arguments on this point often seek to rebut rationalizations of skillful Indian image-making as *merely* instinctive (and thus similar to the mode of "apish" imitation identified by Das)—a position his opponent in the Valladolid debate, Juan Ginés de Sepúlveda, defended by arguing that "we can see how certain small animals, such as bees and spiders, can make things which no human mind could devise."[66] For Las Casas, by contrast, Indian mimetic images resulted from the same kind of deliberative execution as European artworks. In his *Apologetic Summary History* (1555–59), he praised Indian featherwork, also mentioned positively in the *Brief narration*, on the grounds that it seems "to exceed all human ingenuity [*ingenio humano*]": its makers achieve "with their own natural colours everything that they and all other excellent and first-rate painters are capable of painting with brushes."[67] Crucially, this observation supports the larger argument that Indian groups have an artisan caste, one of six political classes always found in a rational, self-governing republic—an assertion that clearly makes reference to the Aristotelian conception of the ideal human being as a sociable, city-building creature.

It is certainly possible, then, that viewers of *Hunting of Deer* familiar with the favorable accounts of Indian image-making in travel books or in the works of Las Casas could have viewed the hunters' deerskins with admiration, as an indication of Timucuan technological sophistication or even "ingenious" artistry.[68] Yet, once again, the engraving resists being pinned down. The subtleties of design highlighted in period descriptions of hunting disguises are downplayed in de Bry's rendering of them. His depiction contrasts the living deer, shown in varied poses and lively movement, with the slack, lifeless deerskins, whose limbs hang limply motionless. Whereas the faces of the two foreground stags are alert and expressive, additional linear shading on the animal heads worn by the hunters lends those parts of the disguise a desiccated, rigid quality. The text accompanying the engraving underlines that the deer were successfully deceived, but the image suggests something more—that the hunters' presence was needed to bring the disguises to life. The men's muscular limbs can be seen moving beneath the inert covering of the deerskins, and their eyes glint through the holes in the masks.

The palpable lack of animation in the disguises enforces, finally, a disconnection between the perspective of the *Brief narration*'s reader and that of the stags and the hunters, who in their different ways uphold the fiction that the deerskin is a real animal. The hunters' absorption in their performance and "enlivening" of the disguise indicates, moreover, their strong connection to the nonhuman world. Their disguises are fashioned from the same entity, the deer, that they are attempting to extract from the land, suggesting that what we are seeing here is one phase in a cycle of consumption and replacement that is itself *part* of nature. This resonates with the text that accompanies *Hunting of Deer*, which notes that the Indians protect their arms from the bowstring with tree bark "as they were taught by nature." Recalling the chapter's earlier discussion of innate disposition, the phrase seems to encapsulate conflicting attitudes latent in the engraving's response to the hunters, permitting us to see them as either innately proficient in manipulating their environment, or—like the animal that cannot change its inclinations—as inseparable from nature.

Probing tensions like this, I have argued that *Hunting of Deer* offers a paradoxical view of the Indian hunters. Far from simply likening them to animals, it shows them successfully engaging in a type of hunting that was central to elite self-definition in Europe. At the same time, the techniques used by the men—miming the quarry's behavior, deciphering its perceptions, and feigning its appearance with an artfully made disguise—must have provoked an uncertain reaction from at least some readers of the *Brief narration*. The Timucua hunters' close engagement with the deer signals the imperfect capacity of hunting, including in its European forms, to establish a secure human-animal boundary. Readers might have tried to stabilize their view of the hunters by relating the engraving to ideas of innate human difference, correlated to variation between animals, which had a long history in the West and which anticipate later discourses of race. To the extent that de Bry's image would have invited contemplation in these terms, it reflects on the limits of European human exceptionalism as well as Indian otherness, even as it promises to offer us a sight "such as we have never seen before."

NOTES

1. Recent overviews of racial thought in the Western tradition include Hannaford, *Race*; Bartlett, "Medieval and Modern"; Kidd, *Forging of Races*; Wells, "Race and Racism." In this chapter, I will use the word Indian to refer to the indigenous peoples of present-day North America (in preference to alternatives such as Native American or Amerindian) because it is the term that occurs most frequently in the primary sources cited here. For the issues surrounding terminology, see Dickason, "Concept of *l'homme sauvage*," 7; Berkhofer, *White Man's Indian*, 5–6; Harris, "Forms of Indography."
2. Kupperman, *Settling with the Indians*, 101–2; Malone, *Skulking Way of War*, 80–81, 85, 127; Parrish, *American Curiosity*, 215–58.
3. De Bry, *Brevis narratio*; de Bry, *Der ander Theil*.
4. Jaenen, *Friend and Foe*; Lestringant, *Huguenot*; Milanich, *Timucua*, 67–92;

Dupuigrenet-Desroussilles, "*La Floride française*," and other essays in this journal special issue.
5. The book also includes two maps and several shorter texts containing navigational and geographic data about Florida. For Le Moyne's biography and oeuvre, see Hulton, *Work of Jacques Le Moyne*. No drawing for *Hunting of Deer* survives.
6. Ribault, *Whole & True Discouerye*; Laudonnière, *L'histoire notable*.
7. For the historical Timucua, see Ehrmann, "Timucua Indians"; Fishman, "Old World Images"; Milanich, *Timucua*.
8. Waage, "Non-Human."
9. Jacoby, "Slaves by Nature?"; Pagden, *Fall of Natural Man*; Anderson, *Creatures of Empire*; Höfele, *Stage, Stake, and Scaffold*.
10. Lestringant, *Huguenot*; Lestringant, "Staged Encounter"; van Groesen, *Representations of the Overseas World*; Martel, "Timucua"; Olson, "Markers."
11. Divided into categories these are: deerskin preparation (de Bry, *Brevis narratio*, nos. 1, 37, 38, 39); culinary practices (5, 23, 24, 28); hunting (6, 25, 26, 36); agricultural tools made from animal products (21); use of animal products in religion (35).
12. Martel, "Timucua," 15.
13. Flügel, *Psychology of Clothes*; Jones and Stallybrass, *Renaissance Clothing*.
14. Das, "Apes of Imitation," 116–18. Further on imitation and the colonial or postcolonial subject, see Taussig, *Mimesis and Alterity*; Gaudio, *Sound, Image, Silence*, 28–30.
15. Das, "Apes of Imitation," 118; see also Greenblatt, "Learning to Curse," 567–68; Hamlin, *Image of America*, 6.
16. Cummins, *Hound and the Hawk*; Cartmill, *View to a Death*; Manning, *Hunters and Poachers*, 4–34.
17. Crane, "Ritual Aspects"; Yamamoto, *Boundaries of the Human*, 99–115.
18. Balis, *Rubens*, 50–55; Cartmill, *View to a Death*, 52–75.
19. For the origin of the word, see Jouanna, *L'idée de race*, 1315–26; Miramon, "Noble Dogs," 200–201; Boulle, "La construction," 158–62; Smith, *Nature*, 140–43.
20. Miramon, "Noble Dogs," 202.
21. Miramon, "Noble Dogs," 200–203.
22. Smith, *Nature*, 140.
23. Overviews include Bartlett, "Medieval and Modern"; Chaplin, "Race"; Brown, "Beyond the Great Debates"; Braude, "Sons of Noah"; Heng, "Invention of Race"; Kim, "Critical Race." For racial discourse in premodern France, see Devyver, *Sang épuré*; Jouanna, *L'idée de race*; Boulle, "La construction"; Aubert, "Blood of France."
24. Clichtove, *Traicte*, n.p: "tresnoble et ancienne rasse"; cited in Jouanna, *L'idée de race*, 1316.
25. Clichtove, *Traicte*, n.p. (ch. 8): "nous voyons les bestes sans raison estre divisees et distingues par icelle diversite, en telle maniere quil en y a aulcunes que sont veues avoir en elles une generosite et noblesse de couraige, procedant de nature. Comme sont le lyon, le elephant, le cheval et le chien. Les aultres ont en elles une ignobilite de nature, comme sont le loup, lours et lasne"; cited with discussion in Jouanna, *L'idée de race*, 441.
26. Saint-Julien, *De l'origine des Bourgongnons*, 125: "Nous trouvons toutesfois en chacune contree des haraz particuliers, esquels les chevaux sont trop plus genereux, & appreciez que les autres. Entre les chiens il y a des races si recherchees, que ceux qui ayment la chasse s'estiment n'avoir petit contentement, quand ils en peuvent recouvrer"; cited with discussion in Jouanna, *L'idée de race*, 124–25.
27. Cited with translation in Nirenberg, "Race and the Middle Ages," 79 n. 31: "Car si des bons chevaux et des bons chiens de chasse / Nous sommes si soigneux de conserver la race, / Combien plus doit

un Roy soigneusement pourvoir / A la race, qui est son principal pouvoir?" For further poetic examples, see Jouanna, *L'idée de race*, 754–69.

28. Nicot, *Thresor de la Langue Françoyse*. For the complementary idea that *mésalliance*, or marriage between unequal partners, was comparable to the unnatural breeding of different species, see Aubert, "Blood of France"; White, "Forms of Wildness," 14–15.

29. Jouanna, *L'idée de race*, 69–107, who gives examples such as Plutarch's anecdote about the trained and untrained hunting dogs of Lycurgus. For French elites' resistance to the idea that those born outside the "race" of the nobility could change their nature, see Jouanna, *L'idée de race*, 98. Huguenot views could be more nuanced, e.g. Ribault's account of his rise from humble origins in Laudonnière, *L'histoire notable*, 17v–18.

30. For the later reception of this theory, see Pagden, *Fall of Natural Man*, 15–56; Anderson, "Beast Within," 305–7.

31. Aristotle, *Politics*, I: 5; cited with discussion in Jacoby, "Slaves by Nature?" 95.

32. Jaenen, "Les Sauvages Ameriquains," 49; Chaplin, "Race," 175, 178.

33. Jouanna, *L'idée de race*, 367–77; Jaenen, *Friend and Foe*, 12–40.

34. Ginzburg, *Clues, Myths*; Eamon, "Science as a Hunt"; Eamon, *Science and the Secrets*; Gage, "Some Stirring"; Lambert, "Subversive Somatology."

35. References to *jugement* or *jugement et cognoissance* occur in the titles of chapters that describe how to decipher signs left by the quarry; see du Fouilloux, *Vénerie*, 73–83. For hunting as an epistemological pursuit, see Lambert, "Subversive Somatology," 79–82; Chamayou, *Manhunts*, 70.

36. Du Fouilloux, *Vénerie*, 1–25.

37. Du Fouilloux, *Vénerie*, 12: "Et parce qu'auiourd'huy les Princes ont fait mesler les races des Chiens fauves ensemble, ilz en sont beaucoup plus fortz, et meilleurs a courir le Cerf."

38. Nicolas cited with translation in Jaenen, "Les Sauvages Ameriquains," 48. For further examples, see Strachey, *Historie*, 84; Morton, *New-England's Memoriall*, 70.

39. Purchas, *Hakluytus Posthumus*, 44; Hakluyt (discussing Indians encountered by Martin Frobisher) cited in Hamlin, *Image of America*, 12. For further examples, see Miner, "Wild Man," 89; Pagden, *Fall of Natural Man*, 68; Hamlin, *Image of America*, 105; Chamayou, *Manhunts*, 29–42.

40. De Bry, *Brevis narratio*, no. 25; translation modified from Faupel and Lawson, *Foothold in Florida*, 24.

41. The engraving shows European red deer, not a species native to America; see Faupel and Lawson, *Foothold in Florida*, 167. Its depiction of the hunters is also similar to roughly contemporary images of European ancestral groups, though these tend to be later; see e.g. the deerskin-wearing Germanic warrior in Cluverius, *Germaniæ antiquæ*, lib. I, 360, III.

42. The main descriptions of disguise stalking are in Swanton, *Indians*, 312–21; Anderson, *Creatures of Empire*, 22–23, 29–30; Parrish, *American Curiosity*, 243–44. For the archaeological sources, see Cushing, "Exploration," 388–94; Sundstrom, "Archaic Hunting Practices"; Shaffer and Gardner, "Wolves."

43. Sundstrom, "Archaic Hunting Practices," 159, 163.

44. Pareja, *Francisco Pareja's 1613 Confessionario*.

45. Ehrmann, "Timucua Indians," 188; Milanich, *Timucua*, 170, 175.

46. For Iberian and French responses to Timucuan "idolatry," see Lestringant, "Staged Encounter"; Olson, "Markers," 196–209.

47. Swanton, *Indians*, 312–21.

48. Lambert, "Subversive Somatology."

49. Lambert, "Subversive Somatology," 81, citing Willerslev, "Not Animal," 648. Further on imitating

the quarry, see Ortega y Gasset, *Meditations*, 139–43; Marvin, "Wild Killing," 24.
50. De Bry, *Brevis narratio*, 8 (Satouriona: "consedit Indico more, hoc est summa tellure, simiae aut alterius animalis instar"); no. 14 (dogs: "atque canis ferae alicuius"); no. 17 (hermaphrodites used in place of beasts of burden/oxen: "jumentorum loco"). Translations modified from Hulton, *Work of Jacques Le Moyne*, 121, 144, 145.
51. For a discussion of hunting as "embodied choreography," see Despret, "Responding Bodies"; Lambert, "Subversive Somatology."
52. A stag with its face reflected in a stream as it drinks, unaware of danger, could figure the defenseless Christ in religious painting, for which see Campbell, *Temptation in Eden*, 76.
53. Blake and Santos, *Arthur Golding's "A Moral Fabletalk,"* 138. The version of the fable cited here is from a c.1580s English translation of the Latin version of the *Warachtighe fabulen*.
54. Blake and Santos, *Arthur Golding's "A Moral Fabletalk,"* 172; my emphasis.
55. Van der Straet, *Venationes Ferarum*, nos. 32 (deer), 73 (starlings), 87, 68, 79, 95; translation of caption to no. 73 in Bok-van Kammen, "Stradanus," 453. For further examples in the European hunting tradition, see Martelli, "Nets, Lures."
56. Van der Straet, *Venationes Ferarum*, no. 16; translation modified from Bok-van Kammen, "Stradanus," 290.
57. Martel, "Timucua," 20 (quotation), 15.
58. Krech, *Ecological Indian*, 151–71.
59. De Bry, *Brevis narratio*, no. 1; translation modified from Hulton, *Work of Jacques Le Moyne*, 139. For the value of depictions designated by the term *ad vivum*, see Balfe and Woodall, "Introduction."
60. De Bry, *Brevis narratio*, no. 39; translation in Hulton, *Work of Jacques Le Moyne*, 151; see also Laudonnière, *L'histoire notable*, 38v.
61. Smith, *Complete Works*, I: 165; see also Strachey, *Historie*, 83.
62. Swanton, *Indians*, 315, 316, 314.
63. Cited in Parrish, *American Curiosity*, 243.
64. Doran, "Native American Ethology," 19.
65. For the Valladolid debate, see Pagden, *Fall of Natural Man*, 119–45; Vacano, "Las Casas." For period translations of Las Casas and the reception of his ideas in France, see Atkinson, *Nouveaux horizons*, 137–68, 206–11; Jaenen, *Friend and Foe*, 12–40; Hamlin, *Image of America*, 15–21, 37–46. For de Bry's knowledge of Las Casas, see Conley, "De Bry's Las Casas."
66. Cited in Pagden, *Fall of Natural Man*, 136.
67. For featherwork in the *Brief narration*, see de Bry, *Brevis narratio*, 14; translation in Hulton, *Work of Jacques Le Moyne*, 125. Las Casas cited with translation in Russo, "An Artistic Humanity," 359. Further on European responses to Indian image-making, see Pierce, Gomar, and Bargellini, *Painting a New World*, 95–102; Russo, *Untranslatable Image*, 85–89; Domenici, "Missionary Gift Records," 95–102; Lira, "Bartolomé de Las Casas," 227–31.
68. Pagden, *Fall of Natural Man*, 74.

WORKS CITED

Anderson, Kay. "'The Beast Within': Race, Humanity, and Animality." *Environment and Planning D: Society and Space* 18, no. 3 (2000): 301–20.

Anderson, Virginia DeJohn. *Creatures of Empire: How Domestic Animals Transformed Early America.*

Oxford: Oxford University Press, 2004.

Aristotle. *Aristotle's Politics*. 2nd ed. Edited and translated by Carnes Lord. Chicago: University of Chicago Press, 2013.

Atkinson, Geoffroy. *Les nouveaux horizons de la Renaissance française*. Paris: Droz, 1935.

Aubert, Guillaume. "'The Blood of France': Race and Purity of Blood in the French Atlantic World." *William and Mary Quarterly*, 3rd series, 61, no. 3 (2004): 439–78.

Balfe, Thomas, and Joanna Woodall. "Introduction: From Living Presence to Lively Likeness: The Lives of *ad vivum*." In *Ad Vivum? Visual Materials and the Vocabulary of Life-Likeness in Europe before 1800*, edited by Thomas Balfe, Joanna Woodall, and Claus Zittel, 1–43. Leiden: Brill, 2019.

Balis, Arnout. *Rubens Hunting Scenes*. Translated by P. S. Falla. London: Harvey Miller Publishers, 1986.

Bartlett, Robert. "Medieval and Modern Concepts of Race and Ethnicity." *Journal of Medieval and Early Modern Studies* 31, no. 1 (2001): 39–56.

Berkhofer, Robert, Jr. *The White Man's Indian: Images of the American Indian, from Columbus to the Present*. New York: Vintage, 1978.

Blake, Liza, and Kathryn Vomero Santos. *Arthur Golding's "A Moral Fabletalk" and Other Renaissance Fable Translations*. Cambridge: Modern Humanities Research Association, 2017.

Bok-van Kammen, Welmoet. "Stradanus and the Hunt." PhD diss., Johns Hopkins University, 1977.

Boulle, Pierre. "La construction du concept de race dans la France d'Ancien Régime." *Outre-mers* 89, no. 336–37 (2002): 155–75.

Braude, Benjamin. "The Sons of Noah and the Construction of Ethnic and Geographical Identities in the Medieval and Early Modern Periods." *William and Mary Quarterly* 54, no. 1 (1997): 103–42.

Brown, Kathleen. "Beyond the Great Debates: Gender and Race in Early America." *Reviews in American History* 26, no. 1 (1998): 96–123.

Campbell, Caroline, ed. *Temptation in Eden: Lucas Cranach's Adam and Eve*. London: Courtauld Institute of Art in association with Paul Holberton, 2007.

Cartmill, Matt. *A View to a Death in the Morning: Hunting and Nature through History*. Cambridge, MA: Harvard University Press, 1993.

Chamayou, Grégoire. *Manhunts: A Philosophical History*. Translated by Steven Rendall. Princeton, NJ: Princeton University Press, 2012.

Chaplin, Joyce. "Race." In *The British Atlantic World, 1500–1800*, 2nd ed., edited by David Armitage and Michael Braddick, 173–90. Basingstoke, UK: Palgrave Macmillan, 2002.

Clichtove, Josse. *Le traicte de La Vraye Noblesse, translate nouvellement de Latin en Francoys*. Paris: Jehan Longis, c.1533.

Cluverius, Philippus. *Germaniae antiquae libri tres*. Leiden: Lodewijk Elzevier, 1616.

Conley, Tom. "De Bry's Las Casas." In *Amerindian Images and the Legacy of Columbus*, edited by René Jara and Nicholas Spadaccini, 103–31. Minneapolis: University of Minnesota Press, 1992.

Crane, Susan. "Ritual Aspects of the Hunt à Force." In *Engaging with Nature: Essays on the Natural World in Medieval and Early Modern Europe*, edited by Barbara Hanawalt and Lisa Kiser, 63–84. Notre Dame: University of Notre Dame Press, 2008.

Cummins, John. *The Hound and the Hawk: The Art of Medieval Hunting*. London: Weidenfeld & Nicolson, 1988.

Cushing, Frank Hamilton. "Exploration of Ancient Key Dwellers' Remains on the Gulf Coast of Florida." *Proceedings of the American Philosophical Society* 35, no. 153 (1896): 329–448.

Das, Nandini. "'Apes of Imitation': Imitation and Identity in Sir Thomas Roe's Embassy to India." In *A Companion to the Global Renaissance: English Literature and Culture in the Era of Expansion*, edited by Jyotsna Singh, 114–28. Oxford: Blackwell, 2009.

Davis, David Brion. "Constructing Race: A Reflection." *William and Mary Quarterly* 54, no. 1 (1997): 7–18.

de Bry, Theodor. *Brevis narratio eorum quæ in Florida Americæ prouĩcia Gallis acciderunt*. Frankfurt am Main: J. Wecheli, 1591.

———. *Der ander Theil, der newlich erfundenen Landschafft Americæ, von dreyen Schiffahrten, so die Frantzosen in Floridam ... gethan*. Frankfurt am Main: J. Feirabendt, 1591.

de Dene, Edewaerd. *De warachtighe fabulen der dieren*. Bruges: P. de Clerck, 1567.

Despret, Vinciane. "Responding Bodies and Partial Affinities in Human-Animal Worlds." *Theory, Culture & Society* 30, no. 7/8 (2013): 51–76.

Devyver, André. *Le sang épuré: les préjugés de race chez les gentilshommes français de l'Ancien Régime (1560–1720)*. Brussels: Editions de l'Université de Bruxelles, 1973.

Dickason, Olive Patricia. "The Concept of *l'homme sauvage* and Early French Colonialism in the Americas." *Revue française d'histoire d'outre-mer* 64, no. 234 (1977): 5–32.

Domenici, Davide. "Missionary Gift Records of Mexican Objects in Early Modern Italy." In *The New World in Early Modern Italy, 1492–1750*, edited by Elizabeth Horodowich and Lia Markey, 86–102. Cambridge: Cambridge University Press, 2017.

Doran, Thomas. "Native American Ethology and Animal Protectionist Rhetoric in the Long Enlightenment." *Humanimalia* 12, no. 1 (2020): 1–49.

du Fouilloux, Jacques. *La Venerie de Jacques du Fouilloux ... Avec plusieurs receptes et remedes pour guerir les chiens de diverses maladies*. Poitiers: De Marnefz et Bouchetz frères, 1561.

Dupuigrenet-Desroussilles, François, Darrin McMahon, and Martin Munro. "*La Floride française*: Florida, France, and the Francophone World." *Journal of Transnational American Studies* 8, no. 1 (2017): 1–4.

Eamon, William. "Science as a Hunt." *Physis* 31 (1994): 393–432.

———. *Science and the Secrets of Nature: Books of Secrets in Medieval and Early Modern Culture*. Princeton, NJ: Princeton University Press, 1994.

Ehrmann, W. W. "The Timucua Indians of Sixteenth Century Florida." *Florida Historical Quarterly* 18, no. 3 (1940): 168–91.

Faupel, W. John, and Sarah Lawson, eds. *A Foothold in Florida: The Eye-Witness Account of Four Voyages Made by the French to that Region and Their Attempt at Colonisation, 1562–1568*. East Grinstead, UK: Antique Atlas, 1992.

Fishman, Laura. "Old World Images Encounter New World Reality: René Laudonnière and the Timucuans of Florida." *Sixteenth Century Journal* 26, no. 3 (1995): 547–59.

Flügel, John Carl. *The Psychology of Clothes*. London: Hogarth Press, 1930.

Gage, Frances. "'Some Stirring or Changing of Place': Vision, Judgement and Mobility in Pictures of Galleries." *Intellectual History Review* 20, no. 1 (2010): 123–45.

Gaudio, Michael. *Sound, Image, Silence: Art and the Aural Imagination in the Atlantic World*. Minneapolis: University of Minnesota Press, 2019.

Ginzburg, Carlo. *Clues, Myths, and the Historical Method*. Translated by J. and A. Tedeschi. Baltimore, MD: Johns Hopkins University Press, 1989.

Greenblatt, Stephen. "Learning to Curse: Aspects of Linguistic Colonialism in the Sixteenth Century." In *First Images of America: The Impact of the New World on the Old*, edited by Fredi Chiappelli with Michael Allen and Robert Benson, vol. 2: 561–80. Berkeley: University of California Press, 1976.

Hamlin, William. *The Image of America in Montaigne, Spenser and Shakespeare: Renaissance Ethnography and Literary Reflection*. New York: St Martin's Press, 1995.

Hannaford, Ivan. *Race: The History of an Idea in the West*. Washington, DC: Woodrow Wilson Center

Press; Baltimore, MD: Johns Hopkins University Press, 1996.

Harris, Jonathan Gil. "Forms of Indography." In *Indography: Writing the "Indian" in Early Modern England*, edited by Jonathan Gil Harris, 1–21. New York: Palgrave Macmillan, 2012.

Heng, Geraldine. "The Invention of Race in the European Middle Ages I: Race Studies, Modernity, and the Middle Ages." *Literature Compass* 8, no. 5 (2011): 315–31.

Höfele, Andreas. *Stage, Stake, and Scaffold: Humans and Animals in Shakespeare's Theatre*. Oxford: Oxford University Press, 2011.

Hulton, P. H., ed. *The Work of Jacques Le Moyne de Morgues: A Huguenot Artist in France, Florida and England*. London: British Museum, 1977.

Jacoby, Karl. "Slaves by Nature? Domestic Animals and Human Slaves." *Slavery and Abolition* 15, no. 1 (1994): 89–99.

Jaenen, Cornelius. *Friend and Foe: Aspects of French-American Cultural Contact in the Sixteenth and Seventeenth Centuries*. Toronto: McClelland and Stewart, 1976.

———. "'Les Sauvages Ameriquains': Persistence into the 18th Century of Traditional French Concepts and Constructs for Comprehending Amerindians." *Ethnohistory* 29, no. 1 (1982): 43–56.

Johnson, Robert. *Nova Britannia: offering most excellent fruites by planting in Virginia, exciting all such as be well affected to further the same*. London: Samuel Macham, 1609.

Jones, Ann Rosalind, and Peter Stallybrass. *Renaissance Clothing and the Materials of Memory*. Cambridge: Cambridge University Press, 2000.

Jouanna, Arlette. *L'idée de race en France au XVIe siècle et au début du XVIIe*. Lille: Université de Lille III, 1976.

Kidd, Colin. *The Forging of Races: Race and Scripture in the Protestant Atlantic World, 1600–2000*. Cambridge: Cambridge University Press, 2006.

Kim, Dorothy. "Critical Race and the Middle Ages." *Literature Compass* 16, no. 9–10 (2019): 1–16.

Krech, Shepard, III. *The Ecological Indian: Myth and History*. New York: Norton, 1999.

Kupperman, Karen Ordahl. *Settling with the Indians: The Meetings of English and Indian Cultures in America, 1580–1640*. Totowa, NJ: Rowman and Littlefield, 1980.

Lambert, Shannon. "Subversive Somatology: Embodied Communication in the Early Modern Stag Hunt." *Public* 30, no. 59 (2019): 78–87.

Laudonnière, René Goulaine de. *A notable historie containing foure voyages made by certayne French captaynes unto Florida*. Translated by "R.H." London: Thomas Dawson, 1587.

———. *L'histoire notable de la Floride située ès Indes Occidentales*. Paris: G. Auvray, 1586.

Lestringant, Frank. "A Staged Encounter: French Meeting Timucua in Jacques Le Moyne de Morgues." *Journal of Transnational American Studies* 8, no. 1 (2017): 1–10.

———. *Le huguenot et le sauvage: l'Amérique et la controverse coloniale en France, au temps des guerres de religion, 1555–1589*. Paris: Aux Amateurs de Livres, 1990.

Lira, Obed Omar. "Bartolomé de Las Casas and the Passions of Language." PhD diss., Harvard University, 2017.

Loomba, Ania, and Jonathan Burton, eds. *Race in Early Modern England: A Documentary Companion*. New York: Palgrave Macmillan, 2007.

Malone, Patrick. *The Skulking Way of War: Technology and Tactics among the New England Indians*. Baltimore, MD: Johns Hopkins University Press, 1993.

Manning, Roger. *Hunters and Poachers: A Social and Cultural History of Unlawful Hunting in England, 1485–1640*. Oxford: Clarendon, 1993.

Martel, Heather. "Timucua in Deer Clothing: Friendship, Resistance, and Protestant Identity in Sixteenth-Century Florida." *Atlantic Studies* 10, no. 1 (2013): 13–33.

Martelli, Cristina Arrigoni. "Nets, Lures, and Camouflage: Capturing Birds in Late Medieval North and Central Italy." *Reinardus* 27 (2015): 1–32.

Marvin, Garry. "Wild Killing: Contesting the Animal in Hunting." In *Killing Animals*, edited by The Animal Studies Group, 10–29. Urbana, IL: University of Illinois Press, 2006.

Milanich, Jerald. *The Timucua*. Oxford: Blackwell, 1996.

Miner, Earl. "The Wild Man through the Looking Glass." In *The Wild Man Within: An Image in Western Thought from the Renaissance to Romanticism*, edited by Edward Dudley and Maximillian Erwin Novak, 87–114. Pittsburgh, PA: University of Pittsburgh Press, 1972.

Miramon, Charles de. "Noble Dogs, Noble Blood: The Invention of the Concept of Race in the Late Middle Ages." In *The Origins of Racism in the West*, edited by Miriam Eliav-Feldon, Benjamin Isaac, and Joseph Ziegler, 200–216. Cambridge: Cambridge University Press, 2009.

Morton, Nathaniel. *New-England's Memoriall: or, A brief Relation of the most Memorable and Remarkable Passages of the Providence of God*. Cambridge, MA: S.G. [Samuel Green] and M.J. [Marmaduke Johnson], 1669.

Nicot, Jean. *Thresor de la Langue Françoyse, tant ancienne que moderne*. Edited by Aimar de Ranconnet. Paris, 1606.

Nirenberg, David. "Race and the Middle Ages." In *Rereading the Black Legend: The Discourses of Religious and Racial Difference in the Renaissance Empires*, edited by Margaret Greer, Walter Mignolo, and Maureen Quilligan, 71–87, 335–45. Chicago: University of Chicago Press, 2007.

Olson, Todd. "Markers: Le Moyne de Morgues in Sixteenth-Century Florida." In *Seeing across Cultures in the Early Modern World*, edited by Dana Leibsohn and Jeanette Favrot Peterson, 193–212. Farnham, UK: Ashgate, 2012.

Ortega y Gasset, José. *Meditations on Hunting*. Translated by Howard Wescott. New York: Scribner, 1972.

Pagden, Anthony. *The Fall of Natural Man: The American Indian and the Origins of Comparative Ethnology*. Rev. ed. Cambridge: Cambridge University Press, 1986.

Pareja, Francisco. *Francisco Pareja's 1613 Confessionario: A Documentary Source for Timucuan Ethnography*. Edited by Jerald Milanich and William Sturtevant. Translated by Emilio Moran. Tallahassee: Florida Division of Archives, History and Records Management, 1972.

Parrish, Susan Scott. *American Curiosity: Cultures of Natural History in the Colonial British Atlantic World*. Chapel Hill: University of North Carolina Press, 2006.

Phoebus, Gaston. *Livre de chasse*, c.1387. Bibliothèque nationale de France. Département des Manuscrits, Français 616.

Pierce, Donna, Rogelio Ruiz Gomar, and Clara Bargellini. *Painting a New World: Mexican Art and Life, 1521–1821*. Denver: Frederick and Jan Mayer Center for Pre-Columbian and Spanish Colonial Art, Denver Art Museum, 2004.

Purchas, Samuel. *Hakluytus Posthumus: or Purchas His Pilgrimes*. New York: AMS Press, 1965.

Ribault, Jean. *The Whole & True Discouerye of Terra Florida*. Edited by Jeannette Thurber Connor. Gainesville: University Press of Florida, 1974.

Russo, Alessandra. "An Artistic Humanity: New Positions on Art and Freedom in the Context of Iberian Expansion, 1500–1600." *RES: Anthropology and Aesthetics* 65/66 (2014/2015): 352–63.

———. *The Untranslatable Image: A Mestizo History of the Arts in New Spain*. Translated by Susan Emanuel. Austin: University of Texas Press, 2014.

Saint-Julien, Pierre de. *De l'origine des Bourgongnons et antiquité des estats de Bourgongne*. Paris, 1581.

Shaffer, Brian, and Karen Gardner. "Wolves in Sheep's Clothing: Prehistoric Depictions of Mimbres Hunting Disguises from the American Southwest." *Visual Anthropology* 12, no. 1 (1999): 1–11.

Smith, John. *Complete Works of Captain John Smith (1580–1631)*. Edited by Philip Barbour. Chapel Hill: University of North Carolina Press, 1986.

Smith, Justin. *Nature, Human Nature, and Human Difference: Race in Early Modern Philosophy*. Princeton, NJ: Princeton University Press, 2017.

Strachey, William. *The Historie of Travell into Virginia Britania (1612), by William Strachey, Gent*. Edited by Virginia Freund and Louis Wright. London: Hakluyt Society, 2010.

Sundstrom, Linea. "Archaic Hunting Practices Depicted in a Northwestern Plains Rock Art Style." *Plains Anthropologist* 34, no. 124, part 1 (1989): 149–69.

Swanton, John. *The Indians of the Southeastern United States*. Washington, DC: Smithsonian Institution, 1946.

Taussig, Michael. *Mimesis and Alterity: A Particular History of the Senses*. New York: Routledge, 1993.

Vacano, Diego von. "Las Casas and the Birth of Race." *History of Political Thought* 33, no. 3 (2012): 401–26.

van der Straet, Jan (Johannes Stradanus). *Venationes Ferarum, Avium, Piscium*. Antwerp: Ph. Galle, c.1580.

van Groesen, Michiel. *The Representations of the Overseas World in the De Bry Collection of Voyages (1590–1634)*. Leiden: Brill, 2008.

Waage, Frederick. "The Non-Human in New World Encounter Narratives of the English Renaissance." *Canadian Review of Comparative Literature* 38, no. 3 (2011): 344–55.

Wells, Andrew. "Race and Racism in the Global European World before 1800." *History Compass* 13, no. 9 (2015): 435–44.

White, Hayden. "The Forms of Wildness: Archaeology of an Idea." In *The Wild Man Within: An Image in Western Thought from the Renaissance to Romanticism*, edited by Edward Dudley and Maximillian Erwin Novak, 3–38. Pittsburgh, PA: University of Pittsburgh Press, 1972.

Willerslev, Rane. "Not Animal, Not Not-Animal: Hunting, Imitation and Empathetic Knowledge among the Siberian Yukaghirs." *Journal of the Royal Anthropological Institute* 10, no. 3 (2004): 629–52.

Yamamoto, Dorothy. *The Boundaries of the Human in Medieval English Literature*. Oxford: Oxford University Press, 2000.

Reframing Whiteness in the Zoo
Snowflake the Gorilla in Modern Media

Elizabeth Tavella

ON NOVEMBER 24, 2003, THE FAMOUS GORILLA WITH ALBINISM KNOWN AS SNOWFLAKE or Copito de Nieve died of skin cancer at the Barcelona Zoo, where he had been transferred after being captured while still an infant in Equatorial Guinea in 1966.[1] Because of his rare physical traits, he quickly became a celebrity with high exhibition value, attracting millions of visitors from around the world during the thirty-seven years he was forced into a life in captivity. Not only was he physically trapped in a cage for his whole life, but he also continues to be trapped in contemporary cultural imagination. Since he first made the cover of the *National Geographic* in March 1967 he has become a popular cultural phenomenon, inspiring novels, short stories, movies, and graphic novels worldwide, all of which embed him within human narratives that distort or erase his subjectivity.[2] This general tendency toward misrepresentation also affects his cultural legacy, extending even to outer space, where an asteroid was named in his honor.[3] The combination of these cultural manifestations played—and continues to play—a major role in rendering him an icon of Western civilization, while also framing his life narrative in symbolic terms, mostly through metaphors expressing uniqueness, solitude, and exceptionalism.

An aspect that is largely left unquestioned is how his body has become a marker of racialization due to his whiteness and, as a consequence, how this physical feature has been idealized and represented in different forms of media. As with other literary examples in which nonhuman animal characters become a projection of racialized discourses, such as in the case of the white whale in Moby Dick, the process of racialization that Snowflake was subject to is not neutral either.[4] The contemplation of racial whiteness that the zoo employed as a means of exploitation for human consumption and capitalist greed recurs, over and over again, on the literary page as well as in visual representations. Nonhuman primates have always permeated human imagination as beings who live "in the borderlands," in a space that challenges the ontological foundations of hierarchical binary oppositions such as human/animal and nature/culture.[5] The racialization of gorillas and their association with Blackness have a long history tied to the underlying racist logic of evolutionary theory and eugenics that has deeply affected Western cultural discourses about members of disenfranchised groups.[6] Snowflake's identity is still constructed within this liminal tension, but because of his whiteness, he undergoes a privileged process of humanization, yet is animalized based on anthropocentric assumptions responsible for labeling his physical and cognitive abilities as inferior compared to standards of normative humanity.

In this chapter, I question the cultural mechanisms that render these narratives seemingly acceptable by analyzing a variety of representations with Snowflake as protagonist that illustrate how his albinism has been characterized in racialized terms, as well as the consequences of conceptualizing the animal-human binary along racial lines. Through a framework located at the juncture of racial politics, disability studies, and decolonial theories, I argue that the notion of whiteness and its supremacy have shaped not only Snowflake's identity but also the identity of the other characters within the stories. In order to fully unveil how racial considerations have affected Snowflake's existence, I analyze Western and Guinean histories, cultural representations, and perspectives, which will further highlight the central role zoos play in promoting and supporting an optic built on oppressive structures of power and knowledge. In discussing the meaning and implications of a racist optic, Judith Butler reminds us that "the visual field is not neutral to the question of race; it is itself a racial formation, an episteme."[7] A close reading of these examples will, therefore, demonstrate that Snowflake's cultural representations are a consequence of this oppressive epistemology and that a new optic, conscious of the deep ties between speciation and racialization, is required to subvert the white gaze as well as the mentality that allows for zoos to continue to exist.

SNOWFLAKE IN WESTERN THOUGHT

The practice of naming a nonhuman animal is never neutral, especially in zoos, where it serves a primarily human function to construct a narrative that would encourage the public to associate with, and thus care about, the named individual.[8] In Snowflake's case, his name bears a history of assimilation and subjugation. He was originally named by his first human capturers Nfumu Ngui, meaning "white gorilla" in Fang language, which immediately draws attention to his white hair and light skin pigment. However, it was only once he arrived at the Barcelona Zoo that the focus on his whiteness acquired a more racialized connotation. He is in fact remembered as Floquet de Neu in Catalan, Copito de Nieve in Spanish, and Snowflake in English. The slightly altered Western name, in all its translations, adds an extra layer of meaning that has deeply influenced the gorilla's cultural representations. The values and perceptions that the word "snowflake" evokes contribute to the gorilla's normative association with purity and uniqueness. This process of translation represents a first clear sign of cultural imperialism, being inextricably linked to the colonial exploits of Europe in Africa. In fact, not only did the zoo erase the native nomenclature, which only reinforces the institution's controlling role, but it also created the premises for the white gaze to flourish. As a consequence, his body becomes the carrier of these superimposed marks, and his whiteness is taken as a cue of relatedness.

In Western representations, Snowflake generally tends to be inscribed into a narrative where he stands as a symbol of solitude and human alienation, given the rareness of his health condition, which is viewed as the main cause of his desolation. This is the case, for instance, in the song "Copito de Nieve de Barcelone" by French songwriter Enzo Enzo, which establishes the trope of solitude in combination with a process of projective identification, which is particularly stressed in the refrain "you and I are alone." As a result of a tension between humanization and animalization, Snowflake's relation to the singer gradually shifts from being considered a friend to an accomplice, and finally a clone, the final step that completes the process of assimilation.[9] While the zoo as a space is not explicitly mentioned, a direct allusion to the bars demarcating an enclosed area represents the first level of separation between them, further stressed by emphasizing the physical distance between Paris and Barcelona. However, it is only once she expresses her desire to go one hundred thousand years back in time to overcome their inability to communicate that it is possible to discern the real obstacle preventing a true encounter: the species barrier. By imagining a regression to a prehuman evolutionary stage, the human species is implicitly framed within the song as more developed based on ableist assumptions of linguistic superiority.[10] The sameness-difference dichotomy is further reinforced through the racialization of Snowflake's whiteness. In fact, besides explicitly referring to his hair as white, his whiteness is also mentioned in direct opposition to the Blackness of another ape, as they are imagined romantically embracing while posing for a photograph. By incorporating both anthropomorphic and zoomorphic features, the grotesque vignette of the two gorillas craving to be in the spotlight on one hand evokes the theatrical staging of animality in the zoo; on the other, it offers a glimpse into the intertwined construction of species and race.[11]

A much more overt representation of racialized tropes can be found in the live-action/CGI feature film *Copito de Nieve*, released in Spain in 2011.[12] After his death, the film industry participated in taking advantage of the gorilla's success to make an animated film based on problematic representations of reverse discrimination. In this romanticized version of his arrival at the Barcelona Zoo, he is depicted as a young talking gorilla living in the house of the zoo vet and acting as a playful sibling to his child, thus enabling a process of identification with young human viewers while normalizing the practice of keeping wild animals as pets, which transforms the concept of animal captivity into a positive and enriching experience.[13] Once Snowflake is transferred to the zoo, at first the other three gorillas living in the same enclosure marginalize him because he is white, an act that risks spreading the myth of reverse racial discrimination into children's imagination.[14] The racialization of gorillas as Black beings is a widespread phenomenon in Western popular culture, disseminated, for instance, by the King Kong movies or Tarzan, and that also infiltrates this film. In particular, the portrayal of the father gorilla as threatening and aggressive perpetuates negative images that result in the demonization of Black masculinity.[15] While the purpose of the tale is to promote an edifying message on the acceptance of diversity, it actually upholds harmful racial and gender stereotypes that stimulate oppressive ways of seeing and knowing. Among these is the notion of Blackness arising from dirt. In fact, in the hope of being considered a "normal" gorilla, which will culminate with his escape from the zoo to go visit a witch who will give him a potion that is supposed to turn his hair black, Snowflake first attempts to color his arm black by using mud, a gesture that can perpetuate the linking of "othered" individuals to things that require cleansing, both on a physical and moral level. Besides the multitude of racial stereotypes, the film also normalizes the spectacularization of otherness as well as freak-show narratives by framing Snowflake's albinism as a marker of difference that is exploited to entertain an audience eager to scrutinize non-normative bodies.[16]

In the 2013 English-dubbed version, during the process of adapting the movie into the receiving culture, a series of directorial choices have a drastic impact on gender and racial dynamics, particularly visible in the relationship between the father gorilla and Snowflake. Not only is Snowflake now portrayed as a female gorilla, but by choosing the voice of a Black man to dub the father gorilla and, conversely, the voice of a white woman for Snowflake, the racialized component of the story is even more evident to the public subliminal perception.[17] Clearly, the anthropomorphized animal characters are coded as Black and white as well as along strict gender binaries. The shift in gender, then, besides distancing viewers from the real-life gorilla who inspired the story, also reinforces the correlation between sexism and racism in ways that echo the infamous King Kong narrative.[18] The exposure to such shifts and biases at an early age contributes to influencing young people's race-related beliefs and attitudes in ways that can be detrimental to social relations for all the individuals involved, no matter their species.

Besides being represented in media and popular culture, Snowflake has also been rendered as a literary character. Perhaps the most notable example is his short but significant appearance in Italo Calvino's last book of fiction, *Palomar*.[19] Palomar is a man on a solitary quest for knowledge who is eager to reduce the complexity around and inside of him by finding a set pattern in the world that would reduce it to its basic mechanisms. Observation is the key to his mode of thinking, and it is precisely for this reason that everything in the book happens filtered through his gaze. The short text titled "The Albino Gorilla," dedicated to his encounter with Snowflake in the Barcelona Zoo, is a meditation on loneliness, captivity, the burden of being unique in the world, and mortality.[20] As Robert Harrison rightly affirms, "the more one ponders Calvino's vignette about the albino gorilla, the more it seems that it is not really about the albino gorilla at all, but about Mr. Palomar, who sees in the ape an image of something unutterable and enigmatic in himself."[21] The solitude trope is once again unequivocally employed, as well as the replication of a racialized optic, which has yet to be fully explored. In fact, by using Snowflake as a prompt for his metaphysical reflections, Palomar constructs Snowflake's identity based on his own whiteness and cognitive abilities, which are taken as the parameters through which he assimilates or discriminates against the gorilla on an ontological level. An analysis of Palomar's construction of the categories of "human" and "animal" will therefore demonstrate that his inability to overcome an anthropocentric framework is deeply tied to his inability to escape the social construction of whiteness, which the zoo is responsible for further normalizing and validating.

The text begins with Palomar approaching the walled garden yard where Snowflake is kept on display. He quickly makes his way through the crowd amassed in front of the glass delimiting the enclosure, which represents the first visible and tangible barrier between himself and Snowflake. Immediately, he characterizes Snowflake in racialized terms by bringing attention to his white hair. By recognizing his skin color as being "like that of a human of the white race," Palomar is displacing corporeal racial markers onto the gorilla and reproducing race hierarchies shaped by anthropomorphic tropes. However, while he notices similarities between himself and Snowflake, he nonetheless maintains a distance simply by establishing a comparison that serves the purpose of positioning the category of "Animal," of which Snowflake represents a universal model, beneath the "Human" represented by Palomar. Syl Ko's redefinition of the term "human" can help clarify who Palomar is actually representing: "Human means a certain way of being, especially exemplified by how one looks or behaves, what practices are associated with one's community, and so on. So the 'human' is just a conceptual way to mark the province of European whiteness as the ideal way of being homo sapiens."[22] From Snowflake's perspective, his whiteness is actually what sentenced him to a life in captivity and to being considered a living phenomenon. Whereas in Palomar's eyes, this physical trait is responsible for triggering a series of metaphysical reflections that lead to Snowflake's ontological reconfiguration based on Palomar's criteria for defining the "human." In both cases, what remains unvaried is that Snowflake is inscribed into a human narrative according to which "human" viewers arbitrarily define how he should be conceptualized. Palomar's definition of "human" also affects how he perceives the other gorillas in the enclosure: they are in fact described as less attractive because of their Blackness, which is particularly evident when Palomar notices the presence of a "female great black gorilla carrying a baby in her arms." Not only then is his optic racialized, but it is also gendered. Additionally, by stressing that the whiteness of his hair cannot be inherited, he is framing Snowflake's whiteness not as a genetic alteration but as a human-like trait that grants him a privileged status. While making these observations, he is also inadvertently pointing to the zoo's breeding program that, in real life, genetically exploited Snowflake in the attempt to bring to life another white gorilla of inestimable economic value. This emblematic case makes evident the inherent capitalist logic of the zoo and its reliance on systemic reproductive exploitation as well as on heteronormative standards of sex.[23] At the same time, it also unveils the zoo's efforts to promote the commodification of whiteness through Snowflake's body, taken as an aesthetic model that must be glorified, reproduced, and visually consumed.

The first phase of assimilation, due to their shared whiteness, continues in Palomar's description of Snowflake's gaze "charged with desolation, and patience and boredom." The perceived similarities between them stimulate in Palomar a momentary biased empathic response that does not extend to the other gorillas in the enclosure. He describes it as "a resignation at being what he is, sole exemplar in the world of a form not chosen, not loved, all the efforts of bearing his own singularity, and the suffering at occupying a space and time with his presence so cumbersome and evident."[24] By attributing Snowflake's sense of solitude to his albinism and framing his whiteness as the cause of his social exclusion, not only is Palomar extending racial thought onto other animal species, but he also seems unable to recognize the true cause of his isolation: the forced imprisonment in the zoo. Snowflake's state of captivity is in fact used exclusively as an entry point to make anthropocentric metaphysical considerations instead of being morally questioned. As soon as Palomar's gaze moves away from Snowflake's face and starts scanning the rest of his body, the initial process of identification is reversed. Triggered perhaps by what Susan Bernstein has defined as "the anxiety of simianation," which she invokes to describe a discomfort over evolutionary ties between humans and other primate species, what now prevails are the physical traits of difference.[25] Palomar's transition to a description based on contrast and opposition is introduced by comparing Snowflake, who is now standing completely still, to "an immemorial antiquity, like mountains or the pyramids." While his ontological status is somewhat questioned through this comparison, since Palomar is unsure whether to perceive him as part of nature or as a model of a primordial stage of human civilization, he still classifies him as inferior to "humans" and compares him exclusively to inanimate objects. A quick scan of Snowflake's body reveals, from Palomar's perspective, little resemblance to the body of a "human": "In place of a nose, the nostrils dig a double chasm; the hands, hairy and—it would seem—not very highly articulated, at the end of the very long and stiff arms, are actually still paws, and the gorilla uses them as such when he walks, pressing them to the ground like a quadruped."[26] After undergoing a brief process of humanization, Snowflake is now animalized and segregated into the category of "animal." Palomar's ableist remarks frame Snowflake's body as being less developed compared to those of humans, an assumption that can be detected also at a semantic level through the recession of the hands to the status of paws. The sight of his hands, perceived as evolutionarily inferior, is what causes Palomar to once again reevaluate Snowflake's ontological privileges. The process of animalization is stressed even further by depicting Snowflake as a quadruped who uses his hands to walk. By contrast, bipeds are indirectly framed as those who have freed their hands from locomotor functions and therefore show a more civilized behavior.[27] Thus, based on Snowflake's physical appearance, Palomar's assertions place him in a relation of either identity or alterity to himself: Snowflake's whiteness confers a "human-like" status upon him, while any trait perceived as different is the cause of his exclusion from the "human" domain. In other words, for Palomar, to humanize means inscribing Snowflake within the circle of white people, while to animalize means marginalizing him based on his ape-like traits.

After describing Snowflake's body in terms of sameness and difference, Palomar applies the same epistemological method to his cognitive abilities, in particular to his ability to create meaning. In fact, Palomar starts speculating about the car tire that Snowflake holds in his "arm-paws" and whether he might be ascribing a symbolic value to it.[28] In asking himself what the tire could signify for him—a toy, a fetish, or a talisman—Palomar provisionally extends to him the ability to create and use symbols. However, while this approach may be interpreted as an effort to access the gorilla's consciousness, Palomar is still thinking through a human-specific framework, according to which Snowflake should be able to make symbolic associations and abstract conceptualizations based on a reference map and system of signs grounded in human culture.[29] Soon after, Palomar connects the act of holding the tire to a need to "allay the anguish of isolation, of difference, of the sentence of being always considered a living phenomenon not only by the visitors to the zoo but also by his own females and children." While with this statement Palomar is to a certain degree recognizing Snowflake's state of vulnerability and solitude, he still projects his own sense of existential isolation onto the situation he observes and, as a consequence, constructs it as his own. During this phase of ontological assimilation and extension of cognitive abilities, he also makes selective and gendered assumptions since he does not extend the privileges offered to Snowflake also to the female gorilla in the enclosure. In fact, for Palomar, she maintains a practical relationship with the car tire, she just "sits in it as if it were an easy chair, sunbathing and delousing her infant," while for Snowflake the contact with the tire has an affective, possessive, symbolic meaning, from which he "can have a glimpse of what for man is the search for an escape from the dismay of living . . . a first daybreak of culture in the long biological night." In making such a drastic distinction between their relationship with the tire, a clear racial and gender hierarchy is established, since Palomar now projects a privilege onto Snowflake not only for being white but also for being male.[30] Snowflake is therefore elected by Palomar as the only being who is able to potentially bridge the gap between "human" and "animal" due to the characteristics that allow him to be considered for inclusion into the "human" category.

Snowflake, however, is still missing language, the ultimate clause for admission into human ontological consideration. For a moment, it seems like he is about to break the wall of silence that is responsible for his segregation to an inferior status. He is in fact about to reach "the springs from which language bursts forth, to establish a flow of relationships between his thoughts and the unyielding, deaf evidence of the facts that determine his life." Ultimately, though, he does not gain access to the symbolic and is unable to create human meaning. Based on Palomar's anthropocentric conception of language and cognition, Snowflake remains stuck in a pre-symbolic condition, a pre-linguistic semiotic universe. It is, however, important to note that what Palomar perceives as silence is, in reality, a consequence of an act of silencing, since he does not take into consideration the possibility of the existence of other languages and forms of communication beyond the human.[31] In this mental and moral framework, the absence of (human) language is equivalent to absence of thoughts, which is used as a parameter to discriminate and deny liberty, autonomy, and dignity to nonhuman animals. Palomar's analysis of Snowflake remains one-dimensional in its focus because connecting with the gorilla's emotions and understanding *his* language and *his* culture is never really a priority. His remarks are in fact made with an inward eye aimed ultimately at understanding his own identity. It is this focus and this priority that form his chief epistemological limit.[32] Palomar is well aware of this limit and constantly struggles to accept it as he questions the reliability of human reason throughout the book; he knows that instilled prejudices influence the human gaze, alter his intentions, and impoverish his perceptions, but he still tries to overcome them despite his tendency to failure.[33] In this case, the physical barrier erected by the zoo creates an extra layer of separation that makes it impossible for Palomar to reconcile their distance. When his thoughts come to an end, the human-animal barrier remains insurmountable, he is unable to find satisfying answers to his metaphysical questions, and a new ontology for Snowflake is impossible to formulate. But how can a new ontology be formulated if nonhuman animals are conceptualized as inferior beings through the lens of whiteness? It is inevitable that a hierarchy of power, structural discrimination, and ontological separation would subsist. The zoo in which Palomar's reflections take place represents the visual and physical enclosure of a much larger system of beliefs and norms. Its very existence, based on domination and captivity operating within a colonialist framework, justifies and supports Palomar's paradigmatic anthropocentrism rooted in arbitrary value judgments.

A similar formulation also operates in *Últimas palabras de Copito de Nieve* (Snowflake's Last Words, 2004) by Spanish playwright Juan Mayorga. In an interview, the director of the play, Andrés Lima, defines the scope of the play in a humanist framework and suggests reading it as "a metaphor of the human being and of the society in which we live. Copito behind the bars is like us in our homes. The text discusses two questions: on one side it talks about death, on the other it turns the gorilla into a mirror of the human being."[34] According then to this explicit declaration of authorial intent, the gorilla's lived existence is herein employed as a metaphor of human existential crises. At the same time, as Linda Materna notes, the play stages an act of animal resistance to subjugation, which invites "the audience to interrogate the moral and physical confinement and servitude in which the societal guardians of legitimate power and authority hold them."[35] While the play somewhat challenges the colonialist framework of animality, it does not however question the problematic Black/white dichotomy that characterizes the narratives based on Snowflake's lived experience.

Inspired by Snowflake's death, Mayorga's play is centered around the last hours of his life. By granting him a high degree of linguistic competence, Snowflake learns to speak through the words of canonical Western philosophers and delivers his last will, which consists of existential reflections over the contemporary "man" and the experience of death. Set in a cage-like environment, Snowflake shares the stage with two other ontologically hybrid characters: the guard, who stands in for a zookeeper, and a Black gorilla. By blending anthropomorphic and animalistic features in each one of them, the trio comes to embody the threshold of the human/animal divide, a space where power dynamics and hierarchies clearly still persist. In fact, while the author attempts to disrupt human exceptionalism and to blur the lines between species, the adoption of an ableist rhetoric that reproduces the Black/white racial dichotomy makes the logic of inclusion/exclusion at times even more striking. This liminal space of ontological reconfiguration is not accessible to the two gorillas in the same ways; the only one who is guaranteed some level of humanization is, once again, the white gorilla. The racialized distinction between Black and white bodies is once again extended to nonhuman animals and their life experiences, which has critical consequences for the audience's perception. While the biopolitical elements of the play bring to the surface the politics of animalization in human society, the social construction of whiteness still prominently controls the narrative.[36] In fact, the Black gorilla's cognitive—and ontological—inferiority is accentuated by a quadruped walk and reproduced on a discourse level particularly by his use of simplified syntactic structures. It is clear then that the two gorillas are not granted the same treatment due to a color-coded assignment of privileges: "because he [Snowflake] was white, because he looked human."[37] As already seen in the case of Calvino's Snowflake, the projection of anthropomorphic characteristics combined with the racialization of his white body creates a hierarchy of discrimination. However, Snowflake too does not gain full access to human privileges. In fact, as a subject assimilated into the dominant human culture, he has access to a more privileged status while still being victim of othering mechanisms. In speaking the words of Western philosophers, he acts *like* an erudite human being, but will never fully be one: he is granted the status of "exemplary citizen" without the freedom of movement outside of his assigned zoo enclosure; he is a famous celebrity, but at the service of the West; he is a literary icon, but acts as an empty signifier whose life and experiences have constantly been distorted to fit into human narratives. The representation of Snowflake's embodied experience mediated through human reason and culture is therefore still rooted in colonialist and racialized discourses that interfere with the possibility for Snowflake to truly speak in his own voice.[38] While the play has been convincingly interpreted as an allegory of immigration, the questions of citizenship and social integration are not really extended to nonhumans, whose political voices are most often exploited as vehicles for the struggles of other disenfranchised social groups.[39] In order to overcome this process of erasure, as Eva Meijer suggests, "we need to challenge human exceptionalism together with the view that there is a binary opposition between 'the human' and 'the animal.' We should pay attention to the variety of ways in which other animals speak and act politically, and search for ways to form new, better relationships with them."[40]

In contrast to this representation of Snowflake speaking profusely, in the graphic novel *Il Re Bianco* (The White King, 2005) by Davide Toffolo, Snowflake remains totally silent.[41] In the prologue of the latest edition, the author defines the book as a travel diary imbued with autobiographical elements and, at the same time, a reconstruction of a life, a biography. This double project is reflected in the structure of the book, which alternates two storylines: the author's journey to visit Snowflake from Italy to the Barcelona Zoo and the sketches of the gorilla's major life events from birth to death. Calvino's *Palomar* functions as a clear intertext, confirmed by a quote from "The Albino Gorilla" serving as an epigraph, which immediately transports readers back to that literary atmosphere. As already seen in the previous examples, in the graphic novel, the human main character sees himself in Snowflake, a projection that culminates in a presumed shared state of loneliness. This process of emotional identification is directly connected to a humanizing process that, however, never reaches a stage of full completion. Once again, in fact, he remains stuck in a liminal space between the ontological categories of "human" and "animal": "It's like watching yourself in the mirror. So similar to us and yet so alien. And now, that he has cancer, he is a caricature of men."[42] Besides inscribing him within a discourse of otherness as a result of a stigmatizing alien rhetoric, his embodied experience of cancer is obscured by the metaphorical purpose it has to serve and turned into a symbol of a universal condition of contemporaneity.[43]

The racialization of his body is undeniably at play also in this work. The appropriation of his whiteness in the hands of the West is reiterated when the fictional version of Benito Mañé, the Indigenous Ntumu Fang responsible for capturing Snowflake, states that "they bring him to Europe, in a big house where people can watch him. He looks more like them, white as he is."[44] A full-page illustration leaves no further doubt about the zoo's intention to capitalize on his whiteness. Standing like a trophy advertising himself, Snowflake holds a sign over his neck that reads "I'm the most famous gorilla in the world. I'm white like you. I live in the Barcelona zoo. Come visit me. You've never seen a phenomenon like me."[45] His white body, then, turned into a symbol of Western civilization, acquires a universal value that can be monetized for visual consumption. The spectacularization of his persona is further stressed in another illustration depicting Snowflake as a personification of Elvis Presley, followed by the words "A life violated by the rules of spectacle."[46]

The author appears to be committed to offering a counternarrative to the dominant story constructed by the zoo by depicting Snowflake as a silent giant assimilated, against his will, into Western culture. He also rewrites the story of his capture from different perspectives, including a sarcastically romanticized version "slightly more Shakespearean," to show the hypocrisy that comes with conveniently minimizing the violence and trauma that Snowflake experienced for the sake of profit. However, while Snowflake receives special treatment, to the point of being appointed king, as the title of the book suggests, the natives of Equatorial Guinea are used as convenient plot devices that rely on racist stereotypical tropes. In fact, not only is their facial individuality drastically reduced compared to the white zoo visitors in Barcelona, but their physical features recall blackface iconography. In the first chapter, the author creates a direct comparison between a female gorilla giving birth to Snowflake and a woman in Rio Muni who, after being sexually assaulted by another resident of the village, fears she will give birth to a child with albinism.[47] Besides sexualizing the female Black body, this juxtaposition also inscribes the questions of difference and social acceptance into a color-coded narrative that constructs the concept of race through animalized imagery. The textual narration further reinforces a dehumanizing rhetoric, rooted in speciesism, particularly through ape-like comparisons used as prompts for laughter: "You're ugly like a monkey, Alfonso." "Shut up, mono negro."[48] The Black natives are therefore depicted as savages driven by sexual instincts whose culture is reduced to superstitions and folktales in sharp contrast with the civilized life of the Western city.

While the Black fictional characters are not given narrative space to reclaim their identities, in the epilogue, Snowflake regains his Fang name as well as his real-life physical appearance, which is restored through a memorial photograph placed on the last page of the graphic novel. Finally, even if only after his death, he can return home. The author draws himself stepping inside the zoo enclosure where Snowflake lies and carrying him onto his shoulders all the way back to Africa, to Equatorial Guinea, where he was born. This redemptive gesture, which demonstrates the healing power of literature—or arts, more broadly—to create space for imaginative liberation, can be interpreted as the author's act of reparation on behalf of Western culture. However, Snowflake's liberation is still dependent on a white savior narrative that strips away his agency and does not fully recognize his power to liberate himself. While this message may be unintentional, its presence indicates that it is still deeply entrenched in Western culture and suggests that whiteness operates in this artwork in both subtle and overt ways.

NFUMU NGUI IN GUINEAN THOUGHT

While Western representations of Snowflake tend to predominate in our cultural history as a consequence of his long-lasting assimilation into European culture and imagination, he has also been captured in Guinean thought, where his symbolic role takes a stronger political turn. Besides being swiftly mentioned in Juan Manuel Davies's novel *Siete días en Bioko* (Seven Days in Bioko, 2007), in which his whiteness is once again framed in racialized terms, he is the protagonist of the poem "Salvad a Copito" (Save Snowflake) by Francisco Zamora Loboch.[49] A closer look at this poem sheds light on the lesser-known history of imperialism that lies behind his capture as well as on the process of idolization of his whiteness at the hands of the West. To fully understand these questions, it is worth remembering that Equatorial Guinea was still a Spanish colony when Snowflake was captured in 1966 and that white colonizers, at the time, were funding the capturing of gorillas.[50] The romanticized versions of Snowflake's life before he was shipped to Spain, promoted by the zoo and mainstream media, completely erase the link between the Barcelona Zoo and Spain's colonizing project. In fact, the Barcelona Zoo was affiliated with the Ikunde Zoological Adaptation and Experimentation Center, a facility in Equatorial Guinea intended for the study of the local flora and fauna, mainly for commercial purposes.[51] The hunting of gorillas in the area of Rio Muni was also facilitated by invasive logging operations that radically disrupted the gorillas' habitat and ecosystem. Meanwhile, the Barcelona Zoo was having a hard time recovering from economic losses mainly due to the Spanish Civil War, and Snowflake's acquisition was pivotal in getting the zoo back on financial track. As Benita Sampedro Vizcaya affirms, "the capture, deterritorialization and public exposition of the unique gorilla is a political act, in all its dimensions, an act saturated with ideology."[52] Zamora Loboch is also a deterritorialized subject who lived most of his life as a migrant outside of Equatorial Guinea. Because of the post-independence regime in his home country, he was forced to remain in Spain, where he had originally moved to complete his studies. Not only his identity, then, but also his literary production are characterized by liminal properties. Generally classified as exile literature, his writing maintains a marginalized position in the Spanish national literary landscape. Its lack of visibility both on the editorial market and in canonical circles mirrors the sense of alienation he experiences as part of the phenomenon of diasporization, which contributes to a lack of social integration in the colonizing country.[53] The tension between having to conform to modes of cultural appropriation to fit into Western society and the active resistance to assimilation is the result of the hybrid position he embodies.

Living at the interstices of two countries and two cultures is a condition the writer shares with Snowflake. However, instead of focusing on their shared traits, the poet takes as a starting point of his poetic reflections the trait that sets them apart: the gorilla's whiteness. Clearly constructed in racialized terms, although this time from a decolonial perspective and with poignant sarcasm, the poet calls attention to the privileged treatment Snowflake has received because of his "white covering and blue eyes." As a consequence of the elevated status conferred by his whiteness, he was transformed into a model citizen perfectly assimilated into Western culture and society: he had access to hot water and heating, "got to enjoy a baby bottle" from the first day he arrived in Barcelona, and made prestigious "friends at the Ministry."[54] This last reference evokes Snowflake's real-life visit to the Barcelona City Hall on Saint Joseph's Day to celebrate the mayor José Maria de Porcioles's birthday. His physical presence at the city hall, photographed sitting on the mayor's chair, is yet another reminder that Snowflake was a living trophy, a materialization of Spain's colonial endeavors in Africa.

By listing the various privileges Snowflake was granted—and by framing them as such—the poet is indirectly invoking all the nonwhite Guineans who are denied those same basic privileges, the "other classmates" who can't hold back their admiration "when they hear the tamer say [Snowflake's] name." Snowflake's celebration in Spain becomes then a means to uncover broader problems regarding citizenship, immigration, and the formation of transnational identities. At the same time, Snowflake's embodied experience of imprisonment in the zoo is invoked through the synecdochal imagery of the "civilized bars," which stresses the violence of the assimilation process constitutive of colonial practices while reminding readers of the literal cage he is forced to live in. Snowflake's racialized whiteness is particularly emphasized in the poet's sarcastic reference to the gorilla's "beautiful name of detergent," which immediately hints at the history of an idealized racial purity promoted in detergent advertisements.[55] But the whitening process goes even further. In fact, the poet extends it also to Snowflake's interiority by defining him as the only gorilla in the world "de alma blanca," all in capital letters. The choice in the wording echoes the trope of the Black body with a white soul, which invalidates whiteness as a positive signifier representing the necessary moral improvement to humanize the Black. The fabrication of Snowflake's interiorized whiteness may also be a reference to Spain's systemic conversion to Christianity of the population of Equatorial Guinea, used as another means to have control over an individual's spiritual and secular literacy.[56] Suddenly, the poet's cynicism takes a different turn, revealing the real price the gorilla had to pay for his privileged status: he has been converted into a commodity in a capitalist society that celebrates his whiteness, the one trait that took over his whole being and forced him into a life in captivity.

With this poem, readers finally have access to a critical perspective of the white culture that has transformed Snowflake into one of their kind, the same culture that fed him pig flesh, dairy products, and Coca Cola.[57] As a consequence of his upbringing within consumerist culture, he literally incorporated capitalism into his diet: his assimilation to Western culture is complete. While the tension between humanization and animalization still reproduces a Black/white dichotomy, it finally acknowledges and problematizes the racialized framework surrounding his existence. Once again, Snowflake stands on a threshold, this time as a symbol of the colonial link between Barcelona and Equatorial Guinea and, by extension, of the exile condition of the Guinean migrants in Spain, which the poet also experienced, who struggle to express their identities without having to display a white soul in a Black body. In bringing to light his lack of decisional power over his life, what remains ostensibly visible is only his whiteness, manipulated by his Western captors to look like a privilege, while his identity is gradually erased. When the poet affirms that Snowflake was able to avoid "anopheles mosquitoes and sentimental neocolonialism," what this really means is that when he was taken away from his home, the jungle of Rio Muni, he was displaced against his own will and incorporated into an ideological machine that damages him and all the individuals—humans and nonhumans—whose identities resist colonial conformations.

CONCLUSIONS

While Snowflake may be the only known gorilla with albinism, the process of racialization he was subject to is not an isolated case. Another gorilla is currently experiencing the consequences of white supremacy in a colonial setting. The name she was given is Anaka, and she lives in the Atlanta Zoo, where she was recently placed at the center of media attention. For her sixth birthday, zoo authorities circulated photographs of her that reveal a lighter pigmentation on her left hand. Immediately, close-ups of her hand went viral on social media and news outlets, describing it as "remarkably human-like," "like [the hand] of a child who played in the dirt," which denote that she is simultaneously humanized and animalized through a racialized optic. These two quotes point, on one side, to the persistent mental association of Blackness with dirt and, on the other, to her partial access to a "human" status because of her white skin patches. This "uncanny resemblance" is, however, not sufficient for her to fully breach the species barrier since she ultimately remains segregated into the "animal" category. While zoo officials clarified that the lighter pigmentation on her hand is nothing but a "cool birthmark," considering it has not changed since birth, still this physical mark has been made into an ideological and ontological marker of racialization that functions as a visual reminder that white is the norm for accessing "human" privileges.

Similarly to Snowflake, Anaka's whiteness represents a marketable product to be exploited and consumed. Her example is further confirmation that the racist framework supporting the existence of zoos has not ended with the closure of human zoos. While the individuals on display have changed, the mobile notion of "animal" has yet to be eradicated. In the effort to reconceptualize multispecies relationships, a new optic is needed that would effectively dismantle a system of oppression and discrimination rooted in white supremacy, which heavily impacts anyone who is seen and treated *like* an "animal" regardless of their species.[58] The various representations of Snowflake analyzed in this chapter demonstrate that the process of racialization he is subject to is a manifestation of the Western conceptualization of the "other" and that, even if unintentionally, they participate in the cultural production of whiteness. As Kalpana Seshadri-Crooks affirms, "whiteness orders, classifies, categorizes, demarcates and separates human beings on the basis of what is considered to be a natural and neutral epistemology."[59] The same epistemology based on separations and hierarchical classifications, intrinsic to the logic of colonialism, regulates zoos. In order then to dismantle race as a regime of looking it is necessary to also dismantle zoos and the mentality that keeps them alive. Only after this paradigm shift can Snowflake be free.

NOTES

1. I avoid the term "albino" to emphasize the individual rather than framing his condition as a descriptive marker and to refrain from perpetuating stigmatizing language and derogatory labeling.
2. Riopelle, "Snowflake," 442–48.
3. The asteroid 95962, discovered by Spanish astronomer José Manteca, was renamed Copito, making him a symbol of Spain's contribution to space colonization. Representations of Snowflake survive also in several products of merchandising, including a commemorative stamp issued fifty years after his death.
4. On the question of whiteness, particularly in American literature, see Morrison, "Unspeakable Things Unspoken," 1–34; Babb, *Whiteness Visible*.
5. Haraway, *Primate Visions*, 1.
6. Glick discusses at length the cultural process of "blackening" gorillas in Western tradition as well as the racist trope of "aligning the species with the rhetorics of Blackness, poor adaptability and 'devolution'"; "Ocular Anthropomorphisms," 57.
7. Butler, "Endangered/Endangering," 15–22.
8. For a more in-depth discussion of this question, see Braverman, "Naming Zoo Animals," 92–110; Borkfelt, "What's in a Name?," 116–25.
9. "Mon copain gorille / Mon complice, mon clone / Copito de Nieve de Barcelone."
10. Me dis "que n'ai-je cent mille ans de moins. Pour pouvoir lui parler."
11. "[Il] Faut le voir, enrouler ses bras blancs contre un grand singe noir qui se croit son amant, posant pour la photo en starlette de gala."
12. Originally in Catalan, the film is directed by Andrés G. Schaer with the title "Floquet de Neu."
13. As an example, the day Snowflake has to be transferred from the apartment in Barcelona where he was temporarily housed to the zoo is compared to the first day of school. By making this

comparison, the imprisonment of nonhuman animals is framed as a nonlasting experience that provides learning opportunities and new friendships.

14. The racial connotation of his social exclusion is made even more explicit by one of the young gorillas who acknowledges that he "totally got judged by the color of [his] fur" as well as when he is jokingly compared to "a powdered doughnut."
15. The 1933 sequel film *The Son of Kong* reinforces this racialized narrative by depicting the son of King Kong as a white gorilla who is smaller in size—thus displaying more "human"-like physical features—and much friendlier towards the white colonizers. Not only is he perceived as less of a threat, but he also ends up sacrificing his life to save the white human protagonist (also known from the original movie as Kong's captor).
16. Unsurprisingly, Snowflake says to himself, "I guess maybe I am a freak." For a discussion of the blurred lines between institutions that profit from animality on display, namely, freak shows, circuses, and zoos, see Johnson, "Zoos, Circuses, and Freak Shows," 57–74.
17. The father is interpreted by Keith David, and Snowflake by Ariana Grande.
18. On the sexist-racist linkage in King Kong, see Affeldt, "Exterminating the Brute," 139–69.
19. Calvino, *Palomar*. The English translation is by William Weaver, *Mr. Palomar*. For a reading of this novel from an animal studies/posthumanist lens, see Bolongaro, "Calvino's Encounter," 105–27; Rohman, "On Singularity and the Symbolic," 63–78; Harrison, *Juvenescence*, 23–28; Iovino, *Italo Calvino's Animals*, 47–59.
20. While he owes his name to an astronomical telescope on Mount Palomar in California, Palomar is nearsighted. The contrast between his physiological deteriorating eyesight and his name, which functions as a signifier of his epistemological scope, has deep philosophical implications connected to broader questions related to humans' access to knowledge and understanding of the world. Palomar is, in fact, a man who looks at the world through the objective lenses of a powerful telescope, and yet his reading, staged as an epistemological exercise, remains fragmented and ultimately inconclusive. On the connection between optics and epistemology, see Calvino's essays "Light in Our Eyes," in *Collection of Sand*, 114–22, and "Visibility," in *Six Memos*, 81–99.
21. Harrison, "Towards a Philosophy of Nature," 431; *Juvenescence*, 22–28.
22. Ko and Ko, *Aphro-ism*, 23. Italics in the original text.
23. During Snowflake's thirty-seven years in captivity, twenty-two offspring by three different mothers were born and none of them inherited his albinism. The British zoo veterinarian David Taylor was hired to collect sperm from Snowflake for artificial insemination. He narrates the experience in one of his autobiographical books: "To take the semen from Snowflake would require me to use electro-ejaculation. This entails inserting a probe into the rectum at just the right spot in relation to the prostate gland and the nerves, which trigger the muscular contractions of ejaculation, and applying a brief pulse of electric current. Though not dangerous, it is unpleasant for the patient (or so I am assured by the man who custom-built our probes for various sizes of animals; he assiduously tried out the one made for great apes on himself—without, of course, any anesthetic). Snowflake would have to be given a general anesthetic—after all, even for the best of reasons, bull gorillas don't take kindly to zoo vets walking up and sticking something that looks rather like a black plastic truncheon into their fundament." In *Vet on the Wild Side*, 45–46.
24. Calvino, *Palomar*, 81.
25. Bernstein, "Ape Anxiety," 250–71. As Ritcher states, "Apes constitute a special case of the uncanny missing link: they denote men's close biological relationship with the animal world, while simultaneously staging the cultural difference which separates men from animals"; in *Literature after Darwin*, 62.
26. Calvino, *Palomar*, 82.

27. Interestingly, these parameters can be applied also to humans who do not conform to a normative standard of biped being. A great literary example can be found in Indra Sinha's *Animal's People: A Novel*, in which a nineteen-year-old boy from the city of Khaufpur is named Animal for the deformed and misshapen spine that causes him to navigate his world on both his arms and legs. For a close reading of this novel, see Parry, "Animal's People," 15–62.
28. Typically, car tires are considered a source of "enrichment" and are offered to zooed animals as an attempt to break the monotony of their life in captivity.
29. There is a multitude of cognitive studies interested in the ability of apes to create (human) meaning. The method employed is always the same: training animals to use human language. This method is not only intrinsically anthropocentric, but it is also based on vocal communication and logocentrism, which means not taking into consideration other potential forms of communication. As examples of this approach see, for instance, Addessi et al., "Preference Transitivity and Symbolic Representation"; Boysen, "The Impact of Symbolic Representations," 489–511.
30. This passage brings to surface the parallels and overlaps between androcentrism and anthropocentrism theorized by Plumwood in "Androcentrism and Anthropocentrism," 119–52. It must also be noted that the female gorilla remains without a name. As already illustrated, the practice of naming has a great impact on how zooed animals are characterized and perceived as individuals. Not extending this privilege to her has obvious repercussions on how her identity is constructed.
31. For an overview of the language of great apes, see King, *The Dynamic Dance*. For an analysis of animal language in a philosophical and political framework, see Seshadri, *HumAnimal*; Meijer, "Political Nonhuman Animal Voices," 221–34.
32. As Safina affirms, "We look at the world through our own eyes, naturally. But by looking from the inside out, we see an inside-out world," which is exactly what is happening to Palomar; *Beyond Words*, 2.
33. An example that further demonstrates the failed logic of Palomar's epistemological efforts can be found in the short text *The Naked Bosom* in which, while he observes a sunbather with "her bosom bared," he searches for a way to not "perpetuate the old habit of male superiority." After several attempts to escape the limits of his own gaze he remains unable to surpass his epistemic limits. Calvino, *Mr. Palomar*, 9–12. For a compelling close reading of this passage, see Bloom, *Reading the Male Gaze*, 122–25.
34. "Una metáfora sobre el ser humano y la sociedad en la que vivimos, ya que Copito en la red es como nosotros en nuestra casa. [El texto] se trata a través de dos vías: por una parte habla de la muerte y por otra pone al gorila como espejo del ser humano"; *El Pais*, September 14, 2004. The play was first staged in Madrid in Nuevo Teatro Alcalá in 2004. For a discussion of the role of the "Animal" on stage in Mayorga's plays, see Rubio, "El animal como personaje," 1–13.
35. Materna, "I've never loved you."
36. Mayorga makes explicit parallels between the prison and the zoo, particularly when the taming manual used in the zoo is designated "Guantanamo Bible," making reference to the infamous detention center in Cuba. See Beilin, *In Search of an Alternative Biopolitics*, 152. For a theoretical discussion of the logic of the zoopticon within these spaces, see Morin, *Carceral Space, Prisoners and Animals*, 119–42.
37. "Porque era blanco. Porque parecía humano."
38. On the links between colonialism and animality, see Montford and Taylor, eds., *Colonialism and Animality*.
39. The Black gorilla is explicitly defined as "sin papeles" (undocumented). For a more in-depth analysis

of Mayorga's discussion of the city as a zoo, see Corces, "When Animals Speak," 269–78.
40. Meijer, *When Animals Speak*," 7–8.
41. Toffolo, *Il Re Bianco*.
42. "È come guardarsi allo specchio. Così simile a noi e allo stesso tempo così alieno. E ora poi, malato di cancro. La caricatura di un uomo"; Toffolo, *Il Re Bianco*, 66.
43. On the use of cancer as metaphor, see Sontag, *Illness as Metaphor*.
44. "Lo portano in Europa, in una grande casa dove la gente lo può guardare. Assomiglia più a loro, così bianco"; Toffolo, *Il Re Bianco*, 79.
45. "Sono il gorilla più famoso del mondo. Sono bianco come te. Vivo allo zoo di Barcellona. Vieni a trovarmi? Sono un fenomeno come non ne hai mai visti"; Toffolo, *Il Re Bianco*, 84.
46. "Una vita violata dallo spettacolo"; Toffolo, *Il Re Bianco*, 92.
47. "Dio, fa' che non sia bianco" (God, don't let him be white); Toffolo, *Il Re Bianco*, 20. For a thorough discussion of the conflation between albinism and racial identity, see Pickett Miller, *Deconstructing the Albino Other*.
48. Toffolo, *Il Re Bianco*: "Sei brutto come una scimmia, Alfonso," 11, and "Sta' zitto mono negro" (black monkey in Spanish), 6.
49. Zamora Loboch, "Salvad a Copito," 9. On Snowflake's short appearance in Davies's novel, see Lewis, *Equatorial Guinean Literature*, 142–43.
50. Equatorial Guinea reached independence only in 1968. The official language, also for literary expression, is Spanish.
51. The center was founded in 1957, with the financial support of Barcelona's ethnology museum and city hall, and operated until the country's independence. The primatologist Jordi Sabater Pi was responsible for the research projects conducted at the center, together with Antoni Jonch, the director of the Barcelona Zoo.
52. Vizcaya, "Salvando a Copito de Nieve," 309.
53. In response to this invisibility, he writes, "La pequeña Guinea Ecuatorial, con apenas 600 000 habitantes, más de la mitad de ellos casi analfabetos, es una auténtica potencia literaria en español que ha producido una ingente obra en el idioma de Cervantes tanto desde el exilio como en el interior del país, y que merece reflexión y admiración.... Merecemos respeto porque nadie nos ha regalado nuestros versos, nuestros cuentos, nuestras humildes novelas, nuestras obras de teatro"; Zamora Loboch, "La increíble aventura," 52. For a more in-depth discussion of this liminal condition, see Odartey-Wellington, "Postnational or Postcolonial?," 199–214.
54. He was even issued with an ID card that lists as his address the Parc de la Ciutadella, i.e., the Barcelona Zoo.
55. Martin-Márquez, *Disorientations*, 344.
56. Claretian missionaries had a central role in this process. See Misioneros Claretianos, *Cien años de evangelización*. See also Pujadas, *La Iglesia en la Guinea Ecuatorial, Fernando Poo*.
57. During his first months in Barcelona, Snowflake lived with the veterinarian Román Luera Carbó and his wife Maria Gracia Luera, known as "Mama Gorila." As she affirms in an interview included in the documentary written and produced by Karen Partridge, "Le enseñó a comer jamón york, comía yogurt, le había dado coca cola." "Snowflake: The White Gorilla," *Nature*, written and produced by Karen Partridge, season 23, episode 8, aired June 9, 2008 on PBS.
58. A convincing theoretical framework that permits one to envision a new optic through a multidimensional lens is proposed by Ko in *Racism as Zoological Witchcraft*.
59. Seshadri-Crooks, *Desiring Whiteness*, 56.

WORKS CITED

Addesi, Elsa, et al. "Preference Transitivity and Symbolic Representation in Capuchin Monkeys (*Cebus apella*)." *PLOS One* (June 11, 2008).

Affeldt, Stefanie. "Exterminating the Brute: Sexism and Racism in *King Kong*." In *Simianization: Apes, Gender, Class, and Race*, Racism Analysis, vol. 6, edited by Wulf Dietmar Hund, Charles Wade Mills, and Silvia Sebastiani, 139–69. Zürich: Lit Verlag, 2015.

Babb, Valerie Melissa. *Whiteness Visible: The Meaning of Whiteness in American Literature*. New York: New York University Press, 1998.

Beardsworth, Alan, and Alan Bryman. "The Wild Animal in Late Modernity: The Case of the Disneyization of Zoos." *Tourist Studies* 1, no. 1 (2001): 12–21.

Beilin, Kararzyna Olga. *In Search of an Alternative Biopolitics: Anti-Bullfighting, Animality, and the Environment in Contemporary Spain*. Columbus: Ohio State University Press, 2015.

Bernstein, Susan. "Ape Anxiety: Sensation Fiction, Evolution, and the Genre Question." *Journal of Victorian Culture* 6, no. 2 (2010): 250–71.

Bhabha, Homi. "Of Mimicry and Man: The Ambivalence of Colonial Discourse." *Discipleship: A Special Issue on Psychoanalysis* 128 (1984): 125–33.

Bloom, James D. *Reading the Male Gaze in Literature and Culture*. New York: Springer, 2017.

Bolongaro, Eugenio. "Calvino's Encounter with the Animal: Anthropomorphism, Cognition and Ethics in Palomar." *Quaderni d'Italianistica* 30, no. 2 (2009): 105–27.

Borkfelt, Sune. "What's in a Name? Consequences of Naming Non-Human Animals." *Animals: An Open Access Journal from MDPI*, no. 1 (2011): 116–25.

Boysen, Sarah T. "The Impact of Symbolic Representations on Chimpanzee Cognition." In *Rational Animals?*, edited by Susan Hurley and Matthew Nudds, 489–511. Oxford: Oxford University Press, 2006.

Brander Rasmussen, Birgit, ed. *The Making and Unmaking of Whiteness*. Durham, NC: Duke University Press, 2001.

Braverman, Irus. "Naming Zoo Animals." In *Zooland: The Institution of Captivity*, 92–110. Stanford, CA: Stanford University Press, 2013.

Butler, Judith. "Endangered/Endangering: Schematic Racism and White Paranoia." In *Reading Rodney King/Reading Urban Uprising*, 15–22. New York: Routledge, 1993.

Calvino, Italo. "Light in Our Eyes." In *Collection of Sand*, translated by Martin McLaughlin. London: Penguin Books, 2013.

———. *Palomar*. Translated by William Weaver. New York: Harcourt Brace, 1985.

———. "Visibility." In *Six Memos for the Next Millennium*. Cambridge, MA: Harvard University Press, 1988.

Corces, Laureano. "When Animals Speak: Staging Representations of Africa." *Afro-Hispanic Review* 28, no. 2 (2009): 269–78.

Domínguez, César, and Theo D'haen, eds. *Cosmopolitanism and the Postnational: Literature and the New Europe*. Leiden: Brill, 2015.

Glick, Megan H. *Infrahumanisms: Science, Culture, and the Making of Modern Non/Personhood*. Durham, NC: Duke University Press, 2018.

———. 'Ocular Anthropomorphisms: Eugenics and Primatology at the Threshold of the 'Almost Human.'" *Social Text* 30, no. 3 (2012).

Gutiérrez Carbajo, Francisco. "El animal no humano en algunas obras teatrales actuales." *Anales de la Literatura Española Contemporánea* 34, no. 2 (2009): 453–78.

Haraway, Donna Jeanne. *Primate Visions: Gender, Race, and Nature in the World of Modern Science.* New York: Routledge, 1989.

Harrison, Robert Pogue. *Juvenescence: A Cultural History of Our Age.* Chicago: University of Chicago Press, 2014.

———. "Towards a Philosophy of Nature." In *Uncommon Ground: Rethinking the Human Place in Nature*, edited by William Cronon, 426–38. London: W.W. Norton & Co., 1996.

Hund, Wulf Dietmar, Charles Wade Mills, and Silvia Sebastiani, eds. *Simianization: Apes, Gender, Class, and Race.* Racism Analysis, vol. 6. Zürich: Lit Verlag, 2015.

Iovino, Serenella. *Italo Calvino's Animals: Anthropocene Stories.* Cambridge, UK: Cambridge University Press, 2021, 47–59.

Johnson, Sammy Jo. "Zoos, Circuses, and Freak Shows." In *Disability and Animality: Crip Perspectives in Critical Animal Studies*, edited by Stephanie Jenkins, Kelly Struthers Montford, and Chloë Taylor, pp. 57–74. London: Routledge, 2020.

King, Barbara J. *The Dynamic Dance: Nonvocal Communication in African Great Apes.* Cambridge, MA: Harvard University Press, 2004.

Kivel, Paul. *Uprooting Racism: How White People Can Work for Racial Justice.* Gabriola Island, BC: New Society Publishers, 2017.

Klein, Hugh, and Kenneth S. Shiffman. "Race-Related Content of Animated Cartoons." *Howard Journal of Communications* 17, no. 3 (2006): 163–82.

Ko, Aph. *Racism as Zoological Witchcraft: A Guide to Getting Out.* Brooklyn, NY: Lantern Books, 2019.

Ko, Aph, and Syl Ko. *Aphro-ism: Essays on Pop Culture, Feminism and Black Veganism from Two Sisters.* New York: Lantern Books, 2017.

Lee, Keekok. *Zoos: A Philosophical Tour.* New York: Palgrave Macmillan, 2005.

Lewis, Marvin A. *Equatorial Guinean Literature in Its National and Transnational Contexts.* Columbia: University of Missouri Press, 2017.

Malamud, Randy. *Reading Zoos: Representations of Animals and Captivity.* New York: New York University Press, 1998.

Martin-Márquez, Susan. *Disorientations: Spanish Colonialism in Africa and the Performance of Identity.* New Haven, CT: Yale University Press, 2008.

Materna, Linda. "'I've never loved you': Juan Mayorga's Últimas Palabras de Copito de Nieve and the Politics of Animal Captivity." *Ovejas Muertas*, September 28, 2017.

Mayorga, Juan. *Últimas palabras de Copito de Nieve.* Madrid: Naque Editora, 2004.

Meijer, Eva. "Political Nonhuman Animal Voices: Rethinking Language and Politics with Nonhuman Animals." In *Animals and Their People: Connecting East and West in Cultural Animal Studies*, edited by Anna Barcz and Dorota Lagodzka, 221–34. Boston: Brill, 2018.

———. *When Animals Speak: Toward an Interspecies Democracy.* New York: NYU Press, 2019.

Misioneros Claretianos. *Cien años de evangelización en Guinea Ecuatorial, 1883–1983.* Barcelona: Editorial Claret, 1983.

Montford, Kelly Struthers, and Chloë Taylor, eds. *Colonialism and Animality: Anti-Colonial Perspectives in Critical Animal Studies.* New York: Routledge, 2020.

Morin, Karen A. *Carceral Space, Prisoners and Animals.* New York: Routledge, 2018.

Morrison, Toni. *Playing in the Dark: Whiteness and the Literary Imagination.* New York: Vintage Books, 1993.

———. "Unspeakable Things Unspoken: The Afro-American Presence in American Literature." *Michigan Quarterly Review*, no. 28 (1989): 1–34.

Ndongo-Bidyogo, Donato, and Mbaré Ngom, eds. *Literatura de Guinea Ecuatorial: Antología.* Casa de

Africa 8. Madrid: SIAL Ediciones, 2000.

Odartey-Wellington, Dorothy. "Postnational or Postcolonial? Reading Immigrant Writing in Postnational Europe." In *Cosmopolitanism and the Postnational*, ed. César Domínguez and Theo D'haen. Leiden: Brill, 2015

Parry, Catherine. "Animal's People: Animal, Animality, Animalisation." In *Other Animals in Twenty-First Century Fiction*, 15–62. New York: Palgrave Macmillan, 2017.

Phatoli, Relebohile, Nontembeko Bila, and Eleanor Ross. "Being Black in a White Skin: Beliefs and Stereotypes around Albinism at a South African University." *African Journal of Disability* 4, no. 1 (May 2015).

Pickett Miller, Niya. *Deconstructing the Albino Other: A Critique of Albinism Identity in Media*. Lanham, MD: Lexington Books, 2020.

Plumwood, Val. "Androcentrism and Anthropocentrism: Parallels and Politics." In *Ethics and the Environment* 1, no. 2 (1996): 119–52.

Pujadas, Tomás. *La Iglesia en la Guinea Ecuatorial, Fernando Poo*. Madrid: Iris de Paz, 1968.

Riopelle, Arthur J. "Snowflake: The World's First White Gorilla." *National Geographic* magazine 131, no. 3 (March 1967): 442–48.

Ritcher, Virginia. *Literature after Darwin: Human Beasts in Western Fiction, 1859–1939*. New York: Palgrave Macmillan, 2011.

Rohman, Carrie. "On Singularity and the Symbolic: The Threshold of the Human in Calvino's 'Mr. Palomar.'" *Criticism* 51, no. 1 (2009): 63–78.

Rubio, Gema Gómez. "El animal como personaje en el teatro de Juan Mayorga." *Tonos Digital* 30 (2016): 1–13.

Safina, Carl. *Beyond Words: What Animals Think and Feel*. New York: Henry Holt and Co., 2015.

Seshadri, Kalpana Rahita. *HumAnimal: Race, Law, Language*. Minneapolis: University of Minnesota Press, 2012.

Seshadri-Crooks, Kalpana. *Desiring Whiteness: A Lacanian Analysis of Race*. London: Routledge, 2000.

Sinha Indra. *Animal's People: A Novel*. New York: Simon & Schuster, 2007.

Sontag, Susan. *Illness as Metaphor*. New York: Vintage Books, 1979.

Taylor, David. *Vet on the Wild Side: Further Adventures of a Wildlife Vet*. New York: St. Martin's Press, 1990.

Toffolo, Davide. *Il Re Bianco*. Milano: BAO Publishing, 2018.

Vizcaya, Benita Sampedro. "Salvando a Copito de Nieve: Poesía, globalización y la extraña mutación de Guinea Ecuatorial." *Revista de Crítica Literaria Latinoamericana* 29, no. 58 (2003): 303–16.

Weheliye, Alexander G. *Habeas Viscus: Racializing Assemblages, Biopolitics, and Black Feminist Theories of the Human*. Durham, NC: Duke University Press, 2014.

Wells, Paul. *The Animated Bestiary: Animals, Cartoons, and Culture*. New Brunswick, NJ: Rutgers University Press, 2009.

Zamora Loboch, Francisco. "La increíble aventura de la literatura de Guinea Ecuatorial." In *Quaderni di Letterature Iberiche e Iberoamericane* 2 (2012): 51–53.

———. "Salvad a Copito." In *Poetas Guineanos en el exilio* (antología). N.p.: Documentos U.R.G.E., [198?], 9.

Of Prey, Sex, and Gender

The Miseducation of Henrietta Forge
Whiteness and the Equestrian Imagination in C. E. Morgan's The Sport of Kings

Angela Hofstetter

BEFORE MASTERY OF THE ALPHABET COMBINED RANDOM LETTERS INTO *NATIONAL VELVET* and *The Black Stallion*, before next-door neighbor Mrs. White took me to see Lipizzaner stallions dance at Gaillard Auditorium and ignited a lifelong passion for baroque horses and dressage, there were Thoroughbreds and the Kentucky Derby. This pageantry stretched out all summer from the Preakness to the Belmont as long-limbed colts and occasional fillies raced for the Triple Crown, but it was the Run for the Roses that held the most acreage in my juvenile imagination. In kindergarten at Ashley River Baptist Church on Savannah Highway in Charleston, South Carolina, Mrs. Price and Mrs. Buckeaster taught me rudimentary block letters so I could spell out my future dream job in a little manila book with a red and blue boy and girl embossed on the front: horse breeder, just like the storied names announced by broadcasters of the winners draped in roses. The first Saturday in May colored everything: My mother Vera had recently lost her battle with lung cancer; I saw her heaven as a field of Kentucky bluegrass where angels were foals with wings. I sought solace in playing stable, an interspecies variation of house where I was filly, rider, vet, racehorse, and mommy-breeder, even more earnestly after I learned from Alma Faye, my new stepmother, that I had been adopted, a bastard, as that dead woman wasn't even my real mother. Little did Alma Faye know then that she had met her match in bigoted cruelty when she married Jack Ansel, the recent widower who shopped at the Piggly Wiggly deli where she worked after he took a fancy to her six-year-old daughter from a previous marriage to a trucker in Hollywood, Florida.

My childhood love of horses reflected desire for connection with something beautiful, powerful, and kind to carry me away from unfortunate, frequently scary circumstances. My love of Thoroughbreds was something else, an inchoate ache for a respectability that transcended unstable circumstances and unknown parentage. Meticulous notebooks filled with Derby winners, their ancestors, the names of jockeys, and other childish musings were a way to imagine inclusion in a society less precarious.

Although I became a teacher instead of a breeder, horses were never far away. Such longings always find a way to resurface. I reveled in the privilege to teach equestrian texts both beloved and haunting, ranging from Anna Sewell's *Black Beauty* to Alfred Hitchcock's *Marnie* to Percival Everett's *Wounded*, embracing the ability to engage in deep conversation about what

---

CONTENT WARNING: This chapter discusses sexual assault.

these stories say about our entangled lives on this beleaguered planet. Exploring that tension between the literal and figurative animal opened a gap where love could meet intellectual inquiry. Teaching tales that granted dignity and subjectivity across species while exposing how figurative animals naturalized systemic injustices across what we now understand as an intersectional spectrum underpinned my pedagogy and shaped the best parts of who I am. A life worth living.

But there is always the shadow, especially when playing in the dark.[1]

Willful blinders tamped down what haunted my psyche until C. E. Morgan's *The Sport of Kings* forced me to plumb the subterranean realms of my existence as a Southern white woman where the horses frolicking in imaginary paddocks don't seem so naive, where the enclosures are traced in red lines instead of white fences. Reflecting on the representation of the Thoroughbred as a cultural metaphor in Morgan's magisterial Southern Gothic during a tumultuous time when everyone felt acutely aware we were living actual history added an urgency to a novel that felt more like prophecy than fiction: #metoo; widespread protests against racial injustice after the agonizing video of the police officer's knee on the neck of George Floyd, who called out for his momma; government lockdowns due to a global pandemic that kept us all on stall rest; Ibram X. Kendi's *How to Be an Anti-Racist* and Isabel Wilkerson's *Caste* becoming bestsellers; armed protestors showing up outside the postponed Kentucky Derby seeking justice for Breonna Taylor; the post-election insurrection where the Confederate flag breached the interior of the Capitol for the first time in history.

This was not the first time I had thought about whiteness embodied in Anglo-American equestrian cultures; it was a key theme of my doctoral dissertation. Looking back, I'm struck by a sentence in my chapter about Gary Ross's 2003 film *Seabiscuit* I wrote as Barack Hussein Obama was about to be inaugurated as the forty-fourth president of the United States: "The elegance and beauty of the Thoroughbred underwrites the residual imperial values that inform a society weary of illegal immigration, feminism, and other accompanying horrors of liberalism."[2] My words might have functioned as the thesis of this essay on *The Sport of Kings* if I hadn't revisited *Playing in the Dark*, Toni Morrison's seminal work about whiteness and the literary imagination when the world was on fire. "It seems both poignant and striking," Morrison writes, "how avoided and unanalyzed is the effect of racist inflection on the subject."[3] Her words shattered my ability to analyze Morgan's novel from the safe, (ostensibly) post-racial distance of someone not personally implicated as I had been more able to do when writing my dissertation. How would it change the stakes of this chapter about Thoroughbred racing and racism if I took my status as the subject responsible for the interpretation seriously? This is not neutral territory: Having grown up under a man who still believed in the War of Northern Aggression and had no trouble telling the hostess in a Carey Hilliard's not to sit his family next to "Blacks" (his polite term for public spaces that curbed his speech), I intimately knew another world outside of the polite academic universe I now inhabited. Repressing discussions of race and genes did not silence their power in American culture, a fact political shifts in 2016 laid bare. Writing about them in a detached, scholarly voice did not silence their power in me, a fact political shifts in 2020 laid bare.

The election of the forty-fifth president only eight years after Obama's election illustrated the hold this metaphor had on the American imagination. During his reelection campaign, Donald J. Trump openly appealed to a mostly white Midwestern crowd: "You have good genes. A lot of it is about the genes, isn't it? Don't you believe? The racehorse theory. You think we're so different? You have good genes in Minnesota."[4] Such a naked assertion idealizing eugenics had not been publicly made on an American stage since we ostensibly entered the "post-racial" era; the thunderous applause his remarks received highlights the importance of works that interrogate our origin stories as part of anti-racist projects.

This was not the first time Trump called on racehorse theory, an intellectual heritage whose stubborn roots go back to Anglo-American traditions that even revolutions presumably founded on liberty cannot stamp out. Only Thoroughbreds bred to other Thoroughbreds can be registered and raced, a segregation enforced without exception at every track even if a grade (mixed breed) horse could run just as fast—or even faster. The belief that applying these rules to humans improves society reveals an important reason why the nature vs. nurture debate is so politicized. Understanding humans to be solely (or at least mostly) the product of their breeding makes social justice reforms concerning race, gender, and class irrelevant because social inequality is viewed as the natural and therefore immutable result of breeding. Such biological determinism enshrines racial purity and binary norms of gender. Reproductive responsibility trumps reproductive rights as "superior" men must breed to "superior" women for the improvement of the white race as a whole. Although in the American iteration of racehorse theory, class is messier than in its British counterpart, traces of aristocracy based on bloodlines remain in the complicated discourses surrounding white supremacy.

Carol Case's *The Right Blood: America's Aristocrats in Thoroughbred Racing* details how "the seasons of [aristocratic] lives were inextricably tied to the Thoroughbred"; these aristocrats were "entirely comfortable with horses, foaling them, sleeping beside them in the stalls, and riding and showing them."[5] Such intimacy naturalized power and privilege as a product of good breeding, human and equine, even for those who sought class affiliation rather than individual contact with individual horses. Case asserts that the breed functions as a totem with "rites that celebrate" through which "members of the clan intensify their sense of community." In short, groups "can establish themselves as superior when they associate themselves with animals that are viewed as superior."[6] Such a totem exposes much about contemporary America—particularly as racial and economic inequality become nakedly apparent. Its "clan" belies the American mythology of equality and unlimited mobility by emphasizing pedigree and purity as prerequisites to enter the race. Though it does not displace the affection for other "breeds," the love affair with the Thoroughbred reveals an increasingly conservative trend in the social landscape of America as 2045 (the year when the Census predicts America will become a minority white country) rapidly approaches. What will blood tell then?

But somehow—reading this novel, *The Sport of Kings*, at this moment—Thoroughbreds, breeding, sexual violence intersected with the ugly truth of race in America that complicates celebrating survivors at a time when so many other lives are being lost. This chapter situates memoir, literary criticism, race theory, and primary texts about eugenics alongside contemporary accounts following #metoo, Black Lives Matter, and presidential politics, entangling stories of sexual violence with the legacy of white supremacy through analyzing a Southern Gothic novel replete with lynchings, incest, and ghosts of a past forever present. It's a deeply personal reading of a novel that shook me to the core, forcing me to consider the stakes for a Southern white woman attempting an anti-racist reading of a novel like C. E. Morgan's *The Sport of Kings* at a moment when uncomfortable truths undermine the admirable desire to believe all women. In short, a voyage into the underbelly of identity politics that always leads us back to our childhood in an effort to reframe the internal dialogue, to find the right question to link the powerful collective "we" with its shadow, implicated self.

THE RIGHT TO BE WELL-BORN

The union between horse-breeding and American eugenics cannot be overestimated, as *The Right to Be Well Born, or Horse Breeding in Relation to Eugenics* by W. E. D. Stokes, the president of the Lexington-based Patchen Wilkes Stock Farm in the early twentieth century, illustrates: "I have always believed that, if the problem of producing great racehorses could be solved, much light could be thrown upon the question of human inheritance. I believed this, because the highly organized racehorse is more like the high-bred man in his physical and nervous constitution than any other animal."[7] Such attitudes gained particular vigor among the American scientific community, which gave significant credence to livestock breeders; even reformers "possessed an ingrained sense that 'good Americans' could be bred like good racehorses."[8] Reproductive rights activist Margaret Sanger promoted policies for the "creation of a race of Thoroughbreds."[9]

Metaphors don't kill; people do. But cultural metaphors like the Thoroughbred shape our mind, enabling us to deceive ourselves into believing in our innate superiority while simultaneously dehumanizing entire races.[10] At first glance, exploring how equestrian metaphors circulate in American culture might seem to be another absurd indulgence in white-girl pony madness, rather than what I hope it really is, an effort "to examine the impact of notions of racial hierarchy, racial exclusion, and racial vulnerability on nonblacks who held, resisted, explored, or altered those notions."[11]

The racehorse theory explains the underlying "birther" controversy Trump and the alt-right manufactured to delegitimize the Obama presidency (although his mother was from Kansas, his father was from Kenya). If we can say that the American presidency is the Kentucky Derby of elections, we can see how such remarks reflected the Jockey Club logic of exclusion. No matter how fast you run, no matter where you are born, no horse is even permitted entry in the race without proper breeding and the official papers to prove it, something the election of the forty-fourth president directly defied.[12]

This unwieldy combination reflects the desire for a hereditary, predominantly white ruling class to make America great again. It also encompasses the paradox of caste as even the offspring of Man O' War or Secretariat fall on hard times, neglected and forgotten in barbed-wire pens instead of four-board paddocks until opportunity knocks and they can trust the old adage "blood will tell"—much like the forgotten of the Rust Belt who have also been dismissed by the Left as deplorables and want to stake their claim to the Thoroughbred totem. According to this logic, proof of pedigree is simply common sense, enabling the purity of the Thoroughbred to become mythic and its rites to unite disparate groups under its banner—white supremacy as a large umbrella that simultaneously denies and reinforces class hierarchy. Roland Barthes points out, "That is why myth is experienced as innocent speech—not because its intentions are hidden—if they were hidden, they would not be efficacious, but because they are naturalized."[13] Such naturalization is further legitimized by the very materiality of the equine body, joining the unlikely constellations of desire and purity in discussions of breeding and demographics, which lead to measures to control female sexuality, to break in women in pink hats "ruined" by feminism.

BLACK MASCULINITY AND THOROUGHBREDS

To understand what forces have shaped our minds is to accept Morrison's challenge to make a "serious intellectual effort to see what racial ideology does to the mind, imagination, and behavior of its masters."[14] Or, as I would like to do here, its mistresses. What we will find won't be pretty, truths C. E. Morgan unflinchingly depicts in *The Sport of Kings*. This flawed chapter represents my grappling with the role art and literary criticism can play in anti-racist explorations: an attempt at real reckoning rather than the virtue signaling of another smug white liberal woman sucking the oxygen out of the room, seeking comfort when called out. (My greatest fear is that this chapter will be another example of this.)

I want to think about how animal metaphors naturalizing racism perpetually breathe new life into Jim Crow by blurring the boundaries of art and life in a genealogy of two contemporary blondes whose miseducation forms a misbegotten tapestry of gender and race relations in the American South: Angela Dawn Bryant (linked by a culture stronger than nature to Carolyn Bryant, denouncer of Emmett Till) and Henrietta Forge, heroine of *The Sport of Kings*. I completed a PhD in comparative literature with a focus on the Victorians in spite of Daddy's objections that it would make me uppity. Henrietta finished high school under the tutelage of her father, who balked at even minor curriculum changes in Kentucky schools in the wake of the Civil Rights Movement. He devoted hours to instructing her in biology and anatomy, the classics from Xenophon to Homer, and rules of breeding—horse and human. Both of our overattentive fathers provided daily lessons about avoiding the Black male rapists in our midst (a curriculum more D. W. Griffith than Ida B. Wells), even though the red lines that kept them out of our neighborhoods did little to protect Henrietta or me from sexual assault in the horrifically complicated Southern Gothic of our lives.[15]

Dylann Roof undoubtedly saw himself through this code of chivalry as he entered Charleston's historically Black AME church and massacred nine parishioners engaged in Bible Study. Seated in a black Hyundai instead of on a famed stallion like Robert E. Lee's Traveler, Roof believed so strongly in the myth of the Black rapist that he could calmly tell the worshippers gathered in Mother Emanuel that it was his duty to kill: "I have to do it," responded the exceptionally slender young man whose bowl haircut is becoming as iconic as Hitler's mustache as he shot a twenty-six-year-old poet and barber trying to make sense of the senseless massacre in the basement of a historic church: "You rape our women and you're taking over our country. You have to go."[16] The shooter punctuated his proclamation with another volley of bullets that ultimately left nine dead before he got into his vehicle and fled north. Roof fought desperately to represent himself at trial to prevent his act from being seen as a sign of mental illness. He wanted to be part of a larger Heroic Narrative that elevates even the most downtrodden to Southern Gallantry, to the Thoroughbreds who constitute the world of white supremacy.

I am one of the women Roof sought to protect.

Herein lies an uncomfortable paradox that accepting Morrison's challenge to look at what racism does to the mistresses demands: the very men we call on to hurt our "aggressors" sometimes hurt us with impunity. Hurt people hurt people. But does that exonerate us when we manipulate the system for dubious purposes? What in our education binds Henrietta and me to Roof as well as Carolyn Bryant and Amy Cooper (who made false allegations about an African American man birding in Central Park)? What are the lessons about purity, race, and breeding taught even to little girls for whom beloved Thoroughbreds only remained a metaphor? Can Morgan's commitment to "playing in the dark" help answer these questions?

THE SPORT OF KINGS

The Sport of Kings dazzles in its breadth; her daring attempt at the Great American Novel audaciously marries William Faulkner's *Light in August* to James Baldwin's *Notes of a Native Son* via Jane Smiley's *Horse Heaven*. Nominated for the Pulitzer, her 2016 book charts the Forge clan's triumph over the uncharted territory of what eventually becomes Paris, Kentucky. Manifest Destiny writ large: young patriarch Samuel leaves his Virginia home accompanied only by a slave given the name Ben. Their future Kentucky dynasty is literally forged by contact with the unforgiving wild land that ultimately yields to their determination. Blood and Soil.[17] The generational weight passed down to the present-day inhabitants of Forge Run Farms is so ineffably vast that current patriarch Henry imagines the lineage as "It." Oral history bolstered by troubling ledgers records settling the property, acquisition of land deeds, Italian furniture, silver, Audubon paintings, livestock, and, from the not-so-distant past, humans. The story closely follows three generations from the 1950s until the early 2000s: John Henry, Henry, and Henrietta—focusing mainly on the latter two's cultivation of a Thoroughbred breeding operation worthy of inscribing the Forge legacy in the history of the Run for the Roses.

The origins of their wealth become problematic when juxtaposed against the family of Allmon Shaughnessy, a groom at Forge Run Farms. In contrast to the Forge line, kept as carefully as the Jockey Club Stud Book, the heritage of the son of absentee father Mike "that fucking Irish fuck" Shaughnessy and Marie, the African American daughter of the Cincinnati Reverend and a long-dead and much-mourned mother, is only recorded in property deeds Allmon will never see. His patriarchal ancestor's name can be found along with eleven other slaves in Edward Cooper Forge's 1827 will, "scrawled in a curly, filigreed script. . . . One negro Man named Scipio, $1000."[18] Somewhere in the Reverend's rantings, Allmon has heard the name Scipio, but he doesn't know exactly what it means. He thinks it might be the name of a star.

Along with this absence of family history is the lack of the legacies that comprise wealth or even security, something Allmon and his mother Marie see little of in their lives. Morgan charts the cruel systemic forces that tear the body as well as the spirit down as they fall further and further into abject poverty in forgotten parts of Cincinnati, as his mother's untreated lupus ravages her flesh (and would ultimately have taken Allmon if suicide had not). In spite of Allmon's exceptional intelligence and poetic soul, beautifully depicted in a tragic story he wrote that gutted his teacher, he ends up incarcerated for a crime he did not commit before being put back inside for one he did when racked with grief at Marie's funeral. There, he enters a prison training program, teaching inmates how to groom horses. This is the Bluegrass State, and hot-blooded horses demand skilled caretakers with courage, sensitivity, and tact whose lives matter far less than the pedigreed property. Allmon excels in handling these frequently dangerous animals and ends up being hired and subsequently seduced by Henrietta, whose proprietary gaze, as she interviews him, lingers over every inch of his muscled body. The tragic outcome of this Southern Gothic variation on mating a lady to a groom unsettles notions of victimhood and purity.[19] Rather than write *The Sport of Kings* as an interracial love story or a modern White Savior narrative with Henrietta as Allmon's heroine or his sympathetic victim, Morgan avoids the animal clichés that typically dehumanize African American males. These she reserves mostly for Henrietta, Daddy's little Ruffian—a woman both victim and victimizer.[20]

The dawning awareness that Henry takes young Henrietta into his bed after his wife leaves him for another man is mostly an unnamable unease until a bedroom scene that follows a bourbon-fueled dinner at the Genealogical Museum of Central Kentucky. The knock that chills the blood comes "when she was stumbling out of her dress, her hair fallen around her shoulders and her mascara smeared from rubbing." Time slows as the antique ceramic knob creaks on its ancient hinges, Henrietta drunkenly gripping the bedpost to remain upright: "Come in, Daddy."[21] We've been preparing for this moment since she was a much smaller girl, watching Henry groom Henrietta: when he removes her from school because she was scolded for using a racial slur; when he takes her in to watch a novice stallion breed a mare when she was thirteen on Valentine's Day; the way the handsome and wealthy divorcé never dates; the way he obsesses over teaching her about the benefits of line breeding even as she protests it's like incest. Something seems off: A beloved farmhand notices she won't hug full-body anymore. The vet notices an uncomfortable physical intimacy more like lovers than father and daughter. The school sends her to see a urologist before her father removes her from their care.

Because men of wealth and privilege don't do such things, no one trusts their eyes to see what is happening in plain sight.

Morgan establishes the family cruelty necessary to reinforce their superiority early on. Their ancestral legacy is actually a curse that prevents even ordinary love from circulating—between man and wife, father and child, human and animal. We first meet Henry as a child being punished for a cruel prank that kills a neighbor's bull. His father, John Henry, ties him to the whipping post once used for slaves and savages him. John Henry is unconcerned about teaching kindness to animals or even abusing his child. He literally beats the idea that most lives only matter as property into the tender body of his little boy.

Upon discovering his overly attentive mother Lavinia is having an affair with a farmworker named Filip, an outraged Henry tells his father John Henry with full knowledge of the consequences in the Jim Crow South: the Black man will be lynched for outraging the white woman deemed incapable of giving consent. In a perversely oedipal turn, the knowledge adds swagger to the teenager's step as his humiliation of his father sets in motion the unspeakable acts to follow. John Henry does not kill his wife, but he rapes and lands "three hard blows against her head, high enough on the back of the skull so the bruise would not show and where there was no danger of breaking her neck" because only "an animal visibly damages its mate." John Henry further teaches his son that "the poor white serves a useful purpose from time to time" because the "unfathomably stupid and passionate" who "would kill a Catholic but couldn't define one" also "have a keen sense of right and wrong undiluted by relativism" and "carry out justice with alacrity." "'Manners are morals,'"—John Henry repeats what his grandfather taught him—and "'a gentleman always minds his manners . . . until he can no longer afford to.' That's when the Klan comes in handy. They're more discreet these days than they used to be."[22] John Henry's words show the way that class and white supremacy forge an unholy union to uphold Jim Crow even when social conditions are changing; their refusal to see anyone not of their bloodline as more than property warps their souls and justifies their wanton cruelty to man and beast. This is a triumph he won't be able to replicate as easily when his own daughter becomes involved with the Black Irish groom decades later and the relativism his father detested has gained some, but not enough, sway. He won't even know for certain if the carefully linebred Forge heir gestating in Henrietta's womb is his.

Henrietta's gender does not soften the Forge worldview that everything and everyone is just something to own. Even the horses they devote their lives to—carefully raising from babies until they are ready to race or breed—are just objects admired for what they can do for the family honor. The mawkish sentimentality that makes the childhood horse books difficult for adults to read plays no part in her story. You cannot imagine lost scenes of Henrietta cloistered with Misty of Chincoteague, sneaking to the barn in horsey pajamas to give an ancient gelding a stolen sugar cube. Henrietta learns to ride as perfunctorily as she learns to have sex, never taking real pleasure in either. Nature and nurture shape this odd relationship to Thoroughbreds and lovers: her father only comes to admire the breed after watching a particularly cruel breaking in of a young, spirited filly. The horse's complete submission to violence thrills him, setting his life on an unalterable course to seek glory in the Kentucky Derby: "He'd seen the ruling strength of the breaker's body, how dominant it was—a man like more than a man—and how quickly the larger, braver thing succumbed to the one who refused to alter his path, the one who offered no concessions."[23]

It was also this love of conquest that put the baby in Henrietta—whether it was from her father's desire for a perfect heir or Henrietta's seduction of her groom. All of the complicated history of race and consent, the legacy of lynching, are put into play as she, Allmon's wealthy employer, "forms a noose of her arms and slips it over his head, drawing his body near." As the coupling continues, they try to find some common ground as their hard hearts soften—but only to a point. Henrietta is quickly nasty when he does not perform sexually: "Is this always a problem for you?" she asks. "Naw, I just . . . it's not my fault," he stammers. This enrages her, and she resorts to words that whip him with their cruelty: "You know what the problem is with people like you?" she spat. "Self-pity. It's always someone else's fault." Allmon rages back: "Like what—like Black? You're all spoiled inbred racist motherfuckers, but you don't even know it! You're so blind, you can't tell when the person standing in front of you is half-white!" The proud heiress can only scoff at her groom, who wants to claim some of the blood that fuels her pride: "I'm sorry, but if you don't look white, you're not white. At least in the real fucking world."[24]

We never get to know what kind of mother Henrietta would have been if she had been able to reconcile with Allmon in a loving way. Before Allmon learns of her pregnancy, Henry successfully sends the groom away with promises of future wealth if the prize filly Hellsmouth wins the Kentucky Derby. Henrietta was beginning to engage in her own anti-racist inquiry, which the birth of her baby may have solidified for her, by looking at the lie behind the myth:

> Henrietta: Oh, come on, the Throughbred was a late hybridization, a mongrelization. That's why they're so strong.
> Henry: The breed is genetically pure.
> Henrietta: No, they married the sturdy English mares to the fast Moors—
> Henry: Blood will always tell.
> Henrietta: They were looking for free forward motion! Don't you understand?
> Henry: Purity builds the empire.
> Henrietta: They made the world modern![25]

Henrietta was doing nothing less than assaulting the lie white supremacy works so hard to cover up, correcting the fundamental misperception of racial purity naturalized in this breed of horse because, paradoxically, the Thoroughbred itself is of mixed blood. Originally descended from the legendary three sires known as the Godolphin Barb, the Byerly Turk, and the Darley Arabian, the combined speed and stamina needed for racing made these elegant animals the widespread preoccupation of a decidedly horsey nation and its rebellious colonies. In "The Thoroughbred as Cultural Metaphor," Richard Nash sees the ascendancy of the breed as a sleight of hand where English nationalism triumphs over Orientalism: "Like most origin stories, it is a tale considerably more complicated than the fable of tripled paternity most often told. Not only is it a tale implicated in the traffic between kings, emperors, and sultans of the East and West, but it is also inflected by the emerging traffic between the families of royals, aristocrats, and merchants as well."[26] The transatlantic translation of this metaphor gets mightily compromised by slavery and the racist myths bred to justify an inhuman institution. As their ledgers, wills, and account notebooks remind us, for families like the Forges, breeding humans was not merely a theoretical proposition.

Even readers not particularly knowledgeable about horse breeding cringe at Henry's obsession with breeding equine siblings as he desperately tries to re-create Secretariat's greatness at Forge Run Farms. His linebreeding for perfection ultimately results in the magnificent filly Hellsmouth, who will win the Kentucky Derby, but our horror of his obsession stems from his desire to breed another "Thoroughbred" Forge with his daughter. Henry is no run-of-the-mill pedophile who seeks unspeakable pleasure with children for lust. Morgan depicts the brutal narcissism of aristocratic families like the Forges, where nature and nurture foster an inability to see anything other than themselves as subjects of an indelible truth to be perpetuated at all costs.

Henry's mother Lavinia never reflected on how she internalized white supremacy until love began to dismantle the values that decreed Filip was only three-fifths of a human being. In a monologue to a sleeping Henry, unable to hear her literally and symbolically, she talks about "love being something that can only occur between equals." Lavinia acknowledges that she previously had not considered Filip as an equal because "he's Black and he drinks too much." The change occurred after Filip "kissed her with his eyes." "He looked into me," she cries. "No one had ever done that before. Then I was completely and totally ashamed . . . of the glaring inequality that existed between us . . . and from that moment on, against every impediment, I strove to become his equal."[27] Sadly, her internal transformation does little to save Filip's life, and no one ever truly "hears" her repudiation of racism but the reader. Her tale of transformation remains as unwritten as Scipio's, the utter silencing of any stories that debunk purity and white pride.

Although Henrietta was also on the cusp of an internal change that echoes the journey of the voiceless Lavinia, Morgan's invocation of slavery never lets us forget what strands the lovers in a past that is all too present: "Her arms were around him like iron bands." She still cannot understand how she is part of a brutal constellation, that their bodies are entangled in a web that is greater than their individual feelings. After he is flooded with traumatic memories that abruptly end their lovemaking, Henrietta says, "Allmon, tell me why you are not free with me." Dumbfounded, the enraged man rails against the innocence white Americans cling to: "White people—! Y'all don't get it. You really don't . . . Y'all fuck up our lives for fucking hundreds of years and then you tell us we aren't free?" Allmon's words reflect the painful reality inflicted by even "nice white people" who clumsily navigate the odd coexistence of a post-racial yet still white-supremacist present. Morgan depicts how deeply Henrietta has internalized not just ambient racism, but the perverted pride in ownership inherited from her ancestors that dehumanized even the man she is unexpectedly growing to love: "What Henrietta said next shocked her, because she once believed the very opposite, but she recognized the truth of it as soon as it was on her tongue. 'It's not the body I want; it's the man.'" But her default mode gets the best of her in spite of her better intentions. After Henry intervenes to send Allmon away with their prize filly Hellsmouth to the training track to separate the lovers forever, Henrietta rails against the man she loves while she is pregnant (something he did not know when Henry bought him off): "'You know what you are? A stereotype: Are you really going to walk away?'" Her fury escalates with "invective and senseless wounds flowing out her mouth" until "that one vile word, coined long ago and wielded like a white man's axe" escapes her mouth and divides them forever.[28] These tragic scenes show that their groping toward something better is still haunted by the legacy of rape, race, and lynching that doomed Filip and Lavinia, even though Henrietta and Allmon are in the twenty-first century and the promise of their future child points to something better.

I squirmed through Henrietta's pregnancy, propelled by a morbid curiosity to know if the child's sire is Henry or Allmon. The unspeakable acts that broke her were unnamable because her address bore the hallowed name of her ancestors: Forge Run Farm, the inherited legacy of brutal dominion over flora and fauna, beauty and beast in this karsty region of the Bluegrass State. I wept bitter tears when Henrietta died. The handsome heiress succumbed during a difficult childbirth, choosing her son's life over her own. The mystery of the child's paternity was solved by the brown skin. I should have known it was coming; Henry nicknamed her "Ruffian"—the famous filly who competed against the colts but ultimately broke down and had to be destroyed—foreshadowing her pitiless existence where she lived in the gaps between privilege and cruelty as she began to scrutinize the impact of white supremacy on the soul she inherited, like her grandmother before her. Sadly, it was too little, too late for her or Allmon. When angry, she couldn't help but fall back on the Forge pride.

Morgan is ambivalent about the possibility of Henry's redemption. The hardened racist grows to love his grandson in a way he had never loved before, bestowing the name of Samuel, the original Forge patriarch, on the beautiful little baby. To the shock of the world, he repudiates the world of Thoroughbred horse racing, bringing his Triple Crown contender home to become a sort of pet. She ends the tale right before the election of President Obama, musing about the possibility of a Black president someday, something neither Henrietta nor Allmon ever live to see. Although Allmon shoots himself, the tragedy of his death feels horribly inevitable as he cannot escape the intergenerational trauma that leads him to die on the very ground his ancestor Scipio escaped.

Say his name: Allmon Shaughnessy.

Another heavy toll paid to Blood and Soil.

RETURN TO CAROLINA

Morgan's unsettling conclusion offered no solace; Henrietta's story plunged me backwards into a past that became terrifyingly present in elusive snapshots of dramatic scenes that rooted my feet to the floor and stole my breath with little warning. No wonder I had repressed them! They began with the recent decline of my stepmother Alma Faye, who sought forgiveness before her death from a child she had never protected or even loved by sharing her lasting terror of a man dead nearly fifteen years. Whether it was the lingering effect of the stroke or the fear of facing her God, the story that I was a crazy liar that had held strong since I left home nearly thirty years ago vanished over plates of fried shrimp, okra, red rice, and hush puppies. Believing me was her final gift, settling doubts of my sanity that had haunted me since kindergarten.

Why was no one able to see that red lines render the hurt inside them invisible?

Because nobody really cared about what happened behind the closed doors of 808 Browning Drive, Charleston, South Carolina, 29407. That coveted corner lot. There were larger issues at stake. It was the 1970s; people were forgetting their place, walking right over the division between East Oak Forest and Maryville. In fact, Maryville, the historic first African American town in South Carolina, sent its children to Albemarle Elementary alongside the kids from East Oak. Even local restaurants—Bessinger's, Sambo's, the cafeteria behind the Coburg Cow—only segregated by smoking or nonsmoking. Neighborhoods were the last stand.

"The goddamned government can make my daughters go to school with 'em, but they can't make me live with 'em," bellowed my father, six-foot-plus Jack Ansel, who glared at the house catty-cornered to ours as he used brute force and size 13s to sink the For Sale sign deeper into the earth. That Friday night, he took us to Perkin's on Savannah Highway for "breakfast at supper" to issue a stern warning about the son of the new family who had just moved in across the street: "Don't leave the house or the fenced-in backyard," followed by, "Don't play in your very own front yard or you'll get raped by that r*t**d n*****boy."

I did not know what rape meant; neither did my new stepsister. My new stepmom Alma Faye from Green Pond did, and she shook. Even if someone had found a nonconsensual path to Alma Faye's tender spaces, rape was a word reserved for a Black man. Or boy. For Jack Ansel, proud son of a Carolina Klansman, even a seventy-five-year-old dutiful citizen who goes to church, pays his taxes, raises his children, and mows his lawn … is just a boy. A dangerous boy who thinks of nothing—not Civil Rights, not God, not James Baldwin, not where his kids will go to college, not even what he is going to have for lunch or where he might use the facilities in the loosely Confederate conditions that informally exist after the abolition of Jim Crow—nothing except White Women. Jack's girls were in danger because of this "goddamnedn*****r*t**d," and he was not going to stand for it. "Check please," he told the waitress, unconcerned if anyone in the whole place heard every word he said.

The only reliable image I can conjure is a little boy with close-cropped hair in a Hang Ten T-shirt, raising his hand in the friendly gesture known to children worldwide as an invitation to play if the prejudices of their parents did not intervene. Because of this boy, his mother, and his father, a small nuclear unit who only followed the dictates of the American dream by moving into three bedrooms with white shutters and a long porch on Browning Drive, every single white family on every single street—Byron, Barrett, Longfellow, Shelley—raced to put up a For Sale sign to protect their children. The houses were quickly purchased by African American families who still predominate in the middle-class neighborhood to this very day.

Now, those For Sale signs weren't wrong: the families who feared for the safety of their kids were right to be afraid of the predator with a predilection for young flesh who lived on Browning Drive.

They just had the wrong address.

CONCLUSION

Sometime in 1975 or 1976, the Bryant family gathered to watch *Mandingo*, which features a horrific scene of a Black man boiled alive for sleeping with a white woman. Details of the outing are very blurry. I don't remember which theater. All that I remember was a vague fear that any Black boy I ever knew too well would be badly hurt. Alma Faye learned an alternate lesson that survived four brain tumor operations, a stroke exacerbated by diabetes, and early dementia. Her only remaining fear was of the Black male rapist. She would carefully stack used Coke glass bottles against her window to warn of an impending attack. When she was hospitalized at the Medical University of South Carolina, she fretted constantly that a Black man was going to come in her window, even ten floors up. The fact that it was her deceased husband who had sexually assaulted her blood daughter and her stepdaughter as well as his children from previous marriages never undid the big lie of race and rape.

Roger Ebert's 1975 review of the film described it as "racist trash, obscene in its manipulation of human beings and feelings, and excruciating to sit through in an audience made up largely of children." "This is a film I felt soiled by," he continued, and "if I'd been one of the kids in the audience, I'm sure I would have been terrified and grief stricken."[29]

We were—for life. Such moments don't necessarily form in coherent narratives expressed with concrete detail in linear time. They enter the marrow.

I couldn't have named it when I was writing down the sires and dams of Kentucky Derby winners in block script, but it was the pedigreed legacy that makes the Thoroughbred such a powerful cultural metaphor to those anxious about their place in the white world. Following Toni Morrison's advice to seek out texts that explore what white supremacy does to those who cling to its false doctrines, finding the ways that such narratives have fundamentally shaped our worldview, whether we like it or not, makes unpacking cultural metaphors like the Thoroughbred a necessary evil. Interrogating the darker recesses of how this metaphor functions in minds like Henrietta's and mine must be more than solipsistic self-help if we are to heal the primal wound of America—particularly as the "racehorse theory" reasserts itself in rallies across America. Uncoupling the Thoroughbred as a cultural metaphor from general pony madness forces a confrontation with the subtle and not-so-subtle ways our society continues to echo Henry Forge's assertion that purity builds empire as anxiety over America's waning imperial status and changing demographics mounts. It's more than a subtle dog whistle, a naturalized symbol of white supremacy that doesn't overtly challenge American innocence.

I certainly did not want to lose mine. But how could it be otherwise? A child of that man, of that city where the first shots of the Civil War were fired, where Dylann Roof massacred nine people in Bible Study, where classmate Walter Scott was struck five times while running away from a police officer over a broken taillight. As I try to make sense of the thoughts I've shared here, the words of Diane Roberts resonate: "The white woman writing about race is necessarily a double agent, both acting as 'mistress' in controlling her characters and her plot, and identifying with them."[30] I don't fully understand why I cannot get this quotation out of my head. Somehow, it seems to indicate the double bind of writing this essay, of trying to let go of my control as mistress of this narrative to see where it might take me. Frankly, of being afraid where it will take me. It got closer to the personal truths of a pony-mad middle-aged Becky than I desired at the outset, ones that make me want to go back and reframe this as only a reading of C. E. Morgan's novel—to hide once again behind disciplinary expertise and never have to confront where I fit into this world that loves purebreds.

Yet I take heart in the words of Ijeoma Oluo: "The beauty of anti-racism is that you don't have to pretend to be free of racism to be an anti-racist. Anti-racism is the commitment to fight racism wherever you find it, including in yourself. And it's the only way forward."[31] Henrietta was on the cusp of this journey; I too am on an interior journey that frankly never ends. In the classroom, I will continue to try and teach to transgress (thank you bell hooks for the guidance).

In my personal life, too. Because if we don't apply the uncomfortable racial lens that #metoo asks men to place on their behavior to ourselves and our culture, which values Thoroughbreds above everything else, it's likely that one of the passionate white women currently screaming, "No Justice, No Peace" will be the next to hysterically call 911 when a Black body gets in her way as she ignores the little girl hurting right next door.

NOTES

1. Morrison, *Playing in the Dark*. This paraphrase as well as the title and epigraph only begin to suggest how influential Morrison's work was on this essay and, more importantly, the entire way I see the world.
2. Hofstetter, "Lyrical Beasts," 239.
3. Morrison, *Playing in the Dark*, 11. She is arguing for a fundamental shift in the ways scholars read and write about literature: "Above all I am interested in how agendas in criticism have disguised themselves and, in doing so, impoverished the literature it studies," 8–9.
4. Dickinson, "Trump Preached White Supremacy."
5. Case, *The Right Blood*, 50.
6. Case, *The Right Blood*, 52.
7. Stokes, *The Right to Be Well Born*, 10.
8. Black, *War against the Weak*, 25.
9. Sanger, "Fewer and Better Babies." Although her work is infused with sympathy for the struggles of women during childbirth, it shares uncomfortable attitudes with prominent eugenicists: "Fundamentally, Birth Control aims for the creation of a race of Thoroughbreds. To create this race of well-born generations, we insist that the tested principles of sound agriculture and breeding are directly applicable to the human race, no less than to plants and animals."
10. Djikstra, *Evil Sisters*, 434. This paraphrase comes from the brilliant chapter that analyzes how Hitler's anti-Semitic propaganda machine used imagery from F. W. Murnau's *Nosferatu* to conflate the metaphor of the vampire and the rat.
11. Morrison, *Playing in the Dark*, 11.
12. Another animal metaphor helps us to understand the Obama birther controversy. When the president-elect told reporters he might adopt a "mutt like me," controversy erupted from NBC to the *Hindustan Times*. Even Shepherd Fairey, whose iconic HOPE poster galvanized a generation for Obama, did a special "Mutts Like Me" series to support shelter dogs. The tension gets at why these animal metaphors have so much power! Forty-five, who sees himself as a Thoroughbred, could not tolerate that forty-four, who identifies with shelter dogs and mutts, occupied the most powerful place in the world, because he didn't have the appropriate papers/pedigree.
13. Barthes, *Mythologies*, 9.
14. Morrison, *Playing in the Dark*, 11–12.
15. Curry, "He's a Rapist," 132. Curry's essay explores the limitations of intersectionality when it does not take vulnerability of the Black male body into account, something that profoundly influenced my reading of the relationship between Henrietta and Allmon. Overlooking this "has blinded scholars and disciplines from the historical realities of Black male vulnerability to rape and sexual violence. Black males have been characterized as incapable of being victims of rape and as not being vulnerable to the libidinal coercion of white men and white women. The heteronormative narrative

of racism hides the homoerotic nature of slavery and Jim Crow, and negates both Black men's sexual vulnerability and their manhood. Instead, it is claimed that they are neither able to protect Black women nor able to resist the allure of white women. Their rape by white women becomes unimaginable."
16. Wade, "How 'Benevolent Sexism' Drove Dylann Roof's Racist Massacre."
17. This chant of attendees of the now infamous Charlottesville Unite the Right rally is inextricably linked to the Thoroughbred metaphor as Stokes's pleading illustrates in *The Right to Be Well Born*: "For the sake of our 'American baby,' and the future of our American people, will not our Representatives in Congress pass more stringent immigration laws to stop this inflow of diseased blood? It is time we Americans who have patriotism in our hearts, and gratitude to our ancestors for the privations and sufferings they underwent to give us this beautiful land, assert ourselves and announce to the world that America must be for Americans, and not for the imported scum of the earth," 48–49.
18. Morgan, *The Sport of Kings*, 139.
19. One can see how Stokes's idiosyncratic work taps into key themes in Anglo-American culture that Morgan depicts: "Let me give a curious illustration: I once knew intimately a great, grand proud old family, whose name is now absolutely extinct, sprung from one illustrious ancestor. They had a daughter who . . . . ran away with a young, uneducated, but bright Irish groom, whose ancestral breeding was lost. . . . . Of her . . . . sons . . . . one was exceptionally bright; at one moment he showed his high breeding and, at the next, all the characteristics of a tricky suspicious fellow. Now the peacock! Now the duck! Then to watch the countenances of high-bred people in their intercourse with him, for he is exceedingly clever; now they lean forward to catch his witty sentences; suddenly, they draw back, they have caught a whiff of the stable," 47.
20. The repeated reference to Henrietta as Ruffian, the famed Thoroughbred filly who broke down during her match race with Foolish Pleasure in 1975, both literalizes that he sees her as a Thoroughbred and foreshadows her tragic ending.
21. Morgan, *Sport of Kings*, 363.
22. Morgan, *Sport of Kings*, 56–57, 68–69.
23. Morgan, *Sport of Kings*, 22.
24. Morgan, *Sport of Kings*, 331–33232.
25. Morgan, *Sport of Kings*, 379.
26. Nash, "The Thoroughbred as Cultural Metaphor," 250.
27. Morgan, *Sport of Kings*, 71.
28. Morgan, *Sport of Kings*, 348–50, 373.
29. Ebert, "Review of *Mandingo*."
30. Roberts, *The Myth of Aunt Jemima*, 19.
31. Oluo, Twitter post.

WORKS CITED

Barthes, Roland. *Mythologies*. Translated by Annette Lavers. New York: Hill and Wang, 1972.

Black, Edwin. *War against the Weak: Eugenics and America's Campaign to Create a Master Race*. New York: Four Walls Eight Windows, 2003.

Case, Carol. *The Right Blood: America's Aristocrats in Thoroughbred Racing*. Rutgers, NJ: Rutgers

University Press, 2000.

Curry, Tommy. "He's a Rapist, Even When He's Not: Richard Wright's Account of Black Male Vulnerability in the Raping of Willie McGee." In *The Politics of Richard Wright: Perspectives on Resistance*, edited by Jane Ana Gordon and Cyrus Ernesto Zirakzadeh. Lexington: University Press of Kentucky, 2018.

Dickinson, Tim. "Trump Preached White Supremacy in Minnesota, America Barely Noticed: Touting the 'Racehorse Theory' and the Superiority of Genes to White Minnesotans, Trump Explicitly Embraced Eugenics." *Rolling Stone*, September 22, 2020.

Djikstra, Bram. *Evil Sisters: The Threat of Female Sexuality and the Cult of Manhood*. New York: Henry Holt & Co., 1998.

Ebert, Roger. "Review of *Mandingo*." July 25, 1975. Available at https://www.rogerebert.com.

Hofstetter, Angela. "Lyrical Beasts: Equine Metaphors of Race, Class and Gender in Contemporary Hollywood Cinema." PhD diss., Indiana University, 2009.

Morgan, C. E. *The Sport of Kings*. New York: Farrar, Strauss & Giroux, 2016.

Morrison, Toni. *Playing in the Dark: Whiteness and the Literary Imagination*. New York: Vintage Books, 1993.

Nash, Richard. "The Thoroughbred as Cultural Metaphor." In *The Culture of the Horse: Status, Discipline, and Identity in the Early Modern World*, edited by Karen Raber and Treva J. Tucker. New York: Palgrave Macmillan, 2005.

Oluo, Ijeoma. Twitter post. July 14, 2019. Available at https://twitter.com/ijeomaoluo/.

Roberts, Diane. *The Myth of Aunt Jemima: White Women Representing Black Women*. New York: Routledge, 1994.

Sanger, Margaret. "Fewer and Better Babies." In *The Public Writing and Speeches of Margaret Sanger*. Available at https://sanger.hosting.nyu.edu.

Stokes, W. E. D. *The Right to Be Well Born, or Horse Breeding in Relation to Eugenics*. New York: C.J. O'Brien, 1917.

Wade, Lisa. "How 'Benevolent Sexism' Drove Dylann Roof's Racist Massacre." *Washington Post*, June 21, 2015.

From Apes to Stags

Black Men, White Women, and the Animals That Code Them in Horror Cinema

Jonathan W. Thurston-Torres

When I was an undergraduate, I took a course on "Animals in Film" with Colin Dayan and Jennifer Fay. One of the first films we watched in the class was the original *King Kong* (1933) by Merian C. Cooper and Ernest B. Schoedsack. I had never seen it before, and what struck me in that initial viewing were the racial elements throughout it. It was all black-and-white (making it possibly one of the first black-and-white films I had ever seen by that point), so you really saw Kong as black compared to Fay Wray, seemingly dressed all in white. The tribal island village must have seemed so exotic to contemporary audiences, and they would have agreed with the colonial vision the film portrays. And who can forget the famed scene of the black ape mounting a symbol of modern civilization, the Empire State Building, while being shot down for daring to try to possess white beauty for himself?

After the screening was over though, my reaction was . . . confusion. I did not understand how something so racially troubled and indicative of the United States' racist and colonial past (and present) was considered a film classic that warranted remakes and sequels, including (at the time of this writing) the recent *Godzilla vs. Kong* (2021). In answer to my own meager response paper to the film, Dayan commented that my calling Kong a "slave of civilization" was poignant, that indeed, "without Kong," she said, "there would be no white supremacy, no ideal of whiteness." It was in that moment, and throughout that semester, that I realized that racial histories are intertwined with animal ones, and, in horror cinema specifically, directors advance animals as a means of conversing with cultural ideas about Black masculinity, just like the titular ape in *King Kong*.

Horror cinema itself has a fraught relationship with racial politics. Robin R. Means Coleman presents a history of Black horror cinema (and Black people *in* horror cinema) in *Horror Noire* (2011). The narrative starts with an analysis of Georges Méliès's *Off to Bloomingdale Asylum* (1901): "The film's 'Negroes' were performed by White actors in blackface, who were charged, seemingly, to depict the violence around crossing racial boundaries, the tensions around racial masquerade, and finally the brutish end to the metaphorical White man's burden with the destruction of the Negro."[1] From the literal horrors of dramatic (mis)representation, Coleman moves on to the 1930s to discuss "jungle fever" through *King Kong* and then the zombie, voodoo, and devil films of the 1940s. In these films, as Mimi Sheller has argued, the Haitian zombie story becomes reinterpreted and reshaped by white westerners to create new cultural fears for themselves.[2] Coleman proceeds in this manner all the way to the present day. And these horror films often comment specifically on Black masculinity and specific interracial relationships, those of Black men and white women. As Coleman says, "The real horror [in these films] is the threat made against a White woman."[3]

Yet Coleman overlooks the role of the nonhuman animals in these horror films, and this neglect has been representative of the field, seen elsewhere in Wilson's *Willful Monstrosity* and O'Brien's *Black Masculinity on Film*. Nonetheless, nonhuman animals factor into our racial discourses, and, as Claude Lévi-Strauss (in)famously said, they are good "to think [with]."[4] In Donna Haraway's *Companion Species Manifesto*, she resists the Lévi-Strauss argument that "Dogs are not surrogates for theory; they are not here just to think with. They are here to live with."[5] While the films covered in this chapter engage with the symbolic, I posit that the films respond to real human race history as well as specific animal-human relationships. More specifically—to abuse some alliteration—the specific species matter for these animal-race discourses. For example, how would the race narrative have been different in *King Kong* if the eponymous king was a golden carp? Or a white wolf? Or a monarch butterfly? What is it about the primate nature of Kong that codes to viewers his racialized status and the metaphoric interracial relationship he has with the white heroine?[6] Why is it that the antagonist of *Candyman* is ravaged by and weaponizes bees? And why does Jordan Peele choose a stag to represent Chris in *Get Out*? Horror cinema often invokes the animal—with its specific species—in order to talk about race and enter into these contemporary discourses of race thinking. And this type of reading is markedly different from looking at these films and—perhaps reductively—saying, "These films animalize Blackness." Our interpretation changes when we say, "No, this film ape-ifies Blackness. This one bee-ifies Blackness. This one deer-ifies Blackness." The specific species used matter for a reading of Black masculinity and interracial relationships in horror cinema when they are coded with animals. These arguments echo much of Alexander G. Weheliye's work in *Habeas Viscus*, when he defines racialization as "the political, economic, social, and cultural disciplining . . . of the Homo sapiens species into assemblages of the human, not-quite-human, and nonhuman."[7] This idea is essential for understanding how a golden retriever, for example, can be granted not-quite-human status by white people, while a Black teenager is designated nonhuman.

An awareness of this blend of race studies and critical animal studies shapes our understanding of not just these horror films but also the genre's presentation of Black masculinity and interracial relationships. If, as Jeffrey Jerome Cohen argues, the "monster's body is a cultural body," then what happens at the site where the body is animalized?[8] And not just animalized but [specific species]-ized? In horror cinema, many racist stereotypes have been reified through this animalization, playing into many of the eugenics thoughts of the 1930s. The interracial relationship has—in many ways, even to this day—been characterized as one of bestial violence. However, horror also offers the means to flip the narrative. Horror film can also be transgressive through its animal-race coding, especially when we revisit the question of which species is used to characterize racial difference.

Three films in particular that stand out as potential milestones in the narrative of Black masculinity and interracial relationships characterized through animals in horror cinema are *King Kong, Candyman,* and *Get Out*. They respond to cultural anxieties of their time that are situated within racial discourse, and while the first two do so to advance racism, Peele uses the animal to fight racism. While I do not see in these films a clear trajectory of social progress, there is a sense that the way we use animals—and the way we read animals—matters increasingly, and horror cinema is becoming increasingly aware of that fact. Horror cinema might now be realizing that the animal can indeed be used as a site of resistance when it comes to depictions of interracial relationships.

EUGENICS AND *KING KONG*

At the start of the 1930s, eugenics and "scientific racism" was still dominant in much of American science circles. The American Eugenics Society and Eugenics Records Office were going strong and being funded by tycoons like Rockefeller. And in 1932, "Germany became a senior partner with the United States in the international eugenics movement," with American scientists lauding the work of Hitler and the Nazi Regime.[9] While racial anthropology would start to disprove much of polygenics and eugenics throughout this decade, it was still—and would remain for a few decades more—commonly thought that race was purely biological. So, perhaps it is no surprise that horror cinema of the decade frequently portrayed nonwhite races as primates, marking them as further back on the evolutionary chain in the 1930s perspective. The United States, as Jessica Metzler has argued, held a "public fascination with racialized, filmic representations of apes in studio pictures."[10] At least four horror films of the decade specifically follow this narrative—*Ingagi* (1930), *Island of Lost Souls* (1932), *The Monster Walks* (1932), and *King Kong* (1933). They all work to reify the eugenicist belief of nonwhite races being biologically inferior through an apification.

In the above-mentioned films, a primate serves as the dominant antagonistic force against the white protagonists. In *Ingagi*, a pseudo-documentary portrays African women (really white actresses in blackface) having sex with gorillas, presented as a spectacle of the Belgian Congo. *Island of Lost Souls* tackles Wells's novel *Island of Dr. Moreau* and makes the animal-people all primate in nature, really leaning on eugenicist thought of the time. *The Monster Walks* also plays on the idea that primates—in this case, an ape—are dangerous in their similarity but inferiority to us "normal" humans. And the infamous *King Kong* is well-known for its racial implications, of course.

As Gail Dines notes in "King Kong and the White Woman," the anxiety addressed with such films (and even interracial pornographic texts, Dines argues) is "what happens if Black masculinity is allowed to go uncontained."[11] In this film, the white heroine Ann Darrow is recruited for a mysterious film project that takes the crew to a hidden island populated by non-white tribal peoples. The civilization conducts ritual sacrifice to the apparent god of the island, the gigantic gorilla Kong, and Ann is eventually taken for such a sacrifice.[12] After she is saved by the film crew, however, the film director, Carl Denham, orchestrates a capture of Kong so he can be put on display in New York City. Predictably, this goes horribly wrong, and Kong escapes, taking Ann with him to the top of the Empire State Building, where he is gunned down by planes. And throughout the film, there are these heavily racialized and psychosexual moments that really speak to underlying political messages and contemporary discourses of racial politics and sexuality.

White femininity is definitely sexualized throughout the film. Ann exists to be a sexual object in the film with very little agency. While she is certainly the object of many white men's gazes throughout the film, the three who most view her are Denham, Jack, and, of course, the voyeuristic intended viewer of the film. While on the boat, Denham focuses the camera on Ann, having her enact different emotions, facial expressions, and even scenarios. When asked about his filming practices, Denham recalls a time he was in Africa: "I'd have got a swell picture of a charging rhino, but the cameraman got scared. The damned fool. I was right there with a rifle. Seemed he didn't trust me to get the rhino before it got him. I haven't fooled with cameramen since. Do the trick myself." Here, Denham notes that, for him, filming is connected to wildlife and nature, and he notes it is connected to Africa for him. Denham's lens is a particular one. During this scene of filming Ann, we the viewer see through Denham's camera. She becomes an object and spectacle for *our* amusement, almost breaking the fourth wall. The film within the film encourages the white men of the audience: This woman is yours. Just give her a command, and she will do it. And even outside this scene later, it is up to Jack to come and repeatedly save Ann throughout the film, in his role as the Heroic White Man.

But after landing on the island, we encounter the white colonial vision. The racialized native tribe is engaging in a ritual sacrifice to Kong, which the film crew interrupts. This island becomes a stark contrast to New York City. Everything here is characterized as primitive and therefore inferior or lesser. Everything can only serve to be spectacle and, more generally, an object for consumption.[13] Just as the people are "backward," so too is nature, still having dinosaurs roaming the land. Kong is situated as the island's avatar and god, the epitome of all this perceived backwardness and all this Blackness. And, as the natives believed, Kong loved Ann. He protects her on numerous occasions, but all the white film crew know is that Kong must be stopped and is an active threat to Ann. After all, the way they see it, she is *their* spectacle, not his.

When Kong is brought to New York City, he breaks out of his bondage and takes Ann back before climbing the Empire State Building. He strips away the little civilization Denham had tried to put on him and refuses the role of spectacle. He refuses to "play white." And in doing so, he is ultimately gunned down, still hoping to protect Ann. Denham says of the death, "It was Beauty killed the Beast." While this all speaks volumes about perceptions of racial performativity then, the scene also shows a cynicism toward interracial relationships, a belief that *all* interracial relationships are destined to be Beauty and the Beast tales, where the white woman is always the Beauty and the Black man is always the Beast.

This film, like *Island of Lost Souls*, *Ingagi*, and *The Monster Walks*, corresponds to contemporary notions of eugenics. In Robert Yerkes's (influential American eugenicist from the '20s and '30s as well as a primatologist and chief psychologist for the Army) foreword to *A Study of American Intelligence* (1923), he says, "No one of us as a citizen can afford to ignore the menace of race deterioration or the evident relations of immigration to national progress and welfare."[14] Yerkes was far from alone in his view that nonwhite races were inferior and, therefore, closer to primates.

> [Other] American eugenicists, who realized that their policies would never move as fast or be carried out as thoroughly as was being done in Germany, envied the Nazis and became cheerleaders for Hitler. . . . Thus. . . . many American eugenicists supported Hitler and Nazism intellectually, with moral (or we might say immoral), political, and financial support. After all, American eugenicists had essentially written Nazi ideology and policy.[15]

The natives in *King Kong* resemble this eugenicist view of far-off people of color engaging in portrayed-as-primal activities and showing an almost animal intelligence, only to be crushed in

Kong's wake like insects. Kong's and the tribe's inability to speak "proper" English contributes to an overall image of the barbarity of racial alterity understood by American eugenics arguments. Carl Brigham in his aforementioned *Study of American Intelligence* summed up the dominant arguments alongside his own: "Our results showing the marked intellectual inferiority of the negro are corroborated by practically all of the investigators who have used psychological tests on white and negro groups."[16] The depiction of both Kong and the island's people in the film reveals this vision that is both colonial and eugenicist, offering a capitalist opportunity in this far-off land as well as characterizing the perceived inferiority of the native people as being "natural" or endemic to their skin color.

The Black figure Kong and his infatuation with the white Ann speak to eugenics arguments about the perceived risk of "miscegenation," such as Carl Brigham's from 1923: "We [Americans] must face a possibility of racial admixture that is infinitely worse than that faced by any European country to-day, for we are incorporating the negro into our racial stock, while all of Europe is comparatively free from this taint."[17] That final word, *taint*, seems to be the ultimate risk in *King Kong*—not that Kong will actively hurt Ann, but that she will somehow be tainted by his Blackness. As Denham hints in his final lines of the film, it is known by at least some characters that Kong would not intentionally hurt Ann, and, in fact, he does much to protect her. If killing Kong was to be read as an act of defense, it was not as defense from violence but as defense from the potential for tainting that Brigham warns against.

When we look closely at *King Kong*, we see more than just an elision occurring, one of the Black human and the nonhuman ape: we see a cautionary tale about the perceived taboo of interracial relations. We see a popular narrative emerge that stems from both older and contemporary eugenics literature that Black humans are both less intelligent and closer to primates. Indeed, Kong's species is used to dehumanize Blackness and promote a specific racial order and hierarchy that resembles a species order, where not just *man* comes out as the top of the food chain, but specifically the *white man*. The vision of *King Kong* reifies this eugenic fantasy and weaponizes the black primate to conflate racial Blackness with, to use a phrase of Yerkes, "almost [but not quite] human" status.

BEES AND THE PHALLIC STINGER OF *CANDYMAN*

About sixty years after *King Kong*, considerably after the Civil Rights Movement was considered over, the American '90s was a decade full of new variations of racism and changes to the popular racial discourses. The London *Telegraph* was calling the America-based Pioneer Fund a neo-Nazi organization.[18] Star of *The Golden Palace* (the spinoff of *The Golden Girls*) Blanche Devereaux argues with a Black hotel manager about the allowance of a Confederate flag.[19] And Supreme Court associate judge nominee Clarence Thomas was accused of sexual harassment by Anita Hill in 1991, and his interracial marriage was also questioned by the public: "Many blacks questioned the 'blackness' of a man who embraces a conservative philosophy and is married to a white woman."[20] And Black masculinity sees a new animal avatar in horror cinema, and this time in insect form.

Candyman begins with graduate student Helen Lyle learning about the eponymous antagonist for a research project. The film is set in Chicago, where we follow Lyle as she traverses the different classes of life, from a nice dinner with Professor Purcell to Lyle's own apartment, to the housing project known as Cabrini-Green, where Candyman seems to thrive. For most of the first half of the film, we are trying to fit together the pieces of the puzzle of the urban legend alongside Lyle, listening to her interviews and following her investigations.

But it's not until around the middle of the film that we truly get Candyman's backstory. It starts with the simple, yet telling, "Candyman was the son of a slave." After the Civil War, his father created a machine for mass production of shoes, and that gave them quite a fortune. Candyman went to "the best schools," and he grew up in "polite society," eventually becoming a talented artist known for doing portraits for upper-class families to showcase their wealth. However, his hamartia, it would seem, was love: "He was hired by a rich [white] landowner to capture his daughter's virginal beauty. Of course, they fell deeply in love, and she became pregnant." The landowner's revenge was swift:

> Her father executed a terrible revenge. He paid a pack of brutal hooligans to do the deed. They chased Candyman through the town to Cabrini Green . . . where they proceeded to saw off his right hand with a rusty blade. And no one came to his aid. But this was just the beginning of his ordeal. Nearby there was an apiary. Dozens of hives filled with hungry bees. They smashed the hives and stole the honeycomb . . . and smeared it over his prone, naked body. Candyman was stung to death by the bees. They burned his body on a giant pyre . . . then scattered his ashes over Cabrini Green.

And this violence is what created the Candyman as he appears in the film: a murderer with a hook for a hand and bees at his disposal. By the end of the film, it's fire that once again destroys him, making Lyle the new urban legend.

Violence in Candyman's origin story, though, is racialized, sexualized, gendered, and socioeconomically classed. It is clear in the film that he became this "monster" because of a generations-past racist landowner. That racism is also gendered: it is not just because he is Black that he is killed, but because he is a Black *man* who fell for the landowner's white daughter. After all, Candyman's own backstory prioritizes informing the viewer about what schools he went to and how the money was passed down in his family; likewise, even in death, it is because the landowner *paid* "a pack of brutal hooligans to do the deed." At a glance, the bees seem like only a trivial aspect of his death and the violence inflicted on him.

Despite Candyman's origin story as victim, though, his role as monster-antagonist in the narrative seems to serve as a natural progression, as if we should now read Lyle as the next white woman "victim" of Candyman's rapacious nature. The origin story stands at odds with the main plot of the film. As Natalie Wilson argues in *Willful Monstrosity*, "This framing story references America's historical obsession with 'miscegenation,' one which fueled the construction of black men as sexual beasts threatening white femininity. Yet, in *Candyman* this history is used not to condemn white male supremacy and its horrors, but rather to cast the black male protagonist as monstrous."[21] If anything, the film's main plot only further serves to *defend* the intentions of the murderous landlord, as Candyman now targets a new white woman, Lyle, both physically and sexually, encouraging viewers to hope for someone, anyone, maybe even a "pack of brutal hooligans," to take Candyman out before the protagonist is killed. Interracial relationships here are characterized by that intense violence: in both the past and the present in the film, death and violence follow whenever a Black man falls for a white woman. And the bees are soon to follow, too.

The bees in this film serve as more than just a feature of Candyman's backstory and one of his weapons of choice. They also speak to the socioeconomic class of the white characters of the past, connecting the landowner's family to a real-world family that innovated the Illinois and American beekeeping industry. The bees further engage with the common myths of bees acting as symbols for sexual violence and penetration, as I show later in this section.[22] By using both historicist and comparatist approaches, one can see the bees in *Candyman* as actually signifying more than just an image of general violence. These combined layers of meaning paint a picture of Candyman that contributes to contemporary race discourses.

In real life, bees have an interesting history in the time surrounding the American Civil War, making it curious that *Candyman* situates the apiary in the context of a wealthy white landowner's domain in Chicago. It is hard not to think of the Battle of Antietam (1862):

> As the 132nd was advancing on the Roulette farm, a shot from a Confederate battery slammed into the Roulette bee yard. The result must have verged on the macabre. Some men dropped their muskets and ran into nearby fields, while others slapped their clothes and batted at the angry honey bees, Apis mellifera L. In the meantime, more Confederate artillery shells and bullets were finding their marks among the Union troops.[23]

With bees being so formidable in the historic past and part of the Civil War (see Miller for even more examples), the success of apiculture comes into question for us. And where did American beekeeping really, pardon the pun, take flight? Would you believe it was actually in Illinois, where *Candyman* is set? The Dadant family settled in the United States around the time of the Civil War and became an immediately successful beekeeping industry. Their own webpage (yes, they are still successful today as one of the largest producers of beekeeping equipment in the United States) says this of their Civil War past: "By the end of the Civil War, Charles had nine colonies of honeybees, and traveled with his young son, C. P. Dadant across the Mississippi River to sell honey and beeswax in a neighboring town. His interest in making quality candles grew from his love and knowledge of beekeeping."[24] While one can easily envision the Dadant family to be the landowners of *Candyman*, with their interest in both fire and bees, what is perhaps more productive is seeing the ways that the film was addressing not just race in isolation through its bee imagery but also class, tying the two together in complex ways.

This literary tradition of the sexual bee becomes weaponized to dangerous extremes in *Candyman*. Jean Cooper in particular speaks to the erotic implications of the bee: "[Bees], with Cupids, are ravishers of flowers and hearts and personify a *kiss* [my emphasis] which extracts honey but pierces the heart; a symbol which is found both in Greek and Oriental erotics. The sting of a bee has phallic connotations."[25] As Cooper's work came out the same year as the *Candyman* film, it is fascinating to see the kiss evoked here. It is that same erotic but deadly kiss that binds Candyman to Lyle in the present in the film. It is one of the only actual uses of the bees for Candyman, who usually uses his hook to murder, not the bees. Even when he is preparing for the kiss, he strips, revealing his ribcage and showing the bees in a horrific yet erotic display. The bees, therefore, are an extension of his sexual desire.

In the context of the film's racial politics, the bees are an animal signifier for Candyman's desire for white women—coded in the film as inappropriate. In the past, they serve as a weaponized, wealthy whiteness that punishes interracial sex. In the present for the film, the bees perhaps stand for the same thing, only this time punishing the white woman for her willingness to kiss a Black man. Indeed, the film makes it seem as if Helen *deserved* her eventual death for submitting to him. Coleman, too, reads the apian kiss into race relations: "The moment of miscegenation is punished as 'bees stream from his mouth. Thus . . . horror operates here to undermine the acceptability of interracial romance.'"[26] The film relies on bees, therefore, not just to add to "monstrosity" or simply to animalize Candyman, but also to speak to these larger race issues.

DEER HUNTING AND WHITE FAMILIES IN *GET OUT*

However, animals do not have to have a negative impact on race representation in horror. Jordan Peele's award-winning 2017 film *Get Out* manages to create a consistent animal narrative that works to speak *against* both racism in history and in horror cinema—namely, using deer.[27] *Get Out* is a film about Chris, a young Black man, going to meet his white girlfriend Rose's parents. However, (spoiler alert), the family's children, including Rose, work to bring Black people to the house to be trapped in a eugenics experiment where the elders of the family can take over their exoticized Black bodies. By the end of the film, Chris manages to escape Rose, her family, and the house and make it back to safety, leaving the carnage of the white family behind him. The film largely plays off of racial tropes in horror films. For example, rather than the Black character dying first, he's the main character, and he survives! Rather than staying in the house and investigating as the average white horror protagonist does, Chris immediately tries to "get out" once he knows something's up.

The deer here has several important inclusions in the film, spread out over three major scenes. The first involves Chris and Rose hitting a deer on the way to her parents' house. The second scene has Rose's dad making statements about deer and deer hunting that closely align with the way their family hunts Black people. And the final scene of interest is when Chris actually weaponizes a trophy deer head to attack the family in his escape from the house near the end of the film. Each of these scenes contributes to an overall narrative about the deer in the context of race discourse.

One important symbolic shift in Peele's story is that the chosen species is *not* a predator or otherwise coded as inherently violent or aggressive. Peele goes with the deer/buck/stag, more of a docile prey animal. Donaldson and Kymlicka call the deer a "liminal animal," a "non-domesticated species who [has] adapted to life among humans."[28] Indeed, the deer navigates both the domestic and the wild, both in real life and in *Get Out*, reflecting its multifaceted nature of adorable fauna, agricultural pest, object of "redneck" hunting rites, and frequent threat to automobile windshields everywhere. *Get Out* takes these multiple roles and negotiates them alongside racial narratives in unique ways for the horror cinema genre.

Early in the film, Chris and Rose are driving down to the Armitage house. While talking, Rose hits a deer in the road, causing it to go into the woods. After the car stops, Chris goes out into the woods to see "if it's okay." He locks eyes with the deer after following its wail before returning to the car, where a police officer interrogates the couple. While the officer starts by telling them they should have called animal control, he starts harassing Chris specifically for his driver's license, not really caring to see Rose's because she is not the person of color here. This is a very tense scene until the officer finally lets the couple leave.

This scene brings up a lot of connections throughout the film. The deer's death reminds Chris of his own mother's death, and we start to see how Chris, too, is a "deer in the headlights" when faced with his own internal guilt. In the police scene, Chris barely gets a word in edgewise, caught between the two white people talking over him, one of whom is a police officer. The juxtaposition of the deer accident against the police conversation is uncanny. Just as a white woman does not see the deer in time, so too do the officer and woman look over and talk over Chris, objectifying him and refusing him the right to speak.

Another scene that invokes the deer happens when the couple finally make it inside the Armitage house. Throughout the house, we see a number of taxidermied deer heads. This image is an immediate contrast to the previous scene. Where Chris felt sympathy toward the hit deer, here the deer is an object of status, a premonition of the danger to come. When Rose tells her father, Dean, that they hit a deer coming in, he responds, "You know what I say. One down... a few hundred thousand to go.... Those things are everywhere up here, Chris; like rats. The damage they've done to the ecology alone." And then the tour begins immediately afterward. Dean's words echo a lot of eugenics rhetoric alongside that of trophy hunting, and they also bring to mind the interracial connotation behind a "buck."

In Keith M. Harris's analysis of filmic black masculinity, he discusses Donald Bogle's *Toms, Coons, Mulattoes, Mammies, and Bucks* (1973) in terms of its "catalogue of stock figures, archetypes, and tropes of blackness."[29] One of the titular tropes is of course the "buck," which Harris understands as "overly sexual, and therefore contained, black men."[30] This long-standing archetype of Black men as both sexual and contained speaks to American beliefs of animal domestication and animal control. In rural areas, deer seem to multiply (I say this as someone who grew up in rural Tennessee), and that phenomenon becomes coded in rampant sexuality and becomes a perceived problem for civilization to thrive. The idea of the racial "buck" relies on similar codes of sexuality and domestication. Dean talks in these specific terms, too. He says, "those things are everywhere," hinting at that sexuality, but also gestures toward the perceived need for population control through the common rhetoric of calling out "damage they've done to the ecology alone."[31] And yet, in response to these beliefs he holds, he actively hunts deer and keeps their heads as trophies for the house, much as he objectifies and fetishizes Black people in his family's sickening multigenerational hunts.

The final deer scene in the film occurs when Chris manages to break free of his bondage and wrest one of the trophy deer heads off the wall. He then runs Dean through with its antlers, killing him, as well as setting off a fire in the house when the fallen Dean knocks over a lit candle. The scene speaks a lot to role reversal. As this is definitely a turning point in the film, where Chris is finally able to work his way out of the house, it is empowering to see him be able to take this frequent symbol of victimhood in the film and use it against Dean. Further, the scene speaks to a continuation of the hunting metaphor throughout the film.

Suddenly, his "prey" status is a tool of agency as opposed to a hindrance. Dean's "trophies" are now viable weapons, and Chris no longer has to look down at the dying deer with empathy; instead, he is able to, in a way, team up with the deer to make his escape. If we were to read the deer as a vehicle for discussing race, then we see that Chris is taking up his own Blackness and a kind of multigenerational history (the "bucks" of the past) and wielding *that* against Dean. He actively resists the "buck" imagery of filmic traditions, eschewing his relationship with Rose and refusing to be "contained." He leans on the liminal status of the deer symbolically to subvert Dean's expectations as well as the horror genre's.

In *Racism as Zoological Witchcraft: A Guide to Getting Out*, Aph Ko reads in *Get Out* white supremacy as a form of "zoological witchcraft," where "the white people and the one Asian guest engage in racial rituals anchored to stripping the Black body of its essence and repurposing it to empower their own fantasies." These rituals contribute to the film's discourse of animal-race politics in such a way that what is animal and what is racial other are blurred together in ways that defy the categorical thinking of intersectionality. Being white in this film is to be consumptive. Being Black in this film is to be a target for a zoological "racial zombification."[32] And the animals here are not "just a metaphor for the violence people of color experience. Jordan Peele shows us how animals are *simultaneously* a casualty of white supremacist violence."[33] The elision of anti-racism and animal rights activism that Aph Ko sees here, seen also through Boisseron's work, speaks volumes about the depth of animal-race work done in the film, but it is the transformation of filmic racialized animality that makes the film really transgressive, in its pointing to films of the past and responding to those tropes with intentionality.

The film relies on animal imagery in a race horror setting to transgress against previous conventions. In some ways, Peele uses similar ontological patterns: it's the *Black* character who gets an animal avatar. The animal connects to violence in the relationship. Also, the animal engages in a plot-like structure all on its own. Just as King Kong moves from the island to the city and Candyman's bees move from past to present, *Get Out*'s deer move from passive to active. However, where Peele diverges from these conventions is on the overall critical level. The deer becomes a site of resistance for Peele, a place for him to show Black struggles today, in horror cinema, and even on an animal-symbolic level, and *at the same time* the deer too is racialized and interpreted as a fellow victim of white supremacy.

ANIMALS AS A SITE OF RESISTANCE

We see with *Get Out* a way to incorporate animals in race horror cinema that actually *resists* racist traditions. The film actively engages in a metaphoric paradigm in horror film by associating the Black man in an interracial relationship with a specific animal, but then disrupts that paradigm by changing the type of species. Peele ignores the predatory or violent animal imagery often associated with Black sexuality in horror (like the primate of *King Kong* or the bees of *Candyman*) and takes an often-used animal racist slur, turning it into an emblem of empowerment and agency. By the end, we see his work to reappropriate "buck" for Black Americans, placing power in the shared commonalities between Chris and the hunted buck. Peele, as Boisseron envisions in *Afro-Dog*, "show[s] how those two subjectivities, the animal and the black ... can defiantly come together to form an interspecies alliance against the hegemonic (white, human, patriarchal), dominating voice."[34]

Boisseron speaks heavily to the possibility for joint activism when it comes to critical race theory and critical animal studies. In her introduction to *Afro-Dog*, she outlines a goal of hers: "[*Afro-Dog*] engages in a corrective tactic, as it seeks to counterbalance a recent discourse that has served the animal cause by utilizing race as a leverage point. The challenge, however, is to be mindful of not over-correcting this imbalance by emphasizing black suffering to the detriment of animal suffering, and thus re-inscribing the contention."[35] This balance is important, too, when analyzing horror films. In *Get Out*, for example, the film is anti-racist at the same time that it's anti-hunting. Dean does not just represent a person who kills Black people as part of a generational scheme; his initial introduction also speaks to his stance of pro-hunting. *Get Out* makes a point here that Black people are one of many other hunted animals in the United States, occupying ultimately the same hierarchical position.

As both scholars and consumers of film, when watching these kinds of films, we should make sure not just to ask the question of "Why animals?" but also, "Why this specific species of animal?" As these three case studies have shown, species matters, and the creative decisions that dictate the species often respond to both contemporary and historical traditions of race/racism and animal domestication. If horror is what Jeffrey Jerome Cohen says and is a response to cultural anxieties, then let's explore how the animals of race-focused horror are used and *can* be used to respond to both racism and animal issues in the world outside of the screen.

NOTES

1. Coleman, *Horror Noire*, 15.
2. Sheller, *Consuming the Caribbean*, 168.
3. Coleman, *Horror Noire*, 52.
4. Lévi-Strauss, *Totemism*, 89.
5. Haraway, *Companion Species Manifesto*, 5.
6. For convenience's sake (and brevity's), when using the term "interracial relationships" in this chapter, I am talking specifically about Black man–white woman relationships.
7. Weheliye, *Habeas Viscus*, 43.
8. Cohen, "Monster Culture," 12.
9. Sussman, *The Myth of Race*, 114.
10. Metzler, "Lusty Ape-men," 31.
11. Dines, "King Kong," 292–93.
12. It would be remiss not to give credit to whom Daniel O'Brien calls the "king among bit players," Noble Johnson, who plays the native chief in this scene. O'Brien discusses much of Johnson's racial stereotyping and the ways that Johnson navigated race in cinema given his light skin tone; *Black Masculinity on Film*, 55.
13. See "Eating the Other," in bell hooks, *Black Looks*.
14. Yerkes, "Foreword," vii.
15. Sussman, *The Myth of Race*, 109–10.
16. Brigham, *A Study of American Intelligence*, 190.
17. Brigham, *A Study of American Intelligence*, 209.
18. MacIntyre, "The New Eugenics."
19. Sotkin, "Camp Town Races."
20. Williams, "In a 90's Quest," 1.
21. Wilson, *Willful Monstrosity*, 95.
22. While bees also have some positive connotations—"busy as a bee," for example—the ones in the film are certainly presented as monstrous and an extension of both Candyman's and the white landowner's monstrosity, so my analysis does prioritize the more violent characteristics of the insect.
23. Miller, "Historical Natural History."

24. Dadant, "Our History."
25. Jean C. Cooper, *Symbolic and Mythological Animals*, 30–31.
26. Coleman, *Horror Noire*, 190, quoting Pinedo, *Recreational Terror*, 131.
27. I was most inspired to watch the film when I heard Annette LePique's conference paper at MMLA in 2019 on Black masculinity and the buck imagery in *Get Out*.
28. Donaldson and Kymlicka, *Zoopolis*, 210.
29. Harris, *Boys, Boyz, Bois*, 41.
30. Harris, *Boys, Boyz, Bois*, 41.
31. Interestingly, Dean ignores the countless accounts of damage done to the ecology by white people alone, such as the eradication of wolves in New York.
32. Ko, *Racism*, 65.
33. Ko, *Racism*, 64.
34. Boisseron, *Afro-Dog*, xxv.
35. Boisseron, *Afro-Dog*, xiv.

WORKS CITED

Boisseron, Bénédicte. *Afro-Dog: Blackness and the Animal Question*. New York: Columbia University Press, 2018.

Brigham, Carl. *A Study of American Intelligence.* Princeton, NJ: Princeton University Press, 1923.

Cohen, Jeffrey Jerome. "Monster Culture (Seven Theses)." In *Monsters*, edited by Brandy Ball Blake and L. Andrew Cooper, 11–33. Southlake, TX: Fountainhead Press, 2012.

Coleman, Robin R. Means. *Horror Noire: Blacks in American Horror Films from the 1890s to Present*. New York: Routledge, 2011.

Cooper, Jean C. *Symbolic and Mythological Animals*. Bloomington: Indiana University Press, 1992.

Cooper, Merian C., and Ernest B. Schoedsack, dirs. *King Kong*. 1933; Manhattan, NY: Radio Pictures. DVD.

Dadant. "Our History." Available at https://dadant.com.

Dines, Gail. "King Kong and the White Woman: Hustler Magazine and the Demonization of Black Masculinity." *Violence Against Women* 4, no. 3 (1998): 291–307.

Donaldson, Sue, and Will Kymlicka. *Zoopolis: A Political Theory of Animal Rights*. Oxford: Oxford University Press, 2011.

Haraway, Donna. *The Companion Species Manifesto: Dogs, People, and Significant Otherness*. Chicago: Prickly Paradigm Press, 2007.

Harris, Keith M. *Boys, Boyz, Bois: An Ethics of Black Masculinity in Film and Popular Media*. New York: Routledge, 2006.

hooks, bell. *Black Looks: Race and Representation*. New York: Taylor & Francis, 2014.

Ko, Aph. *Racism as Zoological Witchcraft: A Guide for Getting Out*. New York: Lantern Books, 2019.

Lévi-Strauss, Claude. *Totemism*. Translated by Rodney Needham. Boston: Beacon Press, 1963.

MacIntyre, B. "The New Eugenics." *(London) Sunday Telegraph*, March 13, 1989.

Metzler, Jessica. "Lusty Ape-men and Imperiled White Womanhood: Reading Race in a 1930s Poe Film Adaptation." In *Adapting Poe: Re-Imaginings in Popular Culture*, edited by Dennis R. Perry and Carl H. Sederholm, 31–44. London: Palgrave, 2012.

Miller, Gary L. "Historical Natural History: Insects and the Civil War." *American Entomologist* 43 (1997): 227–45.

O'Brien, Daniel. *Black Masculinity on Film: Native Sons and White Lies.* New York: Palgrave Macmillan, 2017.

Peele, Jordan, dir. *Get Out.* 2017; Universal City, CA: Universal Pictures. DVD.

Pinedo, Isabel Cristina. *Recreational Terror: Women and the Pleasure of Horror Film Viewing.* Albany, NY: SUNY Press, 1997.

Rose, Bernard, dir. *Candyman.* 1992; Culver City, CA: TriStar Pictures. DVD.

Sheller, Mimi. *Consuming the Caribbean: From Arawaks to Zombies.* London: Routledge, 2003.

Sotkin, Marc. "Camp Town Races Aren't Nearly as Fun as They Used to Be." *Golden Palace* 1, no. 11 (December 4, 1992).

Sussman, Robert Wald. *The Myth of Race: The Troubling Persistence of an Unscientific Idea.* Cambridge, MA: Harvard University Press, 2014.

Weheliye, Alexander G. *Habeas Viscus: Racializing Assemblages, Biopolitics, and Black Feminist Theories of the Human.* Durham, NC: Duke University Press, 2014.

Williams, Lena. "In a 90's Quest for Black Identity, Intense Doubts and Disagreement." *New York Times*, November 30, 1991.

Wilson, Natalie. *Willful Monstrosity: Gender and Race in 21st Century Horror.* Jefferson, NC: McFarland & Co., 2020.

Yerkes, Robert. "Foreword." In Carl Brigham, *A Study of American Intelligence.* Princeton, NJ: Princeton University Press, 1923, v–vii.

Queer Trouble at the Origin
Steven Cohen's Cradle of Humankind (2012)

Ruth Lipschitz

SOUTH AFRICAN PERFORMANCE ARTIST STEVEN COHEN'S TWELVE-MINUTE VIDEO PERformance *Cradle of Humankind* (2012) takes place at the eponymous UNESCO world heritage site outside of Johannesburg. The site's paleontological status as one of the origin sites for the ancestral emergence of *Homo sapiens* bears witness not only to "Darwin's hunch" that humanity originated in Africa, but also to the fact that the contested and racialized theorization of hominid evolution itself is inextricable from the abstraction called "animal."[1] The evolutionary projection of who counts as "human" has its origins in eighteenth-century comparative anatomy and is foundational to the racist logics of colonialism, National Socialism, and South African apartheid. This projection is indivisible from, and shaped by, the desire to secure the racial, ideological, and scientific threshold that aligns whiteness and "the human," and separates both from animalized humans and primates.[2] In this chapter, I argue that the fraught nature of the threshold itself, and the racialized logic of "separation," is at issue in the animalized queer politics of Cohen's *Cradle of Humankind* (2012).

The Cradle of Humankind (2012) begins with a near-naked Cohen cautiously picking his way across the bushveld of the Swartkrans, wearing leopard-print platform stiletto heels and a corseted tutu. A teeth-baring, taxidermied Chacma baboon is sewn onto the front of his corset so that the baboon obscures Cohen's face and body. The baboon is also affixed to the tutu's skirt and is posed with his/her legs splayed and genitals exposed; his/her palms are upturned.[3] The awkward stiffness of the baboon's placement contrasts with Cohen's semi-balletic movement as he brings his hands to the baboon's face and arches his arms above his own head. Much of the video involves tracking Cohen across the active paleontological site (its string grid still visible) and his descent into the Sterkfontein Caves and Wonder Cave. Performing alongside Cohen in this piece, and in the more controversial live stage performance that shares its name, is his former childhood nanny, surrogate mother, recurrent collaborator, longtime muse, and friend, a then ninety-two-year-old Nomsa Dhlamini. Dhlamini makes her first appearance in the artwork prior to the video track's descent into the caves. Seen as a close-up from below, imposing and immobile, she wears all black with a model of the lunar landing craft on her head and prismatic glasses. Once inside the Sterkfontein caves, however, she is shown nearly naked and wearing a fiber-optic "grass" skirt. At the entrance to the underground cave is an in-process excavation of an embedded skeleton that evidences the site's paleontological yield.

Still partially hidden by the stuffed baboon attached to his corset, Cohen makes his way into the cave, caressing the baboon's chest as the camera hovers on his/her glazed eyes, elongated nose, and open mouth, and trailing down, lingers on Cohen's stiletto heels. Using exaggerated hand movements, Cohen draws attention to his flexible wrist and articulated hand, both heralded as paleo-anthropological signifiers of the evolutionary "progress" toward the emergence of *Homo sapiens*. He then throws a flare up into the cave and emerges, out of the darkness, sans stilettos and his baboon frontage, yet wearing a glowing white corset with a taxidermied baboon posterior and tail attached. Tiny tree-like appendages appear in hornlike fashion on his head, and notably, it is only after he has rid himself of the baboon tutu that he pretends to climb the cave wall.

The camera pans across the Wonder Cave's rock formations as Cohen moves through the space with a deliberate and apparently uncoordinated gait, as if miming learning to walk upright. His movement is overlaid by what sounds like shrieking monkeys, and thereafter, Cohen encounters Dhlamini. With visible affection, Cohen takes her unfolding hands, and they converse in a grunting, panting, chattering language as the camera pans across the cave's wet rocks, stalagmites, and lit stalactites. After shuffling closer to the camera's focal point, Dhlamini, with animal horns still visible, turns to meet the viewer's gaze. The video ends with her confrontational close-up.

Critical commentary has thus far concentrated on the stage version of the video and Cohen's controversial reenactment of the racialized and animalized tropes of colonial politics within it. This debate has also questioned whether the "humanizing" effect of Cohen and Dhlamini's relationship mitigates that brutalizing history's re-presentation.[4] In relation to the relatively under-researched video version, however, I am less interested in the notion of humanization and more in the ways in which the video work puts the determining limit of "the human" into question.[5] Thus, my approach to the work analyzes the politics of "becoming human" that play out through its formations of race and animality across sex, gender, race, and species. The work engages what Jacques Derrida calls "limitrophy": a thickening of the notion of the limit by, as he writes, "what sprouts or grows at the limit, around the limit, by maintaining the limit, but also what *feeds the limit*, generates it, raises it, and complicates it."[6]

My reading of *Cradle of Humankind*'s limitrophic complication of the racialized and gendered construct "human," and thus of the abstraction "animal" that sustains it, turns on what Irene Bronner has elsewhere called Cohen's practice of "self-othering" through "hyperbolic" reenactment—a process, Cohen writes, conditioned by his status as a "white, Jewish, faggot."[7] Rather than interpret this statement as a form of identity politics, Cohen's visual language of, as Rebecca Rossen writes, "spectacle, degradation and irreverence" links to the performative politics of citation.[8] More particularly, to performativity's transgressive disarticulation of the nexus of power and knowledge that Judith Butler sets out in her *Bodies That Matter*.

Butler's theory of performativity draws on the work of Michel Foucault and Derrida and not only narrates how power is produced, circulated, and consolidated through discourse, but also opens up that process to sites of instability. Consequently, the normative sex/gender and race identifications, and the sociopolitical relations of inclusion and exclusion they effect are made available to intervention. Butler aligns Foucault's notion of the productivity of power through knowledge with Derrida's concept of iteration, in which, in order to be meaningful, every mark must be conditioned by both repeatability and difference. Consequently, its every inscription is both recognizably "the same" yet different. Since the regulative formations of power/knowledge require repetition to naturalize and maintain themselves, this discursive organization of power, Butler argues, must be open to the interruptive force of iteration, and thus, to subversive resignification. For Butler, then, performativity is both the instrument and interruption of hegemonic heteronormativity. It is both the medium through which social exclusions are naturalized, and the means through which this exclusion is exposed as a function of the ideological power that circumscribes what Butler calls the "domain of intelligible bodies." As an organization of power, Butler writes, this zone gains its coherency through the simultaneous construction of "a domain of unthinkable, abject, unliveable bodies."[9]

However, Butler argues that read through Julia Kristeva's theory of abjection, the excluded body, since it is produced through iteration, is not "outside" meaning or social relation. Rather, what is excluded is constitutive of that very relation, or as she puts it, is "internal to that system as its own nonthematizable necessity." In other words, the repetition that appears to secure the relation of power/knowledge through the internalization of normative sex/gender and race identity is fundamentally insecure, even anxious. Anxious, because every iteration exposes both the subject and the discursive regulatory regime through which they gain their social and ontological coherence to a potentially disruptive difference. Translated into the frame of race and animality—or, in Cohen's terms, into the identification "white, Jewish, faggot"—the non-heteronormative, abject other is at once the legible core of social and subjective identity formation and its disarticulated other; at once that which both secures and threatens the organizational limits of race, sex/gender, and species.[10] And it is the articulation of these very limits, I suggest, that is at stake in the site-specific video version of *Cradle of Humankind*.

In the sections that follow, I return to the video performance to situate its evolutionary "progress" narrative both within the Cradle of Humankind's "origin" story and, to borrow Kay Anderson's pithy phrase, within "the ontological infrastructure of European animality."[11] I set out the coordinates of what Cary Wolfe calls "a discourse of species," and Claire Jean Kim, the "zoologo-racial order" that link the "Jew-Animal" to, in Zakiyyah Jackson's terms, "the animality of black(ened) female flesh."[12] The *Cradle of Humankind* stages, at the purported "origin" of humankind, an ambiguous proximity to "the animal" that the West's so-called evolutionary "sciences" and their racial taxonomies endeavored to settle. As I will show, it does so by concatenating corporeality, Blackness, woman, animal, Africa, whiteness, Jew. This is a proximity all the more threatening, for it is not just any animal that *Cradle of Humankind*'s citational politics summons and mimes as it performs the becoming of "becoming human." As the echo of the Darwinian term "mimicry" suggests, the work signals its evolutionary currency by employing, across the racialized corporealities of "the Jew" and "the Black," that most abject, but also most mobile, figure in the West's racializing discourse of animality, the ape.[13] It does so, however, not to underwrite the production of European heteronormative sovereignty, but to trouble it, queerly.

ORIGIN: THE PRIMATE SCENE

In contextual terms, the *Cradle of Humankind*'s narrative progression appears at first to correspond to the popular image of human progress as an inevitable "march" from primate "ancestor" to erect (hu)man. This movement not only positions itself as linear, directional, and sequential, but belies an ideological conception of the relation human/animal/primate. Here, "becoming human" is a "civilizing" process that unfolds precisely in, and as, distance from the animal. In *Civilisation and Its Discontents*, for example, Freud theorized that some sort of "organic repression" of man's animal self allows him to negotiate the world through sight rather than smell and, consequently, stand erect and walk upright.[14] More than simply a psychosocial intervention into the "onset" of human civilization, this framing of the human/animal binary speaks, as Cary Wolfe notes, of a relation in which to become "human" is also to presume to already "know" what/who is "animal."[15] If "the animal" signifies as the debased and excluded other to man, it does so to make available a politics of animalization that, as discourse of "race science" demonstrates, produces animalized humans. However, following Butler, since the abject, cast-aside, and excluded body is also lodged within the binary opposition as its "constitutive outside," "the animal" is always already "lying in wait," as Wolfe writes, "at the heart of . . . that fantasy figure 'the human.'"[16] Both expelled and all too close, no animal stalks the human quite like the primate, but it is precisely the relation to the primate that the West's question of evolution and purported "science" of racial taxonomies desired to secure.

The paleoanthropological search for an evidentiary dividing line between the higher primates and what scientific racism termed the "lower limits of humanity" gained impetus with Robert Bloom and John T. Robinson's 1947 discovery at the Cradle of an *Australopithecus africanus* skeleton (the so-called Mrs. Ples).[17] Mrs. Ples appeared to confirm the 1924 findings by comparative anatomist and paleontologist Raymond Dart. For Dart, the *Australopithecus africanus* signaled the "missing link" between human and ape. Indeed, in 1925, Dart published his identification of the hominin as the "man-ape of South Africa."[18] A proposed "intermediate between living anthropoids and man," the construct of man-ape is, however, underwritten by a racist colonial and apartheid imaginary that aligns ape with "prehuman" and both with an Africa remade as "primitive" and "savage," and consequently, resignifying Blackness as not "human enough," subhuman.[19]

While, as Amanda Esterhuysen points out, a linear and sequential model of human development has been challenged by a multibranching model of hominid evolution, the concept of the "missing link" and the "progress" narrative it sanctions nonetheless cling to the Cradle of Humankind's identity as an origin site.[20] However, the concept of origin that the site—and by extension, Cohen's performance—offers is not simply evolutionary; rather, it has been deployed to sustain the Western "scientific" imagination that shaped the project of white supremacy across raced and sexed bodies made "animal." Paradoxically, though, the Cradle's status as origin has also been used to consolidate a post-apartheid politics of origin that is served up in the quest for a unified, and indeed, "post-racial" South African commonality. Both framings of origin are at work in Cohen's primal/primate scene.

Cohen's tutu-wearing "man-ape" announces a queer organization of race, gender, and species from the outset. However, the performance also hits all the key anthropocentric and racial markers that found human exceptionalism as white and Western. These include the primacy of the human hand, the "discovery" of fire, and Cohen's emergence from darkness (or metonymically, from Africa as the "dark continent") sans baboon costume. Here, his distance from the "animal" is underscored by his decorative tree headpiece, which suggests the "ability" to organize nature to serve his own image.

While Cohen's presentation seemingly affirms his ultimate "liberation" from the "animal" (his wearing of a taxidermied baboon's posterior and tail is not immediately apparent), the question of the "animal" summoned by Dhlamini's representation cannot be as easily cast aside. For her representation—her partial nakedness and her "Blackness"—is haunted by the vexed history of Sarah Bartman (Saartjie Baartmann), an indigenous Khoikhoi woman exhibited in London and Paris between 1810 and 1815 under the name "Hottentot Venus."[21] To a salacious and voyeuristic European public, as well as to comparative anatomists such as Georges Cuvier, her distinctive racial and sexual difference (pendulous breasts and protruding buttocks or steatopygia) offered evidentiary proof of the so-called "animalized sexuality" of the Black female.[22] Cuvier, for instance, compared Bartman to an orangutan and dissected her upon her death in 1817.[23] For Cuvier, as Sander Gilman notes, the apparent difference of her genitals (the so-called "Hottentot

Apron") testified not only to the "pathological" nature of female sexuality in general, but to the purportedly "primitive" nature of the Hottentot, who, Cuvier asserted, were the "lowest of the human species."[24]

However, while Dhlamini's presence necessarily calls up Bartman as the West's paradigmatic exploitative encounter with the Black female body, this history sits alongside the evident warmth of Cohen and Dhlamini's relationship.[25] Their emotional connection—Cohen calls her his surrogate mother—transforms their shared private language into a connection built upon mutual recognition and respect for difference. In the context of the cave of origin, however, Dhlamini's maternal surrogacy also acts metonymically: Dhlamini appears not just as Cohen's maternal surrogate, but as the African Eve that birthed "us" all. Indeed, read this way, Cohen's narrative of a common ancestor, a mother to Black and white alike, appropriates the "Out of Africa" origin story and reconciliatory nationalism promoted by then president Thabo Mbeki's program of African Renaissance, to which Dhlamini's prismatic glasses and lunar module headpiece also relate.

As Esterhuysen writes, Mbeki's African Renaissance looked both forward to a technologized Africa and backward, recovering silenced African history.[26] Mbeki's Africa implicitly challenges the racist thesis of Africa as negation espoused most virulently in Hegel's "Lectures on the Philosophy of World History" (1822–1828). Hegel states, for example, that "man as we find him in Africa has not progressed beyond his immediate existence . . . [as] nothing consonant with humanity is to be found in his character."[27] It is against this construction of Africa as a dark and savage continent that Mbeki's words at the official opening of the Maropeng Visitor's Centre at the Cradle of Humankind World Heritage Site in 1999 resonate. Mbeki's explicit recourse to a human commonality of origin—a mother Africa—recasts the Enlightenment construct of universal personhood that denied Black subjectivity into an African universalism: "These rocks and stones . . . are the voices of our distant ancestors, who still lie buried in them. The voices of my ancestors and yours!"[28] It is in keeping with this sentiment that Cohen offers the quintessentially queer version of New-South-African post-apartheid "post-racism": "we're the same ape in different drag."[29] Phrased differently, what Cohen and Mbeki problematically suggest, and what the final video image of Dhlamini contradicts, is that if "we" all have a common ancestor (an African Eve), then racial differences cannot possibly matter; and further, if we are all "the same ape," then racial difference cannot possibly signify animal difference.

BLACKNESS AND ANIMALITY

However, as the staying power of anti-Black racism demonstrates, if the journey into universalized humanity passes by way of a monogenetic African origin, it does so only to consolidate itself in whiteness: that is, to be human is precisely not to be "in common" with either Blackness or animality.[30] It is no accident that Cohen's visibly whitened body is revealed at the very moment he emerges, without baboon tutu and heels, from the darkness that preceded the discovery of fire. Nor does the soundtrack of screeching baboons that precedes the moment Cohen encounters Dhlamini/"Mother Africa" reinforce a sense of shared primate origin that Cohen's claim of "same ape in different drag" suggests.[31] Instead of healing the ontological scabs of racialized humanity, *Cradle of Humankind* picks at them, making visible what Achille Mbembe calls the "metatext about the animal" through which Europe imagined Africa and invented itself.[32] More to the point, *Cradle of Humankind* plots the production of a masculinized sovereign whiteness as the determining threshold of "the human" by invoking its proximity to its excluded terms—"black(ened)" female, animal, Jew.[33]

As Mbembe, Kim, and Jackson variously note, the Enlightenment's philosophical and scientific production of European modernity's normative category of the "universal self" is inextricable from the bestialization of the Black body. In the writings of, for instance, Kant, Jefferson, Hegel, Hume, et al., and in the taxonomies of Comte de Gobineau, Cuvier, Houston Stewart Chamberlain, Robert Knox, Ernst Haeckel, et al., African Blackness is reduced to nothing but an animal body, without access to reason, restraint, or religion. Yet, while the animalized African embodied Blackness itself, as Bartman's life and death demonstrate, no body embodied animality quite like the Black female, sexualized out of the realm of white womanhood by virtue of her very animality.[34] In both of Europe's ontologizing regimes, the Great Chain of Being as well as the racist biological determinism that supplanted it and reified its prejudices as "science," the closeness of the African and the ape was nothing less than self-evident and inconclusively "verified" by physical anthropology, craniology, and comparative anatomy.[35] As Kim writes, "Apeness and blackness were hammered out in intimate relation in the crucible of the Western imaginary, each taking shape with the other in mind."[36] To borrow Jackson's words, "'the animal' and the 'black' are not only interdependent representations but also entangled concepts" that require racialization and sexualization for their interarticulation.[37] Moreover, Kim asserts, although Europe's "whitened" universalized humanity operates in a closed loop, as the founding terms of the "zoologo-racial order," the relation between "Black" and "animal" is also "perpetually open" so that both "imagined entities . . . are produced as indeterminate relative to one another."[38] Thus, in the taxonomic structure of the human types such as Knox's *The Races of Men* (1850), the "ape" and the "African" are both mutually supporting terms and without closure. As such, they were available to be deployed against Aryan Europe's other site of sexualized and animalized violence—"the Jew."[39]

SIMIAN SEMITICS

If Cohen stands in for the Caucasian human type, scientific racism's masculine universal, he does so queerly, displacing the Aryan masculine with a hyperbolic and seemingly parodic "whiteness" of "the Jew." Anti-Semitism provides another set of signifiers around whiteness and masculinity that make sense of Cohen's self-presentation: his exaggerated pallor, his self-consciously graceful gestures, the sensual way he strokes the baboon's fur, the way the camera lingers on his stilettos, the taxidermied baboon attached to his tutu (the corset and tutu itself), the disembodied baboon posterior, his awkward gait as he stumbles away from his animal "self" toward Dhlamini. Abstracted from any trace of individuality, Cohen's self-conscious status as "white, Jewish, faggot" takes on the anti-Semitic tropes that proliferated in the wake of nineteenth-century Jewish emancipation.[40] Fueled by the anti-Semitic belief in the purportedly insidious and contaminating nature of Jewish assimilation and acculturation into Western European society, the Jew as a threat to racial hygiene reaches its death-bearing conclusion in National Socialism's "Final Solution," the Holocaust. In attaching the taxidermied baboon, genitals exposed, to his whitened body, and in having the stuffed baboon's sex change unpredictably between male and female in the course of the video, Cohen literalizes the anti-Semite's fantasized figure of the ugly, degenerate, carnal, simian-like, feminized Jew—"small, black, and hairy all over"—that hides behind the veneer of white Europe.[41]

Reenacting the paranoiac racism of supposed Jewish difference, Cohen's whiteness signals not the triumph of assimilation, but the falsity of the "the Jew's" claim to the biological purity of white European society. Thus constructed, the "truth" of the Jew's imagined perverse, sexualized animality (the effeminate corset and the baboon posterior) cannot but remain visible. Marked by the "animal," the inscription of sexual and racial deviance turns his whiteness and his masculinity into empty signifiers even, and especially, as he "apes" being human. Indeed, this very appearance of being European, born of the assimilated Jew's supposed innate talent for mimicry, one "that surpassed the achievements of the most developed apes," made the racist fixing of Jewish difference as animal difference all the more urgent. For the anti-Semite, this animalizing embodiment marks the Jew's constitutive difference as always-already (hyperbolically) visible. It also renders corporeal the supposed degeneracy of his moral character that restricted him to mere parasitic imitation in the first place. As such, the "truth" of the assimilated Jew's aping of "the human" reveals not only an essential animality, but a duplicitous threat to the authentic human's self-creation.[42] The horrifying implications of this logic are clear in the field guide to the *Untermensch* issued by Heinrich Himmler's SS Main Office in 1942: "This creation of nature [the Jew], seemingly wholly of the same sort [*gleichgeartet*] biologically [as the human], with hands, feet, and some sort of brain, with eyes and a mouth, is all the same a totally different, a terrifying creature. . . . Not all those who appear human are in fact so."[43]

ANIMAL-BLACK-JEW

For Theodor Fritsch, a leading nineteenth-century anti-Semite who published the frequently updated *Handbook of the Jewish Question*, "God created the Jew as a buffer between humans and apes."[44] Liminal and contaminated, Fritsch argues, and potentially a separate species, the Jew is neither human nor ape but a bastardized corruption, what Chamberlain called a "mongrel race" produced through interbreeding with Africans.[45] The "Jewish-Negroid" racialization of the ape and the sexualization of Black female animality coalesce in what Knox called the "African character of the Jew."[46] In other words, the Jew's supposed sexual and racial degeneracy, and thus the threat of evolutionary retrogression he embodies, gains its legitimacy and readability through the readily available language of bestialized Blackness and "pathological" female sexuality.

At once hypersexual and irrational, the association between feminine sexuality and the Jew was both decidedly unvirile and innate. In his *Sex and Character* (1903), Otto Weininger diagnoses the effeminacy of the Jew as a threat to the male principle of reason itself. In what is perhaps the most emblematic instance of "Jewish self-hatred," Weininger's fevered book is as deeply misogynistic as it is anti-Semitic, and in a proposition that finds its echo in Nazi social engineering, he argues that modernity itself has become "Judaized" and feminized. As such, Weininger concludes that both women and Jews are working to corrupt the achievements of "the Aryan mind and spirit" by pushing the carnal lure of materiality. Here human/animal, reason/body, man/woman, Aryan/Jew, culture/nature, and health/disease are all overlaid in a synergy of defilement symbolized by the perverse conclusion that circumcision renders the Jew "essentially feminine." Thus besieged by their debased corporeality, Jews, Weininger writes, have no access to reason, hence "no self, therefore no self-respect . . . just as women have no real dignity."[47] In a culture where Blackened female flesh, as Jackson writes, represents the nadir of human evolution, "the abyss that divides organic life into 'human' and 'animal,'" the corrosive power of the assimilated Jew's hypersexed effeminate animality threatens nothing less than the potential abyssal decline of Aryan society.[48] That is, were it not, Weininger argues, for the Jew's lack of virility, his potency would be drained both by his "effeminization" and closeness to the primitivizing sexuality of Blackness. While, as Ritchie Robertson notes, it took the trial of Oscar Wilde to link effeminacy with homosexuality, the Jew's aberrant sexuality had, by the twentieth century, become aligned with male homosexuality.[49] Like the Jew, the term homosexuality, as Siobhan Somerville points out, bears the traces of its own miscegenetic bastardization (an adulterated combination of Greek *homos* and Latin *sexualis*) and gains its ideological coherency from the same eugenicist discourse that shaped the so-called impurity of "the Jew" and racial inferiority of "the Black."[50]

LIMITROPHIC INTER/INTRA-ARTICULATIONS: APING THE APE

In his *Progress and Evolution of Man in Africa* (1961), British paleoanthropologist and archaeologist Louis Leakey announced that "Africa's first contribution to human progress was the evolution of man himself."[51] Precisely who counts as "man," and thus "human," is the silenced ideological fulcrum around which theories of humanity's African origin turn. Leakey's statement validated a thesis of, and a locus for, a theory of hominin evolution in which *Homo sapiens* emerged gradually from apelike ancestors. But if Darwin's evolutionary model held out the possibility of mankind's "missing link," it also, as Somerville writes, modeled "a continuity between the 'savage' and 'civilized' races" that enabled the construction of racial and sexual difference through species difference.[52]

If the Cradle of Humankind imagines itself as a paleoanthropological expression of the universalized transition from animality to humanity, Cohen's *Cradle of Humankind*'s performative intervention foregrounds the racialized and animalized foundation of that universalism. It does so through an exaggerated and non-normative coarticulation of race, sex, and species that places animalization as the very condition under which "becoming human" also involves a heterosexualized "becoming white." Cohen's "ape-man" stands as queer reiteration of scientific racism's fantasized projection of the primate (and primal) contiguity of a "savage femininity" and the Jew that produces a zone of "the less human, the inhuman, the humanly unthinkable."[53] His participation in the zone of exclusion that constructs, following Butler, "bodies that matter" repeats the Jew's purported apish talent for imitation. At the same time, however, aping "the ape" simultaneously transgresses the intelligibility of the threshold of "the human" since its queer syntax interrupts the coordinates of race, sex, and species. With exaggerated artifice, Cohen self-consciously inhabits the site of that discursive convergence called "Jew-Animal," only to reveal that the self-identical heteronormative subject called "human" *is* only in the continued abjection of his others. Rather than cohere to mime his inclusion in the human race, Cohen's performance of "becoming human" refuses resemblance and exposes, rather than forecloses, the "zoologo-racial order" that renders illusory any notion of the "human" as a "natural" consequence of the transcendence of animality. The work speaks not only to the violent instrumentalization of a singular threshold between the "human (animal) and (nonhuman) animal," but also its insecurity.[54] It does so, moreover, not by flattening racial, sexual, and species difference, nor by equalizing inscriptions of racial, sexual, and species oppression and violence. Rather, it demonstrates the ways in which, in the racist logic of the West's organization of the "human," race, sex, and species are co-constitutive. Their interoperation installs a foundational excess that the term "animal" is supposed to shore up but does not. Instead, as the inclusive exclusion, in Butler's terms, the abject "constitutive outside" to the "human," the "animal" remains all too close, threatening to spill over and disarticulate its primal, and primate, foundations. It is for this reason, humanization is not, as Jackson notes, an antidote to the politics of animalization but its regulatory code.[55] And consequently, the "animal" is, as both Cohen's queer iteration of whiteness and Dhlamini's final confrontational gaze suggest, not the excluded other to a universalized humanity; rather, it is its troubling disciplinary origin.

NOTES

1. Kuljian, *Darwin's Hunch*.
2. Dubow, *Scientific Racism*, 21–23.
3. Two stuffed baboons are used interchangeably throughout the video, so that the baboon attached to the corset alternates between male and female, and the shape and sharpness of the exposed teeth also differ.
4. Bronner, "Slow Rhythm," 34; and Smit, "The Search."
5. The concept of humanization necessarily suggests that the ontology of being human is already known and settled, and thus quantifiable according to a scale that marks its separation from that abstraction termed "animal."
6. Derrida, *The Animal*, 29. Emphasis in original.
7. Bronner, "Slow Rhythm," 34.
8. Rossen, "Jews on View," 59.
9. Butler, *Bodies That Matter*, xi, 225.
10. Butler, *Bodies That Matter*, xi, 37.
11. Anderson, "Modern Ontologies," 57.
12. Wolfe, *Animal Rites*, 6; Kim, "Murder and Mattering," 10; Geller, *Bestiarium Judaicum*, 2; Jackson, *Becoming Human*, 14.
13. Geller, *Bestiarium Judaicum*, 2; Gilman, *The Jew's Body*, 169–71.
14. Wolfe, *Animal Rites*, 6; Freud, *Civilisation and Its Discontents*.
15. Wolfe, *Animal Rites*, 6–7.
16. Wolfe, *Animal Rites*, 6.
17. Dubow, *Scientific Racism*, 44.
18. Dart, "*Australopithecus africanus*: The Man-Ape of South Africa."
19. Dubow, *Scientific Racism*, 42–44. That the racist conflation of primate, "prehuman" and "not human enough" still holds sway is borne out in the wake of social media and the press coverage of Lee Berger et al.'s 2018 discovery of *Homo naledi* in the Sterkfontein Cave system. See de Robillard, "In/On the Bones."
20. Its centrality is such that the primate-to-human march is the logo for the Cradle of Humankind itself. See https://www.maropeng.co.za/; and Esterhuysen, "If We Are All African," 281. Dubow, *Scientific Racism*, 44.
21. The bibliography on Sarah Bartman/Saartjie Baartmann is extensive. For historical and art-historical

approaches to the reuse of Baartmann in contemporary art see, for example, Willis, *Black Venus*; Abrahams, "Images of Sara Bartman"; Magubane, "Which Bodies Matter?"; Gilman, "Black Bodies, White Bodies"; Fausto-Sterling, "Gender, Race, and Nation"; and Tuvel, "'Veil of Shame.'"
22. Gilman, "Black Bodies, White Bodies," 212.
23. Dubow, *Scientific Racism*, 23.
24. Gilman, "Black Bodies, White Bodies," 212; Dubow, *Scientific Racism*, 23.
25. In the controversial stage version of this work performed at the Grahamstown Festival in 2012, the animalization of the Black female body was overt. Signalling the histories of denigration and exploitation of the Black body, Cohen shackles Dhlamini and puts taxidermied lion paws on her hands. See Smit, "The Search for a More Desirable Origin," for a detailed description of this version of the *Cradle of Humankind*.
26. Esterhuysen, "If We Are All African," 281.
27. Hegel, "Lectures," 127.
28. Mbeki, cited in Esterhuysen, "If We Are All African," 281.
29. Cohen, interview by Grid Lab, cited in Smit, "The Search," 4. The phrase "New South Africa" and the associated concept of the "Rainbow Nation" were products of a post-apartheid imagined community (in Benedict Anderson's sense). Anchored in shared democratic values enshrined in the South African Constitution, these phrases speak of the warm embrace of mutuality as opposed to supposedly fractious differences.
30. Kim, "Murder and Mattering," 15.
31. Cohen, interview by Grid Lab, cited in Smit, "The Search," 4. On the Cradle of Humankind's origin narrative, *Homo naledi*, and the racialization of the concept of an "apish ancestor," see de Robillard, "In/On the Bones," 1–26.
32. Mbembe, *On the Postcolony*, 1.
33. Jackson, *Becoming Human*, 1.
34. See Gilman, "Black Bodies, White Bodies," 204–42.
35. Jackson, *Becoming Human*, 8.
36. Kim, "Murder and Mattering," 15.
37. Jackson, *Becoming Human*, 28.
38. Kim, "Murder and Mattering," 20.
39. The ape was not the only signifier of Jewish animality. Geller's *Bestiarium Judaicum* (5–6) lists the menagerie of animals Christian Europe employed to animalize Jews prior to the biological anti-Semitism of scientific racism.
40. Bronner, "Slow Rhythm," 34.
41. Gilman, *Jewish Self-Hatred*, 8.
42. Geller, *Bestiarium Judaicum*, 108, 116.
43. Cited in Geller, *Bestiarium Judaicum*, 17.
44. Geller, *Bestiarium Judaicum*, 129.
45. Cited in Gilman, *The Jew's Body*, 174.
46. Knox cited in Gilman, *The Jew's Body*, 175.
47. Robertson, "Historicizing Weininger," 24.
48. Jackson, *Becoming Human*, 6.
49. Robertson, "Historicizing Weininger," 35.
50. Somerville, "Scientific Racism," 258.
51. Cited in Dubow, *Scientific Racism*, 45.
52. Somerville, "Scientific Racism," 258. Darwin's model of evolution focuses on animal biology and

makes no claims for any application of evolution to human sociality, but as Rutledge M. Dennis points out, its appropriation by Social Darwinists such as Herbert Spencer provided the founding logic for a racial hierarchy of human types. Dennis, "Social Darwinism," 244.
53. Butler, *Bodies That Matter*, xi.
54. Geller, *Bestiarium Judaicum*, 2.
55. Jackson, *Becoming Human*, 17.

WORKS CITED

Abrahams, Yvette. "Images of Sara Bartman: Sexuality, Race and Gender in Early Nineteenth-Century Britain." In *Nation, Empire, Colony: Historizing Gender and Race,* edited by Ruth Roach Pierson and Nupur Chaudri, 220–36. Bloomington: Indiana University Press, 1998.

Achinger, Christine. "Allegories of Destruction: 'Woman' and 'the Jew' in Otto Weininger's *Sex and Character*." *Germanic Review: Literature, Culture, Theory* 88, no. 2 (2013): 121–49.

Anderson, Kay. "Modern Ontologies of the 'More-Than-Animal' Human: Provincializing Humanism for the Present Day." In *Interrogating Human Origins: Decolonisation and the Deep Human Past*, edited by Martin Porr and Jacqueline M. Matthews, 56–71. London: Routledge, 2020.

Bronner, Irene. "Slow Rhythm with Nomsa Dhlamini in Steven Cohen's *Cradle of Humankind*." *De arte* 92 (2015): 34–49.

Butler, Judith. *Bodies That Matter: On the Discursive Limits of 'Sex.'* London: Routledge, 1993.

Dart, Raymond. "*Australopithecus africanus*: The Man-Ape of South Africa." *Nature* 115 (1925):195–99.

Dennis, Rutledge M. "Social Darwinism, Scientific Racism and the Metaphysics of Race." *Journal of Negro Education* 64, no. 3 (1995): 243–52.

Derrida, Jacques. *The Animal That Therefore I Am*. Translated by David Wills, edited by Marie-Louise Mallet. New York: Fordham University Press, 2008.

De Robillard, Benita. "In/On the Bones: Species Meanings and the Racialising Discourse of Animality in the *Homo naledi* Controversy." *Image & Text* 32 (2018): 2–26.

Dubow, Saul. *Scientific Racism in Modern South Africa*. Cambridge: Cambridge University Press, 1995.

Esterhuysen, Amanda. "'If We Are All African, Then I Am Nothing': Hominin Evolution and the Politics of Identity in South Africa." In *Interrogating Human Origins: Decolonisation and the Deep Human Past*, edited by Martin Porr and Jacqueline M. Matthews, 279–92. London: Routledge, 2020.

Fausto-Sterling, Anne. "Gender, Race, and Nation: The Comparative Anatomy of 'Hottentot' Women in Europe, 1815–1817." In *Deviant Bodies: Critical Perspectives on Difference in Science and Popular Culture*, edited by Jennifer Terry and Jacqueline Urla, 19–48. Bloomington: Indiana University Press, 1995.

Freud, Sigmund. *Civilisation and Its Discontents*. Translated by James Strachey. New York: Norton, 1961.

Geller, Jay. *Bestiarium Judaicum: Unnatural Histories of the Jews*. New York: Fordham University Press, 2017.

———. "The Jewish Animot." In *Jews and the Ends of Theory*, edited by Shai Ginsburg, Martin Land, and Jonathan Boyarin, 142–63. New York: Fordham University Press, 2019.

Gilman, Sander. "Black Bodies, White Bodies: Toward an Iconography of Female Sexuality in Late Nineteenth-Century Art, Medicine, and Literature." *Critical Inquiry* 12, no. 1 (1985): 202–42.

———. *Jewish Self-Hatred: Anti-Semitism and the Hidden Language of the Jews*. Baltimore, MD: Johns

Hopkins University Press, 1986.

———. *The Jew's Body*. London: Routledge, 1991.

HaCohen, Ran. "The 'Jewish Blackness' Thesis Revisited." *Religions* 9, no. 7 (2018): 1–9.

Haraway, Donna J. *When Species Meet*. London: University of Minnesota Press, 2008.

Hegel, Georg Wilhelm Friedrich. "Lectures on the Philosophy of World History." In *Race and the Enlightenment: A Reader*, edited by Emmanuel Chukwudi Eze. Oxford: Blackwell, 1997.

Jackson, Zakiyyah Iman. *Becoming Human: Matter and Mattering in an Antiblack World*. New York: New York University Press, 2020.

Kim, Claire Jean. "Murder and Mattering in Harambe's House." *Politics and Animals* 3 (2017): 1–15.

Kristeva, Julia. *Powers of Horror: An Essay on Abjection*. Translated by Leon S. Roudiez. New York: Columbia University Press, 1982.

Kuljian, Christa. *Darwin's Hunch: Science, Race and the Search for Human Origins*. Auckland Park, South Africa: Jacana Media, 2016.

Lipschitz, Ruth. "Abjection." In *Edinburgh Companion to Animal Studies*, edited by Lynn Turner, Ron Broglio, and Undine Sellbach. Edinburgh: Edinburgh University Press, 2018.

Lipschitz, Ruth, and Benita de Robillard. "Race and 'the Animal' in the Post-Apartheid National Symbolic." *Image & Text* 30 (2017): 73–93.

Livingstone Smith, David, and Ioana Panaitiu. "Aping the Human Essence: Simianization as Dehumanization." In *Simianization: Apes, Gender, Class, and Race*, edited by Wulf D. Hund, Charles W. Mills, and Silvia Sebastiani, 77–106. Vienna: LIT Verlag, 2015.

Magubane, Zine. "Which Bodies Matter? Feminism, Poststructuralism, Race and the Curious Theoretical Odyssey of the 'Hottentot Venus.'" *Gender and Society* 15, no. 6 (December 2001): 816–34.

Mbembe, Achille. *On the Postcolony*. Berkeley: University of California Press, 2001.

McAfee, Noëlle. *Julia Kristeva*. London: Routledge, 2003.

Peterson, Christopher. "The Aping Apes of Poe and Wright: Race, Animality, and Mimicry in 'The Murders in the Rue Morgue' and *Native Son*." *New Literary History* 41, no. 1 (2010): 151–71.

Robertson, Ritchie. "Historicizing Weininger: The Nineteenth-Century German Image of the Feminized Jew." In *Modernity Culture and 'the Jew,'* edited by Bryan Cheyette and Laura Marcus, 23–39. Cambridge: Polity Press, 1998.

Rossen, Rebecca. "Jews on View: Spectacle, Degradation, and Jewish Corporeality in Contemporary Dance and Performance." *Theatre Journal* 64, no. 1 (2012): 59–78.

Shongwe, Nthabiseng. "Cradle of Humankind Inspires New Play by Steven Cohen." Available at https://www.maropeng.co.za.

Smit, Sonja. "The Search for a More Desirable Origin: Steven Cohen's *The Cradle of Humankind* (2011)." *Liminalities: A Journal of Performance Studies* 11, no. 5 (2015).

Somerville, Siobhan. "Scientific Racism and the Emergence of the Homosexual Body." *Journal of the History of Sexuality* 5, no. 2 (1994): 243–66.

Tuvel, Rebecca. "'Veil of Shame': Derrida, Sarah Bartmann and Animality." *Journal for Critical Animal Studies* 9, no. 1–2 (2011): 209–29.

Willis, Deborah, ed. *Black Venus: They Called Her Hottentot*. Philadelphia: Temple University Press, 2010.

Wolfe, Cary. *Animal Rites: American Culture, the Discourse of Species and Posthumanist Theory*. Chicago: University of Chicago Press, 2003.

#RateASpecies
Reviewing Animal Commodities on the Internet

Soledad Altrudi

CONSIDER THE FOLLOWING TWEET, WHICH ACCOMPANIED A ONE-STAR RATING IN A comment: "Received item, tried tasting but now my mouth is numb. Not even slightly banana flavored. Don't buy!"[1] Seemingly, this reads like a typical product review (a negative one in this case) that anybody might come across while shopping online. Yet, this tweet was in reference to an *Ariolimax comumbianus*, otherwise known as the yellow banana slug, and part of a popular albeit short-lived hashtag that circulated during the first half of 2018, #rateaspecies.[2] Focused on the animal's color, this collection of fewer than twenty words swiftly casts a living creature as an edible consumer good that is found wanting and thus should be subsequently disregarded, and it does so in a potentially comical way. Even if one finds this funny, once the laughing subsides, it is hard to ignore the unsettling feeling that takes its place, which speaks to the ways these sets of text and images cast nonhuman others.

Animals in visual culture have been widely studied, and there is a long tradition of critical analysis of animal representation in media, from photography to television to cinema.[3] This research has shown the systematic othering and artificial staging of the lives of nonhuman animals, who are often depicted in ways that ascribe to tried-and-tested recipes on films and TV, from individuals living impossible dramas to characters in coming-of-age stories, that ultimately reproduce those dominant human-nonhuman animal relations they simultaneously obscure.[4] The scope of this critical research is not surprising as, in general, communication and media studies have successfully revealed the ways in which wider systems of power, such as classism, sexism, racism, imperialism, and so forth, inform many sociocultural products and representations as well as political and economic practices. Indeed, media studies have "the unique capacity to understand and interpret both the confluence of forces that shape the effect of a message as it travels across the circuit of communication and the confluence of forces that affect one's relationship to systems of communication and power."[5]

Certainly, the work of Black feminist scholars has been instrumental in moving this understanding forward by demonstrating how those systems of power produce intersecting oppressions.[6] Yet, communication studies continue to suffer from a "practical anthropocentrism that privileges human interaction and relegates the communication efforts of the more-than-human world to the margins of the discipline."[7]

INTERSECTIONALITY FOR THE NONHUMAN

Communication and media studies are uniquely positioned to provide significant contributions in the context of the Anthropocene, an era marked by the disappearance not just of species but of entire ecosystems as a result of anthropogenic forces. But while critically exploring how animals are mediated and represented matters more than ever, these analyses need to systematically incorporate nonhumans into the fold as they set out to explore how the different systems of power that affect humans intersect. This is why Plec argues that animals need to be included when analyzing how we constitute meaning, and that the role of communication needs to be further developed in the construction and transformation of human relationships with what she calls, borrowing from Abram, the "more-than-human" world.[8] A first step in this direction would be to explore what Wolfe calls the "cross-pollination of speciesist, sexist, and racist discursive structures," as this would help the debates in the humanities and social sciences break free from what the author calls an "unexamined framework of speciesism" in which they remain locked.[9] Considering all this, what I suggest in this chapter is that communication and media studies should work harder to effectively problematize the material and discursive oppression that humans exert towards other nonhumans—particularly animals, but not only—*in conjunction with* or as *it intersects with* the oppression of racially othered humans, taking up the opportunity to interpret and study said oppression as the result of a morally speciesist-anthropocentric system of values.

This complex intersectionality has not been lost to a series of scholars whose work centers on critical animal studies (CAS), "an academic field of study dedicated to the abolition of animal exploitation, oppression and domination" that began to formalize in the early 2000s and that fundamentally argues for "an interdisciplinary and multidisciplinary intersectional and multi-movement approach for a total liberation."[10] While the radicalism and the praxis that CAS embodies have relegated it to the periphery of communication studies, its theoretical endeavors have openly been taken up in the work recently started by Núria Almiron, who, along with others, has introduced the subdiscipline of critical animal and media studies (CAMS).[11] What this subfield proposes is that the current (mis)treatment of othered animals is the result of public consent supported by a morally speciesist-anthropocentric system of values, and that media and communication play a significant role in the perpetuation of those speciesist or anthroparchal ideologies. Here, they draw directly from Cudworth, who has coined the term "anthroparchy" to refer to a system or society in which humans have socially formed relations of power over other species, a domination whose social and ecological effects are co-constituted with other complex forms of domination such as patriarchy, capitalism, and orientalism (in a sort of "relational matrix") and are determined by specific spatialized and historical formations.[12] Presented as an unavoidable step forward, CAMS seeks to expand the critical communication and media field beyond views of humanitarianism and social justice that exclude nonhuman others by deeming them morally irrelevant, something that is no longer defensible from either an ethical or a scientific perspective.

In what follows, the chapter turns to the #rateaspecies hashtag and feed to demonstrate that a critical media analysis of animals on the Internet, one that draws on animal and media studies but also fundamentally considers speciesism vis-à-vis racism in a neoliberal capitalist context, can shed light on how these systemic oppressions intersect and are at work even in the "silliest" instances of online, nonhuman other representation. However, before doing so, a cautionary note is in order: considering species as an added axis in critical, intersectional analysis does not mean that we have entered a post-race scenario. The animal is not the new Black, as assuming so presupposes that society has progressed beyond Blackness in considerations of personhood and that the racial question is passé.[13] As Armstrong and Boisseron argue, comparisons between slavery and race with animals have worked to serve only animal rights and negatively impact African Americans (and the Afro-Caribbean community at large) as it can trivialize the human condition, demonstrate racial insensitivity, or reinscribe a discriminative approach that was meant to be rejected in the first place.[14] At the same time, Kim notes that this comparison can be harmful to the nonhumans as well who, when deployed in rhetorical defenses of Blackness, become mere instruments for measuring degrees of anti-Blackness.[15]

Thus, calling out attempts at analogizing Blackness with animality that mean to serve the plight of one over the other is fundamental, as they only work to perpetuate "a rivalry that traps the contenders in a paradigm that precludes any chance for the escape of either from this hierarchical measuring system."[16] The commonality resides, rather, in the intersectional space one inhabits by condemning discrimination against minorities *and* opposing animal oppression. The answer then is not to feed the system that inevitably pits Blackness (or other racialized minorities) against animality, but rather to bring attention to the system that created it in the first place and turn the intersectional bond into defiance. In that same vein, we must also call out rejections of (feminist or other) theorizing about animals on the grounds that this diverts attention to other pressing human needs, because the very presumption that these efforts are opposed to each other arises not only from the binary premise that human and animal needs are in conflict, but from an assumed status hierarchy that positions humans' needs as paramount. Thus, intersectionality can be articulated as an instrumental tool in exposing embedded and entangled patterns of oppression without obstructing the idiosyncrasies of each.

ANIMALS ON THE INTERNET

Animal representation in the media has been widely studied, especially in what pertains to wildlife photography and documentary, as well as animal characterization on TV. But how do animals appear online? When it comes to nonhumans and the Internet, some of their physical encounters (that is, between animals' bodies and the Internet's materiality) have been documented, but there is no systematic study of this intersection.[17] Similarly, although the phenomenon of cats on the Internet has been somewhat studied, digital encounters between animals and the Internet (that is, when animals "go online") are in dire need of more critical scholarly attention.[18]

On Friday, March 9, 2018, the Oregon Zoo went to Twitter and posted a message saying, "It's Friday, let's rate some species. #rateaspecies." As more animal conservation institutions "got in on the fun," numerous tweets started to appear in which different animals were given Amazon-like reviews and ratings.[19] While it is possible to find some tweets for the months of April and May, most of the activity occurred between the 9th and 14th of March, which left over 150 individual tweets.[20] Although the lifespan of the hashtag was somewhat short, it went viral on social media during that weekend—meaning the content became "contagious" as it spread quickly and widely on the Internet.[21] For example, many of the posts from the Oregon Zoo received over 2,000 likes and around 700 retweets. Furthermore, the thread continued to get extensive press coverage thereafter.[22] One of these articles reported that the person who started this got the idea from an Amazon review he read that described hiking boots in a language that, to him, could also be deployed to describe a river otter.[23] So, the second tweet the Oregon zoo posted, which showed an image of an otter, read: "Overall very good first impressions. Sturdy built, totally winter-ready and waterproof. Only comes in brown but that's actually a plus for me."[24]

The majority of the images that circulated in this thread under the #rateaspecies hashtag were high-definition, close-up shots of species that offered a tremendous amount of detail and effectively presented a dramatic hyperreal nature, one characterized by the lack of reference to humans.[25] Just as with wildlife photography, these images and accompanying texts continue to structure human-animal relations in specific ways through their representation of animals not only as providers of entertainment and spectacle but also as expendable resources to be exploited and dominated.[26] In this case, animals who live in cages or other zoo and lab enclosures were mixed with text in a humorous way and presented as entertainment that humans who use social media get to consume, laugh at, and discard as they move on to the next thing.

Although it is not clear what the purpose behind these tweets was—other than to amuse, entertain, and bring attention to the emitting institutions—what is evident is that these images and text do not construct nonhumans as subjects but rather present them as objects to be mocked. While the objectification of animals as entertainment is nothing new, what further complicates this online trend is that animals are openly referred to and talked about via the language of commodities. Here an animal is a "unit," "model," "thing," "must-have," and "purchase" that gets *rated* depending on "efficiency," "disruptive design," "inspired mechanical engineering," "convenient size," "multi-directional front end," etc. In the words tweeted by the Monterey Bay Aquarium to describe a marine mammal (and its posted spectacular photograph): "Invented its own niche with seamless software/hardware integration. Absolute head-turner and conversation starter. Sorry, no headphone jack: the future is here."[27]

On the one hand, the mapping of commodity language onto animals is what makes these tweets humorous and what made this go viral, together with other media coverage that touted this as "quality fun," precisely because of the cognitive and linguistic distance between the semantic universe that is used to refer to the animals in these pictures and the one employed in relation to purchased goods, which is normally quite large for the majority of the population. Likely, it is precisely this linguistic "transgression" by which otters are described *as if* they were a pair of boots that makes these tweets effectively humorous.

On the other hand, the fact that this language is so openly used in conjunction with animals without eliciting any abhorred reactions or any questioning is problematic and symptomatic of the morally speciesist-anthropocentric system that underlies popular media, and which CAMS seeks to make visible. So although meant as a joke, the treatment of animals in these tweets nonetheless reflects the exploitative nature of certain aspects of human-animal relations because, as Molloy has noted, the popular construction of animal imagery and discourse is intrinsically connected to "a wider set of processes by which animals are commodified and the norms of human-animal relations established and sustained."[28]

Although much has been written in relation to the indissociably connected oppression of nonhuman animals and the development and perpetuation of capitalism, it has mostly focused on the animal-industrial complex.[29] However, the argument put forward here is that just as words such as "cattle," "meat," "poultry" or "livestock" serve to objectify other animals by casting their very existence in terms of the industries that use and kill them for profit, the words used in these tweets continue to frame their existence as commodities that can be consumed in a social media "free" market. Thus, these seemingly innocuous forms of entertainment, namely, the juxtaposition of hyperreal images with commodity-oriented language as well as their massive circulation in digital spaces, work to reify the objectification of animals that already occurs in other areas of our capitalist society.

Furthermore, the fact that the actual name of the species (which, in itself, is another categorical human construction derived from the natural sciences) is not mentioned makes it easier to continue to remove the real animal and be left with a simulacrum of an animal as a digital object.[30] This way of looking constitutes a damaging "deanimalization" because, in presenting us with a disembodied animal figure, it releases us from having to attend to the real animal in its concrete physical and material context.[31] This is particularly problematic in this case because most of the animals depicted in these images are "wild" (as opposed to domestic, farm, or feral) but live in captivity, as denoted by the fact that most of the images come from the Twitter handles of zoos.[32] Therefore, remarking on the primary senders of these tweets—namely, zoos, aquariums, science centers for marine life, SeaWorld, etc.—allows us to recapture the real animal by creating the space to interrogate the institutional contexts and related practices that mark the lives of these animals.

Interestingly, it is not just commodity words that attach to animals but also the globalized capitalistic logic in which they trade, as people *rate* animals not just regarding their efficiency as products but also regarding their expected availability. In this discursive context, animals become objects that can be purchased and owned at any time, just like any other *thing*, and who get a lesser score if they can't be purchased everywhere. For example, in one tweet a bird was presented as interchangeable with a Roomba, described as something that can be acquired on a whim or with equal ease by a human, but also as "less than" the robot vacuum machine because it demonstrates unwanted, uncontrolled behavior. In another, a spider is touted for being available in many colors just like fashionable commodities are, but also rated down for not being available everywhere, which is the expectation for globally exchanged goods.

As might have been noted by now, the hashtag is not "rate an animal," but rather "rate a *species*." This suggests a taxonomic classification of kinds, types, or varieties that also works as a sociocultural assignation. Indeed, "species" is constituted by and through human hierarchies where ideas of animality and nature are entangled in the constitution of race, gender, class, and other human differences.[33] Furthermore, the use of "species" produces a situation where the animal presented in the image must stand in representation for the whole species it belongs to, a reductive move that signals an essentialist treatment of animals much like the one Derrida denounced, and not unlike the one deployed around the categories "women" or "Black."[34]

Furthermore, looking at this thread of tweets from a media-studies perspective reveals how critiques of human use of other animals are consistent with those applied to similar analyses of gender, race, ethnicity, sexuality, disability, and other markers of difference. For example, the California Academy of Sciences questioned an albino crocodile's identity as a crocodile because of his "lack" of the colors commonly present in members of this species: "NOT AS EXPECTED. Color not as shown (not even CLOSE!), supposed to be predator but just sits on heated rock all day and let turtles walk all over him. . . . "[35] There is a direct parallel between the "color not as shown" derogatory remark directed towards this crocodile and the stigmatization and othering of Black people with albinism. This genetic condition, in which a body lacks a pigmented epidermal layer, challenges ideas of race, especially the ideal of race for people of color and various ethnicities. For example, albinos in South Africa and Zimbabwe that are "supposed to be" black, much like the crocodile is "supposed to be a predator," face enormous social consequences, including poverty, a life of exclusion, and even death.[36] Just as the very visible color difference of the crocodile affects its identity as a "proper" crocodile, so does the whiteness of the body of the person with albinism complicate its identity. Martin wrote that "The white negro body presented a fantasy of racial transformation, and the belief that under specific conditions black skin could turn white and the African American could be indistinguishable from the European."[37] Yet as Miller reminds us, this white skin does not accrue white privilege as "the ghost of their blackness remains."[38] Ultimately, although targeted towards a crocodile, the words in this tweet evidence the social constructions that make color equivalent to authenticity.

Similarly, when describing the use of animals as media to facilitate human interaction, Adams mentions that a problematic connection between the words used to describe invasive nonhuman species and immigrants usually emerges, and this becomes evident in a tweet that refers to a situation where an "immigrant" species, exotic to the area of Florida—where the marine laboratory that sent the tweet is located—is pitted against unhappy local fish only to then get eaten as they appear to be tasty.[39] As with racial categorizations, the boundaries that differentiate species are not "natural" but "actively made, maintained, politically charged, and fashioned to serve some needs more than others, inviting new essentialisms even as they alert us to important differences."[40] Thus, while some natural scientific data may have a role in determining which nonhuman species are "native" or "invasive," much of this pertains to what Jørgensen calls the cultural category of "belonging," something determined entirely by humans based on judgments on the appropriateness (or inappropriateness) of a species in a place.[41] That tweet, then, is predicated on a "nativeness standard" and thus reifies the idea that a taxon does not belong where it does not "naturally" occur, obscuring the fact that said "nativeness" is always negotiated through cultural preferences.[42]

Although this notion of "alien" threatening "native" species by "intruding" where they don't belong has been prominent in various fields of science, such as conservation biology and restoration ecology, for some time now, the invasive species/native species trope is unequivocally a product of the neoliberal age, as it "reflects anxieties specific to the global project of breaking down all political, spatial, and natural barriers to market expansion and flourishing."[43] Thus, barely displaced in the kingdom of fish is what Comaroff and Comaroff found in the realm of plants, namely, "a distressingly familiar crusade: the demonization of migrants and refugees by the state and its citizenry alike," who—like the fish in the tweet mentioned above who kept appearing despite being unwanted—are accused of spreading wildly out of control.[44] Thus, it is through tweets like these that

> we are reminded of the conjoined logics of race and species but now it is species that is a metric of raciality rather than the other way around—that is, the construction of "invasives" as heedless, destructive, and hyper-fertile aliens draws from white imaginings about nonwhite immigrants, especially Latinos. Invasives take on color, and nature as the space that they threatened is raced, too, as white.[45]

Again, that biologists "sometimes attribute to immigrant species some of the same characteristics that nativists and xenophobes have ascribed to immigrant humans," such as the veiled claim of excessive breeding present in the aforementioned tweet authored by a marine laboratory in Florida, is not necessarily new; what is novel is the reach that this particularly pernicious discourse can have as it goes viral on social media and is absorbed as "entertainment" by wider segments of individuals.[46]

In aesthetics terms, the animals depicted on the Twitter thread are also touted for being "fuzzy," "stylish," "adorable," for "matching everything" and having "extra fluff," and finally for being "too cute." As Malamud has noted, since the human gaze directed at nonhuman animals in visual culture parallels Mulvey's male gaze, animals are typically valued for their cuteness "in a way that is feminized, and derogatorily so: cute animals are like dumb blondes."[47] In one animal cutification example, a tweet depicted a pink marine creature that was described as knowing how to perform for the camera and had "cute" bodily features, namely dark pink gills. In another, a nonhuman was "top rated" for "cuteness, rarity and grace" and positively described as well as for its ability to come "in a variety of colors and patterns" and double "as a ballet movement coach."[48] Overall, both are feminized representations of animals that also seem to be demarcating the spaces these species are allowed and meant to inhabit, a "domestic" space where they flourish This discourse evidences "cutification" as a distinctive representational style that is usually employed by media targeted towards children and that is meant to attract empathy and affective sentiment while distracting from the real situations of the nonhuman animals depicted.[49] Moreover, we see traces of deeply entrenched racialized constructions of bodies; specifically, while black female bodies used to be (and arguably still are) categorized as lascivious, these feminized "white" animal bodies are described as graceful and cute.[50]

CONCLUSION

The #rateaspecies "amusing and informative" online hashtag discussed here represents and reifies the cultural human/animal binary that permeates our society, in parallel to the white/nonwhite and men/women dichotomies. While not *explicitly* racist or speciesist itself, the thread nonetheless constitutes what Plec would call a "contemporary cultural example of the ways in which racist and speciesist ideologies are rendered into innocent entertainment."[51]

Interestingly, this #rateaspecies Twitter thread was actually turned into a book the following year titled *Animals Reviewed*, published by the Association of Zoos & Aquariums. Stating that while you "can't put a price" on animals, still "you can rate them," the publication recounts its origin story and proceeds to reproduce some of the so-called "overzealous tweets of wildlife affection."[52] The introduction is written from an unquestioned, anthropatriarchal position that affirms that these animals "have also evolved to bring us joy" and that implies that the hashtag benefited humans, as it resulted in an "outpouring of animal therapy from every corner of Twitter." The justification is that this hashtag and subsequent publications hope to inspire the next generation of wildlife defenders, whose conservation efforts are deemed fundamental to the preservation of nonhuman animal species.

Yet, while one can recognize that the intention behind the publication of this association was to extol these animals and their virtuousness, the question still remains: must this be done through the gendered and racialized language of commodities? What lies at the heart of the matter, then, is that the zoo employee who started the thread could so easily conjure the image of his favorite otter as he was reading an Amazon description for hiking boots. This de-animalizing responds to the same systemic logic through which specific human bodies, specifically Black bodies, are also dehumanized—namely, a white normativity that classifies peoples of color as nonhuman bodies.[53]

The point here is, again, not to pit or compare "Blacks and animals" to make a favorable case for animal liberation from zoos, but to show that the underlying values in these tweets find their roots in the same objectifying and othering systemic logic that positions Black individuals as a lesser form of human and animals as a lesser form of species, only to enshrine a very particular form of human as the only legitimate one. Like racism, speciesism is a symptom of oppression, and so, when looking at these popular representations of animals online, we must remember that "the power to re-present another species is an act of domination."[54]

Further inquiries into animal representation on the Internet should not only shed light on practices or uses similar to this one but should also focus on the ways that animals appear online other than as entertainment to be consumed and disposed of, namely, as data and objects of surveillance as well as anthropomorphized pets to be owned and made cute in what is, for certain animals such a raccoons, possums, or rats, a total annihilation of their feral animality. This research should work to recuperate the notion that humans and animals stand in social relationships to each other and that animals are just as constitutive of human societies as their human counterparts, even when accounting for the variance across time and space and the contingency of animals' social location.[55] But, we also need to consider the power relations articulated through such relationships, as Cudworth invites us to do. That is why, although communication and media studies have the capacity to yield a unique analysis of online animal presence and representation, this endeavor needs to embrace an intersectional approach as the treatment of animals in the media works to reify their position as Other in similar ways and through analogous oppressive practices that systematically subject other human Others to alternate positions.

NOTES

1. Muir Woods NPS, "Does NOT taste like Bananas," Twitter, February 27, 2020, 1 p.m. https://twitter.com/MuirWoodsNPS/status/1233089591638396928.
2. A hashtag is a phrase or a keyword marked by a hash sign, commonly used on social media platforms to label or specifically identify certain content. Created by Twitter, this function allows users to easily sort through content and follow topics that are of interest to them.
3. For example, see Baker, *Picturing the Beast*; Brower, *Developing Animals*; Burt, *Animals in Film*; Chris, *Watching Wildlife*; Mills, *Animals on Television*; Mitman, *Reel Nature*; Daston and Mitman, *Thinking with Animals*; and Malamud, *An Introduction to Animals and Visual Culture*.
4. Mitman, *Reel Nature*; Cole and Stewart, *Our Children and Other Animals*.
5. Mejia, "The Epidemiology of Digital Infrastructure," 238.
6. For example, the seminal works of Crenshaw, "Demarginalizing the Intersection of Race and Sex," and Hill Collins, *Black Feminist Thought*. Also see Noble and Tynes, *The Intersectional Internet*.
7. Plec, "Perspectives on Human-Animal Communication," 1.
8. Plec, "Perspectives on Human-Animal Communication," 1–6; Abram, *The Spell of the Sensuous*.
9. Wolfe, "Human, All Too Human," 564–75; Wolfe, *Animal Rites*.
10. DeMello, *Animals and Society*, 5; Nocella, Sorenson, Kim, and Matusoka, eds., *Defining Critical Animal Studies*, xxii. It should be noted that this complex intersectionality has not been lost, though, to feminism. In the early 1970s, ecofeminists started to call attention to the fact that cultural discourses were constructing a dichotomy between women and nature (including animals) on one side, and male-dominated, Western, human culture on the other, which rendered women in closer material proximity and relation to the environment and nonhumans. See Salamone, "The Prevalence of the Natural Law within Women." Furthermore, part of the literature for what would become CAMS refers to the critiques of animal treatment elevated in the 1980s by ecofeminists.
11. Almiron, Cole, and Freeman, "Critical Animal and Media Studies," 367–80.

12. See Cudworth, *Developing Ecofeminist Theory*.
13. See Gossett, "Blackness, Animality, and the Unsovereign."
14. Armstrong, "The Postcolonial Animal," 413–20; Boisseron, *Afro-Dog*.
15. Kim, *Dangerous Crossings*.
16. Boisseron, *Afro-Dog*, xv.
17. See, for example, Carter, *Submarine Cables and the Oceans*; Oremus, "The Global Internet Is Being Attacked."
18. Miltner, "'There's no place for lulz on LOLCats'"; Berland, *Virtual Menageries*; White, *A Unified Theory of Cats on the Internet*. For exception, see Linné, "Cows on Facebook and Instagram," 719–33.
19. Khosla, "Zoos Are Rating Animals Online ."
20. The thread can still be accessed at twitter.com.
21. Berger, *Contagious*.
22. Stone, "Zoos and Science Museums"; Felton, "Zoos Go Viral."
23. Debczak, "#RateaSpecies? Zoos Share Amazon-Style Reviews."
24. Oregon Zoo, "Overall very good first impressions. Sturdy built, totally winter-ready and waterproof. Only comes in brown but that's actually a plus for me," Twitter, March 9, 2018, 1:30 p.m. https://twitter.com/oregonzoo/status/972147659761795072.
25. The characterization of what is depicted in these images as "hyperreal" borrows directly from Debord, who, looking at the circulation of images in society, argues that reality is partially apprehended as it unfolds in a pseudo-world solely as an object of contemplation, where nature becomes a dramatic hyperreal nature. See Debord, *The Society of the Spectacle*; and Altrudi, "Connecting to Nature through Tech?," 124–41.
26. See Mitman, *Reel Nature*; Chris, *Watching Wildlife*; and Scott, "Popularizing Science and Nature Programming," 29–35.
27. Monterey Bay Aquarium, "Invented its own niche with seamless software/hardware integration. Absolute head-turner and conversation starter. Sorry, no headphone jack: the future is here," Twitter, March 9, 2018, 9:25 a.m. https://twitter.com/montereyaq/status/972161528131551233.
28. Molloy, *Popular Media and Animals*, 1.
29. The animal-industrial complex is commonly understood as "the globally operating capitalist network facilitating the total exploitation of other animals captivated in its industries." See Nibert, ed., *Animal Oppression and Capitalism*, 35. See also Twine, "Revealing the 'Animal-Industrial Complex,'" 12–39.
30. Baudrillard, *Simulacra and Simulation*.
31. See Berland, *Virtual Menageries*.
32. Anderson has noted that zoos are cultural institutions, human adaptations of the ensemble of life forms that bear the name "nature" (see Anderson, "Animals, Science, and Spectacle in the City"). But zoos and aquariums are also entertainment facilities, by which Laidlaw means capitalist entities that commodify and exploit other animals while striving to enhance their brand (see Rob Laidlaw, "ZooBiz," 71–99).
33. Cudworth, "Beyond Speciesism," 39–55.
34. It is precisely to combat the assembling of the plurality of living creatures in the figure of an animality that is primarily defined by its opposition to humanity that Derrida develops the concept of "l'animot." See Derrida, Mallet, and Willis, *The Animal That Therefore I Am*.
35. California Academy of Sciences, "NOT AS EXPECTED. Color not as shown (not even CLOSE!!!)," Twitter, March 9, 2018, 12:42 p.m. https://twitter.com/calacademy/

status/972211077663641600.
36. Baker et al., "The Myths Surrounding People with Albinism," 169–81.
37. Martin, *The White African American Body*, 41.
38. Pickett Miller, *Deconstructing the Albino Other*, 11.
39. Adams, "Animals as Media," 26–43. Mote Marine Lab, "0 stars," Twitter, March 20, 2018, 6:33 p.m. https://twitter.com/motemarinelab/status/976270427021561856.
40. The Multispecies Editing Collective, "Troubling Species," 5.
41. Jørgensen, *Recovering Lost Species in the Modern Age*.
42. Chew and Hamilton, "The Rise and Fall of Biotic Nativeness."
43. Kim, *Dangerous Crossings*, 152.
44. Comaroff and Comaroff, "Naturing the Nation," 627–51, 645.
45. Kim, *Dangerous Crossings*, 153.
46. Sagoff, "Why Exotic Species Are Not as Bad as We Fear," B7.
47. Malamud, "Looking at Humans Looking at Animals," 154–68, 158.
48. Ocean Networks, "Top rated for cuteness, rarity and grace," Twitter, March 14, 2018, 3:50 p.m. https://twitter.com/Ocean_Networks/status/974055271898087425.
49. For "cutification," see Cole and Stewart, *Our Children*, 98.
50. Rodrigues, "White Normativity," 71–79.
51. Plec, "(Black) 'Man v. Cheetah,'" 149.
52. Association of Zoos & Aquariums, *Animals Reviewed*, 1.
53. Rodrigues, "White Normativity."
54. Merskin, "Media Theories and the Crossroads of Critical Animal and Media Studies," 11.
55. See Benton, *Natural Relations*, and Cole and Stewart, *Our Children*.

WORKS CITED

Abram, David. *The Spell of the Sensuous: Perception and Language in a More-Than-Human World*. New York: Pantheon Books, 1996.

Adams, Tony E. "Animals as Media: Speaking through/with Nonhuman Beings." In *Perspectives on Human-Animal Communication*, edited by Emily Plec. New York: Routledge, 2013.

Almiron, Núria, Matthew Cole, and Carrie P. Freeman. "Critical Animal and Media Studies: Expanding the Understanding of Oppression in Communication Research." *European Journal of Communication* 33, no. 4 (2018): 367–80.

Altrudi, Soledad. "Connecting to Nature through Tech? The Case of the iNaturalist app." *Convergence* 27, no. 1 (2021): 124–41.

Anderson, Kay. "Animals, Science, and Spectacle in the City." In *Animal Geographies: Place, Politics, and Identity in the Nature-Culture Borderlands*, edited by Jennifer Wolch and Jody Emel. London: Verso, 1998.

Armstrong, Philip. "The Postcolonial Animal." *Society and Animals* 10, no. 4 (2002): 413–20.

Association of Zoos & Aquariums. *Animals Reviewed: Starred Ratings of Our Feathered, Finned and Furry Friends. #RateASpecies*. Portland, OR: Timber Press, 2019.

Baker, Charlotte, et al. "The Myths Surrounding People with Albinism in South Africa and Zimbabwe." *Journal of African Cultural Studies* 22, no. 2 (2010): 169–81.

Baker, Steve. *Picturing the Beast: Animals, Identity, and Representation*. Manchester: Manchester

University Press, 1993.

Baudrillard, Jean. *Simulacra and Simulation*. Ann Arbor: University of Michigan Press, 1994.

Benton, Ted. *Natural Relations: Ecology, Animal Rights and Social Justice*. London: Verso, 1993.

Berger, Jonah. *Contagious: Why Things Catch On*. New York: Simon & Schuster, 2013.

Berland, Jody. *Virtual Menageries: Animals as Mediators in Network Cultures*. Cambridge, MA: MIT Press, 2019.

Boisseron, Bénédicte. *Afro-Dog: Blackness and the Animal Question*. New York: Columbia University Press, 2018.

Brower, Matthew. *Developing Animals: Wildlife and Early American Photography*. Minneapolis: University of Minnesota Press, 2011.

Burt, Jonathan. *Animals in Film*. London: Reaktion Books, 2002.

Carter, Lionel. *Submarine Cables and the Oceans: Connecting the World*. UNEP-WCMC Biodiversity Series no. 31, 2009. Available at https://www.unep-wcmc.org/resources-and-data.

Chew, Matthew, and Andrew Hamilton. "The Rise and Fall of Biotic Nativeness: A Historical Perspective." In *Fifty Years of Invasion Ecology: The Legacy of Charles Elton*, edited by David Richardson. Oxford: Blackwell Publishing, 2011.

Chris, Cynthia. *Watching Wildlife*. Minneapolis: University of Minnesota Press, 2006.

Cole, Matthew, and Kate Stewart. *Our Children and Other Animals*. Farnham, UK: Ashgate Publishing Group, 2014.

Comaroff, Jean, and John Comaroff. "Naturing the Nation: Aliens, Apocalypse, and the Postcolonial State." *Journal of Southern African Studies* 27, no. 3 (2001): 627–51.

Crenshaw, Kimberle. "Demarginalizing the Intersection of Race and Sex: A Black Feminist Critique of Antidiscrimination Doctrine, Feminist Theory and Antiracist Politics." *University of Chicago Legal Forum* (1989).

Cudworth, Erica. "Beyond Speciesism: Intersectionality, Critical Sociology and the Human Domination of Other Animals." In *The Rise of Critical Animal Studies*, edited by Nik Taylor and Richard Twine. London: Routledge, 2014.

———. *Developing Ecofeminist Theory: The Complexity of Difference*. New York: Palgrave Macmillan, 2005.

Daston, Lorraine, and Gregg Mitman. *Thinking with Animals: New Perspectives on Anthropomorphism*. New York: Columbia University Press, 2005.

Debczak, Michele. "#RateaSpecies? Zoos Share Amazon-Style Reviews of Animals on Twitter." Mental Floss. Available at https://www.mentalfloss.com.

Debord, Guy. *The Society of the Spectacle*. New York: Zone Books, 1967.

DeMello, Margo. *Animals and Society: An Introduction to Human-Animal Studies*. New York: Columbia University Press, 2012.

Derrida, Jacques, Marie-Louise Mallet, and David Willis. *The Animal That Therefore I Am*. New York: Fordham University Press, 2008.

Felton, James. "Zoos Go Viral on Twitter after Leaving Hilarious Amazon-Style Reviews of Their Animals." IFLScience, 2018. Available at https://www.iflscience.com.

Gossett, Che. "Blackness, Animality, and the Unsovereign." *Verso* (blog), September 8, 2015. Available at https://www.versobooks.com.

Hill Collins, Patricia. *Black Feminist Thought: Knowledge, Consciousness and the Politics of Empowerment*. New York: Routledge, 2009.

Jørgensen, Dolly. *Recovering Lost Species in the Modern Age: Histories of Longing and Belonging*. Cambridge, MA: MIT Press, 2019.

Khosla, Proma. "Zoos Are Rating Animals Online and It's Too Good." *Mashable*, March 10, 2018. Available at https://www.mashable.com.

Kim, Claire Jean. *Dangerous Crossings: Race, Species, and Nature in a Multicultural Age*. New York: Cambridge University Press, 2015.

Laidlaw, Rob. "ZooBiz: The Conservation of Business?" In *Animal Oppression and Capitalism*, vol. 2, *The Oppressive and Destructive Role of Capitalism*, edited by David Nibert. Santa Barbara, CA: Praeger, 2017.

Linné, Tobias. "Cows on Facebook and Instagram: Interspecies Intimacy in the Social Media Spaces of the Swedish Dairy Industry." *Television & New Media* 17, no. 8 (2016): 719–33.

Malamud, Randy. *An Introduction to Animals and Visual Culture*. New York: Palgrave Macmillan, 2012.

———. "Looking at Humans Looking at Animals." In *Critical Animal and Media Studies: Communication for Nonhuman Animal Advocacy*, edited by Nuria Almiron, Matthew Cole, and Carrie P. Freeman. New York: Routledge, 2015.

Martin, Charles. *The White African American Body: A Cultural and Literary Exploration*. New Brunswick, NJ: Rutgers University Press, 2002.

Mejia, Robert. "The Epidemiology of Digital Infrastructure." In *The Intersectional Internet: Race, Sex, Class and Culture Online*, edited by Safiya Umoja Noble and Brendesha M. Tynes. New York: Peter Lang, 2016.

Merskin, Debra. "Media Theories and the Crossroads of Critical Animal and Media Studies." In *Critical Animal and Media Studies*, edited by Nuria Almiron, Matthew Cole, and Carrie P. Freeman. New York: Routledge, 2015.

Mills, Brett. *Animals on Television: The Cultural Making of the Non-Human*. London: Palgrave Macmillan, 2017.

Miltner, Kate. "'There's no place for lulz on LOLCats': The Role of Genre, Gender, and Group Identity in the Interpretation and Enjoyment of an Internet Meme." *First Monday* 19, no. 8, 2014.

Mitman, Gregg. *Reel Nature: America's Romance with Wildlife on Film*. Seattle: University of Washington Press, 2012.

Molloy, Clare. *Popular Media and Animals*. London: Palgrave Macmillan, 2011.

Nibert, David. *Animal Oppression and Capitalism*. Vol. 1, *The Oppression of Nonhuman Animals as Sources of Food*. Santa Barbara, CA: Praeger, 2017.

Noble, Safiya Umoja, and Brendesha M. Tynes, *The Intersectional Internet: Race, Sex, Class and Culture Online*. New York: Peter Lang, 2016.

Nocella, Anthony, John Sorenson, Socha Kim, and Atsuko K. Matusoka. *Defining Critical Animal Studies: An Intersectional Social Justice Approach for Liberation*. New York: Peter Lang, 2014.

Oremus, Will. "The Global Internet Is Being Attacked by Sharks, Google Confirms." *Slate* magazine 15, 2014. Available at https://slate.com.

Pickett Miller, Niya. *Deconstructing the Albino Other: A Critique of Albinism Identity in the Media*. Lanham, MD: Lexington Books, 2020.

Plec, Emily. "(Black) 'Man v. Cheetah': Perpetuations and Transformations of the Rhetoric of Racism." In *Critical Animal and Media Studies*, edited by Nuria Almiron, Matthew Cole, and Carrie P. Freeman. New York: Routledge, 2015.

———. "Perspectives on Human-Animal Communication: An Introduction." In *Perspectives on Human-Animal Communication*, edited by Emily Plec. New York: Routledge, 2013.

Rodrigues, Luis C. "White Normativity, Animal Advocacy and PETA's Campaigns." *Ethnicities* 20, no. 1 (2020): 71–79.

Sagoff, Mark. "Why Exotic Species Are Not as Bad as We Fear." *Chronicle of Higher Education* 46, no. 42

(2000): B7.

Salamone, Connie. "The Prevalence of the Natural Law within Women: Women and Animal Rights." In *Reweaving the Web of Life: Feminism and Non-Violence*, edited by Pam McAllister. Philadelphia: New Society Publisher, 1982.

Scott, Karen. "Popularizing Science and Nature Programming: The Role of 'Spectacle' in Contemporary Wildlife Documentary." *Journal of Popular Film and Television* 31, no. 1 (2003): 29–35.

Stone, Maddie. "Zoos and Science Museums Are Giving Species 'Amazon Reviews' on Twitter, and It's Awesome." Gizmodo, 2018. Available at https://gizmodo.com/earther.

The Multispecies Editing Collective. "Troubling Species: Care and Belonging in a Relational World." *RCC Perspectives: Transformations in Environment and Society* (2016).

Twine, Richard. "Revealing the 'Animal-Industrial Complex'—A Concept and Method for Critical Animal Studies?" *Journal of Critical Animal Studies* 10 (2012): 12–39.

White, E. J. *A Unified Theory of Cats on the Internet.* Stanford, CA: Stanford University Press, 2020.

Wolfe, Cary. *Animal Rites: American Culture, the Discourse of Species, and Posthumanist Theory.* Chicago: University of Chicago Press, 2003.

———. "Human, All Too Human: 'Animal Studies' and the Humanities." *PMLA: Publications of the Modern Language Association of America* 124, no. 2 (March 1, 2009): 564–75.

Of Food and Kin

Civil Rats and the Human Exceptional
A Vegan-Historical Account of the Rat Extermination Act of 1967

Thomas Aiello

IN 1967, AS PART OF A PLAN TO REVITALIZE IMPOVERISHED URBAN AREAS IN HIS BROADER war on poverty, Lyndon Johnson proposed the Rat Extermination Act, a bill to provide $20 million for eliminating rats in a variety of neglected neighborhoods across the country. Taking place amid a series of urban uprisings, the bill was derided by its opponents as the "Civil Rats" bill. The Rat Extermination Act, and the American mid-century relationship with its rat population, has been studied for its proximity to poverty programs, urban renewal, and race, most comprehensively by historian Dawn Biehler.[1] Biehler's scholarship is invaluable, but the one group that does not receive treatment as an equal agent in the historical narrative is the population of rats themselves. Rat extermination appeared as a national issue at the intersection of racial uprisings in American cities and white conservative backlash against them. "Civil rats" as a congressional epithet combined speciesist attitudes against rats with racist attitudes against frustrated protesters, encapsulating the resentments of white leaders toward the latter by scapegoating the former. The American attitude toward rats in the postwar period through the Civil Rights Movement was shaped by a racial politics that held them up as signposts of Black inadequacy for white conservatives and as signposts of governmental neglect for impoverished urban residents, represented here by the citizens of Baltimore, New York, and Chicago. When leaders did make faltering attempts at reconciling the consequences of racialized poverty, then, they focused their attention on the symbols associated with that poverty—rats—over and against the structural racism that created it.

Taking that speciesism seriously through the intersectional lens of race requires respecting the life of the rat as much as that of the human, while still acknowledging their fundamental differences. It is the common position for any deontological conception of animal ethics, spanning from Kant's categorical imperative to never treat anyone only as a means to an end, to Ronald Dworkin's non-relative interests that have total weight in moral calculations. "The basic idea of a right-based theory," Dworkin explains, "is that distinct individuals have interests that they are entitled to protect if they so wish."[2] The position was taken most influentially by Tom Regan. "Inherent value," he argues, "belongs equally to those who are the experiencing subjects of a life."[3] Assuming rats to be experiencing subjects of a life who have inherent value—beings who should not be treated only as a means to an end—shapes the mid-century signposting of rats in new ways and demonstrates how different bigotries intersect in the treatment of groups coded by race and species.

Jonathan Burt has called the rat "a totem animal for modernity." The rat "cannot be separated from human achievement, yet it also stands as a symptom of human destructiveness," argues Burt. It "adapts with humans to the ever more complicated structures and networks that are produced by modernization." And "like other dangerous objects, the rat constantly pushes at the edges of the borders set to contain it." Still, it is clear that "whether the rat is treated as vermin or hailed as a scientific hero or heroine; in all cases the human intention is always eventually to kill it."[4]

The similarities of such codings are rooted in historical antecedents. "We can discover the origins of the practice of racial dehumanization in our long history of managing the nonhuman animal world," argues Kalpana Rahita Seshadri. She sees a real "similarity between our exploitation of nature and animals and of 'inferior' peoples. Yet the exchange between those who work on questions of race and those who concern themselves with animality and human propriety has been minimal." It is a situation she attributes to "the fact that the concepts of 'race' and 'animal' are anthropological/political and ontological categories, respectively, and are therefore tacitly indifferent, if not exclusive, of each other."[5]

As explained by Kay Anderson, marginalized groups have "been variously identified with the discursive spaces of 'wild' nature (as distinct from that proud monument of 'civilisation' known as the city or, alternatively, those counterpoint spaces like 'ghettoes' within the city's 'dark side'). Animality has been a crucial reference point for constructing sociospatial difference and hierarchy in Western cultures. Its meanings have circulated across the nature border and into a politics of sociospatial relations." The Black population was using animals, in this case rats, as a point of differentiation even as the broader populace was animalizing them in other ways.[6]

IN BALTIMORE

In 1940s Baltimore, for example, officials mandated that all homes be "rat-proofed." Inspectors inspected blocks of housing in Black neighborhoods to "remove the last of the rat-harboring nuisances."[7] Even the Baltimore *Afro-American* took up the crusade, arguing that rats "can be seen walking about our streets and alleys at almost any time of the day or night," and chided its readership about cleanliness and prevention. Rat infestation was "a moral problem" and "in community life it becomes a social one. One dirty yard can spoil a neighborhood."[8] That kind of moralizing demonstrated the way Black residents of the city internalized the racist rat comparisons coming from city and state government, but it did nothing to counter such claims; it did nothing to equate the plight of Black Baltimore with white supremacy and the plight of rats with speciesist human assumptions about rats' place in the animal hierarchy and the cavalier attitude with which humans took their lives.

And lives of all kinds seemed to be at stake. "Baltimore's housing problem and rat problem came up about the same time," explained the *Afro-American*. Noting that the rat traps being used by the city looked like houses in miniature, the paper quipped that "there will be no special houses for white or black rats," playing on the fact that human segregation created such problems in the first place.[9] Leaders in Baltimore blamed the poor themselves for rat infestations. "In these heavily rat-infested districts," went one such claim, "most people apparently accepted rat bites as being inevitable." Equating the presence of rats with poverty not only stigmatized the poor, as historians have noted previously, but it also stigmatized rats using a trope of societal derision, making them as disposable as the impoverished themselves. The bites of such rats were common in Baltimore, causing problems as mundane as irritation and as serious as typhus, occasionally even causing death. There was, however, no reciprocity in the human response; mass killing was marshaled in response to occasional and accidental death.[10]

In response to such twentieth-century efforts, the Rodent Ecology Project at the School of Public Health at Johns Hopkins studied the effectiveness of killing campaigns. Poisoning programs killed roughly 60 percent of rats, a population that recovered within a year. The Rockefeller Foundation agreed. "Killing procedures merely make room for more rats to grow up and actually increase the yield of rat flesh per acre per year," the foundation reported. Killing rats "proved an almost endless, tedious, highly repetitive, and expensive job."[11] Rats were lesser than humans, their deaths were necessary to help ease human racial and housing problems, and others were technically doing the killing. Killing rats became "almost endless, tedious, highly repetitive."[12]

Still, that status did not limit human comparisons to nonhuman victims. "Rats do not check in at the resettlement office to discuss desirable housing vacancies," explained the *Baltimore Sun* in 1952. "When the razing crews start to work, the rats high tail it into nearby blocks, taking their fleas, lice, ticks, and disease potential right along with them." After killing programs ran their course in Baltimore, the *Sun* reported that "the new cement in the back yards began to crack. Some of the yards filled up with trash again. The rats, sensing perhaps that the humans' guard is down again, are finding easy pickings in the garbage-strewn alleys, burrowing under once-new concrete yards."[13] Not only was the rat problem a human problem, but the paper was clearly ascribing human-graded intelligence to the rats, whose senses were simply leading them to their own best possible situation. The *Sun*'s narrative sold rat intentionality as, first, existing, and second, sinister—another human-graded intelligence—as the rats were "sensing the humans' guard is down" and took the opportunity to take advantage of their lack of concern. Ascribing sinister motives to rat behavior became the justification for such killings, but counterintuitively, it was also an argument by a human standard *against* killing them.

IN CHICAGO

There was a similar legacy in Chicago. As early as the Great Depression, residents of the city's South Side were complaining of a scourge of rats, threatening their children and food supply, a problem exacerbated by municipal cuts to inspector budgets. In 1933, however, the Woman's City Club and the Chicago Board of Health got an extermination grant from the Civil Works Administration, hiring one thousand unemployed men to kill the rats. There was no effort at prevention, which would have allowed the rat population to migrate away pragmatically, nor at relocation, which was not even considered. There was only extermination. The plan was to use the vulnerability of the unemployed to create killing agents. Killing jobs, from rat exterminators to slaughterhouse workers, are occupied for the most part by those who need the work, not by those enamored with the act of killing. It was an effort, to be sure, aided by the general human revulsion for rats, but economic vulnerability certainly became the final push for any indigent job seeker who otherwise might have been dubious about taking a job that required him to kill animals. The success of the Chicago killing program, then, led to similar efforts in other metropolitan areas, unemployed men hired locally with federal dollars to exterminate rats.[14]

In 1940, a young Black girl died of "rat bite fever," and the *Chicago Defender* complained that she and other poor residents of the city were being victimized by the government's willingness to divert money to a European war effort "to kill men" while ignoring the "need" to kill rats at home. Again, public funds were diverted, and again exterminators protested. Chastising war spending while simultaneously declaring a war on nonhuman sentient beings, however, demonstrated the disconnect in human thinking.[15] As Edmund P. Russell has explained, "The ability of human beings to kill both national and natural enemies on an unprecedented scale, as well as fears about those abilities, developed in the twentieth century partly because of links between war and pest control."[16] Tens of millions of rats had been killed in the United States alone in the first part of the century. There was no reciprocal relationship in the ways that leaders visualized deaths, nor could there be, because the girl's killer lacked intentionality, unlike the killers of rats and of men in the World War II era. The human life was obviously given preference, but in so doing, common tropes of the role of intentionality in visualizations of killing became reversed.

IN NEW YORK

But then there was New York. In 1957, the *Amsterdam News*, the city's most prominent Black newspaper, ran a photo of an African American woman holding a rat that she had killed. Eva Ray stood defiantly holding the dead rat. "'I'm not afraid of any rat,' said Mrs. Ray, which is an unusual statement to come from a woman." The photo is a semiotic oxymoron, its sexist caption at odds with the image of female empowerment. But the strength of the woman comes at the expense of the dead, diminished rat that she holds. It is semiotically oxymoronic in a speciesist sense, then, as well. The dead rat in the photo is weak and insignificant in contrast with the defiant Ray, but her lack of fear in the photo's caption indicates that such animals are a monstrosity to be feared. In both a feminist and anti-speciesist reading of the photograph and its caption, rats are the losers. And in the content itself, that particular rat is the loser, his or her dead body displayed as a meaningless nuisance. Were, for example, a human's dead body displayed in the photograph as a meaningless nuisance, human outrage would have been palpable.[17]

The *Amsterdam News*'s anti-rat crusade was sustained throughout the late 1950s. In an October 1957 editorial, the paper described a rat eating the leg muscle of a sleeping four-month-old boy. "If you have red blood in your veins," the paper explained, the situation should make readers angry. "It should, for if you are a Negro, it could have been but for the grace of God, your child." It was clear that a lack of response to human-rat interactions in inner cities was not based on concern for rats, but instead on a lack of concern by the predominantly white government for the predominantly Black humans living in certain impoverished New York neighborhoods. The racialized nature of the fight over rats among humans was real, and would continue to sway policy decisions. Regardless, the rat-bite incident led to a special program on Harlem housing on New York's CBS television station.[18] In early 1958, the paper reported on three more rat bites, all in aid of a broader study of the deteriorating and fundamentally racialized housing situation in Harlem. "You'd better watch out," the report began, "the rats will be running up the stairs soon!" Again, it was rats themselves that became the signposts of human, racialized failings.[19]

In 1959, in a story about miniscule $5 and $10 fines given to landlords for building-code violations, the *Amsterdam News* claimed that "vicious, flesh-loving rats chalked up 442 bite victims in Manhattan last year, the majority in the Harlem area." The small fines for slumlords provided "Baby Flesh at $5 a Bite!" and created "Conditions Which Enable the Rats to Live Better Than There [sic] Victims." The report included pictures of human children who were

"The Rats' Victims." The presentation of rats as "flesh-loving" monsters hoping to feed on human children, rather than as innocent animals taking advantage of whatever circumstances were available to them to survive, was inaccurate. Such presentations put the focus squarely on the monstrous caricature created, taking it off of the human victims and the very real problems that disproportionately affected Black neighborhoods.[20]

The "flesh-loving" monster rhetoric wasn't necessarily intellectually disingenuous; very few people, white or Black, assumed that humans and other animals were functionally equal. Some 442 human bite victims certainly suffered and deserved better from the racialized politics of redlined white supremacy. Millions of rats also became victims of such racialized politics, exacerbated by the hysterical reporting of those bites that created a moral panic around them. "Baby Flesh at $5 a Bite" demanded nothing less than a disproportionate response from officials, as it always had in response to perceived attacks from those it deemed less than human. In that same edition, the paper apologized for "devoting so much of its front page and its Society Page to rats." But "ridding this community of the rats which plague our children" was too important. It included photos of all of the city commissioners with a role to play in slum maintenance. The only Black face included was that of the man soon to take over as welfare commissioner from the currently sitting white figure, perhaps a mayoral capitulation to the escalating racial tensions over the problems of racialized poverty and redlining. Again, juxtaposed with the real racial politics of government apathy about Black housing conditions was the scapegoating of rats as a "plague," the term calling back to a medieval Europe where one-third of the continent's human population died.[21]

Another 1959 headline trumpeted "The Rats Who Run Harlem," accompanied by photographs of the corpses of dead rats. One letter to the paper responding to the presentation of dead rats on the front page expressed frustration with the human politicians blamed for the problem, arguing, "Let's get a companion picture for the four-legged rats on your front page—one with the two-legged rats."[22] Not only were the politicians framed as the bad guys who weren't aggressively killing rats, but they were signified as bad guys by naming them rats. And as Edmund Leach has argued, when animal names like "rat" are used "as an imprecation, it indicates that the name itself is credited with potency. It clearly signifies that the animal category is in some way taboo and sacred." It was a self-fulfilling prophecy.[23]

After the State Department of Health adopted a plan to require landlords to pay for rat extermination, the *Amsterdam News* reported the news approvingly along with a photo of two humans, one Black and one white, united in common cause and holding a program sign that read, "RATS ARE KILLERS—drive them from your home." This was consistent with the narrative the paper had presented for years. Racial animus between white and Black humans could be improved by slaughtering rats.[24]

In the 1960s, 62 percent of Black families and 35 percent of white families lived in substandard housing, making them vulnerable to at least 14,000 rat bites in the decade, more than half of the victims under the age of two. Those bites could cause rash, vomiting, diarrhea, and other symptoms that needed to be cured with antibiotics. Rat-bite fever, leptospirosis, and salmonellosis were common.[25] Importantly, and undiscussed, all of those diseases were curable with antibiotics. When humans could not afford antibiotics or were left vulnerable to rats, the culprits were other humans and the imagined economies, built on white supremacist assumptions, that created that imbalance.

In response to rent strikes known as "rat marches," New York embarked on a variety of rat-killing programs, destroying the symbol of decay rather than the decay itself, and in the process destroying the lives of thousands of rats and refusing to address the systemic racism happening at the housing level. New York mayor Robert F. Wagner "spoke disheartedly of the enormous amount of public housing that New York City has and how the houses are not kept up after the tenants have been in them for some years," said Lady Bird Johnson. "It was a very discouraging picture."[26] Activists did not concern themselves with the deaths of the rats, but they did point out the city's problem of treating a symptom rather than the causes of urban poverty. "What good is getting rid of rats when you haven't got any heat or lights?" asked one resident. "We can beat off the rats with a stick, but how are we going to keep warm?"[27]

The protestors were Black; the administrators were white. The racial differentiation of the moment matched the power imbalance felt by Black residents every day. Meanwhile, the dead rats were used as a symbol of that imbalance, an afterthought, their lives considered meaningless by comparison, a problem made more problematic by research published that summer from the University of California at Berkeley demonstrating that rats developed larger brains when provided richer lives with more experiences and stimulation. It was a glaring demonstration that rats were thinking, feeling creatures with opportunities for neural growth similar to humans.'[28] And it came as the last gasp of scientific racism was seeking to invalidate the humanity of the African American population. The Tuskegee Syphilis Experiment was begun in 1932 by the US Public Health Service in Macon County, Alabama. Outside of the government, groups like the International Association for the Advancement of Ethnology and Eugenics, the Pioneer Fund, and the National Putnam Letters Committee did their best to stoke the dying embers of a eugenics movement that sought to validate racial discrimination.[29] Protestors, then, were left with little option but to ignore neural studies of rats in order to protect themselves from the consequences of both political and scientific demonstrations of racism.

Responding to long-held complaints by civil rights leaders in 1965, mayor Richard Daley directed the city's Board of Health, Department of Streets and Sanitation, and Department of Buildings to undertake what the *Chicago Defender* called a "3-way assault on rats," an "inner city war." It was the language of human combat, a way of coding rats as an enemy with ill intent.[30]

IN WASHINGTON

Exacerbating the perceived urban problems was federal inaction. "One of the things that slipped through in the early days was a letter drafted somewhere in the bowels of that organization to one of the better mayors in the United States," recalled James C. Gaither, special assistant to the president, "who had written the Secretary saying, 'I've just been told that HEW will not continue funding of the rat extermination program in'—whatever the city was—'because we've been too successful [at killing rats, thus limiting federal appropriations in the future], and I'm enclosing a copy of this incredible letter that I've received from HEW.' And a letter went back from me that somehow got through to him saying, 'Dear Mr. Mayor, I congratulate you on the wonderful rat extermination program you've run for that city.' It was absolutely awful."[31]

The disconnect was also apparent in Washington, DC. While lamenting the District of Columbia's lack of funding for rat control, the *Washington Post* described Clarence Travis, the district's Health Department Vector Control Division director, the leader of the department tasked with rat prevention and eradication, as "the District's Lord High Executioner of Rats."

It was a clever phrase, and effectively true. If, however, the paper referred to the leader of the district's branch of the Humane Society as the Lord High Executioner of Dogs, in response to euthanizations of abandoned pets, the population would have been up in arms and the Humane Society probably would have sued. Again, the linguistics of the rat discourse created a chain of value among living groups of animals, a chain where rats were always at the bottom.[32]

Thus it was that early in Johnson's administration, his Office of Equal Opportunity attempted a series of rat-killing programs under the title Operation Rat. "A rat eradication program for the American People," Operation Rat started in early 1965. Johnson's rival Robert Kennedy had been using rats as rhetorical signposts of urban, racialized poverty that year in response to the Watts uprising, noting that appeals to rioters for law and order neglected to acknowledge that the legal system had not protected poor Black residents "from having to keep lights turned on the feet of children at night, to keep them from being gnawed by rats." In August 1966, special assistant to the president Joe Califano asked Sargent Shriver about the costs of a larger, more comprehensive "program to exterminate the rats in our ghettos throughout the country." Johnson was convinced about the need. He shared "a deep concern over the human injury and anguish brought about by this shameful condition in our cities."[33]

And so, the Rat Extermination Act would be broader than Operation Rat, falling under the aegis of the new Department of Housing and Urban Development.[34] Originally part of that Office of Economic Opportunity spending package, the now freestanding rat bill would have allotted 40 million dollars over two years for killing rats in poor human communities, but conservative representatives balked; they worried about budgetary concerns and heavy spending in minority districts. The bill came to the House floor just three short days after the conclusion of the Newark riots. Newark was a majority-Black city policed by a majority-white force. Unemployment was high, and redlining was commonly used to protect the property values of white citizens and keep the Black citizens in poverty. The frustrated population was responding to those realities, but most immediately, it was responding to another in a long line of police brutality incidents, when two white officers beat a Black taxi driver named John Smith. Four days of violence followed, leaving twenty-six people dead and hundreds injured.[35]

The country had been in flames for much of the previous several months. In a period known as "The Long, Hot Summer," there were more than 150 racial uprisings across the country. In June, for example, there was a week-long uprising in Cincinnati. Then there was Detroit. There was Milwaukee. In Atlanta, SNCC leader Stokely Carmichael told an audience, "We are not concerned with peace. We are concerned with the liberation of Black people. We have to build a revolution." The day prior to the House vote on the rat legislation, the same body voted overwhelmingly for an anti-riot bill designed to punish "professional agitators" who "inflame the people." New Jersey's Frank Thompson derided the effort as a "bill of attainder aimed at one man—Stokely Carmichael." The anti-riot measure passed, 347–70. In the face of the uprisings and of official white hostility toward them, passing any measure seen to benefit those communities was unlikely.[36]

And that made the Rat Extermination Act vulnerable. "The rat smart thing to do is to vote down this civil rats bill, rat now," joked Virginia congressman James Broyhill. "I must say, that's the darndest title for a legislative proposal that you could ever come up with," said Larry O'Brien, then serving as the postmaster general. "That opened itself up to some sick humor. Some wise guy said why don't we just enlist all the cats in the program; we could save a lot of money. It was subjected to a lot of ridicule until we began to look at some of the appalling statistics regarding this problem." Opposition to the law demonstrated Southern conservative desensitization to the death of rats and to the seriousness of the civil rights cause. The death of rats, in fact, could be so easily dismissed because those deaths were ostensibly in service to civil rights, an effort they had been ridiculing since *Brown v. Board of Education* in 1954. *The Democrat* magazine lamented, "To the vast majority of Republicans in the House of Representatives, rats in slums are a matter of great amusement."[37] That was true, but the magazine failed to mention that Southern Democrats, leaders of the opposition to civil rights since *Brown*, were equally dismissive. The lives of rats were of concern to no one in Congress, and the lives of African American residents of segregated urban neighborhoods were not considered by many to be worthy of much more.

While the Johnson administration and its allies saw rats as a signpost of class and racial injustice, conservative critics saw rats as the consequences of the failings of inner-city residents to keep up their neighborhoods. Neither side of the debate, however, sided with the rats. All saw them as a problem to be fixed rather than a group of innocents seeking survival, the same project in which humans were engaged and which legislative leaders were tasked with aiding. "We are spending federal funds to protect our livestock from rodents and predatory animals," Johnson said. "The least we can do is give our children the same protection we give our livestock." Rats were predatory animals rather than victims of similar circumstances that created human poverty. Thus, the debate juxtaposed images of children who had been deformed or killed by rat bites against congressmen making jokes about "civil rats." Both sides assumed human supremacy. No one was concerned about the fate of the rats.[38]

Humorist Art Buchwald further drove home the point, satirically blaming the bill's failure on "U.S. rodent lovers who have been militantly fighting any legislation to control rats." He told the story of the National Rat Association, led by Walter Ferret, who claimed, "The Constitution provides that everyone shall have the right to keep rats in his home, and the NRA has been leading the fight to protect this constitutional guarantee."[39] Buchwald played the lives of rats for laughs. "Whenever anyone starts talking to them about anti-rodent legislation," the fictional Ferret announced, "I wish they would keep the NRA slogan in mind: 'The rats you save may be your own.'"[40]

Civil rights leaders, meanwhile, saw the rat bill as a race issue. In the wake of Newark and other violent uprisings over the summer of 1967, Jesse Gray protested at the Capitol that "rats cause riots." Maimie Reese, leader of the National Association of Colored Women's Clubs, explained that her group had been founded "for the purpose of raising the standard of living for the Negro family. Controlling the rat menace is in line with this goal."[41] For rights leaders, rats were associated with racism and white conservative politics. For white conservative politicians, rats were associated with self-made urban decay. Every side used the rat as the symbol of failure. Such coding made it difficult to see rats themselves—the ones being exterminated en masse—as the victims.

On July 20, the House officially killed the "civil rats" bill 207 to 176 on a procedural vote.[42] The vote came accompanied with more joking language, such as "a high commissioner of rats" and "a rat bureaucracy." Proponents of the bill, however, were frustrated. "Seldom does one find such inconsistency in such a short period," said Republican Theodore Kupferman. "Yesterday, you voted to establish Federal supremacy to suppress violence [with the anti-riot bill]. Today, you voted to incite violence."[43] Kupferman's interpretation of violence, of course, was solely an interpretation of violence against humans, as the bill itself was nothing if not a revelry of violence against the rat population.

The administration paid attention to stories of rat bites and the public fears of rats.[44] It also hoped to participate in crafting the public conversation. A frustrated Johnson administration prepared an advertisement that featured a menacing photograph of a rat. "Cut this out and put it in bed next to your child," the ad read. "Go ahead. Try it if you have the stomach for it. Lay it next to your baby and let him play with it.

"You can't?

"Then you have a lot more imagination than some of the members of our House of Representatives.

"They don't even think real rats are anything to worry about."

The ad listed all of the members of Congress who voted against the bill. Johnson nixed the advertisement as too strong, but it demonstrated the administration's thinking. Frighten humans with rats, then scapegoat the rats for human social problems.[45] Though the advertisement never ran, Johnson was still dedicated to eradicating rats and reemphasized his plan in a wide-ranging policy speech to Congress on urban and rural poverty at the end of August. "The knowledge that many children in the world's most affluent nation are attacked, maimed and even killed by rats should fill every American with shame. Yet, this is an everyday occurrence in the slums of our cities," Johnson proclaimed. "There is no excuse for this national disgrace." He had proposed the Rat Extermination Act to foster both rat prevention and extermination programs. Better garbage collection, code enforcement, and public education campaigns would accompany "house-by-house, block-by-block extermination programs in rat infested neighborhoods."[46]

As explained by Philip Lee, assistant secretary for Health and Human Services, Johnson was still heavily invested in the success of some version of the rat bill, and thus was willing to negotiate.[47] When a compromise was finally reached, Congress moved the rat measure to a health bill, taking it out of HUD and instead sending federal grants to local health departments, where Harry Reuss had wanted it in the first place. "There was always this tug between the people who were interested in health and the people who were interested in housing," said Sidney Saperstein, deputy general counsel at the Department of Health, Education, and Welfare. The administration reluctantly decided to support the health bill amendment, realizing that passage "would be interpreted as a victory for the Administration."[48] Even then, the funds only passed by a slim one-vote margin. The Urban Rat Control Program would ultimately fund fifty-two killing and prevention projects in different American cities.[49]

And so, such discussions would continually repeat themselves. In 1968, after the rat extermination money made it through Congress, Boston playwright Julie Portman produced *Riot*, a series of racially charged historical vignettes that included a white senator complaining about the "civil rats" bill.[50] Also that year, Johns Hopkins and WJZ television in Baltimore ran a documentary titled "Rats, Rats? Rats!" that described the city's failings in rat eradication and the economic and human toll it took on residents of the city.[51] Washington, DC's Anacostia Neighborhood Museum featured a 1969 exhibit to encourage the government's War on Rats. On the other side of the debate, the Black Panther Party provided "pest control" as part of its aid to inner-city residents in places like Detroit and Houston.[52] The People's Free Pest Control Program provided free extermination services to those in vulnerable neighborhoods. "Every effort is made to destroy the nesting and breeding places of harmful pests," the program's founding document proclaimed.[53]

The Black Panthers' minister of culture was Emory Douglas, a revolutionary artist who often depicted the consequences of urban poverty for Black America in illustrations and posters, and the evolution of the rat debate can even be tracked through his work. In the 1960s, for example, rat imagery in his illustrations symbolized the greed of politicians. Richard Nixon, John Mitchell, and others were portrayed as rats. But as the 1960s became the 1970s, Douglas's images of rats accompanied Black slum-dwellers. In an image from July 1970 titled "We Want Decent Housing Fit for Shelter of Human Beings," a woman fights off a horde of rats with a broom and a bucket while standing on a shabby table in a rundown tenement. The caption reads, "When I spend more time fightin the rats, than taking care of my children you know, it makes me realize that I have a right to kill the greedy slumlords who forces me to live in these inhuman conditions." Months later, he produced a similar poster titled "Kill the Greedy Slumlords!" wherein a woman sits with a shotgun while her baby nurses on a bottle next to her. Rats are just below, trying to get the child. The caption reads, "Just wait till that landlord comes around with his hands all stuck out—smiling talkin bout, 'Why Mrs. Mae what a lovely day.'" In a poster from 1971, a woman holds a large rat. The script ironically reads, "Black Misery! Ain't we got a right to the tree of life?"[54] It was a powerful image to humans who had been conditioned to equate rats with human social problems, but it was at the same time literally encouraging the death of an animal as part of "a right to life."[55]

Leo Gehrig, who at the time had been the deputy surgeon general, spoke about the "Civil Rats" bill in 1990, saying, "I remember the rat incident. . . . I guess we've all come to learn that man may be smart but he's not smarter than a rat."[56] Man may be smart, but his intelligence is fundamentally different than that of a rat. Those differences, combined with historical and social coding, turned rats into symbols of urban decay and racialized poverty in the mid-twentieth century, culminating in the 1967 Rat Extermination Act.

Thus, the Civil Rats Act appears different when analyzed through an animal ethics lens. In playing to racial fears stoked by riots and the tenuous danger of living in poverty, municipal and federal governments launched an asymmetrical killing campaign against an animal that was relatively harmless, a human nuisance with a historical stigma only attempting to survive. It was a slaughter built on tiered bigotries: the human supremacy over animals conditioned by the white supremacist assumptions of administrators. White supremacy created redlined, impoverished, and segregated neighborhoods, then turned to human supremacist assumptions to mitigate at least one visible symbol of the many problems that those neighborhoods faced. The extermination of rats was not designed to alleviate Black suffering. It was designed to remove one of the most visible symbols of Black suffering. In the process, the extermination plan ensured that the suffering of everyone who wasn't both white and human would indefinitely continue.

NOTES

1. See, for example, Hirsch and Mohl, eds., *Urban Policy*; Self, *American Babylon*; Sugrue, *Origins of the Urban Crisis*; Georgakas and Surkin, *Detroit*; and Jaffe and Sherwood, *Dream City*.
2. Kant's dictum "So act that you treat humanity, whether in your own person or in the person of any other, always at the same time as an end, never merely as a means" originally appeared in 1785. Dworkin, *Taking Rights Seriously*, 213; Kant, *Groundwork*, 429.
3. Regan, "The Case for Animal Rights," 187.
4. Burt, *Rat*, 18, 15, 12, 15. See also Zinsser, *Rats, Lice and History*, 208–9.
5. Seshadri, *HumAnimal*, 7.
6. Anderson, "The Beast Within," 302.
7. Biehler, *Pests in the City*, 84; and City of Baltimore, *One Hundred and Twenty-Ninth Annual Report*, 17, 39, 73, 235.
8. *Afro-American*, May 6, 1944, 4; and Biehler, *Pests in the City*, 85.
9. *Afro-American*, July 31, 1943, 9; and Biehler, *Pests in the City*, 89.

10. Common ailments like salmonellosis, leptospirosis, and rat-bite fever were not the kinds of illnesses that would spread to epidemic level, so the notion of rat-killing as preventative of a broader medical contagion was not a viable argument, and with the semantic emphasis on poverty, was not an argument that was made. Biehler, *Pests in the City*, 89; and Richter, "Incidence of Rat Bites," 324–26.
11. Biehler, *Pests in the City*, 90; and Johns Hopkins University, Rodent Ecology.
12. Arendt, *Eichmann in Jerusalem*, 289. See also Arendt, "Personal Responsibility," 17–48; and Neiman, "Banality Reconsidered," 305–15.
13. Biehler, *Pests in the City*, 93; and *Baltimore Sun*, March 17, 1952, 2; February 24, 1954, 4.
14. Biehler, *Pests in the City*, 86.
15. *Chicago Defender*, June 22, 1940, 14; December 26, 1963, 5. Rat bite fever is characterized by fever, shivering, joint pain, and headaches. It is technically not caused by rat bites themselves, but instead by the trading of bodily fluids, usually either the urine or mucus of rats. See Cole, Stoll, and Bulger, "Rat-Bite Fever," 979–81; and Blattner, "Comments on Current Literature," 884–86.
16. Russell, "'Speaking of Annihilation,'" 1508.
17. New York *Amsterdam News*, October 5, 1957, 16. The criticism that human dead bodies are more meaningful than rat dead bodies, while understandable, is an example of speciesism and preferential thinking that has neither scientific nor moral backing. The claim of this paper is that there is no moral difference between humans and rats. Both are living, thinking, feeling beings who want to live.
18. New York *Amsterdam News*, October 12, 1957, 1; October 19, 1957, 6, 7.
19. New York *Amsterdam News*, January 4, 1958, 1.
20. New York *Amsterdam News*, July 25, 1959, 1, 10.
21. New York *Amsterdam News*, July 25, 1959, 1, 10.
22. New York *Amsterdam News*, August 22, 1959, 10.
23. Leach, "Anthropological Aspects of Language," 151–65.
24. New York *Amsterdam News*, October 3, 1959, 2; November 14, 1959, 10.
25. Biehler, *Pests in the City*, 107–9; Scott, "Rat Bite," 900–902; Hurley, "Floods, Rats, and Toxic Waste," 242–62; and Clinton, "Rats in Urban America," 1–7.
26. Lady Bird Johnson, White House Diary Collection.
27. *New York Times*, January 11, 1964, 1; January 22, 1964, 1; March 3, 1964, 1; Biehler, *Pests in the City*, 110; and New York *Amsterdam News*, May 30, 1964, 50.
28. Diamond, Krech, and Rosenzweig, "The Effects of an Enriched Environment," 111–19; *Los Angeles Times*, July 31, 1964, 12; and New York *Amsterdam News*, May 9, 1964, 33.
29. Sussman, *The Myth of Race*, 210–34. For more on the Tuskegee Syphilis Experiment, see Reverby, *Examining Tuskegee*; and Jones, *Bad Blood*. For a broader history of the use of Black lives and bodies in American medical experimentation, see Washington, *Medical Apartheid*.
30. *Chicago Defender*, October 27, 1965, 1.
31. Gaither, oral history transcript.
32. *Washington Post*, August 13, 1967, 1; August 14, 1967, A1.
33. Schmitt, *President of the Other America*, 117, 120; "Herb Kramer memorandum," "Operation Rat," "William S. Gaud to Hayes Redmon," "Joe Califano to Sarge Shriver," "Robert C. Wood to H.R. Gross," Subject Files, Agriculture; Scott, *Operation Rat*; and Johnson's Daily Diary entry, April 13, 1966, Johnson's White House Diary Collection.
34. Wood, oral history transcript.
35. Califano, *The Triumph and Tragedy of Lyndon Johnson*, 212; *Report of the National Advisory*

Commission, 57; and Mumford, *Newark*, 191–213.
36. Edsall and Edsall, *Chain Reaction*, 64; *Report of the National Advisory Commission*, 55–56; and McLaughlin, *The Long, Hot Summer of 1967*, 81–138.
37. O'Brien, oral history transcript; *Afro-American*, August 12, 1967, 4; *New York Times*, July 19, 1967, 19; *Boston Globe*, July 22, 1967, 7; and "Republicans Laugh," 3–4.
38. Edsall and Edsall, *Chain Reaction*, 65; Biehler, *Pests in the City*, 111–12; *Wall Street Journal*, August 10, 1967, 12; New York *Amsterdam News*, July 29, 1967, 41; "Rat Extermination Act of 1967," 20 July 1967, H19548–56; Califano, *The Triumph and Tragedy of Lyndon Johnson*, 212–13; "Lloyd Hackler to Larry Levinson," Subject Files, Legislation.
39. *Los Angeles Times*, July 25, 1967, 3.
40. *Los Angeles Times*, July 25, 1967, 3.
41. *Chicago Defender*, August 7, 1967, 6; August 16, 1967, 15; October 30, 1967, 7; *Washington Post*, August 8, 1967, A1, A6; Kahrl, *Free the Beaches: The Story of Ned Coll*, 81; Biehler, *Pests in the City*, 113; and Edsall and Edsall, *Chain Reaction*, 65.
42. "Barefoot Sanders to Lyndon Johnson," *Boston Globe*, 22 July 1967, 7; *Washington Post*, July 30, 1967, B7; *Wall Street Journal*, August 10, 1967, 12; and Califano, *The Triumph and Tragedy of Lyndon Johnson*, 212.
43. *New York Times*, July 21, 1967, 1.
44. See, for example, "Joanne M. Hedge to Jim Gaither," Subject Files, Agriculture.
45. "Cut this out and put it in bed next to your child," and "LBJ memo, 23 September 1967," Subject Files, Legislation.
46. Johnson, "Message on America's Unfinished Business," 24691–24692; and Califano, *The Triumph and Tragedy of Lyndon Johnson*, 212–13.
47. Lee, oral history transcript.
48. "Memorandum for the Honorable S. Douglass Cater and Honorable H. Barefoot Sanders, Jr.," Subject Files, Agriculture.
49. Saperstein, oral history transcript; Biehler, *Pests in the City*, 113; and *Los Angeles Times*, September 20, 1967, 1.
50. *Boston Globe*, January 28, 1968, C10.
51. *Afro-American*, November 30, 1968, 32.
52. Kinard and Nighbert, "The Anacostia Neighborhood Museum," 103–9; and The Rat.
53. "People's Free Health Control Program," 71–73.
54. Douglas, *Black Panther*, 38–39, 45, 80–81.
55. Douglas, *Black Panther*, 103; and Gaiter, "The Revolution Will Be Visualized," 241–54.
56. Gehrig, oral history transcript.

WORKS CITED

Anderson, Kay. "'The Beast Within': Race, Humanity, and Animality." *Environment and Planning D: Society and Space* 18 (2000): 301–20.

Arendt, Hannah. *Eichmann in Jerusalem: A Report on the Banality of Evil*. 1963; New York: Penguin, 1977.

———. "Personal Responsibility under Dictatorship." In *Responsibility and Judgment*, 17–48. 1964; New York: Random House, 2005.

Biehler, Dawn. *Pests in the City: Flies, Bedbugs, Cockroaches, and Rats.* Seattle: University of Washington Press, 2013.

Blattner, Russell J. "Comments on Current Literature: Rat-Bite Fever." *Journal of Pediatrics* 67 (November 1965): 884–86.

Burt, Jonathan. *Rat.* London: Reaktion Books, 2006.

Califano, Joseph A. *The Triumph and Tragedy of Lyndon Johnson: The White House Years.* College Station: Texas A&M University, 2000.

City of Baltimore. *One Hundred and Twenty-Ninth Annual Report of the Department of Health, 1943.* Baltimore, MD: City of Baltimore, 1943.

Clinton, James. "Rats in Urban America." *Public Health Reports* 84 (January 1969): 1–7.

Cole, James S., Ralph W. Stoll, and Roger J. Bulger. "Rat-Bite Fever: Report of Three Cases." *Annals of Internal Medicine* 71, no. 5 (1969): 979–81.

Diamond, Marian C., David Krech, and Mark R. Rosenzweig. "The Effects of an Enriched Environment on the Histology of the Rat Cerebral Cortex." *Journal of Comparative Neurology* 123 (August 1964): 111–19.

Douglas, Emory. *Black Panther: The Revolutionary Art of Emory Douglas.* New York: Rizzoli, 2007.

Dworkin, Ronald. *Taking Rights Seriously.* London: Gerald Duckworth and Co., 1977.

Edsall, Thomas Byrne, and Mary D. Edsall. *Chain Reaction: The Impact of Race, Rights, and Taxes on American Politics.* New York: W.W. Norton, 1991.

Gaiter, Colette. "The Revolution Will Be Visualized: Emory Douglas in the Black Panther Party." In *West of Center: Art and the Counterculture Experiment in America, 1965–1977*, edited by Elissa Auther and Adam Lerner, 241–54. Minneapolis: University of Minnesota Press, 2012.

Gaither, James C. Oral history transcript. Interview 5, May 12, 1980, by Michael L. Gillette. LBJ Library Oral Histories, LBJ Presidential Library. Available at https://www.discoverlbj.org.

Gehrig, Leo. Oral history transcript. Interview 1, February 13, 1990, by Michael L. Gillette. LBJ Library Oral Histories, LBJ Presidential Library. Available at https://www.discoverlbj.org.

Georgakas, Dan, and Marvin Surkin. *Detroit: I Do Mind Dying: A Study in Urban Revolution.* New York: St. Martin's Press, 1975.

Hirsch, Arnold R., and Raymond A. Mohl, eds. *Urban Policy in Twentieth-Century America.* New Brunswick, NJ: Rutgers University Press, 1993.

Hurley, Andrew. "Floods, Rats, and Toxic Waste: Allocating Environmental Hazards since World War II." In *Common Fields: An Environmental History of St. Louis*, edited by Andrew Hurley, 242–62. Saint Louis: Missouri Historical Society Press, 1997.

Jackson, Mandi Isaacs. "Harlem's Rent Strike and Rat War: Representation, Housing Access, and Tenant Resistance in New York, 1958–1964." *American Studies* 47 (2006): 53–79.

Jaffe, Harry S., and Tom Sherwood. *Dream City: Race, Power, and the Decline of Washington, DC.* New York: Simon & Schuster, 1994.

Johns Hopkins University—Rodent Ecology, 1944–1952. Folder 478, box 58, series 200, RG 1.2, Rockefeller Foundation records, projects. Rockefeller Archive Center, Sleepy Hollow, New York.

Johnson, Lyndon. "Message on America's Unfinished Business: Urban and Rural Poverty." 30 August 1967, *Congressional Record*, 90th Congress, 1st sess., vol. 113, part 18, 24688–24693.

Jones, James H. *Bad Blood: The Tuskegee Syphilis Experiment.* New York: Free Press, 1981.

Kahrl, Andrew W. *Free the Beaches: The Story of Ned Coll and the Battle for America's Most Exclusive Shoreline.* New Haven, CT: Yale University Press, 2018.

Kant, Immanuel. *Groundwork for the Metaphysics of Morals.* 1785; New Haven: Yale University Press, 2002.

Kinard, John, and Esther Nighbert. "The Anacostia Neighborhood Museum, Smithsonian Institution, Washington, D.C." *Museum International* 24 (December/January 1972): 103–9.

Kriner, Douglas L., and Francis X. Shen. *The Casualty Gap: The Causes and Consequences of American Wartime Inequalities*. New York: Oxford University Press, 2010.

Lady Bird Johnson's White House Diary Collection. LBJ Presidential Library. Available at https://www.discoverlbj.org.

Leach, Edmund. "Anthropological Aspects of Language: Animal Categories and Verbal Abuse." *Anthrozoös* 2, no. 3 (1989): 151–65.

Lee, Philip. Oral history transcript. Interview 1, January 18, 1969, by David G. McComb. LBJ Library Oral Histories, LBJ Presidential Library. Available at https://www.discoverlbj.org.

McLaughlin, Malcolm. *The Long, Hot Summer of 1967: Urban Rebellion in America*. New York: Palgrave Macmillan, 2014.

Mumford, Kevin. *Newark: A History of Race, Rights, and Riots in America*. New York: New York University Press, 2007.

Neiman, Susan. "Banality Reconsidered." In *Politics in Dark Times: Encounters with Hannah Arendt*, edited by Seyla Benhabib, 305–15. New York: Cambridge University Press, 2010.

O'Brien, Lawrence F. Oral history transcript. Interview 19, April 22, 1987, by Michael L. Gillette. LBJ Library Oral Histories, LBJ Presidential Library. Available at https://www.discoverlbj.org.

"People's Free Health Control Program." In *The Black Panther Party: Service to the People Programs*, Dr. Huey P. Newton Foundation, 71–73. Albuquerque: University of New Mexico Press, 2008.

Prindle, Richard A. Oral history transcript. Interview 1, February 3, 1969, by David G. McComb. LBJ Library Oral Histories, LBJ Presidential Library. Available at https://www.discoverlbj.org.

"Rat Extermination Act of 1967." 20 July 1967, *Congressional Record*, 90th Congress, 1st sess., vol. 113, part 17, H19548–56.

Regan, Tom. "The Case for Animal Rights." In *Advances in Animal Welfare Science, 1986/87*, edited by Michael W. Fox and Linda D. Mickley, 179–90. Washington, DC: Humane Society of the United States, 1986.

Report of the National Advisory Commission on Civil Disorders. New York: Bantam Books, 1968.

"Republicans Laugh as Slum Dwellers Battle Rats." *The Democrat* (July–August 1967): 3–4.

Reverby, Susan M. *Examining Tuskegee: The Infamous Syphilis Study and Its Legacy*. Chapel Hill: University of North Carolina Press, 2009.

Richter, Curt. "Incidence of Rat Bites and Rat Bite Fever in Baltimore." *Journal of the American Medical Association* 128 (June 1945): 324–26.

Russell, Edmund P. "'Speaking of Annihilation': Mobilization for War Against Human and Insect Enemies, 1914–1945." *Journal of American History* 82 (March 1996): 1505–29.

Saperstein, Sidney A. Oral history transcript. Interview 2, June 28, 1986, by Janet Kerr-Tener. LBJ Library Oral Histories, LBJ Presidential Library. Available at https://www.discoverlbj.org.

Schmitt, Edward R. *President of the Other America: Robert Kennedy and the Politics of Poverty*. Amherst: University of Massachusetts Press, 2010.

Scott, Harold George. *Operation Rat: A Rat Eradication Program for the American People*. Washington, DC: US Public Health Service, Office of Equal Opportunity, 1965.

———. "Rat Bite: Epidemiology and Control." *Journal of Environmental Health* 27 (May–June 1965): 900–902.

Self, Robert O. *American Babylon: Race and the Struggle for Postwar Oakland*. Princeton, NJ: Princeton University Press, 2003.

Seshadri, Kalpana Rahita. *HumAnimal: Race, Law, Language*. Minneapolis: University of Minnesota Press, 2012.

Subject Files, Agriculture, NAID 582583, AG 5–1, Pest Control, Box 8. White House Central Files, Lyndon Baines Johnson Presidential Library, Austin, Texas.

Subject Files, Legislation, NAID 591585, LE/AG 5–1, Pest Control, Box 27. White House Central Files, Lyndon Baines Johnson Presidential Library, Austin, Texas.

Sugrue, Thomas J. *The Origins of the Urban Crisis: Race and Inequality in Postwar Detroit*. Princeton, NJ: Princeton University Press, 1996.

Sullivan, Robert. *Rats: Observations on the History and Habitat of the City's Most Unwanted Inhabitants*. New York: Bloomsbury, 2004.

Sussman, Robert Wald. *The Myth of Race: The Troubling Persistence of an Unscientific Idea*. Cambridge, MA: Harvard University Press, 2014.

The Rat: Man's Invited Affliction. Exhibition records, ACMA.M03–081. Anacostia Community Museum Archives, Smithsonian Institution, Washington, DC.

Washington, Harriet A. *Medical Apartheid: The Dark History of Medical Experimentation on Black Americans from Colonial Times to the Present*. New York: Doubleday, 2007.

Wood, Robert C. Oral history transcript. Interview 1, October 19, 1968, by David G. McComb. LBJ Library Oral Histories, LBJ Presidential Library. Available at https://www.discoverlbj.org.

Young, Stephen. "Rats." 22 August 1967, *Congressional Record*, 90th Congress, 1st sess., vol. 113, part 18, 24688–93.

Zinsser, Hans. *Rats, Lice and History*. 1935; London: Routledge, 2007.

The Cry of the Wolf
Exposing the Peril of Racism Lurking in the White Sheep Complex

Rajesh K. Reddy

On the evening of December 28, 2018, Black South African protesters gathered on Clifton's Fourth Beach to slaughter a sheep in ritual sacrifice. White animal activists flocked to the scene in counterprotest, decrying the violence and citing provincial laws prohibiting animal slaughter on public grounds. As reported by the media, the crux of the conflict concerned the alleged ousting of Black beachgoers from the area two nights before, prompting calls for the organized protest to symbolically cleanse the shore of racism. What has gone overlooked, however, is how the sheep had been racialized and transformed into a symbol-cum-warning sign, as underscored by the lone placard staged by her lifeless body that read, "Run Racist Run!!"[1] Indeed, what a close scrutiny of the scene reveals is more than just a mere concern for her life on the part of the animal activists. Rather, what the encounter betrays is their identification with the innocence of the white sheep at the hands of the Black protesters, with the implied claims to their own innocence subverted by the tagging of the body as "racist." Though widely discussed as an isolated incident, the Clifton Beach affair offers insight into the historically fraught relationship between marginalized communities and white-centric constructions of animal rights discourse—both within and beyond the borders of South Africa. The slaughter of the white sheep as a response to systemic racism, then, attests to a sea change in how nonhuman animals are being weaponized for political ends. Indeed, whereas animalizing rhetoric has historically been deployed by those at the center against those at the margins, recent years have witnessed the phenomenon of the center animalizing itself.

What accounts for this paradigm shift, this chapter contends, is the unique appeal that animal rights discourse holds for dominant groups in the face of social justice agitation. In South Africa, the concern for nonhuman animal well-being traces back to Apartheid-era struggles, with advocates of segregation seizing upon the threat animal slaughter posed to white-only spaces. One incentive for opting into the animal protection movement, then, concerned the ethical stance that it offered advocates, allowing them to opt out of, if not oppose, the growing call for equal rights. Owing to pervasive myths such as the *swart gevaar*, or the threat of Black violence waiting to be unleashed upon white society if they were to lose power, the identification with nonhuman animals enabled those at the nation's center to cast themselves as victims vis-à-vis those whom they themselves had marginalized. The symbolic fulfillment of these myths, then, served to justify the case for white rule. A quarter century after the end of Apartheid, the Clifton Beach conflict captures how this white sheep complex, or the impulse of dominant social groups to identify with animal suffering at the hands of marginalized people, continues to inform and functionally segregate the global animal rights movement to the detriment of not only marginalized communities but also animals themselves.

Seeking to engender a more inclusive and effective animal protection movement, this chapter employs postcolonial and critical race theory to deconstruct the white sheep complex and reconcile human with nonhuman rights discourse. In doing so, the chapter approaches the Clifton Beach controversy as a legacy of Apartheid, with many of the inequities it enshrined having been compounded over a quarter-century. Outside the context of beach access, it touches upon present-day barriers in the field of agricultural production and highlights how white South Africans have characterized efforts at land reform as assaults on their livelihoods, if not their lives. In this vein, the chapter examines how, as a product of the agricultural industry, the white sheep at the heart of the Clifton Beach controversy came to symbolize one of their own in the eyes of white South Africans, who projected onto her sacrifice their own perceived innocence and victimization at the hands of the Black crowd.

What this scene captures is the appeal the white sheep complex holds for those in power to manufacture their self-victimization through the rhetoric of animal rights, an impulse that remains as strong today as in the Apartheid era. The harm posed by this white sheep complex proves multivalenced, imperiling both animal and human rights discourses. With regard to the former, it draws critical attention away from the animal-industrial complex, which is predominantly controlled by those in power and which subjects an untold number of animals to untold horrors. As to the latter, the white sheep complex frustrates the call for equal rights by empowering the hegemony to cast itself as the sacrificial lamb of social justice. While the protesters' staging of the scene at Clifton Beach exposed the undercurrent of racism that fueled much of the counterprotest, it is incumbent upon animal advocates to root out the peril of the white sheep complex if human and animal rights discourses are to ever be productively braided.

THE GEOPOLITICAL MAPPING OF RACE AND ANIMALITY

Accounts of the incident that gave rise to the slaughter of the white sheep differ drastically. To appreciate the conflict, one must first be acquainted with the fact that Clifton represents Cape Town's most affluent suburb and boasts some of the country's most expensive real estate. To hear its majority white residents tell the story, Clifton had witnessed an uptick in serious crime. Street gangs had moved into the area. Beachgoers were being mugged on the steps leading to the shore. Older men had been seen plying underage girls with alcohol by the sea. A pair of attempted rapes had also been reported. According to Clifton residents, local police could not be trusted to act upon these and other complaints. In response, local business owners contracted with a private security company called Professional Protection Alternatives (PPA) to restore order to the area. A massive fight on December 16 saw the private security team assist local police in the evacuation of beachgoers. A week later, on the evening of December 26, PPA personnel once again descended upon the shore. By all accounts there was no incident that required their presence. By their own admission, the security team had simply come to enforce the beach's 8 p.m. curfew. What is beyond dispute, however, is that they lacked the legal authority to do so. What has been contested is whether they asked all or only Black beachgoers to leave.

Whether true or not, the allegation recalled the nation's painful Apartheid past. With over 1,600 miles of shoreline, South Africa's beaches represent some of its most prized real estate, and many of its beaches, including Clifton's best, were reserved exclusively for whites in the Apartheid era. The segregation of beaches followed a series of discriminatory laws. For example, the Natives Act of 1923 restricted the urban areas in which Black South Africans could live. The Group Areas Act of 1950 and its successors expanded upon this policy by creating separate residential areas for all races. In 1949, the Railways and Harbours Regulation, Control and Management Act of 1916 was amended to segregate trains. These and related measures were countenanced under South Africa's separate but equal doctrine. Yet the accommodations, like those crafted under its counterpart in the United States, were anything but. Confronted with the stark inequities that followed, courts began to strike down these apartheid regulations in the 1950s. In his review of these rulings, Hanibal Goitom cautions against inferring a judicial championing of civil rights. Rather, he argues, "It was simply based on the courts' reading of the legislature's intention: discrimination without substantial inequality."[2] What this meant was that if lawmakers were content or even desired to see inequalities result, they need only make their preference for inequity clear—which they did.

The legislature dispensed with all pretense of seeking to provide separate but equal facilities when it passed the Reservation of Separate Amenities Act of 1953. The Act empowered private and public entities to establish "any public premises . . . for the exclusive use of persons belonging to a particular race or class."[3] The law tracked the courts' jurisprudence on the separate but equal doctrine by providing that regulations could not be invalidated on the grounds that no separate amenities or premises had been provided for other races. Neither could they be struck down if the premises were "not substantially similar or of the same character, standard, extent or quality."[4] Notably, at the time of its passage, the Act did not define "public premises" to include beaches.[5] The shore fell under the Act's purview following the passage of the Reservation of Separate Amenities Amendment Act of 1960, which expanded the definition of "public premises" to include not just the shore but also the sea itself.[6] In 1972, the power to regulate beach segregation was devolved to local authorities by an amendment of the Sea-Shore Act of 1935.[7] Although localities were empowered to make individual determinations on the matter of beach segregation, the central government exerted pressure to see the status quo maintained.[8]

Whether centrally or locally designed, beach segregation all but ensured that glaring inequities persisted along politically drawn, racial lines. The city of Durban offers a prime example. By 1977, just five years after beach segregation was localized, its city council had allocated 2,100 meters of its coastline to whites, who made up just 22 percent of its population, whereas Black people, who constituted 46 percent of the population, received a mere 650 meters.[9] The inequities of beach segregation, however, entailed more than just the disproportionate allocation of space. Indeed, nonwhite beaches offered fewer if any amenities and were often located in remote areas that were difficult to reach and sometimes dangerous to access.[10] These stark differences were, of course, the result of political design. As Joseph Lelyveld observes, "It took plenty of lawmaking and law enforcement to get the various racial groups segregated on their various beaches, with the most handsome spots, the least windswept, going by scant coincidence to the people who picked the lawmakers."[11] Yet even though the segregation of beaches was realized through the power of a white electorate in an undemocratic system, significant effort was devoted to re-presenting the shore as an apolitical space.

What resulted was an ideological mapping of race as a geographic as opposed to a political construct. Where segregated beaches were sited in close proximity, significant planning went into racial divides informed by the existing landscape. Loath to despoil the natural beauty of the shore, the city of Durban eschewed artificial barriers such as fencing and instead employed natural and existing features such as rock outcrops, piers, and the like. This harmonization of race with the landscape made segregation appear as a natural as opposed to a political construct. In their review of Durban's design, Durrheim and Dixon observe how nonwhite bodies were employed to serve as natural barriers as well. Its designers had gradationally segmented the coastline, which included a "Black," "Indian," "Coloured," and finally a "Multiracial" beach before ending in seven consecutive beaches reserved exclusively for whites. Under this blueprint, even progressive whites who visited the multiracial beach to protest segregation saw their bodies conscripted to whiten this final buffer between Durban's white and other beaches. As Durrheim and Dixon note, this map saw one's legal race mark one's legal space and vice versa, and the harmonization of this overlap implied a temporal coordinate: that of the Apartheid era. This racial, spatial, and temporal mapping of the country's beaches was especially welcomed by its minority white population. First and foremost, beaches presented a reprieve from the economic concerns that dominated city life and created a space for recreation; more than this, however, they promised an escape from the political agitation for equal rights that could not otherwise be avoided in the urban landscape. Whereas racial lines in the city were mapped onto manmade constructs such as streets, beach segregation was deemed to be informed by nature. To question or oppose it would have been unnatural. Thus, it was violators who were seen as politicizing nature.[12]

The struggle against Apartheid was waged on several fronts, and South Africa's segregated beaches proved a unique battleground. In addition to constituting prime real estate, the symbolic value of the country's beaches was not lost on civil rights agitators. Beach activism sent an important message that there could and should be no safe harbor from the call for equal rights. Some of the loudest calls for integration took place in those sites where whites specifically sought refuge from it. This civil disobedience generally took the form of family outings and organized marches that ended peaceably with "black politicians wading famously in the forbidden seas."[13] These benign acts that saw race transgress space, however, were perceived as violence. As Durrheim and Dixon note, activists were said to have "commandeered" beaches, where they "dispossessed" whites and "created a hostile atmosphere" with political chants.[14] As noted earlier, the issue of beach segregation had been delegated to local authorities, who criminalized transgressions. With respect to the city of Cape Town, penalties included 50 rand in fines, or the equivalent of $75, or 50 days of jail time.[15] Although these protests were largely peaceful, they were met with violence. Some of the weapons brandished against protesters included shotguns and water cannons.[16] In Durban, white counterprotesters draped their bodies with political signage, descending with shirts that read "whites only" and shouting at police to "shoot them dead!"[17] Some in Durban suggested that lifeguards be withdrawn whenever Black beachgoers appeared. Although Durban's mayor, Henry Klotz, replied that he would treat the remark "with the contempt it deserves," his tepid support of integration was grounded in self-interest, if not self-preservation. In explaining his rationale for opening some but not all of Durban's beaches to nonwhites in 1987, Klotz appealed to reason: "If we don't give now, [the beaches] will be taken away from us. So why should we not share now?"[18] As one officer who was charged with enforcing beach segregation in Cape Town argued, activists knew that violating segregation laws in large numbers would leave localities little choice: they could either call in provincial riot police, which would lead to national embarrassment on the global stage, or simply leave the violators be. As Lelyveld underscores, this strategy leaned more on "infiltration" than "invasion" such that beach integration might slowly "creep up, like the tides."[19] And it did. Given that the central government would not outlaw beach segregation across South Africa until 1989, local authorities acted under the power vested in them by the 1972 Sea-Shore Act. For many, this shift in posture came in the form of passive acts that did not take an official stance on beach segregation. For example, the city of Cape Town simply stopped posting apartheid signage, and the Administrator of the Cape began to divert funds exclusively to beaches that were open to all races.

Although protests against beach segregation were largely peaceful, they were condemned for disrupting the Apartheid-era blueprint. Whether by virtue of nonenforcement of existing laws or the active or passive integration of beaches, one's race no longer marked one's space. For white beachgoers, the presence of these "alien" bodies wreaked havoc on and even changed the perceived nature of the terrain.[20] For example, white beachgoers complained of being "swamped" by Black bodies, who "flooded" the shores on Christmas and outnumbered whites almost ten to one.[21] What was previously an escape from racial politics now threatened the white consciousness with fears of being drowned, engulfed, or otherwise swept away by this revolutionary tide. This anxiety was informed by the myth of the *swart gevaar*, Afrikaans for "Black Peril." Manufactured by officials of the Apartheid government, the myth prophesized the total annihilation of whites in the country if its Black majority ever ascended to power. Fear of its fulfillment thus justified discrimination on several fronts, including segregation. This loss of the shoreline as a safe haven was seen as a step toward its realization.

This despair, anxiety, and resentment at the imagined loss of this safe haven has been captured by white South Africans' letters to the editor of the *Mercury* newspaper from 1982, the year Durban's first integrated beach was created, to the end of Apartheid in 1994. In their compilation and review of these accounts, Durrheim and Dixon observe how the imagined victims of the Black Peril were not the authors themselves but the white family, whether the author's own or one collectively imagined. For example, one letter to the editor described Black beachgoers in military-like terms, with the author lamenting that white vacationers looking to escape the hardships of the city were "being dominated and intimidated by hordes of largely undisciplined black people.... Looking back a few years, one asks what has happened to the happy family groups that one used to see on our beaches."[22] This imagined domination of white beachgoers by their Black counterparts was troubling in its assertion that the inequities that flowed under the Apartheid regime had now been reversed. In this vein, the author's seemingly innocent question of what has become of the "happy family groups" who used to frequent the city's beaches implies its own answer: the realization of the Black Peril, which has erased them from the map. Of course, the real reason for the absence of the white family is that white families had absented themselves from Durban's integrated shores. As one letter to the editor stated, the "beachfront and the amenities it has to offer are forever lost to whites," with the author adding, "Never again will I take my family near the place."[23] Indeed, those desiring the use of exclusively white amenities looked beyond Durban's integrated beaches to other shores. Despite the fact that white families were removing themselves from these locales, their conspicuous absence was readily capitalized upon to imply the threat of racial violence. Indeed, another letter argued that maintaining separate beaches was "in the interests of all races and to maintain strict control in the interests of racial harmony."[24]

Yet all hope for the return of segregation to integrated beaches, not to mention the existence of segregated beaches themselves, came to an end with the central government's prohibition of beach segregation in 1989. With this mandate, the presence of Black bodies on any of the country's shores no longer constituted a political act. At least with respect to beaches, race was no longer an element that could be mapped onto the geopolitical landscape. Yet opposition to mixed-race beaches remained, coalesced, and even intensified under the view that Black manners threatened this former white family haven.[25] Yet because no real threat in the form of the Black Peril existed and because white beachgoers could no longer suggest its existence by removing themselves to other coastlines, they searched for other means to see the threat of the Black Peril returned. One particular letter to the editor of the *Mercury* captures how this threat was manufactured on the first calendar day of the first year that beach integration had been nationalized:

> I spent New Year's Day on Durban's North Beach and found: 1) Massive overcrowding by blacks. Blacks have completely taken over this beach. 2) The masses of whites who previously flocked to it on holidays were conspicuous in their near total absence, suggesting that they cannot accept what is experienced. . . . 3) The litter on the beach, the promenade, paddling pools, the garden areas and surrounding streets was disgusting. I found rubbish bins empty, but litter strewn everywhere about. . . . One only need compare the position when whites used the beaches in great numbers. Was the same litter problem found? It wasn't. Most blacks discard rubbish wherever they are irrespective of the facilities provided as will be found wherever they gather in large numbers. 4) The bylaws might not have been written because blacks were camping in the beach area and vehicles nearby; they consumed liquor in the streets, and braais had been set up on the pavements in the side and back streets to the annoyance of residents and pedestrians. 5) Combi-taxis were jam-packed everywhere and music blared from many. 6) I saw two black children defecating on the beach and their elders covered the mess with sand. And six black children and three black men urinating in public places without any regard for discretion (or it being unlawful). 7) One had a chicken tethered to a bush (I wasn't able to establish its fate).[26]

Although the author's list of grievances goes on, the consideration of the chicken and her fate in this moment merits scrutiny given the insight it offers into the evolving discourse around race and animality. For the author, the chicken bears mentioning because she represents an alien presence akin to that of those Black beachgoers who have "completely taken over." This symbolic association is underscored by the chicken's literal tethering to the "bush," or the conceptual antithesis of civilization that the native population represents. This animalizing rhetoric deployed against the Other has been studied by numerous postcolonial scholars and is perhaps best characterized by Achille Mbembe's observation that "in the heyday of colonial conquest and occupation . . . a difference of color was a difference of species."[27] This pseudospeciation of the colonized Other saw their bodies branded with animal markers—such as "beast," "barbarian," "savage," and so on—as a means to justify their commodification, exploitation, exclusion, and more. Here, the reference to the chicken in this recreational space and her association with Black beachgoers attests to the transformation of this once-civilized landscape and to underscore which bodies did and did not belong.

Yet the scene the author paints signals a subtle shift in the political exploitation of nonhuman animals. Here, the author's parenthesized concern for the life of the chicken marks her as a target of violence at her owner's hands. Given the author's failure to identify the individual owner, however, the threat to her life may be imputed to any Black male, whether an adult or child. This dynamic throws other details into greater relief, with the author zoomorphizing white beachgoers to encourage an identification between them and the nonhuman animal as victim. To this end, the author notes how whites who once "flocked" to this site are now "conspicuously absent." As such, the Black-run *braais*, or barbecues, resonate with the prospect of racial violence. Immediately after expressing concern for the chicken's fate, the author argues that "it would be folly for a woman and children to attend the beach by themselves in these circumstances; indeed a man's presence would hardly help for the arrogance of many is such that in the event of an altercation it would be foolhardy to remonstrate." Every white beachgoer in the scene—man, woman, and child—has been rendered a helpless victim now that the safe harbor of the white-only beach has been lost to integration. Indeed, the author's remark that the adage of "live and let live is easier said than accepted" takes on an added urgency given this identification with the nonhuman animal victim.[28] This animalization of the white family is significant for its symbolic fulfillment of the Black Peril, which was braided with the equally pernicious myth of the "total onslaught," which forecasted the end of minority white rule and the destruction of the nation if the threat of communism from abroad or as embraced by Black politicians from within was allowed to take root.

The perceived threats posed by the Black Peril, total onslaught, and their analogs were designed to be ambiguous and thus pervasive. It was the psychological impulse of whites to uncover existential threats everywhere they looked. The mere presence of Black bodies was sufficient to trigger fears of their self-prophesized destruction. Another letter to the editor attests to the pernicious nature of the collective myths: "So long as there are differences in colour, standards, culture, religion, habits and language, conflict hangs over us like the sword of Damocles."[29] It is compelling that the author invokes a classical myth to express that of the Black Peril. In it, Damocles, who serves as a courtier to King Dionysus, expresses wonder at his liege's power and fortune. Offering to switch places, Dionysus arranges a sword to be hung over the head of Damocles by a single hair. The point of the story, of course, is to convey the constant fear felt by those in power.[30] The author's application of the story, however, attests to how difference of any kind implicates the demise of the white body politic. The Black Peril and total onslaught, then, conditioned white South Africans to always be fending off danger. In addition, because the myths were contrived to justify undemocratic rule, whites were incentivized to project their demise in the face of all difference. With the desegregation of the country's cities drawing near, the prospect of ritual slaughter in the suburbs provided a visceral opportunity for their self-victimization.

FIGHTING THE TOTAL ONSLAUGHT IN THE WHITE SUBURB

The prospect of animal slaughter presented a dual threat to the historically white neighborhood. The first was posed by the physical reintroduction of farmed animals to the urban landscape. The West had long idealized the city as providing an escape from the natural world; in this dichotomy between rational humans and irrational nonhuman animals, the latter represented the ultimate Other and were thus anathema to civilization and their presence was treated with disdain. The second threat to the white neighborhood centered on the urban discomfort with slaughter. Urban dwellers had grown "unnerved by the 'screaming' and 'groaning' of the livestock awaiting death" in their surrounds. Of course, this discomfort did not mean that meat and other animal products were no longer consumed in white-only urban areas. Rather, Ballard offers, technological advances in transport and refrigeration allowed animal production and slaughter to be conveniently externalized.[31] This physical and symbolic peripheralization of farmed animal rearing and slaughter laid the foundation for the ethical blinkering of white society, permitting it to lay claim to compassion for animals and eat them too.[32] In her seminal work in the area of animal ethics, Carol Adams stresses how farmed animals in the modern agricultural industry have become an "absent referent" through their death and transformation into a consumer product in "meat" that bears no trace of their existence, thereby allowing humans to consume animal products without considering the animals involved.[33] In addition to undermining the Western ideal of civilization, the return of agriculture to the urban landscape re-presented this absent referent in the form of the farmed animal, who broadcast their visceral connection to meat through harrowing bellows and cries.

Given that this uncomfortable reminder coincided with the arrival of new Black neighbors, established white residents saw opposition to animal slaughter as a means to reassert their claim to civilization, oppose integration, and re-absent the absent referent of the farmed animal body. As it related to the reception of new Black residents, Richard Ballard notes that although explicit calls for segregation began to subside leading up to democratic rule in the early 1990s, white "tolerance was conditional upon these 'space invaders' conforming to established values."[34] Neighbors who refused to cease the practice of ritual slaughter, therefore, subverted the image of the neighborhood as a civilized *space*, which implied its return to a less civilized *time*. In this vein, the ritual slaughter of an animal to mark a death in the family, the birth of a child, or the consummation of a marriage was coded as "barbaric" and "primitive."[35] Whether somber or celebratory, these events witnessed these dehumanizing labels applied to the nonwhite body. These marginalized groups who were previously denied entry or exiled from these locales by virtue of their perceived animality under the laws of apartheid now found themselves shunned due to the threat they posed to those same beings with whom they were compared.

Despite claims that race was a nonissue, the threat that the Black Peril and total onslaught posed to the collective white consciousness had not been eradicated but sublimated, and the proximity of animal slaughter to the haven of one's home cleared a platform for its expression. Sensationalized headlines such as "Chaos as neighbours complain about ritual slaying" and "Slaughter in the suburbs" were intended to galvanize and close ranks among whites, who expressed "shock," "horror," and indignation at these practices being carried out in their metaphorical backyard.[36] Of course, the myth of the Black Peril and its analogs encouraged white residents to recast themselves as symbolic victims. One resident, a mother, appealed to the parental instinct and implored society to "imagine what it will do to *our* [emphasis added] children, seeing a cow being killed with knives and spears."[37] Another resident, a man who did not necessarily oppose cultural slaughter, nevertheless insisted that it not be "*inflicted* [emphasis added] on everyone in the area."[38] As these extracts suggest, white residents who had been reacquainted with the absent referent substituted themselves and their families in their place, thereby transforming themselves into the sacrificial victims of their Black neighbors, whose "invasion" they could oppose in the name of self-defense while also re-absenting the farmed animal, whose victimization could be ignored and the connection between animals and flesh conveniently forgotten.

Despite considerable opposition, residential ritual slaughter carried out on one's own property was protected at the constitutional level as cultural and religious practice. Yet the practice and its practitioners were attacked on the grounds that it was cruel and unnecessary. Residential slaughter, however, did not run afoul of local ordinances, as welfare organizations such as the Society for the Prevention of Cruelty to Animals found no violations of cruelty laws.[39] The argument that ritual slaughter was unnecessary also failed. Industrial animal production, whose operations were located an appropriate distance away, had reached such a scale and degree of sophistication that residential slaughter could be relegated to the past. Yet as Ballard argues, ritual slaughter in Zulu and other Southern African traditions had to be carried out in a place of appropriate significance, which often implicated one's home as the only venue.[40]

Indeed, for many who opposed ritual slaughter, the predominant question was not so much *whether* ritual animal slaughter was acceptable, ethically or otherwise, but *where* it was acceptable. Some asserted that the appropriate space was the abattoir or rural farmland; others identified the

Zulu *kraal*, or Black homestead, in light of the African nature of the practice.[41] In contrast, the realm of the historically white suburb was always inappropriate. Given the cultural view that it was sometimes necessary for ritual slaughter to be carried out in the home, headlines petitioning neighbors to "jettison bloodthirsty practices" carried the suggestion that Black practitioners along with Black practices might be cast out on the basis of being both a danger and detritus.[42] Their expulsion would restore the space and time of civilization. In residential battlegrounds where ritual slaughter could not be stopped, some made a strategic retreat to gated communities whose bylaws could protect them.[43] Whether the response of whites was to fight or take flight, the question of why those who wished to practice ritual slaughter could not simply go to the Black farm remained. The answer is that Black farmers had been systematically dispossessed of their lands, with the overwhelming majority of these acres that were supposed to be returned to their rightful owners still in the hands of their white counterparts to this day.

CONFRONTING THE PERIL OF THE WHITE SHEEP COMPLEX AT CLIFTON BEACH

Although the Apartheid era ended a quarter-century ago, its legacy has seen inequities remain, if not grow more glaring. In March 2018, just months before the conflict at Clifton Beach, South Africa was named the world's most inequitable society in a comparison of 149 nations and territories.[44] According to the World Bank, who announced the finding, 70.9 percent of the country's wealth is consolidated in the hands of the top percentile, or 1 percent, of its population; comparatively, the bottom 60 percent collectively hold just 7 percent of the nation's wealth. Race plays a predominant factor in predicting one's economic prospects. Whereas white South Africans account for a tenth of the population, they represent approximately a third of the middle class and two thirds of the elite.[45] This rampant inequality is pronounced in the agricultural sector as well, with white South Africans controlling 72 percent of the nation's farmland. Although the African National Congress (ANC) Party vowed to correct this Apartheid-era disparity when it took control of the government in 1994, less than a quarter of the farmland designated to be restored to Black farmers has been.[46] Against this backdrop, white demands that traditional ritual slaughter be relegated to Black farms neglects to appreciate that the Apartheid era had made it so that there would be far fewer Black farms to see it carried out.

Looking to end this disparity, South Africa's ANC government held months-long hearings in 2018 to debate the expropriation without compensation of private land to benefit disenfranchised Black farmers. Not surprisingly, opponents employed the myth of the Black Peril and its analogs to characterize the return of land to its rightful owners as a race war and genocide. Given the legacy of the Apartheid era's mapping of race onto space and vice versa, the loss of white land naturally spelled the disappearance of white lives.[47] A monument outside Johannesburg featuring rows of crosses beneath a large sign that reads "Farm Murders" had been created to convey this narrative of lost lives. This monument to white victimhood resonated with provocateurs within and beyond the country, particularly in light of the looming prospect of land expropriation, which raised accusations of reverse racism.[48] Heavily criticized for his own history of race-baiting, U.S. President Donald Trump tweeted his intent to investigate the nation's "land and farm seizures and expropriations and the large scale killing of farmers," whom he explicitly identified as white.[49] Notably, this purported mass killing of white farmers has been debunked by the farmer organization AgriSA, which found that just 62 of the country's 20,000 murders from April 2017 to March 2018 were farm-related, making up less than 0.33 percent of all cases.[50] Of course, even these numbers in and of themselves do not attest to race-related or motivated violence. This fact, however, did not temper allegations of a looming Black Peril during the months in which the government discussed the expropriation of white farmland. The opportunity to underscore the threat came with the racialization and slaughter of the white sheep in Clifton just before Christmas Day.

It should first be noted that the call to occupy Clifton Beach was likely based upon a falsehood, yet one that captured a deeper truth. Black beachgoers who were present confirmed that the private security personnel from Professional Protection Alternatives had asked all beachgoers, including whites, to leave in observance of the beach's curfew.[51] However, it should be noted that the private security company had not only been contracted by local business owners of a white-majority area but were also acting beyond their legal authority when seeking to enforce the law. As such, even though the personnel had not deployed their power discriminatorily, the power they did perform was inextricably bound up with white privilege. Indeed, the same security company was accused of closing off a popular road at the behest of residents on New Year's Eve to prevent outsiders from spoiling their celebration. As one of the leaders of the protest argued, private security guards hired by Clifton's residents were often instructed not to "allow black people who appear to look like they are from the townships or criminals onto the beach."[52] The protesters' occupation of the same spot from which they had been cast out—or at least upon which they were not equally welcome—invoked the geopolitical mapping of race and space during the time of Apartheid. The sacrifice of the sheep on these once-forbidden sands, then, was carried out to invoke the spirits of the crowd's Black ancestors and cleanse the shore of racism. As one of the organizers of the protest, Chumani Maxwele, explained, "The offering of the sheep is calling on our ancestors to respond to our trauma at the hands of white people over the years."[53] The counterprotesters who showed up, however, argued that the slaughter of the sheep amounted to a racist act itself.

Given how the Apartheid myths of the Black Peril and total onslaught endured and gained force through an identification with nonhuman animal victims, it is not difficult to see how counterprotesters imagined themselves as the lone white sheep, now a symbolic victim of reverse racism, in a sea of Black protesters chanting political songs. This empathy was amplified by insinuations that the sheep must have been stolen from a farm.[54] Given that the debate over the expropriation of farmland was still roiling the nation, as well as allegations that white farmers were being killed in historic numbers, the suggestion that the white sheep had belonged to a white owner fostered a belief among counterprotesters that they had not only been fleeced but were also witnessing the slaughter of one of their own. This racialization of the white sheep was not lost upon the Black protesters, who, despite stating that her slaughter was a means of communicating with ancestors to address their trauma, posted signage by her lifeless body warning Clifton's white-majority residents to "Run Racist Run!" While this placard has multiple layers of meaning, an unspoken yet unmistakable message to counterprotesters was that if they wished to see themselves as the victims of ritual animal slaughter in a symbolic fulfillment of the Black Peril and total onslaught, then they would be granted that desire.

Yet the placard, whether intentionally or otherwise, offers the white animal advocate a path forward. In explicitly calling out the Apartheid-era impulse to read one's perceived victimization into the slaughter of nonhuman animals, the sign challenges animal advocates to contend with the wolf in the white sheep's clothing, or the ideological predator of racism masking itself as prey. What this provides to animal advocates is an opportunity to consider how animal advocacy has been braided with Apartheid-era ideology and the effort necessary to tease these strands apart. Moreover, doing so will allow animal advocates to see the actual white sheep of their country. And make no mistake. White sheep do exist. As Hylton White observes, Zulu households in South Africa's KwaZulu-Natal province apply racial labels to distinguish Zulu animals from their white counterparts.[55] In the case of poultry, for instance, although Zulu and white chickens may share the same historical origin, the appearance of Zulu chickens varies dramatically between the sexes, as they feature variations in color, plumes, mottlings, and more that allow them to be recognized as individual beings; they also enjoy access to the outdoors and engage in intelligent, species-specific behavior, such as assuming defensive stances and breeding according to their natural ecology. In contrast, white chickens, otherwise known as broiler chickens and battery cage hens, are the product of restricted breeding lines that make them indistinguishable to the eye; their movements are constrained by metal cages, where they are subjected to routine mutilations such as beak trimming to prevent them from cannibalizing one another, and as a result, these chickens of whiteness display confused and deficient minds.[56] Undoubtedly, an animal rights paradigm that hews to abolitionist principles would see both groups saved from slaughter regardless of the difference in their welfare conditions. That said, while this chapter does not embrace the view that animal suffering or sacrifice can be justified, it also does not subscribe to all arguments against it. An animal rights campaign that doubles as a breeding ground for the white sheep complex both furthers the persecution of marginalized groups and predisposes them to assume a hostile stance toward the rhetoric of animal rights. If human and nonhuman rights are to ever become complementary ethics, it is imperative that animal advocates decry this peril—that is, the wolf of racism lurking in the white sheep complex. What a disavowal of the white sheep complex has the power to nurture, then, is a new perspective that can inspire animal advocates to see the actual white sheep in their country, or those animals suffering untold cruelties at the hands of an animal-industrial complex that conceals their slaughter from view.

NOTES

1. Antoni, "Slaughtering Truth."
2. Goitom, "On This Day."
3. Reservation of Separate Amenities Act, §§ 1, 2(1).
4. Reservation of Separate Amenities Act, §§ 3(a), 3(b).
5. Reservation of Separate Amenities Act, §§ 1, 2(1).
6. Reservation of Separate Amenities Amendment Act, § 1.
7. Sea-Shore Act of 1935 §§ 2, 3.
8. For example, the mayor of Durban was rebuked and faced expulsion from the national party in 1988 after opening several of his city's beaches to nonwhites. Claiborne, "Durban's Mayor Rapped."
9. Durrheim and Dixon, "The Role of Place and Metaphor in Racial Exclusion," 436.
10. Durrheim and Dixon, "The Role of Place and Metaphor in Racial Exclusion," 436.
11. Lelyveld, "Apartheid Is Crumbling on Beaches in South Africa," A2.
12. Durrheim and Dixon, "The Role of Place and Metaphor in Racial Exclusion," 433–36, 442–43.
13. Durrheim and Dixon, "The Role of Place and Metaphor in Racial Exclusion," 438.
14. Durrheim and Dixon, "The Role of Place and Metaphor in Racial Exclusion," 438, 442–43.
15. Lelyveld, "Apartheid Is Crumbling on Beaches in South Africa," A2.

16. Lelyveld, "Apartheid Is Crumbling on Beaches in South Africa," A2.
17. Associated Press, "Apartheid Foes March on a Beach," A6.
18. Burns, "Apartheid's Guardians Yield Beachhead to Change," A4.
19. Lelyveld, "Apartheid Is Crumbling on Beaches in South Africa," A2.
20. Durrheim and Dixon, "The Role of Place and Metaphor in Racial Exclusion," 441.
21. Burns, "Apartheid's Guardians Yield Beachhead to Change," A4.
22. Rose, "Letter to the Editor," *Mercury*, January 13, 1988, 10.
23. "Letter to the Editor," *Mercury*, January 19, 1986, 7.
24. "Letter to the Editor," *Mercury*, December 29, 1986, 3.
25. Durrheim and Dixon, "The Role of Place and Metaphor in Racial Exclusion," 444.
26. "Letter to the Editor," *Mercury*, January 1, 1990, 6.
27. Mbembe, "Collision, Collusion, and Refractions."
28. "Letter to the Editor," *Mercury*, January 1, 1990, 6.
29. "Letter to the Editor," *Mercury*, December 29, 1986, 3.
30. The irony of the author's use of the sword of Damocles as a metaphor for the state of the country lies in Dionysus having ascended to power through numerous acts of cruelty committed against his enemies. As such, the many perils that haunted him had been wrought by his own hand.
31. Ballard, "'Slaughter in the Suburbs,'" 1074–75.
32. In addition, concern for the humane treatment of animals had become a marker of one's civilized status.
33. Adams, *The Sexual Politics of Meat*, 66.
34. Ballard, "'Slaughter in the Suburbs,'" 1073.
35. Rawlins, "Eloquence Cannot Take Away Pain."
36. Ballard, "'Slaughter in the Suburbs,'" 1069–70.
37. Msomi, "Slaughter in the Suburbs," 1079.
38. Campbell, "Umemulo Upsets Suburbia."
39. Ballard, "'Slaughter in the Suburbs,'" 1069. Residential farmed animals arguably suffered far less than their counterparts in the industrial animal agriculture complex.
40. Ballard, "'Slaughter in the Suburbs,'" 1072.
41. Ballard, "'Slaughter in the Suburbs,'" 1079.
42. Mellors, "Jettison Bloodthirsty Practices."
43. Ballard, "'Slaughter in the Suburbs,'" 1073–74.
44. Beaubien, "The Country with the World's Worst Inequality Is . . ."
45. World Bank, "Overcoming Poverty and Inequality in South Africa," xvi, 38.
46. Clark, "South Africa Confronts a Legacy of Apartheid."
47. Clark, "South Africa Confronts a Legacy of Apartheid."
48. Schaeffer, "With His South Africa Tweet."
49. Trump, Twitter post.
50. Clark, "South Africa Confronts a Legacy of Apartheid."
51. Antoni, "Slaughtering Truth on the Altar of Racism."
52. "Race Row after Guards Order."
53. "Protesters Slaughter Sheep at Clifton Beach."
54. "Blacks Threaten White Genocide."
55. White, "Beastly Whiteness," 104–13.
56. White, "Beastly Whiteness," 104–7.

WORKS CITED

Adams, Carol J. *The Sexual Politics of Meat: A Feminist-Vegetarian Critical Theory* (New York: Continuum, 2010).

Antoni, Marie-Louise. "Slaughtering Truth on the Altar of Racism—Clifton's Controversy." *Biz News*, January 7, 2019. Available at https://www.biznews.com.

Associated Press. "Apartheid Foes March on a Beach." *New York Times*, September 4, 1989, A6.

Ballard, Richard. "'Slaughter in the Suburbs': Livestock Slaughter and Race in Post-Apartheid Cities." *Ethnic and Racial Studies* 33, no. 6 (June 2010): 1074–75.

Beaubien, Jason. "The Country with the World's Worst Inequality Is . . ." *NPR*, April 2, 2018. Available at https://www.npr.org.

"Blacks Threaten White Genocide on Cape Town's Clifton Beach." *Free West Media*, January 1, 2019. Available at https://freewestmedia.com.

Burns, John F. "Apartheid's Guardians Yield Beachhead to Change." *New York Times*, January 14, 1988, A4.

Campbell, Carol. "Umemulo Upsets Suburbia." *Natal on Saturday*, December 18, 1993.

Claiborne, William. "Durban's Mayor Rapped for Integrating Beach." *Washington Post*, May 12, 1988.

Clark, Christopher. "South Africa Confronts a Legacy of Apartheid." *The Atlantic*, May 3, 2019.

Durrheim, Kevin, and John Dixon, "The Role of Place and Metaphor in Racial Exclusion: South Africa's Beaches as Sites of Shifting Racialization." *Ethnic and Racial Studies* 24, no. 3 (May 2001): 434–50.

Goitom, Hanibal. "On This Day: Desegregation of South African Beaches." *Law Librarians of Congress*, November 16, 2015. Available at https://blogs.loc.gov.

Lelyveld, Joseph. "Apartheid Is Crumbling on Beaches in South Africa." *New York Times*, March 12, 1981, A2.

"Letter to the Editor." *Mercury*, January 19, 1986, 7.

"Letter to the Editor." *Mercury*, December 29, 1986, 3.

"Letter to the Editor." *Mercury*, January 1, 1990, 6.

Mbembe, Achille. "Collision, Collusion, and Refractions: Reflections on South Africa after Liberation." Lecture given on April 27, 2010, at University of Oxford, Oxford, England.

Mellors, N. "Jettison Bloodthirsty Practices." *Daily News*, December 15, 1999.

Msomi, Goodman. "Slaughter in the Suburbs," *Sunday Tribune*, December 12, 1999.

"Protesters Slaughter Sheep at Clifton Beach." *News24*, January 2, 2019. Available at https://www.politicsweb.co.za.

"Race Row after Guards Order Black People off Cape Town Beach." *The National*, December 29, 2018. Available at https://www.thenational.ae.

Rawlins, George. "Eloquence Cannot Take Away Pain." *Daily News*, March 1, 1996.

Reservation of Separate Amenities Act No. 49 of 1953. *Statutes of the Union of South Africa 1953*, Parow, C.P.

Rose, D. "Letter to the Editor." *Mercury*, January 13, 1988, 10.

Schaeffer, Carol. "With His South Africa Tweet, Trump Became a Megaphone for a White-Supremacist Talking Point." *The Nation*, August 24, 2018.

Sea-Shore Act No. 21 of 1935. *Union Gazette Extraordinary*, April 10, 1935.

The World Bank, "Overcoming Poverty and Inequality in South Africa: An Assessment of Drivers, Constraints and Opportunities." March 2018. Available at https://openknowledge.worldbank.org.

Trump, Donald. Twitter post, August 22, 2018, 10:28 p.m. Available at https://twitter.com.

White, Hylton. "Beastly Whiteness: Animal Kinds and the Social Imagination in South Africa." *Anthropology Southern Africa*, no. 34, no. 3–4 (2011): 104–13.

Contributors

Thomas Aiello is professor of anthrozoology, history, and African American studies at Valdosta State University. He is the author of more than twenty books and dozens of peer-reviewed journal articles. His work helped amend the Louisiana constitution to make nonunanimous juries illegal and was cited in the United States Supreme Court as part of its decision ruling them unconstitutional. His most recent books are *The Life and Times of Louis Lomax: The Art of Deliberate Disunity* (2021), *The Trouble in Room 519: Money, Matricide, and Marginal Fiction in the Early Twentieth Century* (2021), and *The Artistic Activism of Elombe Brath* (2021). He holds PhDs in history and anthrozoology and lives in Valdosta, Georgia.

Soledad Altrudi is a PhD candidate at USC's Annenberg School for Communication and Journalism. Her dissertation explores Parque Patagonia and its associated rewilding practices as a political project that not just entails a conservation strategy but also works as a device for ordering human–nonhuman interactions in a highly mediatized environment.

Thomas Balfe received his PhD from the Courtauld Institute of Art, University of London, where he now teaches. He is an art historian specializing in early modern easel painting and graphic art, c.1550–c.1750. His research areas are animal, hunting, still life, and human-animal inversion imagery, and vocabularies of lifelikeness in early modern art writing. His coedited book on the term *ad vivum* and its relation to images made from or after the life was published by Brill in 2019. More recent articles have discussed animal fable painting and the depiction of the hunting dog in Flemish gamepiece still life. His current research focuses on the representation of non-European hunting practices by European artists active in the sixteenth and seventeenth centuries.

Silke Hackenesch is an associate professor at the Institute of North American History at the University of Cologne. She specializes in twentieth-century childhood and adoption studies, African American history, commodity history, and Black Diaspora studies. Silke is the author of *Chocolate and Blackness: A Cultural History* (2017). She has published articles in *Historische Anthropologie, Food and History*, and *Comparativ: Zeitschrift für Globalgeschichte und vergleichende Gesellschaftsforschung*. She has written chapters for *Rethinking Black German Studies, Kinder des Zweiten Weltkrieges*, and *Race & Sex: Eine Geschichte der Neuzeit*. Currently, she is working on a manuscript that analyzes the contested debates the transnational adoption of Black German children elicited in the (African) American community, from civil rights organizations, to social work professionals and individual adoption advocates. Silke serves as a board member for the book series Imagining Black Europe. Her research has been supported by the German Academic Exchange Service (DAAD), the Thyssen Foundation, the German Research Foundation (DFG), the Society for the History of Children and Youth (SHCY), the Alliance for the Study of

Adoption and Culture (ASAC), the University of Cologne, and the German Historical Institute in Washington, DC. Her work has also been featured in the *New York Times*, on *Deutschlandfunk*, and in blogs and podcasts.

Angela Hofstetter shares her rural home in Story, Indiana, with giant dogs, plump horses, and assorted flora and fauna friends from the Hoosier National Forest. She received her PhD in comparative literature from Indiana University in Bloomington, where she fostered a passion for novels of the long nineteenth century and gender studies. A senior lecturer at Butler University, Angela's courses reflect her commitment to a robust intersectionality that interrogates the moral complexity of all animals—human and other. She is currently pursuing an MFA in creative nonfiction at Butler University, focusing on a memoir about trauma and her relationship with her beloved mare Eroika.

Ruth Lipschitz obtained her PhD at Goldsmiths, University of London (2015). She holds a permanent post in the Faculty of Art, Design and Architecture at the University of Johannesburg. The limitrophic interrelation between race and species is at the heart of her unpublished PhD dissertation, "Animality and Alterity," and is explored in "Skin/ned Politics" (in the special issue of *Hypatia*, "Animal Others," edited by Kari Weil and Lori Gruen, 2012), "Abjection" in the *Edinburgh Companion to Animal Studies* (edited by Lynn Turner, Undine Sellbach, and Ron Broglio, 2018), as well as in "Race and 'the Animal' in the Post-Apartheid 'National Symbolic'" (coauthored with Benita de Robillard in *Image & Text* [2017]). Her most recent publication, "*Dance with Nothing but Heart* (2001): Death, 'the Animal' and the Queer 'Taste' of the Other," appears in *Literature and Meat since 1900*, edited by Seán McCorry and John Miller (2019).

Rachel Sarah O'Toole is an associate professor in the Department of History at the University of California, Irvine where she teaches classes on colonial Latin America, the African Diaspora, and sex and gender. Her monograph *Bound Lives: Africans, Indians, and the Making of Race in Colonial Peru* received the 2013 Latin American Studies Association Peru Section Flora Tristán book prize. With Sherwin Bryant and Ben Vinson III, she coedited *Africans to Spanish America: Expanding the Diaspora* (2012), and with Ivonne del Valle and Anna More, she coedited *Iberian Empires and the Roots of Globalization* (2019). She has published articles on the construction of whiteness, masculinity within slavery, African Diaspora identities, indigenous politics, and gender influences on racial constructions, and currently is completing her second monograph regarding the meanings of freedom in colonial Peru.

Rachael L. Pasierowska completed her dual PhD at Rice University, Texas, and the Universidade Estadual de Campinas, São Paulo, in history with a specialization in animal and slavery studies. Her research focuses on the interactions between enslaved Africans in the nineteenth-century Atlantic world (Brazil, Cuba, and the U.S. South) and animals. Pasierowska has published multiple articles, including ones on enslaved children, animals and African American folklore, and animals in the Atlantic world. Following completion of her dual doctorate, Pasierowska accepted a position as lecturer at Sam Houston State University, where she instructs both of the American survey courses. She has been awarded fellowships from all over the country and has been invited to speak at institutions in three continents.

Rajesh K. Reddy directs the Animal Law Program at the Center for Animal Law Studies at Lewis & Clark Law School, where he teaches international animal law and animal legal philosophy, among other courses. He earned his PhD in English from the University of Georgia, with his dissertation focusing on the relationship between human and nonhuman rights in postcolonial literature and discourse. In the legal arena, he has worked for the U.S.-based Animal Legal Defense Fund and the Human Rights Law Network in New Delhi, India. He sits on the board of Minding Animals International and leads the International Subcommittee of the American Bar Association's Animal Law Committee.

Benita de Robillard is senior lecturer in the Interdisciplinary Arts and Culture Studies department at the University of the Witwatersrand in Johannesburg. Her research explores the nomadic meshing of bodies and socialites in the post/apartheid conjuncture, and her recent publications examine the vexed interconstitution of race and animality in this setting.

Mieke Roscher is associate professor for cultural and social history and the history of human-animal relations at the University of Kassel, Germany. Her publications include *Ein Königreich für Tiere* (2009) on the British animal rights movement, the edited volume *Animal Biography* (together with André Krebber, 2018), the *Handbook of Historical Animal Studies* (together with André Krebber and Brett Mizelle, 2021), and numerous articles on animal historiography and agency, the twentieth-century European zoo, and gender in animal welfare. She is currently writing a monograph on the political history of animals in the Third Reich.

Elizabeth Tavella is a postdoctoral fellow affiliated with the Department of Romance Languages and Literatures and the Center for the Study of Gender and Sexuality at the University of Chicago. As a transdisciplinary scholar, Elizabeth's research engages critical animal studies, decolonial methodologies, and queer ecology to investigate intertwined systems of oppression and hierarchies of power via a literary and cultural perspective. Elizabeth's scholarship also addresses how dynamics of race, gender, class, and species inform contemporary practices of food production and consumption. In addition to a forthcoming monograph on spaces of animal confinement, taking into consideration slaughterhouses, zoos, and laboratories, Elizabeth's current work focuses on speculative writing and sites of resistance celebrating multispecies liberated futures through the lens of Indigenous perspectives, Afrofuturist imaginaries, and queer/trans futurities.

Jonathan W. Thurston-Torres is an early modernist who received their PhD in English from Michigan State University. They are a trans scholar living with HIV, and their academic work often considers animals as representative of human diversity, whether in Shakespeare's plays or modern horror film. Their journalistic exposé, *Blood Criminals: Living with HIV in 21st Century Ameria,* was nominated for POZ Magazine Book of the Year, and their novels have been nominated for Lambda Literary Awards.

Index

A

albinism, 97–108, 109n23, 111n47, 163–64
alpacas, 57, 59
American Civil War, 138–39
American Indians, 53–55, 57, 59–60, 65, 73–76, 78–81, 83, 86–88, 88n1, Afro-Andean, 59; Algonquian, 78, 87; Andean, 53–65, 66n10, 66n12, 66n27, 67n58, 67n66, 68n73; Incas, 54–55, 59–60, 62–63, 66n12; Timucua, 74–75, 78–79, 81, 83, 86–88
Anaka the Gorilla, 107–8
animal rights, xii-xiii, 20, 33, 36–38, 40, 44n51, 44n55, 45n60, 142, 161, 175, 177–83, 191–92, 197–98, 200–201
animal-race studies, xi-xii, 15–17, 26, 33, 39–40, 76–78, 133–34, 160, 176
anthropocentrism, xii, 97, 100–103, 110nn29–30, 150, 159–60, 162
anthropomorphism, xi, 99–100, 103, 166
anti-racism, viii, xiii-xiv, 33, 36–40, 118–19, 121, 124, 128, 142–43
Anti-Semitism, 129n10, 152–54, 156n39
apartheid, 33–35, 37–38, 42n20, 44n40, 147, 150–51, 156n29, 191–95, 198–201

B

bats, 68n73
bees, 87, 134, 138–40, 142, 143n22
Boisseron, Bénédicte, xi-xiv, 17, 24–25, 36, 39–40, 142, 161
birds, 59, 62, 121, 163; chickens, 53–54, 57, 65, 196, 201; crows, x; ducks, 130n19; owls, 62; peacocks, 130n19
blackface, x, 105, 133, 135
Black Lives Matter, 15, 26, 43n33, 119
Blackness, x, 16–17, 21, 39–40, 41n4, 97, 99–100, 107, 108n6, 134, 136–37, 141, 149–54, 151–52, 160–65; African Americans, 3, 10–11, 15–17, 21–24, 26, 26n2, 27n3, 75, 121–23, 127, 142, 161, 164, 178, 180, 182–83; Black Africans, x, 12n25, 22, 38–39, 59, 151–53, 191–200; Black children, xi, 3–11, 12n25, 177–78, 181, 196
Black Panthers, 183
breeding, ix, 11, 16–23, 26, 76–78, 90n28, 101, 117–25, 128, 130n19, 153, 164, 201
butterflies, 68n73

C

Calvino, Italo, 100–104
Candyman, 134, 137–40, 142
Catholicism, 53–57, 60, 62, 64–65, 66n10, 66n12, 123
cats, 7, 12n25, 161, 181
Christianity, ix, 23, 53–55, 57, 59, 65, 75, 77, 79, 107, 121, 156n39
Civil Rights Movement, x-xi, 15, 23–26, 121, 175
colonialism, xii-xiii, 16, 19, 23, 34–37, 40, 42n20, 53–57, 59–60, 62–65, 75, 98, 103–4, 106–8, 133, 136–37, 147–48, 150, 192, 196
commercialism, 97, 106–7, 136, 142, 159–63, 197

commodity. *See* commercialism
cows, ix, 8, 37, 57, 198
crocodile, 82, 163–64
cuteness, 164–66
Cynocephali, vii, ix-x

D

Dayan, Colin, 133
Deckha, Maneesha, 17, 38
deer, 73–88, 134, 140–42
disease, 60, 62, 64, 122, 130n17, 153, 177, 179–80, 185n10, 185n15
dogs, vii, ix-xi, 4, 6–7, 9, 12n25, 15–26, 26–27n2, 39, 76–78, 81, 83–84, 90n29, 129n12, 134, 181; German shepherd, 15–26, 28n54. *See also* police: police dogs
domestication, ix, 6–8, 11, 77, 140–41, 143
donkeys, vii, 53–54, 59. *See also* mules

E

eugenics, 18–20, 22, 25–26, 118–20, 134–37, 140, 152–54, 180

F

Ferguson, Missouri, 15, 26–27n2
fish, 62, 164
Floyd, George, 118
food practices, 4–9, 11, 19, 39–40, 54–55, 57, 59, 107, 177
fox, xi

G

gender, vii, 4, 17, 22, 59, 81, 101–2, 105, 118–29, 133–43, 147–55, 159–61, 163–65, 178, 184, 192, 196
Get Out. See Peele, Jordan
goats, 57
guinea pigs, 53–57, 67n36

H

Haraway, Donna, 18, 134
hogs, x, 6, 11. *See also* pigs
horses, vii, ix-x, 3–6, 8, 11, 57, 59, 76–77, 83, 87, 117–26, 128–29
human evolution, 99, 101, 147–54, 156–57n52
hunting, 9, 39, 62, 73–88, 106, 140–43

I

Il Re Bianco. See Toffolo, Davide
immigration, 104, 106, 118, 130n17, 136, 164
Indigenous rituals, 60, 62–65, 68n73, 79, 136
interracial relationships, 122–23, 127–28, 133–43

J

Jackson, Zakiyyah Iman, 15–16, 149
Jews, vii, 19, 148–49, 152–54

K

Kelly Ingram Park, 24–25
Kentucky Derby, x, 117–18, 120, 124–26, 128
King, Martin Luther, Jr., 23–24
King Kong, 99–101, 109n15, 133–37, 142
Ko, Aph, 142

L

language, 8, 55, 65, 74, 76, 79, 102, 137, 162
Latinx populations, 164
"Letter from Birmingham Jail." *See* King, Martin Luther, Jr.
livestock, 5, 7–11, 22, 54–57, 59, 120, 122, 162, 182, 197
llamas, 53–57, 59, 65
lynching, 119, 123–24, 126

M

Mandingo, 127–28
medical racism, 3, 10–11
mixed race populations, 42n20, 59, 124, 129n12, 153, 195
Morgan, C. E., 118–19, 121–26, 128
mules, 6, 11, 57. *See also* donkeys

N

nature v. nurture, 119, 124–25
Nazi regime, 16, 18–22, 26, 135–37, 154

O

otters, 162, 165
oxen, 54, 81, 83–85. *See also* cows

P

Palomar. See Calvino, Italo
Peele, Jordan, 134, 140–43

pets, 9–10, 12n25, 99, 166, 181
pigs, 4, 6, 8, 11, 53–57, 65. *See also* hogs
police, xi, 15–16, 23–26, 26n2, 118, 140–41, 181; police dogs, 15–16, 19–20, 23–26, 26n2
possums, 166
"post-race," xii, 118–19, 126, 150–51, 160
primates, x, 97, 101, 134–37, 142, 147, 149–51, 154–55; apes, vii, x, 75, 87, 99–101, 105, 109n23, 109n25, 110n29, 110n31, 133–37, 149–54, 156n39; baboons, vii, x, 147–48, 150–53, 155n3; gorillas, 97–108, 135; monkeys, 59, 81, 105; orangutans, 150
prisons, 23, 110n36, 122
pumas, 60, 67n58

R

rabbits, xi
raccoons, 166
racehorse theory, 118–20, 128
rats, 166, 175–84
representation, vii-viii, 15, 24–25, 98, 100–101, 104, 108, 120, 134, 139, 159–60, 162–63, 165–66, 175–84, 192–98, 200–201
rhinos, 136
ritual sacrifice, 37–40, 44n55, 54–57, 62, 64, 136, 191–92, 197–201
Roof, Dylann, 121, 128

S

scientific racism. *See* eugenics
sexual assault, 34, 121, 123, 125–28, 129n15, 139, 192
sheep, 33, 35–40, 44n55, 53, 57, 191–92, 200–201
Skabelund, Aaron, 17–18
slavery, ix, x, 3–11, 12n25, 22–23, 35, 39, 59, 122–23, 125, 138
slug, 159
snakes, 54, 60, 62–65, 67n66, 68n73
Snowflake the Gorilla, 97–108
social media, 35, 37, 43n33, 118–19, 129, 159–66, 199
socioeconomic class, xi, 9, 42n20, 44n40, 119–20, 123, 125–27, 138–39, 159–60, 163, 175–84, 192–200
speciesism, xii, 26, 36, 105, 160, 165, 166, 175–78, 185n17
spiders, 60, 87, 163
Sport of Kings, The. See Morgan, C. E.

T

Taylor, Breonna, 118
Third Reich. *See* Nazi regime.
tigers, 83, 85
toads, 60
Toffolo, Davide, 104
Trump, Donald, 118–20, 199

U

U.S. South, 3–6, 8, 10–11, 12n25, 117–19, 121–23

W

whiteness, 24, 26, 37, 97–108, 118–20, 124–25, 128–29, 133, 151–53, 155, 163–65, 201; white gaze, 98, 135–36; white privilege, 17, 97, 101–4, 106–7, 164, 200; white savior narrative, 105, 122, 136; white supremacy, 38, 119, 121, 123–25, 128, 133, 137–38, 142, 150–52, 176, 179, 184
witchcraft, 60, 67n66, 99, 142

Z

Zelinger, Amir, 22
zoos, 97–108, 161–63, 165, 167n32